Sociolinguistic Fieldwork

Looking for an easy-to-use, practical guide to conducting fieldwork in sociolinguistics? This invaluable textbook will give you the skills and knowledge required for carrying out research projects in "the field," including:

- how to select and enter a community
- how to design a research sample
- what recording equipment to choose and how to operate it
- how to collect, store, and manage data
- how to interact effectively with participants and communities
- what ethical issues you should be aware of

Carefully designed to be of maximum practical use to students and researchers in sociolinguistics, linguistic anthropology, and related fields, the book is packed with useful features, including:

- helpful checklists for recording techniques and equipment specifications
- practical examples taken from classic sociolinguistic studies
- vivid passages in which students recount their own experiences of doing fieldwork in many different parts of the world

NATALIE SCHILLING is an Associate Professor of Linguistics at Georgetown University. She has conducted and directed sociolinguistic fieldwork projects in communities ranging from isolated island villages to neighborhoods in the heart of urban Washington, DC, and has taught courses in sociolinguistic fieldwork for more than fifteen years.

KEY TOPICS IN SOCIOLINGUISTICS
Series editor: Rajend Mesthrie

This new series focuses on the main topics of study in sociolinguistics today. It consists of accessible yet challenging accounts of the most important issues to consider when examining the relationship between language and society. Some topics have been the subject of sociolinguistic study for many years, and are here re-examined in the light of new developments in the field; others are issues of growing importance that have not so far been given a sustained treatment. Written by leading experts, the books in the series are designed to be used on courses and in seminars, and include useful suggestions for further reading and a helpful glossary.

Already published in the series:

Politeness by Richard J. Watts
Language Policy by Bernard Spolsky
Discourse by Jan Blommaert
Analyzing Sociolinguistic Variation by Sali A. Tagliamonte
Language and Ethnicity by Carmen Fought
Style by Nikolas Coupland
World Englishes by Rajend Mesthrie and Rakesh Bhatt
Language and Identity by John Edwards
Attitudes to Language by Peter Garrett
Language Attrition by Monika S. Schmid
Writing and Society: An Introduction by Florian Coulmas
Sociolinguistic Fieldwork by Natalie Schilling

Forthcoming titles:

Speech Communities by Marcyliena Morgan

Sociolinguistic Fieldwork

NATALIE SCHILLING

CAMBRIDGE
UNIVERSITY PRESS

CAMBRIDGE UNIVERSITY PRESS
Cambridge, New York, Melbourne, Madrid, Cape Town,
Singapore, São Paulo, Delhi, Mexico City

Cambridge University Press
The Edinburgh Building, Cambridge CB2 8RU, UK

Published in the United States of America by
Cambridge University Press, New York

www.cambridge.org
Information on this title: www.cambridge.org/9780521127974

First published 2013

Printed and bound in the United Kingdom by the MPG Books Group

A catalogue record for this publication is available from the British Library

Schilling, Natalie.
    Sociolinguistic fieldwork / Natalie Schilling.
        pages   cm. – (Key topics in sociolinguistics)
    ISBN 978-0-521-76292-2 (Hardback) – ISBN 978-0-521-12797-4 (Paperback)
1. Sociolinguistics–Fieldwork.   2. Sociolinguistics–Methodology.   I. Title.
P40.S295 2013
306.44072′1–dc23
                                                        2012039594

ISBN 978-0-521-76292-2 Hardback
ISBN 978-0-521-12797-4 Paperback

For my grandfathers: H.C. William Schilling, artist (1905–1964) and Anatol I. Zverev, scientist (1913–1983)

Contents

Figures

Acknowledgements

I am deeply indebted to countless people without whom I could not have learned so much about sociolinguistic fieldwork or written this book. I cannot possibly thank everyone individually in the space of a page or two, but I want everyone involved to know that I value each person's unique contribution.

First, I thank my professors, especially my linguistics and sociolinguistics professors. I am particularly grateful to Walt Wolfram, who took me on my first fieldwork adventures and taught me not only how to do a good study but, more importantly, how to do good deeds, though giving back to the communities we study in any way we can, linguistic, non-linguistic, big or small. Thanks also to the other members of my first-ever fieldwork team, especially Kirk Hazen, who is still out in the field and still giving back to the community.

Second, I thank all the community members with whom I have had the good fortune to work in my various fieldwork projects, in particular the people of Ocracoke, NC; Robeson County, NC; Hyde County, NC; Smith Island, MD; and various neighborhoods in Washington, DC. Thank you for sharing your voices, your homes, and your lives with us. I have been immeasurably enriched academically and personally by getting to know you, and I cherish all of you. I would like to mention a couple of the special friends I made over the course of my fieldwork experiences, some of whom are no longer here to read these words but who live on in our hearts – and sometimes in our recordings: Adolph Dial, Hayes Alan Locklear, and Georgia Locklear from Robeson County; Frances Dize, Pastor Rick Edmund, Janet Evans, Craig Evans, and Melanie Guy from Smith Island (and also my re-found friends Dana Insley and Chris Parks); and my many, many friends on Ocracoke, far too numerous to mention. But thanks at least to Dave and Jen Esham, Melinda Jackson Esham, James Barrie Gaskill and Ellen Gaskell, Candy Gaskill, Chester Lynn, Kenny Ballance, Alton Ballance, and of course Rex and Miggie O'Neal. Here's to all of you: "It's hoi toid on the sound soid."

Third, I have to thank each and every one of my students of sociolinguistic fieldwork, past, present, and future. I have learned just as much from you as you have from me, and I treasure our mutual learning endeavors. Heartfelt and enduring thanks to my first-ever students in sociolinguistic fieldwork at Stanford University, including Angie Kortenhoven, Sarah J. Roberts, Devyani Sharma, and Andrew Wong. I am so proud of all of you, and so profoundly grateful for our enduring collegiality. And of course thank you to all of my students at Georgetown University. I would particularly like to acknowledge the following for sharing their insights, thoughts, and feelings about their sociolinguistic fieldwork experiences: Leslie Cochrane, Jinsok Lee, Jia Jackie Lou, Jermay Jamsu Reynolds, Sakiko Kajino, Jason Sanderson, Corinne Seals, Sheena Shah, Amelia Tseng, Mark Watson, Cala Zubair, and especially Anastasia Nylund and Jen McFadden. Thanks to Barbara Soukup for her generous help with information on and insight into language attitudes and perceptions, and to Janet Fuller for her fieldwork-related insights – and her continuing friendship. Thanks also to my Georgetown University colleagues for their friendship and moral support. Particular thanks to Roger Shuy, Ralph Fasold, Deborah Tannen, Heidi Hamilton, Rob Podesva, Anna Marie Trester, and especially Debby Schiffrin, for her longstanding collaboration in our Sociolinguistic Field Methods classes and for being the inspiration behind our Language and Communication in the Washington, DC, Metropolitan Area (LCDC) project.

I owe many personal thank yous, especially to my family. In particular, I thank Mom and Dad, and my brothers Ron and Rick, for always believing in me. Special thanks also to Aunt Bonny and Uncle Haydon, without whom I would never have gotten to launch my sociolinguistic fieldwork journey in North Carolina.

Finally, I extend my enduring thanks to those who, above all others, truly saw me through this book, from beginning to middle to end, from vague idea to what I hope is a tangible, useful contribution to all who embark on the journey of sociolinguistic fieldwork. Thanks to my very dear friend Jim, for hanging in there with me through even the most difficult times; to Jen McFadden, student, editor, colleague, and friend; to Otto Santa Ana, my writing partner and professional and personal inspiration; and to Chris, who has believed in me, and in this book project, from day one.

1 Introduction

1.1 FOREGROUNDING FIELD METHODS

Empirical data on language in its social context is at the heart of sociolinguistic study. Nonetheless, researchers have lamented that the field methods whereby such data are gathered have always been rather "inconspicuous" (Feagin 2013: 37). Write-ups of research projects focus on results and interpretations – not on how the data from which the findings are drawn were actually obtained. Indeed, Tagliamonte (2006a: 17) maintains that "fieldwork methods may be the best-kept secret of sociolinguistics." In addition, the few publications that do focus on sociolinguistic field methods (e.g. Bailey and Tillery 2004; Bailey, Wikle, and Tillery 1997b; Feagin 2013; Labov 1972a, 1984; Macaulay 2009; Milroy and Gordon 2003; Schilling-Estes 2007; Tagliamonte 2006a; Wolfson 1976) all point to the crucial role that research design and method play in shaping the data and, hence, the conclusions we derive. Further, sociolinguistic research foci have both broadened and become more nuanced, and data-related technology of course continues to transform itself every day. Correspondingly, research methods have become more varied and sophisticated and continue to evolve at a rapid pace.

The purpose of this book is to at last reveal the "secrets" of sociolinguistic fieldwork. It is both a how-to for students and researchers who need to design and conduct studies on language in its social context and a thoughtful exploration of the chief methods in sociolinguistic data collection, including examination of which methods work best for which purposes; evaluation of the strengths and weaknesses, advantages and disadvantages of each approach; and consideration of the theoretical assumptions underlying different methodological approaches. The book covers both quantitative and qualitative methodologies, as well as small- and large-scale studies. However, its chief focus is on how a range of methods and perspectives can be applied to variationist sociolinguistics, or quantitative sociolinguistics, the

1

subfield that has dominated modern sociolinguistic study since its inception in the early 1960s. Thus, in addition to providing practical guidelines, the book also explores several recent and ongoing "turns" in current variationist sociolinguistics, including integrating ethnographic study into traditional survey-based methods; and reconsidering traditional conceptualizations of and methods for studying stylistic variation, including investigating variation as it unfolds in interaction. Also of crucial importance throughout the book are questions of fieldwork ethics, including not only consideration of how to ensure that your research causes no harm but also how your research can actually be of benefit to the communities you study.

   The book is intended to be general enough for use by researchers on spoken, signed, and written language variation. However, where research methods become more specialized (e.g. in considering issues of obtaining high-quality recordings and preserving the confidentiality of identifying information), the emphasis is on methods in spoken language research, since sociolinguistics has been most closely focused on spoken language since its inception and since the "secular," everyday linguistic usages that sociolinguists seek have traditionally been concentrated in spoken registers (though, naturally, this has been changing in recent decades as written electronic communications has become increasingly commonplace). In addition, although human communication encompasses not only the linguistic signal *per se* but also gesture, position, facial expression, etc., this book follows the mainstream of variation study in focusing on the verbal channel, though of course it is necessary to concurrently consider the extralinguistic context that shapes and is shaped by the linguistic signal.

   Throughout the book, methodological and theoretical approaches and issues will be illustrated with examples from sociolinguistic studies ranging from the first foundational studies in the field, to later groundbreaking and paradigm-shifting works, to important ongoing work in the early decades of the twenty-first century. Illustrations will also come from a range of languages and sociolinguistic fieldwork locales from across the globe. At the same time as I provide breadth, however, I will provide depth of detail by drawing many examples from studies with which I have some degree of personal connection, whether through direct involvement with the research project, through direct contact with the project directors or project team, or in my role as advisor to researchers and students who have sought my guidance in designing and conducting projects on language variation in its social setting.

   The necessity for a limited scope is obvious, given the sheer impossibility of representing all of the many types of peoples and places that have been studied since the inception of modern sociolinguistics. But my personal focus is also driven by personal convictions: first, that sociolinguistic research is best conducted from a dual insider–outsider (i.e. participant–observer) perspective, as I discuss in Chapters 3, 5, and 7; and second, that our best reflections upon fieldwork methods are drawn from projects with which we have at least some degree of "insider" involvement during the fieldwork process. I believe our best insights about field methods come not from reading neat and polished accounts, where process almost always takes a back seat to the final analytical product, but rather from the "messy" and necessarily personal experience of fieldwork itself. My insights have been greatly enriched by connection with a wide array of projects throughout the US and the world, and my hope is to share these insights with the range of readers who stand to benefit from this book as they plan, conduct, and consider their own sociolinguistic and related studies.

As a special aid to the beginning researchers who are one of the chief audiences for this book, I highlight the research experiences of students at Georgetown University in a series of insets on "Students in the field." These students have conducted research on a wide range of communities throughout the world, and they have plenty of knowledge to share, including insight into what worked well, what did not work, and what surprises they encountered. They also share with us their emotional experiences. Sociolinguistic fieldwork can be daunting, but it can also be the most rewarding part of being a researcher, in terms of how much we learn about language and life, and in terms of the personal connections we forge as we engage with communities in a mutual learning process.

The text presumes grounding in introductory sociolinguistics, though it will also be useful for any scholar who wishes or needs to gather data on language in its social context; for example, those working in applied linguistics, linguistic anthropology, historical linguistics, and language endangerment.

1.2 SOCIOLINGUISTIC FIELD METHODS: A BRIEF HISTORY AND OVERVIEW

Variationist field methods have their roots in several traditions of empirical language study, including historical / comparative linguistics; the traditional dialectology (dialect geography) that stems from comparative linguistics; and the American descriptivist / structuralist linguistics of the early twentieth century (Chambers and Trudgill 1998:

13–54; Milroy and Gordon 2003: 1–22). In addition, qualitatively oriented approaches to the interrelation between language and society, namely, linguistic anthropology, the ethnography of communication, and interactional sociolinguistics, have played an important role in shaping quantitative sociolinguistics and have exerted increasing influence as variation analysis has developed over the past four decades (e.g. Milroy and Gordon 2003: 1–22).

The first systematic dialect studies were a natural outgrowth of historical linguists' interest in the interrelations between modern languages and language varieties and what these relations could reveal about historical connections and developments. The earliest dialect geographic studies were Wenker's survey of German dialects (1876–1887), Guillieron's survey of French dialects (1896–1900), and Jaberg and Jud's surveys of the Italian dialects of Italy and southern Switzerland in the first decades of the twentieth century. These studies served as the inspiration for the systematic study of American English dialects, initiated with the inauguration of the Linguistic Atlas of the United States and Canada project in 1930. Concurrently, in the early decades of the twentieth century, American descriptivist linguists inaugurated their own tradition of empirical linguistics with their investigations of the structures of Native American languages. (See Chambers and Trudgill 1998: 13–53 for a detailed discussion of the development of variationist sociolinguistics out of traditional dialectology.)

Because of their interest in linguistic history (i.e. diachronic linguistics), early dialectologists concentrated on obtaining data from speakers whose speech was believed to be most reflective of older speech forms – non-mobile, older, rural males with little formal education. And whereas the focus of American structuralist linguists was chiefly on the interrelation of the elements of language at a given moment in time (i.e. synchronic linguistics), they shared with dialectologists a focus on empirical data and linguistic fieldwork, as well as an interest in how similarities across current languages can be revealing of historical linguistic relationships.

However, it was not until the latter half of the twentieth century that diachronic and synchronic linguistics were truly brought together, with the pioneering work of Uriel Weinreich and William Labov and the advent of modern variationist sociolinguistics (Weinreich, Labov, and Herzog 1968). Like historical linguists and traditional dialect geographers, variationists are keenly interested in language change; however, their focus is not typically on long-completed changes but rather on ongoing language change. The pioneering study in this regard is Labov's 1963 study of Martha's Vineyard, an island off the coast of

Massachusetts (New England, USA), in which Labov demonstrated that, contrary to prior belief, it is indeed possible to observe language change in progress, through studying the synchronic patterning of community variation (1963, 1972c: 1–42). Crucially, in order to fully understand language change (and linguistic systematicity), we must investigate variation as it patterns according to both linguistic and social factors. And the social context of language variation is not limited to its patterning across geographic space but extends also to its patterning across social groups (e.g. age groups, social class groups, ethnic groups) as well as to its social meaning for both groups and individuals (e.g. a particular linguistic feature may be seen as a marker of regional identity or associated with a particular character trait).

Because variationists recognize that language variation must be studied across the entire social spectrum, their target populations are much broader than those of traditional dialect geographers, encompassing a full range of age, gender, socioeconomic, and ethnic groups. In addition, because they are focused on ongoing change rather than historic language forms, variationists often center their studies in urban rather than rural locations and may focus on younger populations as well. Some of the many important studies of language variation in urban settings include such pioneering works as Labov's (1966) study of New York City English; Wolfram's (1969) study of African American English in Detroit, Michigan; Cedergren's (1973) study of Spanish in Panama City; Trudgill's (1974) study of Norwich, England; and Macaulay's (1977) work in Glasgow, Scotland. In addition, there have been important ongoing studies of, for example, Montreal French (Sankoff, Sankoff, Laberge, and Topham 1976; Thibault and Vincent 1990; Vincent, Laforest, and Martel 1995) and Philadelphia English (Labov 1994), as well as re-studies of Martha's Vineyard (Blake and Josey 2003; Pope, Meyerhoff, and Ladd 2007), Panama City (Cedergren 1973, 1984), Norwich (Trudgill 1988), and New York City (r) (Labov 1994), among others. Finally, recent and ongoing studies of language variation and change in urban settings increasingly are taking language and dialect contact into account, as evidenced, for example, in Horvath's (1985) study of the socioethnic varieties in Sydney, Australia; Kerswill's studies of dialect contact, dialect leveling, and new dialect formation in southeast England (Kerswill 1996, 2013; Kerswill and Williams 2000, 2002); and Walker and Hoffman's ongoing studies of the highly multiethnic and multilingual city of Toronto, Canada (e.g. Hoffman and Walker 2010).

Variationist sociolinguistics also differs from traditional dialectology and American descriptivist linguistics in terms of what type of speech data is sought, and hence on primary methods of data collection. Dialectologists traditionally relied on lengthy questionnaires designed to elicit information on the use of a variety of lexical, phonological, and grammatical features, sometimes directly (e.g. "Have you ever heard the term 'snap beans' used for the beans that you break in half to cook? If yes, how often would you use that term …?") but more often indirectly ("What word would you use for the beans that you break in half to cook?"; see Bailey, Tillery, and Wikle 1997a). Questionnaires were distributed by mail or by traveling fieldworkers across very large areas (often across a whole country), and there tended to be very few respondents (often a single respondent) from each location within the wider survey area. And again, the social spectrum was typically narrow, with most informants being those who presumably represented the oldest speech forms, especially in European dialect surveys.

The American structuralists also relied on elicited language forms, though their interest was in piecing together the linguistic systems of undocumented or little-studied languages rather than in areal or social variation within well-known languages. Thus, their elicitations focused on obtaining information on the interrelation between linguistic elements rather than isolated items, through such tasks as judgments of "same" or "different," to determine minimal pairs, and sentence permutation tasks, to determine interrelations such as the subject and verb forms constituting the person–number paradigm. Again, though, the number of informants was limited – not just per location but per entire language – and there was typically little or no information on intra-language variation.

Again, because their focus is on intra-language variation, including social variation within populations as well as social and geographic variation across social groups, variationists gather data from many speakers in each community of study. In addition, their data must include many tokens of each of the variable linguistic features they are interested in, not just one or two examples of each, in order to gain a full picture of the linguistic and social factors that condition regularly patterned variability. Finally, variationist methodology has long been rooted in Labov's vernacular principle, which states:

> the style which is most regular in its structure and in its relation to the evolution of the language is the vernacular, in which the minimal attention is paid to speech (Labov 1972a: 112).

To fulfill the need for long stretches of connected, unselfconscious speech, Labov devised the so-called **sociolinguistic interview** – a casual interview designed to approximate the flow of an everyday relaxed conversation, as well as to focus speakers' attention on what they are talking about rather than on their speech itself (Labov 1972a; Wolfram and Fasold 1974). Interviewer questions are kept brief, and interviewees are encouraged to talk at length about topics of interest to them rather than asked to provide concise information on particular language features. Many researchers have modified the basic format of the sociolinguistic interview, and everyone tailors it to suit each individual community under study. In addition, some variationists have questioned the focus on vernacular, unselfconscious speech and have demonstrated how more selfconscious styles lend valuable insight into the patterning of variation and change (Coupland 2001a, 2001b, 2007; Eckert 2000: 213–228; Milroy and Gordon 2003: 49–51; Schilling-Estes 1998). Nonetheless, the sociolinguistic interview as originally conceived remains the most important item in the variationist sociolinguist's fieldwork toolkit. This vital tool will be discussed at length in Chapter 3, including its strengths and limitations in terms of investigating a range of speech styles.

Case study: Investigating change through studying systematic variation – Labov's pathbreaking study of Martha's Vineyard

In the early 1960s, Labov conducted a pioneering study of Martha's Vineyard, an island off the coast of Massachusetts, in the Northeastern US (1972c: 1–42). His focus was on the apparent increase in the production of the /ay/ and /aw/ diphthongs with centralized rather than low nuclei, a development which seemingly was taking place at the same time as the island was being transformed from a traditional, self-sustaining maritime community to a magnet for vacationers and new residents from mainland communities. An increase in centralization would be unusual, since historically the centralized forms developed into today's diphthongs with low central nuclei, and we do not typically expect a community to reverse a language change, or "turn its back on the history of the English language" (Labov 1972c: 25).

In order to investigate whether the suspected movement away from [aɪ] and [aʊ] toward increasing [əɪ] and [əʊ] was indeed taking place, Labov conducted tape-recorded interviews with numerous islanders, representative of important community social groups. Through subsequent quantitative analysis (i.e. counting all tokens of centralized and non-centralized /ay/ and /aw/ in the recordings and noting the linguistic contexts and social factors surrounding each occurrence), Labov was able to demonstrate that the centralization of /ay/ and /aw/ showed regular patterning according to linguistic factors such as following environment. For example, speakers were more likely to produce centralized nuclei for /ay/ before voiceless than voiced obstruents, so that [rəɪt] is more likely than [rəɪd].

In addition, he demonstrated that younger speakers showed more centralization than older speakers. This observation, coupled with data from earlier dialect geographic studies (and general information on the history of English), confirmed that the centralization of /ay/ and /aw/ was indeed on the rise in the island community.

Finally, Labov noted a correlation between speakers' orientation to Martha's Vineyard and usage levels for centralized /ay/ and /aw/: Those who positively valued the local community and its traditional ways showed higher usage levels for the centralized variants than those with more neutral or negative feelings toward the island and its traditional inward focus and isolation from outside forces.

Labov's study thus illustrates several key elements of variation theory and its inhering methodology:

1) We can investigate language change in progress through investigating the systematic patterning of language variation in a given population at a single moment in time.
2) To fully investigate the patterning of language variation, we must take into account both the linguistic and social factors that condition and / or correlate with the variable features in question.
3) The social factors that correlate with / condition language change include not only readily observable demographic factors such as age, occupation, and ethnicity, but also, and perhaps most importantly, attitudinal and identificational factors such as orientation toward one's local community.

1.3   ENRICHING QUANTITATIVE SOCIOLINGUISTICS WITH QUALITATIVE DATA / METHODS

Though essentially quantitative in nature, variationist sociolinguistics shares much in common with the qualitatively oriented disciplines of linguistic anthropology, the ethnography of communication, and interactional sociolinguistics, since all are focused on the interrelation of

language and society / culture. Central to anthropological / ethnographic approaches is a concern for coming to understand cultures
and communities from the perspectives of their members, through
long-term participant-observation in community life. In addition to
gathering copious amounts of language data, variationists too seek
community understandings, though often the variationist focus is
more linguistic than cultural, since language change and linguistic
systematicity remain central concerns. Labov's Martha's Vineyard
study is a model not only in its careful linguistic analysis but also in
its concern for uncovering the sociocultural meanings of the linguistic
features under study for the people who use them. Other, larger scale
sociolinguistic studies in urban contexts have sometimes sacrificed
sociocultural depth for linguistic and social breadth, as well as for
replicability across communities, and relied on pre-imposed social
categorizations and meanings, for example by dividing the community
into "typical" socioeconomic groups based on "typical" measures of
income, education, occupation, etc., rather than uncovering more
nuanced local categorizations (e.g. Eckert 2000: 16–25, 2005; Rickford
1986). However, variationist sociolinguistics has never really strayed
far from its ethnographic roots and its focus on the local as well as the
global, as evidenced, for example, as early as Labov's studies of the local
meaning of features of African American Vernacular English among
Harlem youth in the 1960s and continuing with Milroy and Milroy's
studies of the local meanings connoted by use of traditional vernacular
forms among members of various types of social networks in Belfast,
Northern Ireland, in 1975–1981 (1985). As our studies have progressed,
there has been ever-increasing recognition that the social meaning and
hence regular patterning of language variation (and the course of
language change) is best understood by combining broad-brush surveys
using sociolinguistic interview methods with in-depth ethnographic
analysis of local sociocultural meanings, practices, and categories.

    A model study exemplifying the synergistic union of quantitative
variationist and qualitative ethnographic methods is Penelope Eckert's
Linguistic Variation as Social Practice (2000). Eckert's work on adolescent
language patterns in a suburban Detroit (Michigan) high school is a
thorough and careful quantitative analysis of language variation and
ongoing change utilizing the best practices (including field method
techniques) of variationists. Crucially, though, it is grounded in extensive ethnographic observation of the high school under study and of
American high school and adolescent culture more generally, and so
Eckert is able to insightfully examine interrelations between patterns
of variation and change and *local* social categories, meanings, and

practices. For example, she is able to show that particular features associated with a current change in progress correlate more closely with kids' *own* social categories (i.e. the school-oriented "jocks" and street-oriented "burnouts") than their parents' socioeconomic class groups, as defined by "objective" measures imposed from outside community perspectives. In addition, she shows how language variation may play a greater role in demarcating which practices the kids engage in than the groups to which they belong. Thus, for example, among the jock and burnout boys in her study, usage levels for the newest vowel pronunciations are more closely correlated with the activity of "cruising" (i.e. traveling frequently to potentially risky areas of Detroit) than with membership in the jock or burnout social categories (pp. 150–153).

At the same time that variationists are broadening their language studies by including solid ethnographic studies of community sociocultural perspectives, they are also looking more deeply into their data by investigating how variants pattern in unfolding discourse. In this way, they gain understanding not only of the local community meanings of language features but of individual and interpersonal meanings as well. In addition, through such study we come to understand that linguistic variants are not simply reflective of membership in certain social groups or of particular attitudinal postures but that people actively utilize particular features to create and shape individual and group identities and (language) styles, as well as project particular stances – that is, relationships to what is being said and to one's interlocutors (see Section 4.3 for more on the notion of "stance").

Further, just as identities and styles are not fixed but fluid, so too are the meanings of variables malleable and multifaceted. For example, in order to examine the patterning and meaning of one of the most noticeable features of one of the most distinctive dialects of the US, "Pittsburghese," the variety associated with Pittsburgh, Pennsylvania, and the immediate vicinity, Johnstone and Kiesling (2008) combined quantitative study of the production and perception of monophthongal vs. diphthongal /aw/ with analysis of how /aw/ was used in connected speech (interviews and other data-gathering tasks), as well as how people talked *about* /aw/. (They also conducted historical investigation of the rise of Pittsburghese as an entity in its own right.) Their findings revealed that, far from remaining fixed, the meaning of /aw/ has changed drastically – from a highly localized but quite unnoticeable feature of Pittsburgh speech, to a marker of regionality to be avoided in "correct" speech, to a stereotype that can be used to perform the Pittsburgh dialect or Pittsburgh personas.

In addition to having changing meanings, a feature can have more than one meaning at a time, whether across communities, within a single community, or even for an individual speaker. Often, these meanings are related. That is, rather than point to or "index" one particular stance or facet of identity (whether a character trait or demographic category), a variant is often associated with an "indexical field," "a constellation of meanings that are ideologically linked" (Eckert 2008: 464). For example, Eckert (2008: 467–471) discusses how quantitative sociolinguistic studies of practice groups as disparate as Orthodox Jews (Benor 2001, 2004), high school girls who pride themselves on their intelligence and purposeful nonconformity to mainstream social groups (i.e. 'nerds'; Bucholtz 1996, 1999, 2001), and gay men (Podesva 2004, 2006; Podesva, Roberts, and Campbell-Kibler 2002) all show high usage levels for released /t/ in word positions where the usual American English variant would be unreleased or flapped (or possibly also glottalized, deleted or palatalized). All of these studies also include important discourse analytic components that show that these different groups capitalize on many of the same ideologically linked meanings associated with released /t/ in American English: In the US, /t/-release is considered to be hyperarticulate and so can be used to index such qualities as intelligence, carefulness, and precision, all of which are important to all the groups listed above, at least in particular situations, at particular moments in conversational interaction. At the same time, the stances and qualities associated with released /t/ may be associated with different local meanings in each different community of practice – for example, it is associated with nerd *girls* in one context and learned Jewish *men* in another.

1.4 HOW THIS BOOK IS ORGANIZED

This book presents readers with a step-by-step guide to designing and conducting field research on language in its social context, with an emphasis on methods used in variationist sociolinguistic research. Along the way, the various methods, as well as underlying concepts, constructs, and theoretical assumptions are examined and assessed.

In Chapter 2, we start by considering just what constitutes a sociolinguistic study, beginning with what types of linguistic, social, and sociolinguistic questions we might ask, what types of populations we might study (e.g. by considering the question of what constitutes a "speech community"), how to select speakers from within the population (i.e. what type of sample to construct), what types of categories we should group our speakers into, and finally, how to design a re-study of a population previously studied via sociolinguistic methodologies. The latter question is of great importance since variationist sociolinguistic study now has a long enough time depth that current researchers can return to sites investigated decades ago in order to enhance early studies of language change conducted chiefly via the synchronic study of different age groups (i.e. change in "apparent time") with information on change in real time.

Intimately connected to what types of research questions we are asking is the question of what types of data-collection methods will best suit our needs. In Chapter 3, we examine a range of data-collection techniques, including questionnaire-based surveys (whether administered face-to-face, by phone, or online); rapid and anonymous surveys; ethnographic study / participant-observation; and of course the sociolinguistic interview. Again, the focus is on how the various methods can be applied to variationist sociolinguistic study, and each method is both outlined and assessed. For example, we consider how surveys can be used to complement interview-based studies by allowing for broader population coverage, as well as providing information on linguistic features not likely to arise in sociolinguistic interviews. In addition, we consider the pros and cons of different types of surveys – for example, the breadth of Internet-based surveys vis-à-vis those administered face-to-face, as weighed against the decreasing amount of verifiable social information we can obtain from participants as we move from in-person communications to the telephone to Internet-based surveys. We also discuss how to integrate ethnographic methods into sociolinguistic study, since, as noted above, thorough understanding of the perspectives of those we study greatly enriches our knowledge of what linguistic variants and patterns of variation mean to the people who use them, as well as how these meanings arise and are sustained, shaped, and re-shaped in conversational interaction and ongoing community life. Further, we consider the many advantages of the staple of sociolinguistic field methods, the sociolinguistic interview, as well as the criticisms that have been leveled against it, whether in terms of its "unnaturalness" as a speech event (Wolfson 1976), the asymmetrical social and discoursal relations it may foster (e.g. Milroy and Gordon 2003: 61–65), and its perhaps somewhat narrow focus on "vernacular," "unselfconscious" speech (Schilling-Estes 2008).

Since this book is on sociolinguistic field methods and centers on gathering one's own data, it does not treat quantitative (historical) sociolinguistic studies whose chief source of data is pre-existing data from the historical record, or quantitative sociolinguistics relying on pre-existing computerized corpora (e.g. Bauer 2002; Schneider 2013). Such data sources can indeed be invaluable in sociolinguistic and historical sociolinguistic study, but their compilation and analysis is beyond the scope of this book, though we do consider the rudiments of basic database design in Chapter 6. We also consider the use of pre-existing variationist sociolinguistic datasets (as well as analyses and interpretations) in Section 2.4, when we consider methods and issues in conducting real-time studies – that is, re-studies of communities investigated decades ago via sociolinguistic techniques.

Chapter 4 picks up where Chapter 3 leaves off by focusing on stylistic variation, including how to study it and how important it is to obtain data on a full range of speech styles and their social and conversational correlates, as well as to treat stylistic variation as an object of study in its own right, not just as a means to obtaining and recognizing vernacular speech. For example, researchers increasingly are recognizing that styles at the other end of the continuum from unmonitored speech, including even highly selfconscious, overtly performative speech, have a lot to tell us about meanings and perceptions of linguistic features, since in performing variants and varieties we may exaggerate those features or styles that we perceive as most salient and / or most socially meaningful. In addition, it is likely that language changes are carried forward when novel forms are highlighted in individual speech, in ongoing discourse, perhaps in exaggerated performance or through their positioning or function in discourse (e.g. Eckert 2000: 216–219), rather than through the mechanistic workings of linguistic systems that somehow take on momentum apart from human agency. Further, a focus on style reveals that group styles (e.g. dialects) are not mere reflections of pre-existing social meanings and social group memberships (e.g. ethnic, gender, social class groups) but rather are grounded in individual and interindividual stylistic choices in unfolding conversational interaction. Hence, no investigation of the interrelation between language and its social setting, or of language variation and change, can be complete without close examination of the intra-speaker variation through which individual and group identities, styles, and stances are created, sustained, shaped, and changed (Coupland 2007; Eckert 2000; Johnstone 1996, 2000b).

Sociolinguists' views on stylistic variation have changed dramatically since the inception of variation analysis, and so have the means whereby data on different speech styles are gathered. In Chapter 4, we examine how to design research on style from a variety of approaches. The earliest is Labov's (1972c: 70–109) "attention to speech" approach in which style is seen primarily as a reflection of how much attention speakers are paying to their speech itself as they converse, and data from different styles is obtained chiefly in order to identify where true vernacular speech lies. The next main approach is Bell's (1984) "audience design" model, in which style is held to be shaped chiefly by who is in one's audience, or perhaps imagined audience. Crucially, though, style is now seen not only as a reactive phenomenon (i.e. as a reaction to one's audience) but also as proactive to a degree, and it is recognized that speakers sometimes (or often) shift styles to effect changes in interlocutor relations or other situational factors, not simply in response to extralinguistic changes that have already occurred. Finally, we look at current approaches in which speaker agency is primary, and in which speakers use stylistic resources for a host of interactional, social, and identificational reasons – not simply to conform to audience members or to the expectation that they should speak more standardly when speaking more carefully (i.e. when paying greater attention to their speech).

Because earlier views on stylistic variation are rather unidimensional, research design grounded in those approaches can be quasi-experimental and can be confined to the relatively controlled sociolinguistic interview setting, where the researcher can vary the factor of interest (attention to speech, audience) while keeping other situational factors at least fairly constant. When we move into more current approaches, however, we begin looking at data from a range of interactional types, from everyday conversational discourse to stylized public performances, and so the same level of control is not always possible. At the same time, though, we recognize that even the most creative styles make use of pre-existing features with pre-set social associations, and today's researchers in stylistic variation often combine methods that seek to control for and hence isolate various situational factors with investigations into the multifaceted situational and speaker-internal factors underlying even seemingly reactive style shifts. A full array of methods for studying style is thus investigated in Chapter 4.

In Chapters 5 and 6, we move from consideration of underlying research questions and study design to the actual act of entering the field and conducting the study. In Chapter 5, we address such practical issues as how to make initial contacts in the community and how to find study participants, as well as more subtle issues connected with what role(s) the researcher should adopt in the community and in interview interactions. For example, we consider how to gain acceptance into the community while still recognizing that the researcher inevitably remains at least something of an "outsider" (or becomes something of an outsider in researching one's own community). We also consider issues of power inequity underlying the relationship between researcher and research "subject" and urge budding researchers to follow Labov (e.g. 1984: 40–41) in seeking to minimize power differences by stressing their role as learners and community members' status as experts.

Chapter 6 has an even more practical focus and is centered on the crucial issue of ensuring that the data one works so hard to obtain is of excellent audio (and often also video) quality and is subsequently cataloged and stored in an organized manner amenable to variation analyses. Given the rapid pace of technological advances, we outline general specifications for audio and video recording equipment rather than providing specific recommendations. We also offer guidelines for recording techniques that have proven over the years to reliably yield high-quality data. Issues of data accessibility are addressed as well. In particular, we discuss the Internet as something of a double-edged sword. Granted, advances in Internet-based data storage and management technologies make cataloging and sharing data among researchers far easier than ever before. However, the advantages do not come without cost, and researchers must be increasingly careful to guard against unauthorized access to confidential information.

The concluding chapter of this book further explores the role of the researcher in the field by considering how much and what kinds of involvement the researcher should have in the community of study. We consider the question of whether minimal (yet always ethical) involvement is sufficient (or perhaps best, in the interest of scientific objectivity and respect for the research community), or whether researchers should assist the community in various ways, for example in correcting linguistic misinformation when there is a clear need (e.g. Labov 1982), or even actively seeking ways in which the researcher's linguistic knowledge can benefit the research community (e.g. Wolfram 1993). Chapter 7 presents a variety of linguistic outreach programs involving varying levels of community engagement, including early and ongoing efforts by linguists to seek greater educational equity in the classroom for native speakers of non-mainstream varieties of English, linguistic involvement in the legal arena (e.g. identifying dialect discrimination in the courtroom, analyzing language evidence), and current efforts to effect widespread educational reform by working with educators and policy makers to add units on language variation to standard elementary and middle school curricula.

As one increasingly involves oneself in working with communities to effect change through spreading (socio)linguistic knowledge, one inevitably confronts a variety of practical and ethical questions, including issues of power (e.g. who holds the power – the linguistic "experts" or community members who are experts in localized ways of life and ways of understanding) and issues of perspective (e.g. whose viewpoint should we espouse – that of the academic expert, the official community expert, or "ordinary" community members). Finally, we question whether sociolinguists' community engagement must necessarily involve linguistic matters at all. After all, simply lending a listening ear goes a long way, and sociolinguistic researchers, as well as those in related disciplines involving gathering naturalistic data in its natural setting, ideally must be caring listeners, attuned to the nuances not only of how community members talk but also, crucially, what they have to say.

Suggested readings

CHAMBERS, J. K. AND PETER TRUDGILL 1998. *DIALECTOLOGY*. 2ND EDN. CAMBRIDGE UNIVERSITY PRESS. See especially Chapters 2–4.

This classic text provides a comprehensive presentation of the development of dialectology and variationist sociolinguistics, and it presents an insightful discussion of the relationship between the two closely tied subfields of linguistics.

MILROY, LESLEY AND MATTHEW J. GORDON 2003. *SOCIOLIN-GUISTICS: METHOD AND INTERPRETATION*. MALDEN, MA: BLACK-WELL. See especially Chapters 1–3.

Milroy and Gordon's essential textbook in sociolinguistics provides a thorough and highly accessible overview of the field, including methods and issues in sampling and data collection. A range of techniques is outlined, including sociolinguistic surveys, sociolinguistic interviews, and participant-observation.

LABOV, WILLIAM 1972. SOME PRINCIPLES OF LINGUISTIC METHODOLOGY. *LANGUAGE IN SOCIETY* 1: 97–120.

This foundational article on linguistic methods outlines a variety of approaches to gathering data for linguistic study, including methods used by historical linguists, anthropological linguists, psycholinguists (and others working primarily in laboratory settings), formal linguists, and sociolinguists. Labov argues against formal linguists' reliance on the linguistic intuitions of isolated individuals (often the researcher him- or herself) and advocates instead for conducting research on community language as it is used in everyday life in order to gain an accurate picture of language in its full heterogeneity across geographic and social space, as well as over time.

2   Designing the study

As with any project, completing a successful sociolinguistic research project involves a good deal of pre-planning. Fieldwork is time-consuming, emotionally demanding, and often expensive, and there is nothing worse than spending time and energy in the field only to return home realizing that you should have delimited your population differently, obtained data from different groups or individuals, or perhaps more or fewer speakers, or obtained better quality data, whether in terms of recording quality or in terms of what people said or how they said it. I have taught courses in sociolinguistic field methods and supervised students' sociolinguistic research projects for a number of years, and I cannot count how many times students have included in their field reports the phrase, "If only I had . . ."

In this chapter, we take the first steps toward eliminating the "if onlys" by stressing the importance of carefully selecting one's community of study, choosing which speakers to study from within that community, and appropriately categorizing the selected speakers. We also discuss the extra care that must go into planning a re-study of a community previously subjected to sociolinguistic study, for the purposes of obtaining data on language change in real time. While seemingly a re-study would involve a simple replication of previous methods, in actuality replication is by no means "simple"; indeed, exact replication is not really even possible, since even if one manages to record all the same speakers (or the same groupings of speakers, including age, gender, ethnic, and social class groups), using the same interview questionnaire or other survey instrument, the same recording locations, etc., the data-gathering situation will necessarily be different, since the times have changed, and the interviewer and speakers are either different people who were not a part of the original study, or they have aged and changed; hence interviewer and speakers will necessarily interrelate in different ways than in the original study. Obtaining good quality language data are the subjects of Chapters 3 and 4, while good recordings – and record-keeping – are discussed in Chapter 6.

It is very important to know from the outset that before you begin your study, you will be required to apply for and receive approval from your institution's Institutional Review Board (IRB). In addition, projects involving more than one institution will need approval from each entity's IRB, including perhaps IRBs from different countries whose requirements are sometimes surprisingly different from those of one's home culture. IRBs exist to ensure that research conducted on or with human subjects is ethical and will not adversely affect research participants and their communities. They are comprised of experts with experience, knowledge, and wisdom regarding the ethical conduct of research. The requirements they establish are grounded in the careful scrutiny by the scientific community at large of a full range of research studies reaching back for decades, and so their requirements are to be respected and heeded. Researchers who fail to apply for and receive IRB approval prior to data collection will probably not be allowed to use their data in any academic venue, with the possible exception of practice research in the classroom setting. Further, failing to apply for and follow IRB guidelines can have serious implications for *all* research being conducted at your institution, not just your own project, since one researcher's breaches of protocol can result in the revoking of the entire institution's right to do research. Because IRB requirements vary from university to university, they will not be discussed in detail in this book. It is incumbent upon you, a researcher planning to conduct research on human subjects, to research your IRB and its specific requirements. Regardless of IRB requirements, a good researcher is always an ethical researcher, and the topic of fieldwork ethics is recurrent throughout this book.

2.1 SELECTING THE POPULATION: WHAT IS A "SPEECH COMMUNITY"?

When you start thinking about conducting a sociolinguistic research project, chances are that you already have some sort of community in mind that you would like to study. Perhaps you are captivated by the distinctive dialect of a small, rural community or a large urban area, or by how a particular social group relies on creative linguistic usages as a part of its distinctive group identity. Or perhaps you are interested in learning more about a particular community, perhaps a geographically defined neighborhood or a community who comes together for particular social reasons, and you would like to learn in detail how that group uses language, whether particular languages, language varieties or elements of different varieties. There are many different types of communities that you can study, and who and what you decide to study depends on your research interests and, in most cases, helps shape your research questions as well.

As we think about what communities or types of community we as sociolinguists are interested in studying, we must ask ourselves how we define "community" in the first place. Sociolinguists have for decades talked about their studies of various **speech communities**, but exactly what constitutes a speech community has been the subject of much debate. As sociolinguists, we are of course interested in language and linguistic systematicity, but at the same time we maintain that language resides in social space and not simply in the cognitive space of any given individual. Our dual focus means that we have different ideas regarding what the proper object of linguistic study should be. For some of us, it is something chiefly linguistic, perhaps a particular dialect; for others, the object is chiefly social, for example the linguistic usages of people who reside in a particular neighborhood, regardless of whether they all share the same dialect or language. Hence, we find such radically different definitions of the "speech community" as Patrick's "socially-based unit of linguistic analysis" (2002: 577) and Bucholtz's "language-based unit of social analysis" (1999: 203). Researchers who take the former approach focus on linguistic questions, and they use social factors to help them find their answers. For example, many variationists investigate how language changes spread through different types of social groups, in seeking insights into the nature of language change and the language change process. Under the latter approach, researchers' main questions are social in nature, perhaps having to do with social groups, social interactions, or social and individual identity, and they investigate linguistic patterns to help them gain greater social understandings. For example, a researcher may be interested in how people use language in displaying and shaping gender identity.

These seemingly diametrically opposed approaches in reality are simply starting points, for sociolinguists are united in their agreement that language and society are inextricably intertwined and that no study of language could be complete without thorough investigation of its social embedding, nor any question about human society or identity society adequately answered without consideration of the role language necessarily plays in all human interactions and institutions.

Related to the question of whether to start from the linguistic or the social in defining the speech community is the question of how people should be united in order to constitute a community. Do our study participants need to interact with one another, or is sharing a common language variety or another sort of social bond sufficient (e.g. living in the same city, attending the same university)? If we deem interaction to be necessary, must it be of a certain type or quality? Is frequent interaction enough, or must there be some sense of social cohesiveness?

Another major question that arises in considering what constitutes a speech community concerns homogeneity vs. heterogeneity: How uniform must a speech community be in terms of linguistic and / or social characteristics, and in what ways? Given the sociolinguistic focus on linguistic variability, it is not useful to conceive of a speech community as being united in terms of rigid uniformity of language production, since every group of people, and every individual speaker, is linguistically heterogeneous. More useful is the classic Labovian definition, in which a speech community is defined by shared patterns of variability in terms of linguistic production and, equally importantly, shared norms for *evaluating* linguistic usages:

> The speech community is not defined by any marked agreement in the use of language elements, so much as by participation in a set of shared norms. These norms may be observed in overt types of evaluative behavior, and by the uniformity of abstract patterns of variation which are invariant in respect to particular levels of usage (Labov 1972c: 120–121).

For example, Labov (1966) showed that whereas residents of New York City's Lower East Side had quite different usage levels for several defining features of the New York City dialect (e.g. r-lessness, /æ/ raising, /ɔ/ raising) depending on such factors as socioeconomic status, they were united in their common patterns of stylistic variation, with members of all social class groups using lower levels for the dialectal features (vs. their standard counterparts) in more formal, selfconscious speech. These patterns indirectly reveal that residents of the Lower East Side shared an evaluation of the dialect features as less "proper" or "correct" than standard features, regardless of each group or individual's particular usage levels for the New York City features. This evaluation was confirmed in various tasks Labov conducted to gain more direct information on his subjects' language attitudes; for example, soliciting people's overt self-evaluations of their linguistic behavior and conducting interviews focused on language attitudes.

Labov's conception of the speech community has been highly influential – so much so that it is often held to be synonymous with the term "speech community" in sociolinguistics. However, it has also come under criticism, most often because it seems to imply a uniform orientation toward language standards that real communities do not seem to share. For example, does it seem likely that all people in New York's Lower East Side truly devalue their local accent in favor of widely accepted American standards for "correct" speech? Perhaps some people are proud of their New York City dialect, with its connotations of urban savvy and "street smarts," while for some the dialect may have strong positive associations with community identity. Further, a "consensus" model of social class stratification, in which all groups orient toward mainstream norms (e.g. toward higher social class standing, greater material wealth, and more standard English) may be more or less applicable in different settings. For example, Rickford (1986) demonstrated that the community of Cane Walk, Guyana, was better characterized in terms of interclass conflict with respect to social and linguistic attitudes than intergroup agreement. This conflict manifested itself in a sharp linguistic divide between the superordinate and subordinate classes: Those who owned the plantations that formed the backbone of the local economy used a fairly standard variety of English, and those who worked the plantations spoke a variety of English characterized by heavy use of features of the local creole.

However, as Patrick (2002) points out, Labov never intended "shared norms" to mean rigid adherence to a single set of linguistic evaluations but simply orientation toward the same norms. Hence Labov himself highlights the case of Steve K., a young man who overtly rejected the devaluation of the New York City dialect he had begun to internalize in college and purposely chose to *not* speak standard English. Despite his oppositional attitude, Steve K.'s patterns of stylistic variation nonetheless fall right in line with everyone else's. Despite his best efforts, he too produces more standard features in formal contexts than in informal. Hence, he is a member of the Lower East Side speech community, since his patterns of language variation reveal his underlying evaluation of standard English as "better" than the New York City dialect, despite his avowed orientation to the contrary.

Other questions arise as well: for example, there are questions of scale (e.g. Can a country constitute a speech community? What about two people?), contiguity (Must a community be geographically contiguous? What about a virtual community?), and separateness or insularity. Hence, whereas early dialect geographers and anthropologists often focused on populations they deemed to be relatively self-contained and remote from outside influence, in the belief that such communities and their language varieties are more "authentic" and "pure" than those of populations in which there is more intermingling and intercommunication with "outsiders," as the twentieth century has passed into the twenty-first, there has been increasing recognition among social scientists that not only are the world's peoples becoming increasingly interconnected, but in reality there has never been any such thing as a completely insular, "pure" population or language in the first place (Montgomery 2000; Trudgill 1989). Thus, while sociolinguistic investigations of relatively insular, "exotic" or "quaint" communities and their speakers are part of the sociolinguistic canon and have contributed greatly to our understanding of the interrelation between language, society, and identity, a narrow focus on such populations is very limiting since so many populations are *not* insular, and since communities characterized by intermixing and intercommunication are more linguistically dynamic than relatively remote communities and so have more to tell us about language change.

Again, despite the many questions concerning the definition of "speech community," many researchers follow Labov's definition or a close approximation thereof. In addition, for many researchers the default version of a speech community-based approach to sociolinguistic study is the investigation of a fairly large geographically defined population stratified by various demographic characteristics such as socioeconomic class, age, gender, and ethnicity. Such studies are often classified as "Labovian," though Labov has never confined himself to investigating only one particular type of community. Thus, for example, whereas his investigation of the Lower East Side of New York City indeed is focused on a large geographically defined community, his earlier study of Martha's Vineyard (Labov 1963) centers on a much smaller population. Further, both studies move beyond correlations between linguistic and demographic features into such matters as language attitudes and orientation to the local community.

Another angle from which sociolinguists study smaller populations is in terms of individuals' interactional ties or **social networks**. Social-network-based approaches were introduced into sociolinguistics by Milroy and Milroy in the mid-1970s in their studies of Belfast, Northern Ireland (L. Milroy 1980; Milroy and Milroy 1985). Although their studies were grounded in a particular geographic location, the groups Milroy and Milroy studied within Belfast (and the three geographically defined neighborhoods within Belfast upon which they were more narrowly focused) were based on people who interacted with one another rather than simply those who fitted into particular demographic categories. Crucially, too, their analyses of the social embedding of language variation and change were focused not on demographic correlates but on the types of network ties that bound different groups together. A key finding was that interpersonal ties may have more to tell us about language variation and change than social group membership. In particular, dense, multiplex ties; that is, strong ties to relatively few people, in many arenas of life such as residence, work, family, and social life, were found to inhibit linguistic innovation and loose ties to promote it.

This is not to say that social-network-based approaches are incompatible with those focusing on larger communities based on demographic criteria, since larger demographic categories such as socioeconomic class groups are comprised of individuals with particular types of network ties; and further, the class groups that have been shown to lead in language change (often middle classes, rather than upper or lower social class groups) in many cases are characterized by loose ties across social groups rather than dense ties within a single group. Nonetheless, social-network-based studies are different in focus, since their chief social concern is with patterns of interindividual interaction, and the communities they study are typically smaller than those taking a more traditional "Labovian" approach.

Some important variationist studies taking a social network approach include Cheshire's (1982) study of adolescent groups in Reading, England; Nichols' (1983) study of mainland vs. island Gullah speakers in coastal South Carolina; Lippi-Green's (1989) study of locally defined networks in the Austrian Alpine village of Grossdorf; and Eckert's (1989, 2000) groundbreaking work on teenage social groups in a Detroit-area high school – though, as noted in Chapter 1, her work moves beyond social networks to considerations of community of practice (see below). Also important is Labov's early work on the interrelation between vernacular language use and integration into youth gangs in Harlem in the early 1970s (1972b), conducted prior to the introduction of the methodology and terminology of social network analysis to sociolinguistics by Milroy and Milroy.

In addition, social-network-based studies have illuminated the relationship between network strength and the maintenance of localized languages vs. shifting toward wider language norms, as illustrated, for example, in Gal's (1979) study of Oberwart, Austria, which showed a correlation between the maintenance of traditional German / Hungarian bilingualism (vs. an incoming shift to German only) and the degree to which people were integrated into traditional peasant networks; and Zentella's (1997) study of three generations of a Puerto Rican community in New York City which showed a relationship between patterns of Spanish language maintenance vs. shift to English and age- and gender-based social networks.

Whereas a focus on localized social networks helps explicate correlations between patterns of language variation and change and wider scale social groups such as socioeconomic class groups, the relationship between linguistic usages and personal interconnections can be further illuminated by focusing not only on density and multiplexity of network ties but also on *why* people are tied together in the first place – that is, why people come together, what types of interactions they engage in (vs. mere strength of interactional tie), and what types of values and orientations they share (and contest). In other words, our sociolinguistic studies of various kinds of speaker groups can be richly informed by considering them as **communities of practice**. Following researchers in practice theory such as Lave and Wenger (1991), Eckert defines a community of practice as "an aggregate of people who come together around some shared enterprise" and which is "simultaneously defined by its membership and the shared practices in which that membership engages" (Eckert and McConnell-Ginet 1992: 464). Through focusing on shared practices, we gain insight into how social ties and structures are enacted, shaped, and changed in everyday, ongoing interaction, including linguistic interaction. Crucially, we can also look beyond correlations between linguistic and social patterns into *why* we see the patterns that we do – in other words, we can investigate how people use linguistic resources (e.g. linguistic variables, registers, styles, and / or languages) to make social meanings. For example, in her study of "nerd" girls in a California high school, Bucholtz (1999) shows how the girls use hyperstandard grammar and elevated diction, as well as avoid current teen slang terms, to craft an identity purposefully characterized by intelligence and rejection of the values held by the school's various popular groups (e.g. "coolness," hegemonic femininity[ies]). Hence, in focusing on what binds the nerd girls together socially, we are able to see not only which linguistic features the girls use, but also why they use particular types of features and what these features mean.

Bucholtz (1999) also notes a number of other features of community-of-practice-based approaches that render them advantageous for sociolinguistic study. For example, there is more focus on speaker agency, and speaker identities are recognized as fluid rather than fixed, since they are seen as being constituted in ongoing practice rather than as static by-products of "social address" (e.g. demographic categories such as class, age, sex, race; see Eckert 2000) or pre-existing social groups in which membership is typically "given" rather than chosen (e.g. neighborhood groups). Further, whereas social-network-based approaches tend to focus on single networks and their core members, community-of-practice-based approaches recognize that all speakers belong to multiple networks and that peripheral members of one group (e.g. Bucholtz's nerd girls, who are peripheral to the "main" social groups in the school) may very well be central members of another group (e.g. the deliberately constituted "nerd" group).

In addition, focusing on unfolding practices allows us to see not just how individual and group identities, as well as intergroup relations, are constituted but also how they are contested. Thus, for example, even relatively small groups like Bucholtz's nerd girls show varying alignments with "nerdiness" vs. "coolness" in different situations, or even within a single interaction; and we can begin to see how such conflicts play out in larger groups such as the two diametrically opposed social class groups in Rickford's (1986) Cane Walk study, with the subordinate group enacting their opposition to the superordinate group through their marked non-use of the standard language features to which we would expect them to aspire. Indeed, Eckert maintains that it is the community of practice that is the essential link between individual identities / practices and larger social structures such as class, gender, and ethnicity, since people relate to these structures through our localized practice groups rather than directly, as individuals. As Eckert notes, people make sense of their world by building outward from the local, and "Ultimately, categories such as age, class, ethnicity, and gender are produced and reproduced in their differential forms of participation in communities of practice" (2000: 40). Categories can also be subverted in practice groups. For example, although the nerd girls in Bucholtz's study are in some sense bound by existing gender structures (and strictures), they work to subvert stereotypical notions of girls as less intelligent than boys by flaunting their smartness through their noticeably hyperstandard language usages.

As with Bucholtz's study, many variationist studies focused on communities of practice are especially concerned with gender(ed) practices, roles, relations, and identities. For example, Mallinson and Childs (Childs and Mallinson 2004; Mallinson and Childs 2007) show how, even in a very small, isolated Appalachian community of African Americans, neither "women" nor their linguistic usages constitute a monolithic identity. Rather, there are two quite different women's practice groups, the "Church ladies" and the "porch sitters," whose different linguistic usages are both constitutive and reflective of the different things they habitually do as well as their different attitudes and orientations. For example, the Church ladies actively participate in church and community activities and have a positive orientation toward life in small-town Appalachia (a region whose residents are mostly White), practices and attitudes that go hand-in-hand with their low usages levels for features of African American Vernacular English. Conversely, the porch sitters, who have higher usages levels of African American Vernacular English (AAVE) features, enjoy socializing on a group member's porch for gossip and drinks and orient themselves away from their small town toward urban African American culture.

Whereas many studies of language and gender focus on women, especially those who would be considered "atypical" according to hegemonic gender ideologies, Kiesling demonstrates that taking a close-up view of even "normal" (i.e. White, heterosexual) men's practice groups reveals that "men" are no more uniform than women. Hence, in his study of a Southeastern US fraternity (1998), Kiesling shows that, whereas all the men in the practice group are concerned with power, different men orient toward different types of power, with some of them focusing more on the physical power associated with working-class identity and vernacular linguistic usages, and others focusing on institutional power and the standard language forms associated with it. And once we move beyond the "typical," gender identities and gendered linguistic usages get even more complicated, as we saw above for Bucholtz's nerd girls and will see below for a group of homosexual African American male drag queens (Barrett 1995).

A focus on speakers' proactive linguistic usages leads of course to consideration not only of inter- and intra-group language styles but **individual style** as well. The investigation of intra-speaker variation has long been a part of variation analysis, beginning with the earliest uses of the sociolinguistic interview, which was designed to elicit a range of speech styles including, importantly, each speaker's "true" vernacular. The study of stylistic variation has grown progressively more important as quantitative sociolinguists have increasingly realized the importance of speaker agency and the value of looking at how people use linguistic features in unfolding discourse in addition to aggregate patterns of language variation. Some researchers, including Coupland (2007) and Johnstone (1996), have also demonstrated the value of in-depth investigations of the speech styles that characterize particular individuals, including their components, purposes, and effects, in enriching our general understanding language variation and language change. Indeed, researchers focusing on individual styles note that language changes are just as likely, perhaps more likely, to have their origins in the purposefully styled linguistic usages of notable / noticeable individuals as in the unselfconscious usages that Labov and his followers have for decades maintained underlie linguistic innovation (Coupland 1980, 1984, 2001a, 2001b, 2007; Eckert 1989, 1998, 2000; Johnstone 1996, 1999, 2000b; Johnstone and Bean 1997)

A few other researchers take things even further and maintain that linguistic study should *always* begin with the individual, since no two people show the exact same patterns of language variation or use exactly the same repertoire of linguistic features, and so to speak of group styles, including dialects and languages, is to deal in abstractions rather than linguistic reality. Proponents of such individual-centered views include Le Page and Tabouret-Keller (1985) who consider linguistic usages to be "acts of identity" by individuals who choose features, whether of a single "style" or "language" or from across multiple varieties, to bring them linguistically and psychologically closer to those with whom they wish to identify and distance themselves from those from whom they wish to dissociate. Under such a view, the focus is on how individuals use language features to make various meanings – how individuals engage in "languaging" (Becker 1995) – rather than on languages or language varieties as entities, and both social identities and language systems are seen as emergent in interaction rather than as pre-set "givens" (cf. Hopper's "emergent grammar" [1987]). However, as fundamental as individuals are, linguistic features cannot get their social meanings in a vacuum, and so we must always consider the interplay between individuals' proactive use of linguistic features to make social meanings and the longstanding associations between linguistic usages and social groups (e.g. an ethnic group, a gender group), iconic characters (e.g. the old-time fisherman, the nerdy high school student), and interactional stances (e.g. uncertainty, powerlessness) from which interpretable social meanings are necessarily drawn.

In sum, choosing a population for sociolinguistic study very much depends on how we choose to define "community," and even more fundamentally on how we view the interrelation between language varieties, social structures, interpersonal interactions, and personal identity. The roots of sociolinguistics lie in part in dialect geography, and so we often have a propensity to define our communities of study based on geography and some measure of shared linguistic usages. However, our interest in the social as well as the linguistic may lead us to investigate communities as defined in terms of their members' social interactions, including the strength of their network ties and the types of actions that lead them to form ties in the first place. In addition, we may choose to focus on how language variation correlates with social categories or on how categories are constructed and reconstructed in social interaction. Further, our interest in the inter-relation between language and social meaning may lead us to a micro-scopic focus on how linguistic meanings unfold in interpersonal discourse via the proactive use of language variants by "linguistic individuals" (Johnstone 1996). Finally, we may question whether we can indeed delimit a population of study prior to undertaking our investigations or whether the most relevant social groupings (and linguistic usages) will emerge only through extensive systematic observations.

While choosing a community of study involves a host of philosoph-ical considerations, the reader of this book is of course fundamentally interested in the practical question of deciding who and what to study. The approaches outlined above are not and cannot be mutually exclu-sive, since aggregate meanings are constructed in individual inter-actions and, conversely, individuals derive meanings from ongoing linguistic–social associations. Hence, whether you choose to study a geographically defined "speech community," one or more social net-works, a community or communities of practice, or a particular indi-vidual, your study will be richest by keeping in mind that the individual and the localized community comprise the larger commu-nity every bit as much as the individual is constituted in social interaction and in relation to societal structures, norms, and ways of thinking (e.g. attitudes, values, ideologies). Thus, if you choose to study a larger community and aggregate patterns of variation, you will of necessity come to see how individuals sustain and shape wider patterns of language variation, while if you focus on individuals or small com-munities of practice, you will have to consider them against a larger social and linguistic backdrop if you are to speak meaningfully about what particular linguistic usages mean to the people who use and interpret them.

Case studies: The interplay between micro and macro levels of linguistic and social variation

James Walker and Michol Hoffman direct an ongoing large-scale sociolinguistic study of the effects of language contact in Toronto, one of the world's most multilingual cities (e.g. Hoffman and Walker 2010). As part of their study, they are investigating patterns of variation in a number of language features, including stable and changing features of Canadian English (e.g. the stable deletion of word-final t / d in consonants clusters, as in 'understan' for *understand*, and the progress of various elements of the ongoing Canadian Vowel Shift) across ethnic groups, including established groups of Whites (of British and Irish descent) and newer groups of Italians and Chinese. In initially designing their study, they classified speakers into ethnic groups in a very traditional way, according to lineal descent and neighborhood residence. However, based on preliminary observations of language use patterns and their understanding that individual and group self-conceptualizations are vital components of ethnic identity, they subclassified the Italians and Chinese in their study according to each individual's own ethnic orientation, as determined using responses to a questionnaire inquiring about such matters as self-identification, degree of integration into particular social networks, language use, and participation in community activities. Individuals belonging to the "same" ethnic group indeed show differing degrees of ethnic orientation and, in addition, younger speakers show weaker ethnic affiliation than older speakers. Furthermore, patterns of language variation appear to correlate not only with ethnic group membership (as objectively defined) but also with ethnic orientation. Hence, for example, speakers of Chinese descent with a higher degree of ethnic orientation show less participation in certain elements of the Canadian Vowel Shift, namely, the backing of /æ/ and lowering of /ɛ/, than those with lower affiliation to their ethnic group.

This correlation is not readily attributable to language transfer and so is likely to be attributable to speakers' different senses of ethnic identity. In other words, it appears that non-uses of backed /æ/ and lowered /ɛ/ are not mere correlates of objectively defined group membership but *markers* that are associated with Chinese ethnicity among Toronto residents of Chinese descent and can be used or not used to project a greater or lesser degree of ethnic affiliation. As Hoffman and Walker astutely note (2010), such identification of features as actual markers of social identity is not possible through looking solely at large-scale correlations between social groups and linguistic usages but rather must be arrived at through consideration of individual orientations toward the various social groups with which they more and less strongly identify. To put it succinctly, we cannot really understand what global patterns mean without looking locally, into individuals' perceptions of self and group identity.

On the other side of the coin, Barrett (1995) provides an excellent example of how we can understand localized language styles

and particularized linguistic usages through considering them
against the backdrop of broad associations between patterns of
language variation, deep-seated social institutions, and widely
circulating social meanings. His focus of study is a community
of practice – African American drag queens who craft their own
brand of gender and ethnic identity through their linguistic
performances in Texas bars. In order to create and display their
unique identity as drag queens, gays, African Americans, and
men, they do not simply create a brand-new style but rather
craft one through the juxtaposition of several established, even
stereotypical, styles / varieties that normally are not found in
co-occurrence: "White women's language" (characterized by
such features as hyperstandard grammar, "empty" adjectives
like *divine*, and superpolite forms), gay male English (which
shares features with stereotypical White women's language
but has stereotypical features of its own, for example the use
of terms like *fabulous* and *fierce*), and African American English,
a readily recognizable dialect with many distinguishing features
that is also often the subject of stereotypes.

Barrett further notes that the use of these stereotypical styles
does not serve to reproduce stereotypes but rather subverts
them. Hence, for example, the drag queens ridicule, even criti-
cize, White speech and White domination through juxtaposing
White women's English with subject matter and language features associated with African Americans as, for example, in
RuPaul's pronunciation of the stereotypical African American
term *Miss Thang* with a "White" accent (*Miss Thing*). In addition,
the drag queens display their resistance to the hegemonic gender
order (in which heterosexual males dominate heterosexual
women) through juxtaposing gay male language features with
themes and features associated with the dominating standard
variety, as in RuPaul's use of standard phonology to talk
about one day becoming President and painting the White House
pink.

Again, though, as distinctive as is the drag queens' highly
particularized style and the meanings that are projected through
its use, the style only gains its meanings because we recognize
the wider styles of which it is comprised and their various
attendant social meanings, and so it can only be studied through
considering both the local and the global, the subversive but also
the stereotypical.

2.2   SAMPLING THE POPULATION

Once you have selected a community for study, it is in most cases then necessary to devise a principled method for selecting speakers from within the population to include in your study, since in all but the smallest communities it will be impossible to include every individual from the community. In most cases, in selecting your speakers – i.e. sampling your population – you will want to ensure that the speakers you choose are representative of the larger community so that the resultant findings can be generalized to the population at large. Strictly speaking, the only way to ensure genuine representativeness is to obtain a random sample. As we shall see, though, true random sampling is seldom feasible and not necessarily of most benefit to our sociolinguistic research projects. Hence, sociolinguists sometimes use a modified random sampling technique called proportionate stratified random sampling. Most often, though, they use a quite different sampling method: quota sampling or judgment sampling. The matter of sample size is also important and usually one of the first questions beginning fieldworkers ask. However, there is no single straightforward answer, and a number of factors must be taken into account, including the size of your community, your sampling method, how you categorize the speakers in your sample (i.e. stratification; see below), your research questions, and even the very practical matter of how feasible it will be for you to analyze the data you do collect.

2.2.1   Random sampling

Random sampling entails selecting study participants in such a way that each member of the population has an equal chance of being chosen. If you obtain a large enough random sample, it will be statistically representative and your results will be generalizable to the population as a whole. Random samples are typically based on pre-existing lists or sample frames – that is, any list that enumerates the relevant population, such as an electoral register or a telephone directory. Participants are selected randomly from this list, usually by computational means.

   While, at first glance, such sampling may seem quite straightforward, in reality a number of issues almost immediately crop up. First, you must carefully consider the nature of your sample frame, since many seemingly complete or representative lists of community members are already biased before we even begin to sample from them. Hence, for example, telephone directories typically only include those with land lines – a growing concern as more and more people choose mobile phone service only. Further, a telephone directory will not include people with unlisted numbers or segments of the population who cannot afford phone service, choose not to have it, or perhaps are in areas too remote for service coverage.

Even if you feel confident that your sample frame is comprehensive (e.g. perhaps you have generated a list of possible telephone numbers in the area where your population is located to enable inclusion of mobile numbers and unlisted numbers) and you have drawn your sample from that, bias can set in quickly. Hence for example, research experience has shown that it is typically women who answer a household phone, and hence if you are selecting your speakers by random phone calls, you cannot simply invite participation from the first person who answers the phone but rather must devise a way to include male household members (perhaps by asking to speak to the person with the most recent birthday). In addition, it is highly unlikely that the participants you have randomly chosen will all agree to participate in your study, and so the matter of replacement arises almost right away, and you will need to have in place some sort of principled method for ensuring that you do not bias your sample in your inclusion of new speakers. For example, you might find that it is mostly the older speakers on your list who agree to take part in your study, and you will want to be cautious about replacing younger, busier potential participants with older people, since you could easily introduce an age bias into your sample. Or perhaps you will find that those who are most willing to participate in your study are more interested in or more familiar with research projects and have a higher educational level than the population as a whole.

Further issues arise when we consider the nature of sociolinguistic research as compared with other types of social science research in which random sampling is the norm. For example, quite large numbers of participants are usually needed to ensure genuine representativeness. The statistical requirements are complex; however, Neuman (1997) suggests that a good rule of thumb is that for small populations (under 1,000), a sample size of 300 is appropriate, while for large populations (over 150,000), a sample size of at least 1,500 is necessary (cited in Milroy and Gordon 2003: 28). And whereas it is easy to imagine conducting a short, fill-in-the-blank survey on linguistic usages with 1,500 participants, matters become more difficult when we consider that the chief method for collecting data on language variation in its social context is the sociolinguistic interview (see Section 3.3), a semi-structured interview designed to approximate a casual conversation that lasts at least one to one-and-a-half hours. In addition, even if you do have the resources to conduct an appropriate number of interviews, they still need to be transcribed, and until further advances are made in automated speech-to-text transcribing tools, transcribing an interview still takes about ten hours for every hour of recorded speech. Further, there is the matter of actual linguistic and sociolinguistic analysis, the most time-consuming element of all. And even though computational methods are speeding the pace with which quantitative analyses can be conducted, there are always many qualitative components to consider as well (as noted above), and so it is quite likely that a very large body of interview data obtained from a truly representative sample will never be analyzed to the researcher's satisfaction. A classic case to bear in mind is Shuy, Wolfram, and Riley's (1968) foundational sociolinguistic study of Detroit African American English. While this study helped lay the groundwork for quantitative sociolinguistic study and its findings were invaluable, the fieldwork project itself teaches us a valuable lesson about sociolinguistics: In their zeal to obtain as representative a sample as possible, the research team conducted 702 interviews with appropriate participants, only to realize after the fact that they could not possibly analyze their whole body of data in any depth whatsoever (especially given the then-current state of automated technologies), and so they ended up basing their research on only thirty-six speakers, selected not at all randomly but "on the basis of their general suitability" (Milroy and Gordon 2003: 29).

Finally, there is the question of whether random sampling is really necessary or most useful for sociolinguistic study. Sociolinguists over the years have noted that linguistic usage is typically more homogeneous than other behaviors (e.g. purchasing preferences), since people in a given community do need at least a minimal level of common understanding; and so it is probably not necessary to obtain a sample large enough to be statistically representative to conduct a meaningful sociolinguistic study (e.g. Labov 1966: 180–181; Milroy and Gordon 2003: 28–29; Sankoff, G. 1980: 51–52). Even more important than sample size is the nature of the random sample: Sociolinguists are usually interested in seeing how particular linguistic features pattern across certain social factors (e.g. regionality, age, gender, ethnicity), and there is no guarantee that a strictly random sample will yield data from speakers in all the categories of interest, particularly if certain segments of the population are statistically underrepresented (e.g. ethnic minorities, residents of remote communities). Hence, as sociolinguistics has developed over the decades, its practitioners have moved away from the quest for random samples to other techniques that will yield the data of most interest.

Nonetheless, a random sample is still useful for answering certain research questions. In these cases, the researcher does not necessarily have to personally undertake the difficult process of constructing the sample but rather may be able to "piggyback" on a pre-selected random sample by adding questions to a more general survey already carefully designed to eliminate biases and obtain an adequate sample size. Hence, for example, Bailey and his research colleagues purchased a block of survey questions on the Texas Poll, a public opinion poll, in order to obtain information on the distribution of particular grammatical features across the state and across selected age groups (Bailey and Bernstein 1989; Bailey, Wikle, and Tillery 1997b). Of course, they could not ask the non-linguists conducting the poll to conduct sociolinguistic interviews with each survey respondent, but their survey responses on a wide range of features, coupled with the wide coverage of the survey population, yielded a broad picture of linguistic and social variation across a large geographic area, as well as valuable data on probable dialect change (Bailey *et al.* 1991, 1997b).

2.2.2 Proportionate stratified random sampling

If a random sample is desired but the different segments of the population you wish to study are unevenly represented, then it may be best to modify the strictly random sampling method and obtain a proportionate stratified random sample, essentially a random sample that is proportionate based on a certain variable. For example, if the community you are studying includes African Americans and Whites but only a small percentage of African Americans, you can construct a sample via random techniques modified to ensure that it includes the same percentage of African Americans as in the general population. The same technique may be applied if the population is unevenly distributed across geographic area. Hence, for example, in designing their comprehensive Survey of Oklahoma Dialects (SOD, begun in 1991), Bailey and his colleagues constructed a sample for the telephone survey portion of the study that included at least one speaker from even the most sparsely populated counties (and hence more speakers from densely populated counties), since they were interested in seeing how particular features patterned across urban and rural populations and needed to ensure that the sample would not inadvertently leave out speakers from sparsely populated rural areas. The survey yielded the very interesting finding that, whereas certain linguistic innovations, such as the /ɔ/–/ɑ/ merger in word pairs like *caught–cot*, appeared to be diffusing as expected, from densely populated areas to less dense areas (in a so-called hierarchical pattern), the Southern feature *fixin' to* (as in, "I'm fixin' to go" for 'I'm about to go') was diffusing outward from rural to urban areas, in a pattern of contrahierarchical diffusion, as evidenced in its distribution across space and apparent time – that is, in different age groups of speakers, born and raised in different time periods (Bailey *et al.* 1991).

2.2.3 Judgment sampling

Despite the utility of random and proportionate random sampling techniques in answering certain sociolinguistic research questions, most sociolinguists use a third sampling technique that has proven to be well suited for a range of types of studies, quota or judgment sampling. This type of sampling involves identifying in advance the types of speakers you want to study and then obtaining a certain number of each type of speaker – for example, older, middle-aged, and younger speakers; males and females; African Americans and Whites. The categories or "cells" are then filled either randomly, by researcher judgment of suitability / representativeness, or by working through participants' social networks, following Lesley Milroy's "snowball" technique (Milroy and Gordon 2003: 32). Because the categories in our judgment sample come directly from our research questions (e.g. "How is a particular feature distributed across age and gender groups in a given population?"), they enable us to get right to the heart of our research without simply hoping that our sampling technique will yield appropriate speakers or having to build impractically large samples until we have included all the population groups we want. The judgment sample is not random and so technically speaking does not ensure statistical representativeness; however, as noted above, we can usually be confident that the insights we obtain are generalizable to the larger population thanks to the relative uniformity of linguistic vs. other social behaviors.

Of course, deciding which speaker groups are important to study is not necessarily a straightforward matter, and we must base our judgments not simply on pre-determined research questions but on at least basic knowledge of the social groupings relevant to the population of study. If nothing else, we should be familiar with basic demographics, but sometimes more particularized categories will be important as well. Further, our categories may be based at least in part on previous studies of the same or other populations, whether for comparative purposes or because particular categorizations have been shown to yield insight into the questions that most concern us. For example, since variationists are interested in language change, they very often construct samples that include different age groups of speakers, based on the idea that one's basic linguistic usages are cemented during the time period in which their native language and dialect were acquired (see Section 2.4 below on the apparent time hypothesis), as well as a balance of male and female speakers, since many studies show differential diffusion of linguistic innovations across gender groups, with women often leading in adopting language changes. However, it is by no means a given that what was important and relevant in previous studies will prove so in your study, or that you can rely on previous studies in determining all relevant speaker groupings. Indeed, sometimes researchers conduct quite extensive studies of the social aspects of the community before deciding on participant cells, and often modifications occur in the course of study, as unexpected important social groupings are revealed.

Case study: How research questions shape samples: LAUSC vs. ANAE

As an example of how research questions shape judgment samples, let us consider two projects that investigated the same very large speech community, the United States and Canada, from two quite different angles. The first is the Linguistic Atlas of the United States and Canada (LAUSC), a project begun in the early twentieth century with the aim of getting a picture of the traditional dialects of North American, including their dividing lines and characteristic features, before they faded away. Armed with the sociolinguistic knowledge that particular types of speakers are more resistant to change than others (in particular, the non-mobile older rural males, or NORMs, of traditional dialect geographic studies) the researchers in the various subprojects conducted under the LAUSC umbrella constructed samples that included both rural and non-rural areas, older and middle-aged speakers, and speakers with little education as well as those with more. In constructing their maps, they focused mostly on older rural speakers since, again, these speakers were most likely to reflect traditional dialect usages. Various highly detailed dialect profiles resulted from the LAUSC projects, including the Linguistics Atlas of the Middle and South Atlantic States (LAMSAS; Kretzschmar 1994; McDavid and O'Cain 1980), the Linguistic Atlas of the Gulf States (Pederson, McDaniel, Bailey, and Bassett 1986), and the Linguistic Atlas of the Upper Midwest (Allen 1973). Figure 2.1 shows the dialect map resulting from the LAMSAS project, which indicates, among other divisions, a longstanding divide between Northern, Midland, and Southern dialect areas in the Eastern United States.

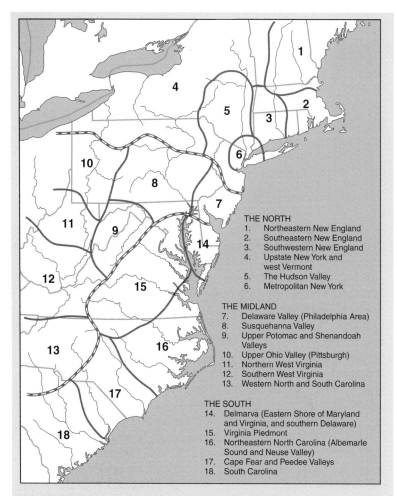

2.1 Dialect areas of the Eastern United States as revealed in the Linguistic Atlas of the Middle and South Atlantic States portion of the Linguistic Atlas of the United States and Canada (from Kurath, Hans, 1949, *Word Geography of the Eastern United States*, Ann Arbor: University of Michigan Press, p. 91, fig. 3).

In contrast, a very recent project on language variation across the US and Canada, the Atlas of North American English (ANAE; Labov, Ash, and Boberg 2006b) has a quite different focus: to obtain the most current picture possible of phonological variation in North America. (For an overview of the research project and some of its important general findings, see Ash 2003.) To this end, the sample, which originally included both urban and non-urban areas, was soon narrowed solely to urban areas, where changes tend to progress most rapidly; and for each location sampled, it was necessary to obtain data from at least one younger woman, since again, women and young people are expected to lead in language change over older speakers and men. The resulting picture in terms of large dialect divisions is not too different from the various LAUSC snapshots, although smaller subdialects seem to be losing their distinctiveness.

The most important, and surprising, finding of the ANAE project is that, contrary to popular and perhaps even previous sociolinguistic opinion, the large dialects of North America are actually getting more rather than less distinctive from one another. Most of the difference lies in vowel systems, especially those of the Inland North (located along the Great Lakes from Rochester, New York, to Chicago, Illinois) and the South. Each of these areas is characterized by a sweeping change in vowel pronunciations (i.e. a vowel shift). However, in each area vowel pronunciations are changing in quite different ways. Thus, for example, the Inland North is characterized by the Northern Cities Vowel Shift, in which, among other features, the vowel in words like *caught* is pronounced lower in the mouth, so that *caught* sounds like *cot*; in turn, the vowel in words like *cot* is pronounced farther forward in the mouth, so that *cot* sounds almost like *cat*. Conversely, in the Southeast, the vowel in *caught* may be lowered, but it also "breaks" into at least a two-part vowel, or diphthong, and so does not sound like *cot*, as it does in the North, and neither is *cot* fronted to *cat*. In addition, the chief characteristic of the Southern vowel system is the pronunciation of the diphthong in words like *time* and *ride* as a one-part vowel, or monophthong, as in [ta:m] for *time* and [ra:d] for *ride*. Other North American dialect areas (e.g. the Midland, the West, Canada) are distinguished from both the South and the Inland North by the merger of the vowels in *caught* and *cot* rather than the preservation of a pronunciation distinction, a merger which is gaining ground in North America even as the Northern Cities Shift and Southern Shift are progressing as well.

In short, the ANAE project reveals that regional dialect differences are alive and well – and even growing – in North America, despite predictions that increased interactions and intercommunications (including mass media) have resulted in the leveling out of dialect variation. Figure 2.2, the overview map resulting from the ANAE project, demonstrates the tenacity of the dialect lines uncovered in the much earlier LAUSC projects, as shown for example, in the Eastern US dialect divisions in Figure 2.1 above.

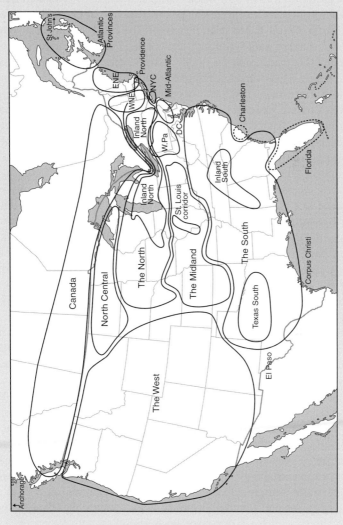

2.2 Dialect areas of the U.S. as revealed in the Atlas of North American English project (adapted from Labov, William, Sharon Ash, and Charles Boberg. 2006, *The Atlas of North American English: Phonetics, Phonology and Sound Change*, Berlin/New York: de Gruyter, p. 148, map 11.15).

As an example of how sampling procedures are shaped not simply by research questions but also by the characteristics of the communities of study, let us again consider two different projects, this time on a much smaller scale. In the early 1990s, Walt Wolfram, together with a team of graduate students of which I was one, launched his sociolinguistic studies in North Carolina with the investigation of Ocracoke Island, located in the Outer Banks island chain off the coast of North Carolina (Wolfram, Hazen, and Schilling-Estes 1999). The focus here was on describing the traditional Ocracoke dialect, distinct from mainland dialects due to its centuries of relative isolation, as well as investigating possible dialect change in the face of economic and demographic change that began taking place in the mid-twentieth century as Ocracoke was gradually transformed from a relatively self-sufficient community centered on a maritime economy to a magnet for tourists, summer beachgoers, and new year-round, full-time residents. In order to investigate dialect change, we needed to sample speakers of different age groups. At the same time, we needed a baseline, a description of the traditional Ocracoke dialect, and so we included in our sample only those islanders we considered to be "ancestral islanders" – that is, those who not only grew up on the island but who could trace their Ocracoke heritage back at least a couple of generations. Furthermore, whereas ethnicity-based variation is important in many Southern US communities, we quickly determined that there was no need to construct a balanced sample of White and African American speakers, since there was only one ancestral Black family on the island.

When the Ocracoke study was well underway, Wolfram and his team designed and conducted a study in a rural community in mainland North Carolina with some related and some different research aims. This community is Robeson County, a tri-ethnic area with a very large population of Lumbee Indians in addition to Whites and African Americans (Wolfram and Dannenberg 1999). As with the Ocracoke study, one of our aims here was to investigate dialect change in the face of gradual emergence from historical isolation, this time due in part to the geographic isolation brought on by very swampy terrain but also to the longstanding social isolation of non-mainstream ethnic groups in US society. Again, we included in our sample different age groups of speakers, as well as a balance of males and females. Another focus, though, was interethnic variation and so, unlike in Ocracoke, we purposely sought to construct a sample including balanced numbers of Whites, Blacks, and Lumbee rather than investigating one ethnic group alone.

Although sampling speakers based on relatively straightforward demographic categories is often very useful (though see Section 2.3

below for a discussion of complexities), sometimes more particularized social groupings are most important to the communities we study and more directly implicated in patterns of language variation and change than overarching categories like gender, ethnicity, and socioeconomic status. And it sometimes takes quite a bit of insight into the community, gained through extensive ethnographic involvement, to uncover the most relevant, locally important social groups. For example, as discussed in Chapter 1, Eckert (1989, 2000) grouped the teens in her study of a Detroit-area high school into categories that had been shown to correlate with patterns of variation and change in previous studies (e.g. gender, socioeconomic class). However, based on her extensive ethnographic work in the school, she realized that the students were more focused on their own locally salient social groups – the school-oriented jocks and non-academically oriented burnouts – than on socioeconomic status based on adult norms, and so she was able to construct a sample that included jocks, burnouts, and "in-betweens" and later to determine that membership status in these groups had more to do with patterns of language variation than did their parents' socioeconomic status.

Finally, despite all our careful planning, we sometimes miscalculate and fail to account for important local social groups in constructing our samples. Conversely, we sometimes begin our studies presuming or supposing that certain social groups are important, but they turn out not to be. For example, early in our studies of the Ocracoke community, we thought that there might be social and linguistic differences among islanders who lived on one side of Ocracoke Village (the Creek) vs. the other (the Point), as well as divisions based on membership in one of the two island churches. Fortunately, we had designed our interviews to include questions inquiring about these and other possible social divisions in the community, and we quickly realized that community members did not see divisions where we had speculated they might exist, and so we did not have to include these rather fine-grained divisions in our final sample but were able to stick with a straightforward sample stratified by age group and gender.

On the other side of the coin, as our studies in Robeson County were proceeding, we came to realize that there were important social divisions we were missing. We had expected, and found, linguistic and social differences across the three area ethnic groups, Whites, African Americans, and Lumbee Indians. What we did not anticipate were the linguistic differences we began to perceive among the Lumbee themselves. After careful observation and discussions with our

study participants and community leaders, we learned that there are
important social divisions within the Lumbee community, based not on
any readily observable demographic characteristic (e.g. socioeconomic
status) but on the particular geographically and historically defined
subcommunity to which each Lumbee belongs. These communities are
not very noticeable or clearly bounded, consisting for the most part of
small rural enclaves, often centered on a church or even a historic
church that no longer exists. However, they are very salient to the
Lumbee, and each is considered to be unique in character, and some
are unique in language use. Although we did not learn about these
communities in time to broaden our sample to include a balanced
sample of speakers from each of the different Lumbee communities (in
fact, we are still unsure exactly how many there are, since different
Lumbee make greater or finer distinctions), we luckily had obtained
enough speakers from several of the different communities, including
the one considered to be the most "authentic" in terms of Lumbee
identity and Lumbee dialect, the Prospect community, to determine
that there were linguistic differences between Prospect and non-
Prospect Lumbee, including the traditional Prospect pronunciation of
words like *time* and *ride* as something like [tɔɪm] and [rɔɪd] as opposed
to the more typical Southern pronunciations ([ta:m], [ra:d]) of the
non-Prospect Lumbee.

STUDENTS IN THE FIELD

In a very different cultural context, Cala Zubair (2012) decided that she needed
to radically reconstruct her sample, and indeed her entire research focus, based on
locally salient social groups she had discovered while in the field. Building on several
years' experience conducting ethnographic and sociolinguistic research in Sri Lanka, she
designed a study to investigate attitudes and ideologies among Sri Lankan university
students toward Formal Sinhala, Colloquial Sinhala, and English. Her original sample
population consisted of English majors, since they presumably would have a high degree
of awareness of, and strong opinions regarding, language in Sri Lanka. However, once
she began conducting interviews, she realized that she had missed a tremendously
important and quite rigid division among university students, between the so-called
"Raggers," who adamantly opposed English (and those who used it), and the
"Anti-Raggers," who viewed English as a means to increased opportunity. Naturally,
all English majors were Anti-Raggers, so Zubair had to go outside her original sample.
However, once she began studying the Raggers, she became so fascinated with them
that she shifted her focus entirely to Ragger linguistic and cultural practices, including

> their invention of new Sinhala words and phrases to avoid using common English ones and their exclusion of Anti-Raggers from campus locations they had declared as "Ragger" territory.

To summarize, we have seen that different communities and different research questions call for different sampling methods and yield populations of different types of composition. Whereas random samples allow for statistical generalizability, they often must be very large and can be quite difficult to obtain, due to the difficulty of finding an unbiased frame on which to base the sample and subsequently selecting and replacing participants without introducing bias. In addition, we can never be sure that a truly random sample will include speakers of all the social groups, or with all the social characteristics, we are interested in studying. Therefore, sociolinguists sometimes use modified random samples that include all social categories of interest. More often, they use judgment samples. We shape our judgment samples according to our research questions, but our judgment samples are also necessarily shaped by the communities we study. And, crucially, we cannot always rely on seemingly obvious demographic factors to determine what types of speakers we want to include in our study, but we must pay attention to locally salient groupings as well. Indeed, we sometimes must ask ourselves whether we can even determine speaker "cells" prior to initiating data collection, or whether the relevant groupings can only unfold once we are already in the field. In order to ensure the ecological validity of our samples and subgroupings, it is vital that we conduct background social, historical, and linguistic research on any community in which we intend to conduct sociolinguistic research; in addition, ideally we will also spend a good bit of time immersed in the community, conducting systematic observations, prior to designing our sample and beginning more targeted sociolinguistic study. There can be quite a wide range of social categories on which we base our judgment samples. What is important is that you have sound reasons for your categorizations, whether "objectively defensible criteria" such as "specifiable sociological and demographic criteria" (Milroy and Gordon 2003: 31), and / or categories uncovered in the course of careful background research or ethnographic study.

Case study: The effects of methods on dialectology

Although it may seem that truly representative random samples are inherently "better" than judgment samples and yield more accurate data on the distribution of linguistic features across social categories, Bailey, Wikle, and Tillery (1997b) demonstrated through careful study of the results of surveys conducted using random vs. judgment samples for two populations, Texas and Oklahoma, that the two types of samples yield quite comparable results, especially once non-sampling-related effects are carefully factored out. The two surveys of Texas speech were the Texas portion of the Linguistic Atlas of the Gulf States (LAGS; Pederson *et al.* 1986), and the Grammatical Investigation of Texas Speech (GRITS; Bailey *et al.* 1991). The former used a judgment sample to obtain mostly older native speakers from certain areas of Texas via face-to-face interaction with informants who were provided with frames designed to elicit various lexical items (e.g. "What word would you use for the beans that you break in half to cook?"). The latter was a random sample conducted via telephone and relied on more direct self-reports rather than less direct elicitation (e.g. "Have you ever used the term 'snap beans' for the beans that you break in half to cook?" If yes, "How often would you use the term: all of the time, some of the time, not very often or never?"). In addition, it included speakers of wider age range (born both before and after World War II) as well as wider areal coverage. The two surveys of Oklahoma speech were the Survey of Oklahoma Dialects telephone sample (SOD-T) and Survey of Oklahoma Dialects field sample (SOD-F). The first was a proportionate stratified random sample including both native and non-native Oklahoma residents as well as both urban and rural speakers, with county population serving as the stratification variable. The latter was a judgment sample, conducted face-to-face. Both SOD-T and SOD-F used self-reports.

The results of the comparisons at first glance suggest that using random vs. judgment samples indeed affects results, as there are significantly different usage levels for most features surveyed via each sampling method (chiefly lexical and grammatical items – for example, *y'all*, *fixin' to*, *might could*, and *snap beans*). However, as noted above, the two surveys for each state are different not only in terms of random vs. non-random sampling but also in terms of population sampled. Once population differences are factored out, usage levels for the linguistic features examined become practically the same, in the case of Oklahoma, and much more congruent, though still not identical, in the case of Texas. Hence, a comparison of SOD-F with SOD-T respondents who are Oklahoma natives from rural areas evens out differences in usage levels for the items *y'all* (singular and plural), *fixin' to*, *might could*, and *snap beans*. Similarly, a comparison of Upper Texas informants in LAGS with native respondents born before World War II in GRITS helps lessen differences for *might could* and *fixin' to*, though the differences in usage levels are still significant. However, Bailey *et al.* maintain that these differences are still not due to sampling differences but are rather due to differences in elicitation technique, since the LAGS survey used less direct elicitations while GRITS relied on direct self-reports. And whereas typically sociolinguists prefer to steer away from direct elicitations, since the frames may color responses (see Section 3.1 on survey questionnaires), in these two cases, self-reports most likely yield a more accurate picture of actual usage levels than indirect elicitations, since these two forms are quite infrequent and very difficult to elicit. For example, the indirect elicitation frame for 'might could' probably occasioned a very wide array of responses, with very few 'might coulds' among them: "When you get something done that was hard work all by yourself and your friend was standing around without helping, you say _____" (Bailey, Wikle, and Tillery 1997b: 57, fn. 15).

The overall conclusion to be drawn from their study on "The effects of methods" is that the effects of random vs. judgment samples seem to have very little to do with survey results compared with other effects such as differences in geographic coverage, age coverage, and elicitation technique. Bailey, Wikle, and Tillery's study thus adds further justification for sociolinguists' reliance on judgment samples, despite criticisms sometimes levied at them for not seeking truly representative samples. However, the different types of samples do serve different purposes: random samples are "clearly best for making inferences about the distribution of linguistic features in a given population" (Bailey *et al.* 1997b: 61), while judgment samples are better for investigating the diffusion of changes across time and space and, in the case of Linguistic Atlas surveys focused on older rural speakers, for establishing historical baselines and delimiting dialect areas (1997b: 61).

2.3 STRATIFYING THE SAMPLE

As noted above, sociolinguists often construct their samples based on particular social groups they determine to be important in the community and / or revealing in terms of the patterning of language variation and change. In other words, the sample is divided or stratified right from the outset. In addition, once our data are collected and preliminary analysis begins, we may decide to make further divisions or different groupings. We have already seen that deciding which groups to include in your sample requires prior research into your community as well as other sociolinguistic studies; further, it is vital to keep an open mind once you begin your study, as unexpected speaker groupings may emerge as relevant. In this section, we take a closer look at the types of groups into which a sample population can be stratified and quickly come to see that even the most seemingly straightforward speaker categories are readily problematized. Further, we have seen that group patterns are grounded in individual usages and that researchers are realizing increasingly that people and their language patterns are much more than the sum of the various demographic and other social groups to which they belong. Speakers are creative individuals who continually enact and shape social groupings rather than simply reflecting them. Individuals also move between social groups, whether throughout the course of their lives, in interactions with people with different group characteristics (e.g. in conversing with a White vs. African American speaker), or even in the course of a single conversation (e.g. I may more closely affiliate with my ethnic identity when talking about heritage and culture but more closely affiliate with my identity as a researcher when talking about science). Hence, the very notion of stratifying a sample according to pre-existing and unchanging social categories becomes problematic, and we have to figure out how to deal with the fact that identities are malleable and multifaceted and that language variation is not merely reflective of pre-existing group and individual identities but co-constitutive of them. Further, individual and group identities often have more to do with people's internal senses of belonging than externally imposed categorizations and, in turn, it has been demonstrated since the earliest days of variation analysis (e.g. Labov 1963) that individual attitudes, orientations, and ideologies are really the driving forces behind language variation and change rather than group membership *per se*. Thus, we must take care to look within group memberships for factors that are truly causative rather than merely correlative (for example, orientation toward or away from the local community as opposed to age group or occupation, as in Labov's classic Martha's Vineyard study).

2.3.1 Problematizing social categories: Social class, ethnicity, gender, and age

In stratifying their research samples, sociolinguists have tended to presuppose social divisions based on traditional demographic categories such as social class, race, sex, and age. At first glance, such categorizations may seem relatively straightforward, but all are fairly readily problematized. For example, social class is a difficult category on a couple of different levels. First is the question of what we mean by social class. In Western society at least, we probably tend to think first of some mixture of economic position and social status, perhaps ascertained by measures such as income, occupation, education, and type of residence / neighborhood. However, economic worth does not always neatly correlate with social standing, and sometimes people who can be grouped into the same economic class may have different social statuses. Hence, for example, in a given community in the US it may be the case that a university professor and an experienced plumber have the same income; however, the professor will be accorded higher status because their occupation is viewed as more prestigious. In addition, the factors that comprise social standing may be quite community specific. For example, in the Lumbee Indian community discussed above, certain community elders have higher social standing than their neighbors and relations, regardless of any demographic measures such as income or occupation; in addition, the Lumbee who are associated with the Prospect community (by lineage more so than by mere residence) are accorded greater prestige as "true" Lumbee than those who belong to other Lumbee subgroups. On the other side of the coin, we can question social class on quite a broad level and ask ourselves whether we can apply the same notion of the "social order" to all types of societies. For example, as noted above, in some communities and cultures social classes may be arranged along a linear hierarchy, with everyone orienting toward the upper social classes, while in other cases, class relations may be characterized by intergroup conflict (Rickford 1986). Furthermore, social or socioeconomic class may not be of equal importance in all societies; for example, social class traditionally has been far more important in Britain than in the US (e.g. Cannadine 1988: cited in Milroy and Gordon 2003: 41).

Even if we reach agreement on what constitutes social class, we still encounter difficulties when it comes to grouping people into classes. For example, do we categorize according to family or individual, given that families often share economic resources yet different members most likely have different occupations, incomes, etc.? Family members with no income have long been problematic in terms of social class categorization, and early findings pertaining to social class, gender, and language variation are blurred by the fact that women were typically assigned a social class based on measures pertaining to husbands or fathers rather than their own individual characteristics. There are also issues of class mobility, and it is difficult to decide whether to group someone of working-class roots but current professional standing into their social class of origin or a higher class. And finally, what is the role of individual and community perceptions of social standing vis-à-vis external measures of social class? It seems likely that such perceptions must come into play and that people will shape, or at least attempt to shape, their speech patterns to accord with how they see themselves. For example, we found in our studies of Ocracoke that one of the wealthiest men on the island also had some of the highest usage levels for the features of the non-standard local dialect. His linguistic behaviors corresponded with other practices that indicated that he considered himself a down-to-earth islander more akin to the rugged fishermen who symbolize the traditional Ocracoke way of life than to the well-to-do, college-educated hotel owner he was. Conversely, in many communities people steer their speech toward more standard varieties than would be predicted of their social class if their occupation warrants. Indeed, this is so commonplace that some sociolinguists have argued that the extent to which the standard language variety is valued in people's daily life – that is, their position in the **linguistic market** – plays a far greater role in shaping patterns of language variation and change than their class background (e.g. Sankoff and Laberge 1978).

Despite the reliance of early variationist studies on social class as defined according to traditional socieconomic measures rather than matters perhaps more directly indicative of social status or community members' perceptions of status and class-related identity, sociolinguists have at least long recognized that social class is a highly complex construct and that categorizing speakers according to socioeconomic status in sociologically and sociolinguistic meaningful ways is by no means a straightforward task.

Similarly, sociolinguists have, at least in theory, relinquished traditional notions of ethnicity and gender as equivalent to biological race and sex, respectively, as they have come to recognize that both are complex social constructs, partly constituted by the very linguistic usages we seek to correlate with them. For example, ethnicity defies ready definition (e.g. is it a matter of bloodline, shared practices and beliefs, or both?), and there are no objective criteria whereby people can be classified into ethnic groups, as evidenced in the fact that ethnic categorizations of the same community or even individual can change over time. Hence, for example, the Lumbee Indians, in the context of the US South and its longstanding bi-racial division between Whites and non-Whites, have at various points in history been grouped with Whites, classified as "persons of color," and referred to as "mixed," and they still struggle for full Federal recognition as *bona fide* Native Americans. In addition, as noted above in the discussion of Hoffman and Walker's (2010) Toronto study, it is likely that language variation correlates better with an individual's self-identification of ethnicity, including degree of affiliation with particular ethnic groups, than outward indicators. Further, as noted above, identities are malleable, and individual ethnic affiliations can and do change, perhaps over the course of a lifespan or even during the progress of a given interaction. Hence, for example, in Schilling-Estes (2004), I show how a Lumbee and an African American in Robeson County who are engaged in a sociolinguistic interview align themselves more and less closely with their own and each other's ethnic groups as they discuss different topics and align themselves differently with respect to what they are talking about. These differing alignments are effected and demonstrated at various levels of language patterning, ranging from the phonological to the discoursal; the study is discussed in more detail in Chapter 4, in our discussion of creative uses of stylistic variation.

We have already discussed several studies in which it is evident that gender, too, is by no means a "given" we can impose upon speakers as we stratify our samples. People may have quite different gender roles, ideologies and self- and other-perceptions in different communities, or even in different segments of the same community, and so gender-based patterns of language variation and of participation in language change may vary both across and within communities. Further, as with the other speaker categories into which we often stratify our samples, people use language variation to shape their gendered identities even as particular conceptions of such identities are reflected or called up (i.e. indexed) in language use. In addition, gender is by no means a simple matter of a male–female dichotomy. Indeed, Eckert (2000) maintains that intra-gender differences can be more important to people than intergender distinction, and people work harder to position themselves as particular types of males or females than simply as one sex or the other. So, for example, the jock girls in her studies are quite different socially and linguistically from the burnout girls, with the latter crafting more of a "bad girl" image, partly through heavy use of innovative language features characteristic of urban Detroit and so indicative of their orientation toward the local, urban, working-class culture rather than the academic, middle-class culture on which the jock girls are focused. Other gender roles fit even less neatly into non-hegemonic gender orders and ideologies. For example, Bucholtz's nerd girls (1999) are "atypical" because they are focused on intelligence and not "cuteness" or sexiness, while the African American drag queens in Barrett's (1995) study are certainly anything but typical in terms of either gender or ethnic categorization but have crafted a unique identity through their unique blend of language features associated with White women, gay men, and African Americans.

Even from the earliest days of variation study, in large-scale urban studies that sought to categorize people according to outwardly identifiable demographic criteria, it was evident that one could not simply speak of women's vs. men's patterns of language variation either within or across communities. For example, both Labov (1966) and Wolfram (1969) found in their studies of New York City English and Detroit African American English, respectively, that gender-based patterns were different in different social class groups, with female–male differences in usage levels for variants undergoing change being greatest in upper working / lower middle-class groups than in lower or higher social classes. In addition, Labov found that whereas women in general used more standard features than men, women showed a greater range of variation across speech styles and were actually less standard than men in casual speech. Hence, neither stratifying one's sample into gender groups nor identifying and interpreting gender-based patterns of language variation has ever been a simple matter, and things have only gotten more complicated as our understandings of the complexities of the social construct of gender (and even the seemingly straightforward categorization of biological sex) have become more nuanced.

Finally, because variationists are interested in language change, we almost always include in our samples speakers of a range of ages since, as noted above, people's current linguistic usages are very often indicative of, or at least give us valuable clues about, the state of the community language variety during speakers' formative years. Hence, it is likely that an older person's speech is reflective, at least to a degree, of older patterns of variation, while younger people will display more linguistic innovativeness. Very often, we stratify our sample according to age group. However, because age is a continuous rather than a discrete variable, it becomes immediately apparent that it can be very difficult to decide where to draw the lines. Do we simply group speakers into balanced divisions based on arbitrary cuts – such as age

20–40 = "younger," age 40–60 = "middle-aged," age 60+ = "older," or do we seek more ethnographically informed categorizations? For example, in our studies of Robeson County, NC, we decided after careful ethnographic and sociohistorical study to make more locally relevant generational divisions based on birth before or after locally important events / time periods that corresponded with greater and lesser degrees of isolation from other populations: speakers born before World War I often traveled or even lived outside the county for extended periods of time for work opportunities; those born between the two World Wars were more locally centered, since outside employment opportunities dried up after the first World War; those born after World War II but prior to school desegregation again came into increasing contact with the outside world; while those born after Robeson County schools were desegregated (in 1970!) also came into more contact with other local groups, namely Whites and Blacks.

Whereas usage levels and patterns for particular variables (e.g. the pronunciation of the vowel in *time* as [taːm] or [tɔɪm]) correlated well with these generational divisions, the patterning of other features made clear that generational divisions are always somewhat arbitrary, no matter how ethnographically informed. It is difficult to decide where to place speakers who fall slightly to one side of the dividing line between age divisions, and we want to be careful to not simply place them where they would make our age-based linguistic patterns most robust. In addition, even if we consider age as a continuous variable rather grouping people into discrete age categories (using tools ranging from a simple scatterplot of usage levels by birth year to statistical methods such as RBrul), we will often see that there may be a good bit of intra-generational variation as well as intergenerational similarity. For example, in considering levels or r-lessness among the Lumbee, we found declining usage levels in speakers of younger and younger age groups. At the same time, in looking within age groups, we also saw declining heterogeneity, since older individuals had quite widely varying usage levels for r-lessness, while younger speakers showed much less scatter. Further, there is the deeper issue of whether chronological age is really what correlates best with linguistic usages or if we also (or perhaps instead) should group speakers according to measures indicative of their life stage (Eckert 1997). For example, it may very well be the case that a 30-year-old who lives at home with his parents, works as a checkout clerk in a convenience store, and spends his evenings socializing with his high school friends, will display more youthful linguistic usages than a 30-year-old with a university degree and a professional career.

2.3.2 Practical considerations for problematic categories and categorizations

We have seen, then, a host of complexities when it comes to stratifying our population samples: social factors such as class, ethnicity, gender, and age resist easy definition, while at the same time individual speakers resist ready categorization into neat social groupings. Further, individual identity is not static or simply a by-product of the social groups to which each person belongs but rather is constituted in the interplay between ongoing linguistic–social associations and the continual unfolding of language and social meaning in interindividual discourse including, crucially, individual and group attitudes, orientations, and ideologies that are highly resistant to objective observation and classification. And while such factors may seem to be of interest chiefly to scholars of sociolinguistic and social theory, in reality all of these complexities present very practical difficulties from the very outset of planning a sociolinguistic study.

Given that individuals, unique and creative though they may be, do indeed consider themselves to be part of various groups and do orient their language usages toward or away from at least the stereotypes associated with certain groups, it is certainly not meaningless to group people into the very groups we often take for granted as "givens," since most likely our speakers do so, too. However, it is important to consider locally salient categorizations (e.g. Church ladies, porch sitters) as well as wider social groups (e.g. gender, ethnicity) in addition to individual attitudes and orientations that may not correspond with outward appearances. Hence, the careful researcher should strive to become ethnographically informed regarding community groupings, as well as psychologically informed about people's internal attitudes, senses of identity, etc., perhaps through relevant questions in sociolinguistic interviews, supplementary interviews focused on issues of identity and attitudes, and / or survey questionnaires.

In addition, I would urge attention not only to social and individual meanings as they exist at a given moment but also to how individuals and groups enact and re-enact social categories and move variously among social groups in discoursal interaction. Even if our focus is on macro-level correlations between social categories and patterns of variation and change, we would do well to pause at least every now and then and look at how speakers and speaker groups use features over time, whether over generations, years, or the course of a particular interaction. For example, a researcher whose chief interest is in how the Northern Cities Vowel Shift is moving through populations of different density and across age and gender groups might design a large-scale survey of various population centers in the relevant geographic area, stratify the sample according to evenly divided age groups and according to female or male "sex" as a stand-in for gender, and then see how the elements of the vowel shift pattern according to region, age, and sex. Such a study is likely to yield great insight into *how* the shift is progressing, but we could gain more insight into why it shows the patterning that it does through augmenting the large-scale survey with sociohistorical study, ethnographic research, and investigation of how the features associated with the shift are used in discourse. For example, perhaps the researcher will discover that certain historical events affected patterns of interaction, attitudes, and the like and hence divide speakers into more sociohistorically meaningful age divisions; or perhaps choose to group speakers into generational cohorts based on measures indicative of life stage rather than mere chronological age. The researcher might also find through ethnographic analysis and investigation of how features are used in interaction that in some communities there are important social factors besides age and gender affecting the progression of the shift. Indeed, this is exactly the case for the Northern Cities Vowel Shift, as demonstrated, for example, in Eckert's high school study, in which she shows that teens' membership in different peer groups, as well as degree of integration into these groups, has a great impact on how readily they adopt (or whether they resist) innovations associated with the Northern Cities Vowel Shift. At the same time, her correlation of linguistic usages with social networks and social practices, as well as her examination of how features are used in discourse, has a lot to tell us about what particular elements of the shift mean, including, for example, "urban" vs. "suburban" or wider orientation.

Issues of stratification are different if we approach our study from a social network or community-of-practice-based point of view. However, social network studies may still involve dividing speakers into demographic groups in addition to determining who interacts with whom and how strongly people in various networks are bound together. Hence, Milroy and Milroy (1985) examined speakers' linguistic usages according to gender / sex and neighborhood residence in addition to their degree of participation in local social networks. And whereas they initially found an overall correlation between network strength and the development and maintenance of localized, vernacular language norms, upon closer inspection they realized that only in the neighborhood where social network scores were quite different in different gender groups (due to different patterns of employment) was there a statistically significant correlation between network strength and vernacularity, with men showing stronger networks and more vernacular language and women showing looser networks and less localized linguistic usages. In other words, it seemed that gender as well as mere strength of network ties is implicated in the maintenance of vernacular norms, though conversely, part of what constitutes gender in this community in the first place is employment roles. In any case, the investigation of gender-based patterns of language use as well as patterns of variation according to network strength led to greater understanding of role of network strength in prohibiting or promoting dialect maintenance and dialect change than would the investigation of a population stratified by network score alone.

Under a community-of-practice-based approach, we may still group speakers into different categories, but this approach, above all others, recognizes that categories are constituted in practices. Hence, our speaker groups may look quite different to the demographically based categories in sociolinguistic studies taking other approaches. Nonetheless, as with traditional "speech community" and social network studies, we will find that linguistic variation correlates with social differences. For example, as noted in Chapter 1, Eckert (2000) found that teens' participation in certain practices (e.g. cruising to dangerous areas of Detroit) actually correlated more closely with particular linguistic usages than with membership in the jock vs. burnout social networks. Similarly, Bucholtz (1999) found that centrality vs. peripherality in the nerd girl group she studied affected the degree to which individuals would use nerdy language features like hyperstandard grammar and avoid non-nerdy features like current slang terms.

2.4   INVESTIGATING LANGUAGE CHANGE IN REAL TIME

As we conclude this chapter on designing the sociolinguistic study, it is important to consider a special kind of study design that is becoming more important as the field of sociolinguistics gains increasing time depth – the re-study of communities that were the subject of sociolinguistic study in decades past in order to add data on language change in real time to the insights gained via the investigation of probable changes in apparent time. Apparent time studies involve investigating the patterning of variation in different generations of speakers in a given community at a single moment in time. If the patterning is unstable, change in the community language variety can be inferred, following the **apparent time hypothesis**, which holds that, for the most part, the core features of an individual's vernacular language variety will be solidified for life by the time they reach their late teens, and so the speech of those in different age groups can be taken as representative of the speech of different time periods. Labov (1963) was the first to demonstrate the efficacy of the apparent time approach, in his classic study of Martha's Vineyard. He found increasing usage levels for the production of the /ay/ and /aw/ diphthongs with a centralized rather than low nucleus among younger and younger age groups, and then confirmed this evidence of apparent change with real-time data from an earlier Linguistic Atlas study of the same area that showed low usage levels for the centralized variants. Subsequently, sociolinguists have used the apparent time construct to infer changes in progress, obtaining real-time confirmation whenever possible from earlier dialectological studies or other evidence on previous stages of the language variety. However, such data were not as directly comparable as desired, since they were not obtained via the same methods as modern sociolinguistic studies (chiefly, the sociolinguistic interview); nor were the data as comprehensive in terms of amount and type of data from each speaker (e.g. connected naturalistic speech as well as elicited items) and from each population segment of each community (e.g. social classes, sexes, races). It has only been relatively recently that quantitative sociolinguistics has had enough time depth that researchers can now design and conduct meaningful re-studies of communities originally investigated via modern sociolinguistic methods.

At first glance, designing a re-study may seem relatively straightforward, since seemingly simple replication of the original study design is all that is required. However, questions start arising right away. The first is who to study: the exact same speakers as in the original study, different speakers of the same age groups as in the original study, and / or speakers of the next generation(s). It turns out that any or all of these groups will provide us with valuable information, but each provides different answers. Panel studies, those involving the same speakers as the original study, provide information on whether individual vernaculars really are stable, per the apparent time hypothesis, or whether there is instability across the life span, so-called age grading. However, they can tell us nothing about whether there has been any change in the community language variety. For this information, we must turn to trend studies – those involving new speakers in the original age groups, as well as younger generation(s). A third possibility is a truncated panel study (Trudgill 1988), in which we do not re-sample from the original age groups but simply add data from younger speakers to the original study. Clearly, conducting a panel study is quite difficult, practically speaking, since it will almost certainly be impossible to locate all original study participants and get them to agree to participate in a follow-up study. Hence, we have to rely on a subset and can only hope that we can obtain some sort of balance across the social groups into which the original sample was stratified. Trend studies are not without problems, either; for example, we have to take care to ensure that our new sample matches the old one as closely as possible on all criteria, not just in terms of age groups but also categories such as social classes, ethnicities, etc. In addition, the population demographics of the community may have changed, and we may have trouble locating new speakers who fit the original social criteria (and indeed have to question whether such speakers would now yield the most accurate picture of language use in the now-changed community). And of course the oldest age group will certainly have diminished in size, if they have not disappeared completely.

The difficulties in designing and conducting re-studies in real time by no means end with the securing of the appropriate speakers. Trudgill (1988) astutely outlines several key issues: In addition to considering who the interviewees are, we also have to think about who the interviewer(s) should be: at first glance, it seems like we would want to use the same person or people as in the original study, to ensure maximal comparability. However, as Trudgill (1988) points out, the original researcher will have aged and otherwise changed and will perhaps have a different effect on interviewees' speech than a younger interviewer with characteristics comparable to those of the original researcher decades ago. Further, there is the issue of the interview questionnaire. Again, it seems logical that one would administer the exact same interview; however, some questions (and / or reading passages and word lists) may be dated and hence more likely to yield puzzled looks (or ridicule) rather than naturalistic speech. In addition, sociolinguistic elicitation techniques themselves have improved over the years, and the researcher must choose between using newer methods more likely to yield naturalistic speech or older methods that more closely parallel those used in earlier studies.

Case study: Norwich revisited

One of the earliest and most instructive examples of a thoughtfully designed real-time study is Trudgill's (1988) re-study of Norwich, England, a community he studied first in 1968 (1974) and then revisited in 1983. Trudgill conducted a truncated panel study, adding speakers born between 1958 and 1973 to the original sample consisting of speakers born between 1875 and 1958. Rather than simply blindly replicating the exact methods and data-gathering situations of 1968, Trudgill realized that no matter what he did, things would not be exactly the same, and so he carefully considered how best to achieve comparable language data. He decided that he was too different from his former self to ensure comparability in terms of interviewer effects, since he was now older, more educated, and no longer simply a "local" with a strong local dialect; hence, he employed a young interviewer from the local area. At the same time, while realizing that part of his old interview were dated (e.g. a reading passage that included older slang terms like "gear" for clothes) and that current researchers had better methods for eliciting vernacular speech than he did in 1968, he nonetheless decided to keep the original interview, since he did not want to risk inadvertently obtaining more genuinely vernacular but less comparable data in the newer study.

Based on his careful research, Trudgill was able to confirm that several apparent changes observed across generations in 1968 were indeed progressing in 1983, including the replacement of /e:/ in words like *face* and *gate* with /æɪ/, and the merger of the vowels in word pairs like *moan* and *mown*. He also found other changes that had gone to completion (the merger of *beer / bear*) or near-completion (the production of /t/ as a glottal stop, at least in casual speech style).

However, his real-time study also revealed that apparent time studies cannot tell us everything. One new feature, the production of /θ/ and /ð/ as [f] and [v], respectively, was not present at all in 1968 but was now widespread among younger Norwich speakers; while another major change, the rapid influx of [w]-like productions of /r/, was incipient in 1968 but disregarded as a minor idiosyncrasy or even a speech defect rather than the important new feature it turned out to be. And whereas the latter change might have been noted if the original sample had been larger, there is no way Trudgill could have observed the former change in the earlier study, since it simply had not yet been introduced. A further admitted limitation of Trudgill's re-study was that it did not include panel as well as trend methodology, and so he could not conclusively demonstrate his impression that certain innovations were being adopted by all age groups while others were confined solely to the youngest speakers.

Trudgill's study thus serves as a model in several regards: it outlines carefully the decisions we must make in designing re-studies that are as comparable as possible to the original studies we seek to replicate, and it demonstrates that as robust as apparent time studies have proven to be, the fullest picture of language change in progress can only be revealed via real-time investigation.

Case study: Martha's Vineyard 1961–1962, 1997–2000, and 2001–2002

The Martha's Vineyard community that served as the basis for Labov's groundbreaking study of change in progress (1963, 1972c: 1–42) has been the subject of two re-studies, each one yielding different results and hence providing a striking demonstration of the effect of research methods on results. The first re-study was conducted by Meredith Josey during 1997–2000 (Blake and Josey 2003; Josey 2004) and had slightly different research foci than the original study. For example, it focused on islanders from only one town rather than towns in the two main island regions, focused on the centralization of /ay/ only rather than on both /ay/ and /aw/, and also focused more intently on acoustic phonetic analysis than was practicable at the time of the original study. The second re-study, conducted by Jennifer Pope in 2001 and 2002 (Pope, Meyerhoff, and Ladd 2007), was intended to replicate Labov's study as closely as possible in terms of sampling procedure, survey methods, and research foci. The same island regions were covered, the same reading passage and word list as in Labov (1963, 1972c) were used, both /ay/ and /aw/ were examined, and the analysis was chiefly auditory, with impressions confirmed by limited acoustic analysis, as in the original work. Blake and Josey (2003) and Josey (2004) determined that centralization was receding rather than expanding in the early 2000s and suggested that the feature seems to have lost its iconic status as a marker of islander speech as islanders have grown to accept the summer people and new residents they initially resisted in the mid-twentieth century. Conversely, Pope, Meyerhoff, and Ladd (2007) found that centralization was indeed alive and well, particularly for /aw/, and that there was still a good bit of tension between ancestral islanders and newer residents and visitors.

Pope *et al.* (2007) suggest that the discrepant findings are due partly to the different research foci but also, crucially, to differences in fieldwork methods and their resultant differences in the researchers' experiences and observations of the island community. Because of their focus on /ay/, Blake and Josey conclude that centralization in general is receding; however, while Pope *et al.* (2007) confirm a decrease in centralized /ay/, they also find centralized /aw/ to be holding steady and indeed increasing. In addition, Pope *et al.* elicited a wider range of speech styles, since they used interview speech, reading passages, and word lists; whereas Blake and Josey report only that they conducted sociolinguistic interviews. Further, the social coverage of the island is much greater for Pope *et al.*, since they sampled residents from all island towns, and since Pope sought connections with down-to-earth islanders (by staying in a youth hostel, hitchhiking around the island, and visiting in the winter as well as the summer tourist season), while Josey interviewed only Chilmark residents she met through her work as an au pair for one of the island's longstanding and wealthier residents in the last spring and early summer of each fieldwork year.

The two researchers' different connections to the island communities yielded not only different types of speech data but also different interpretations of island society and the social meaning of language variation. Blake and Josey rely on income figures and their own experiences to conclude that islanders are now more prosperous and less resentful of outsiders and hence no longer need linguistic markers of separateness such as centralization. However, Pope *et al.* point out that income alone is not a reliable measure of economic well-being (cf. Section 2.3.1 above on social class), especially given the soaring cost of housing on Martha's Vineyard; and there still exists a division between longstanding island fishers and farmers and wealthier (mostly newer) occupants, a distance marked in part by linguistic difference. Pope *et al.* further demonstrate the continued importance of the centralization of /ay/ and /aw/ through direct correlation of usage levels for the island variants with positive, negative, and neutral orientations toward Martha's Vineyard, exactly as Labov had done in 1963.

The two re-studies of Martha's Vineyard thus reveal that whereas one can obtain valuable information on sociolinguistic patterns via a range of methodologies and research foci, it is only

through careful replication of sampling procedures, survey
methods, and, as much as possible, the relationship between
the researcher and those being researched that a full picture of
language change in real time can truly be obtained.

In my own research, I have encountered other, more subtle
difficulties in designing and interpreting the results of real-time
studies: No matter how carefully we design a re-study such that we
replicate the original sample, interview conditions, and interviewer–
interviewee relationship, we can never ensure that the earlier and
later data-gathering session and resultant data are exactly parallel.
This is because no matter how tightly we control for factors such as
setting, participants, and interview techniques, we can never have
complete control over how our interviewees will *interpret* the interview context or interviewer–interviewee relationship. For example,
in the early 2000s, I designed a re-study of Smith Island, Maryland,
in order to determine whether an apparent change toward increasing dialectal distinctiveness observed in the mid-1980s was indeed
being sustained in real time. The study involved both trend and
panel methods, and although it was very difficult to locate original
study participants among the ever-decreasing island population, several original interviewees were re-interviewed. Among these were a
male aged seventeen at the time of the original interview and thirty-
three at the second ("Danny"), and an island schoolteacher in her
mid-twenties in the mid-1980s and late thirties at the time of the
later interview ("Jenna"). It was not possible to replicate interview
conditions as exactly as would be desirable; however, most of the
same differences across time applied to both interviewees. In the
mid-1980s each was interviewed by a fellow islander in their island
home, while in the early 2000s, each was interviewed by the same
two strangers (researchers from a local university) in a less personal
location (the interviewee's business office and the island community
center, respectively).

Given the external contextual differences that seemingly would tend
toward more natural speech in the first interview and more guarded
speech in the second, it is not overly surprising that Danny's later
interview shows lower usage levels for the two local vernacular variants studied: the production of /ay/ with a raised nucleus and production of /aw/ with a fronted rather than backed glide. However, it is by
no means a "given" that his earlier interview represents his "real"
vernacular speech: It is evident from the minute one begins listening

to the earlier interview that Danny is not speaking unselfconsciously but is instead playing a game. In response to the awkwardness of being questioned about his life by someone who really knows all about his life, Danny produces a highly stylized "mock serious" interview, replete with such features as exaggeratedly elevated diction, sing-songy intonational contours, and slow, deliberate pacing (the two parties' frequent laughter is also indicative of the "mock serious" frame). Hence, this is not the way he "really" speaks, and he may very well be exaggerating his usage levels for Smith Island dialect features as part of his performance of an islander giving a serious interview about the community and its speech. Indeed, his later interview is more of a "real" interview, though we cannot know if it yields his "real" speech since it is held in a relatively formal setting.

The second speaker, Jenna, also has quite different interview conditions at the two different time periods. However, in contrast to Danny, her speech is stable with respect to the Smith Island /ay/ and /aw/ variants. Most likely this is because, despite external differences in setting and participant structure, each time she frames the interview in the same way – as an occasion for her to climb up on a soapbox and deliver to an imagined general audience her strong opinions on the lack of adequate funding for the Smith Island school. Hence, for her, what appear to be two quite different speech events are essentially the same thing, while for Danny the events are different (mock vs. serious interview), though not in the ways we would expect (casual interview, less casual interview).

Luckily, the real-time studies that have been conducted since the mid-1990s do reveal that the changes suggested by original apparent time studies are indeed sustained in real time. In other words, researchers *can* rely on the apparent time construct in designing new studies and need not replicate every older sociolinguistic study for conclusive proof of changes in progress. In fact, as Sankoff (2006) notes, apparent time studies if anything underestimate rather than overestimate the progress of change. When trend studies are combined with panel studies, we tend to see individual change in the direction of incoming community changes in addition to change across different age groups of speakers. Hence, most changes seem to be accelerated by age grading. This is especially true when people are aware of the change and the innovative form is socially desirable. Of course, the robustness of the apparent time construct in no way precludes the need or desire for further studies in real time, and it remains necessary to take great care in designing one's re-studies, to ensure that the difficulty of obtaining the appropriate speaker the second time around ends up being worth the effort.

2.5 SUMMARY

In this chapter, we have walked through the first steps in conducting a successful sociolinguistic fieldwork project: carefully selecting your community of study, selecting your sampling method, and stratifying your sample. None of these steps is straightforward. We have examined a number of ways of conceiving of "community," from geographically bounded urban neighborhoods to urban and rural social networks to communities of practice whose participants may or may not be located in the same physical space, and whose make-up is multi-leveled and malleable. We have also considered whether we should start from the "linguistic" or the "social" side of sociolinguistics – that is, choosing a language variety and finding people who speak it or locating a social group of interest and investigating how they speak. We even questioned the reification of "languages" and "dialects" themselves, since every individual uses language slightly differently, and it may be more valid to speak of person's engaging in "languaging" rather than languages or dialects as entities. Further questions arise in considering sampling methods: while random samples are the only type that truly ensure statistical representativeness, they are not very practicable in sociolinguistic study and are not necessarily best suited to our purposes. Rather, judgment samples, involving the selection of speakers who meet the criteria we are interested in studying, are usually more useful for our studies of the patterning of language variation and change across particular social groups. However, deciding how to group our speakers is problematic as well, and we have learned that we probably should not rely on pre-determined, "big picture" categories such as social class, ethnicity, or gender, but rather should consider locally important social groups and social meanings. Finally, we consider the special planning that needs to go into real-time studies, since in conducting community re-studies we ideally want to keep our study conditions as similar to the original study as possible but have to acknowledge that there are some things we simply cannot hold constant, including how participants will conceive of interview interactions in their minds, no matter how carefully we control all external conditions.

We stress throughout this chapter and indeed throughout the book that there is no single best type of community or methodological approach. Rather, we can only gain full understanding of the complex interrelation between linguistic variation and social meanings when we approach our studies from a variety of perspectives, including looking at categories and meanings as both global and local, established and unfolding, and as constructed over the course of decades as well as within particular interactional moments.

Suggested readings ▬▬▬▬▬▬▬▬▬▬▬▬▬▬▬▬▬▬▬

PATRICK, PETER 2002. THE SPEECH COMMUNITY. IN J.K. CHAMBERS, PETER TRUDGILL, AND NATALIE SCHILLING-ESTES (EDS.), *THE HANDBOOK OF LANGUAGE VARIATION AND CHANGE.* MALDEN, MA: BLACKWELL, 573⁻597.

This article presents an in-depth discussion of what scholars of language, historically and currently, have considered to be the proper object of linguistic study. It considers a variety of conceptualizations of "speech community," ranging from Chomsky's notorious "ideal speaker–listener, in a completely homogeneous speech community" to community-centered definitions focusing on shared patterns of linguistic usage and social practice. These include Labov's notion of shared linguistic norms, Hymes' focus on speakers' social rather than linguistic behaviors and ideologies, and LePage's emphasis on individuals' linguistic repertoires rather than on artificially homogenized abstractions such as "dialects" and "languages."

BUCHOLTZ, MARY 1999. "WHY BE NORMAL?" LANGUAGE AND IDENTITY PRACTICES IN A COMMUNITY OF NERD GIRLS. *LANGUAGE IN SOCIETY* 28: 203–223.

Although the bulk of this article investigates the sociolinguistics of one small community, the introductory sections provide a broad overview of different notions of "speech community." Bucholtz urges sociolinguists to adopt socially centered views that see the speech community as "a language-based unit of social analysis" (p. 577) rather than Patrick's (and Labov's) linguistically centered definition of the speech community as "a socially-based unit of linguistic analysis" (p. 577). She provides a useful, point-by-point comparison of the Labovian notion of "speech community" with the socially centered notion of "community of practice."

BAILEY, GUY, TOM WIKLE, AND JAN TILLERY 1997b. THE EFFECTS OF METHODS ON RESULTS IN DIALECTOLOGY. *ENGLISH WORLD-WIDE* 18: 35–63.

As described in detail in the case study in Section 2.2 above, Bailey *et al.* present and compare results of sociolinguistic studies grounded in random vs. judgment samples. Although at first glance sampling methods appear to affect results (i.e. usage levels for particular linguistic features across different generations), both types of samples in fact yield essentially the same results once non-sampling-related effects (population differences, differences in elicitation techniques) are factored out.

CUKOR-AVILA, PATRICIA AND GUY BAILEY 2013. REAL AND APPARENT TIME. IN J. K. CHAMBERS AND NATALIE SCHILLING (EDS.), *THE HANDBOOK OF LANGUAGE VARIATION AND CHANGE*. 2ND EDN. MALDEN, MA: BLACKWELL.

This chapter provides a comprehensive overview of studies in real and apparent time and demonstrates that, when used judiciously, apparent time data is an excellent stand-in for real-time data. The authors also note that, ideally, apparent time studies should be complemented with studies in real time, though real-time data is often quite difficult to acquire and real-time studies require extra care in their design, to ensure comparability across time periods. The issue of change vs. stability across the lifespan of individuals is also treated in detail.

SANKOFF, GILLIAN 2006. AGE: APPARENT TIME AND REAL TIME. *ELSEVIER ENCYCLOPEDIA OF LANGUAGE AND LINGUISTICS*. 2ND EDN. ARTICLE NUMBER: LALI: 01479.

This encyclopedia entry from one of the world's leading experts in real-time study provides a concise yet comprehensive overview of studies in real and apparent time from the pre-Labovian period through the present day. Comparison of original apparent time and subsequent real-time studies from around the world reveal that the validity of the apparent time construct as a predictor of language change in progress can indeed be upheld. In fact, Sankoff concludes that "Far from misleading us about the existence of change, apparent time generally underestimates the rate of change," since adults often do change their language slightly over the course of their lifespan in the direction of ongoing community change.

TRUDGILL, PETER 1988. NORWICH REVISITED: RECENT LINGUISTIC CHANGES IN AN ENGLISH URBAN DIALECT. *ENGLISH WORLD-WIDE* 9(3): 33–49.

In this classic article, Trudgill provides sound general advice to researchers through detailed discussion of his personal decision-making process in designing a real-time study of a community he himself had previously studied. He discusses the necessity of ensuring maximal comparability across time periods, astutely pointing out that even using the exact same elicitation techniques and interviewer(s) will not necessarily yield the "same" interview conditions or speech of the same level of vernacularity. Trudgill also presents insightful discussion and interpretation of his results and observes, along with other researchers in real time, that the apparent time construct is highly useful but must be applied with caution, since some apparent changes will turn out to be cases of age grading and others will have ceased progressing. In addition, the researcher in apparent time may overlook changes in their incipient stages, especially ones that are linguistically or sociolinguistically unexpected.

3   Data-collection methods

In this chapter we cover a range of data-collection methods and instruments, from surveys conducted via questionnaires to sociolinguistic interviews to ethnographic participant-observation. In addition to discussing methods for obtaining data on variable language production, we discuss techniques for obtaining data on perception from within a sociolinguistic framework, including issues related to listeners' identification of features, varieties, and speakers, as well as listener attitudes toward those who use particular features, varieties, and codes. In each case, we discuss both designing and implementing the various techniques, as well as the advantages, disadvantages, and purposes of each. At issue throughout is the question of "authenticity," and we consider whether it is possible or even desirable to seek to remove researcher effects, in an effort to overcome Labov's observer's paradox: "To obtain the data that is most important for linguistic theory, we have to observe how people speak when they are not being observed" (1972a: 113). This chapter concludes with the recommendation that, wherever possible, researchers should seek to use a variety of data-collection methods in each of their studies since, as Labov so aptly put it in the earliest days of variationist sociolinguistics, we most closely approach sociolinguistic truth "by convergence of several kinds of data with complementary sources of error" (Labov 1972a: 97).

3.1 SOCIOLINGUISTIC SURVEYS

3.1.1 Method of administration: Face-to-face or long distance

The earliest dialect studies were conducted via survey questionnaires designed to elicit information on a range of language forms – lexical, phonological, and grammatical. A few early studies employed postal questionnaires, including the first dialect geographic study, conducted in Germany by Wenker, beginning in 1876. However, researchers soon decided that it would be advantageous on a number of levels to send out trained fieldworkers to administer questionnaires in person, and until recent decades, most sociolinguistic and dialectological studies that included a survey component relied on face-to-face rather than long-distance methods. Face-to-face surveys allow more control over who the respondents are, since we cannot know from long-distance surveys whether claimed demographic and other characteristics (e.g. attitudes) are accurate. In addition, administering surveys in person allows us to record responses ourselves (through on-the-spot phonetic transcription or audio recording), to record variable as well as categorical usages (since a single respondent may give more than one response to an elicitation in person but probably not on paper), and to provide and request clarification. In addition, because in-person surveys are usually administered orally, respondents may be more relaxed than when filling out a written form and so produce more naturalistic data.

However, long-distance surveys have their own advantages: They require much less time, effort, and money than in-person surveys and so allow for broader population coverage in a shorter amount of time. In addition, one can argue that respondents may actually feel more rather than less comfortable with long-distance surveys, since the presence of a fieldworker who is either an advanced student or a professor may be intimidating. Technological innovations since Wenker's time have also created new possibilities for long-distance surveys. Telephone surveys offer wide geographic and demographic coverage as well as the ability to audio record (and ascertain the veracity of at least a few speaker characteristics – e.g. gender). In addition, Internet-based surveys allow one to record very detailed information not only on linguistic usages but also on such measures as response time and eye movement. Further, computer-based surveys enable one to relatively easily include computer-manipulated stimuli, in order to test subtle facets of dialect perception. For example, Plichta, Preston, and Rakerd (2005) conducted an Internet survey of people's perceptions of features associated with the Northern Cities Vowel Shift currently taking place in much of the Inland Northern US. Participants from both within and outside the Northern Cities region listened to computer-synthesized words with various degrees of vowel shift (e.g. words ranging along the continuum from [sad] to [sæd]) and then selected whether they had heard, for example, *sod* or *sad*.

STUDENTS IN THE FIELD

Internet-based surveys can be enormously helpful in conducting research on multiple speech communities, allowing researchers to collect data efficiently and inexpensively. They do have potential drawbacks, though, as Jason Sanderson discovered in his study of Gallo and Breton speakers in the communities of Rennes and Brest in Brittany, France. He designed an Internet survey to initiate his study of community identity and to help develop topics for later face-to-face sociolinguistic interviews, thinking that this would allow him to sample a wide portion of the population. He decided to approach potential participants through a Facebook group of Bretons. The group's moderator was supportive and encouraged group members to participate. The initial response rate was good – nearly 400 people responded to his survey. But the generational make-up of the response pool was more uniform than Jason had hoped: the majority of respondents were under age 30, and very few were over 40. Later, in a follow-up Internet survey, Jason had to deal with the unfortunate consequences of one participant's negative comment on the Facebook group site. The comment affected how other participants viewed the survey, and because the group's moderator changed between the initial and follow-up surveys, Jason found himself doing "damage control" without the leader's support. The result of these complications was a significant decrease in the response rate for the follow-up survey.

Whether we do our fieldwork online or face-to-face, all sociolinguists face challenges like these: our sample sizes may be imbalanced, or our connections to informants may be subject to the vagaries of community relationships. But these obstacles can nevertheless be overcome if we remain flexible and open to new opportunities. Despite his setbacks, Jason was able to glean invaluable information from his surveys. In addition, he focused in depth on the more open-ended discussion gathered in face-to-face interviews, giving his project a valuable qualitative component in addition to the quantitative picture the survey provided. His experience shows that successful data collection can take many forms, some of which may surprise us.

Both in-person and long-distance surveys serve very pointed purposes that make them useful sociolinguistic research tools in their own right, as well as useful complements to sociolinguistic interviews and ethnographic–linguistic observations. Namely, surveys allow for greater breadth of coverage, in terms of both population and number of features examined, and in addition allow us to target features that may or may not show up in conversational interviews, as well as detailed information on the patterning of the features we are most interested in.

3.1.2 Types of survey questions / elicitation frames

Sociolinguistic surveys can be composed of different types of questions (more precisely, elicitation frames, since not all items are questions) designed to yield information on different types of research questions. Almost all will elicit basic demographic information, often at the end of the survey; and even those not specifically focused on language attitudes sometimes will elicit information on attitudes and orientations, to see if such matters are correlative with language variation. For example, the first section of the telephone portion of Bailey, Tillery, and Wikle's (1997a) Survey of Oklahoma Dialects (SOD-T) included questions about how residents liked living in Oklahoma and their local neighborhoods, as well as whether they considered Oklahoma to be a southern state. In addition, they even included some items designed to yield insight into individuals' openness to new experiences (and perhaps new language forms) through having them rate how strongly they agreed or disagreed with statements such as: "It's better to have life go along smoothly than to be surprised, even when the surprises are pleasant," "In general, I like to take risks," and "I like to bet on long shots."

Traditionally, dialectological surveys were concerned primarily with eliciting forms and features. In more recent decades, as sociolinguists became interested in vowel system shifts, including the progress of vowel mergers, some survey questionnaires began to include items and tasks designed to elicit judgments of whether or not particular minimal pairs sounded the same or different. In addition, sociolinguists may use elicitation frames reminiscent of those used by structural and generativist linguists (e.g. grammaticality judgments, sentence permutations) in order to learn more about the full range of patterning of particular features as opposed to simple presence, absence, and frequency. Elicitation frames are used not only in survey questionnaires, but they also may serve as a valuable supplement to sociolinguistic interviews, the chief method of data collection since the inception of variationist sociolinguistics. Interviews can only tell us what forms people happened to use on that particular occasion of talk, not which forms they might use on a different occasion, which forms they cannot use, or the full range of environments where a form may and may not be used.

Eliciting forms and features

In order to elicit forms and features, researchers can use either direct (self-reports) or indirect elicitations. Direct elicitations investigate a person's familiarity with a particular form by naming the form in question. For example, Bailey, Tillery, and Wikle's (1997a) Survey of Oklahoma Dialects chiefly comprised direct elicitations, as shown in (3.1) below, which reproduces question 2 of the survey instrument.

(3.1)

> 2.1 Have you heard the term "SNAP BEANS" used for the bean that you break in half to cook?
>
> (1) yes
>
> (If yes)   2.2   How often would you use that term: all of the time, some of the time, not very often or never?
>
>   (1) all   (2) some   (3) not often   (4) never
>
> (2) no
>
> (If no)   2.3   What term would you use?

In contrast, indirect elicitations are designed to prompt a person to *produce* the item of interest. They can take several different forms, such as questions of the form, "What do you call ...?" or fill-in-the-blanks, and they may be used to elicit a full range of linguistic forms. Bailey *et al.*'s SOD-T survey included a number of indirect questions designed to elicit lexical items, for example "What do you call those little bugs that get on you in the grass and make you itch?" (looking for *redbugs* or *chiggers*) and "What do you call the enclosed place where hogs are kept?" (looking for *pig pen* or *sty*). The worksheet used in connection with the LAUSC projects used questions that are a bit more indirect: for instance, "Where did you keep your hogs and pigs?"; "The thing you put in your mouth and work back and forth and blow on it. Do you remember any other names for it?" (looking for *harp, breath harp, mouth organ, harmonica,* etc.). The Linguistic Atlas worksheet also used fill-in-the-blanks to elicit pronunciations and grammatical features: for example, variant pronunciations of the word *yolk* were elicited with the question "What do you call the two parts of an egg? One is the white; the other is ____," while variants of the past tense of *drive* (e.g. *drove, druv, driv*) were elicited with "I wanted to hang something out in the barn, so I just took a nail and ____." Other elicitations can be even less direct: Thus, Bailey *et al.* used the following frames to elicit phonological features, even though they seemed to be lexical elicitations: "When are you most likely to hear an owl hoot?" (to elicit information on the monophthongization of /ay/ before voiceless consonants, as in [na:t] for *night*); "Now what about those large birds that sit on telephone poles and swoop down to kill mice and other small animals, what do you call those?" (to elicit information on the merger of /ɔ/ and /a/ in word pairs like *hawk / hock*).

Eliciting information on structural limitations of forms

In addition to eliciting data on which linguistic features can be used in particular languages and language varieties, linguists need to know which forms and structures cannot be used. Furthermore, if we are interested in language variation, we need to know which environments favor, disfavor, and prohibit variable usages. Because non-use in speech or straightforward elicitation may be due to accidental gaps rather than ungrammaticality, sociolinguists and generative and anthropological linguists must turn to sentence permutation and judgment tasks.

Sometimes these tasks are included in questionnaires and sociolinguistic interviews; in other cases, researchers may return to interviewees to conduct more targeted linguistic tasks subsequent to obtaining conversational speech data from them.

For example, in the first fieldwork study in which I participated, in Ocracoke Island, NC, we appended a number of indirect elicitations (and one direct elicitation) in an attempt to obtain targeted information on various lexical, grammatical, and phonological features. Two features were of particular interest: regularization of past tense *be* to the *were* stem rather than the usual vernacular *was*, as in "I weren't home" or "It weren't me," and the pronunciation of *haven't* / *hasn't* as "hadn't." We had observed the first feature in casual conversations and recorded interviews with islanders, noting in particular that regularization to *were* was largely confined to negative forms ("It weren't me" vs. *"It were me") but were curious about two aspects of the form we were not likely to learn about by observing and analyzing connected speech. First, was the feature stigmatized and so likely to be avoided in direct elicitation? Second, did the feature occur only with the contracted negative and not with *were not*? We never heard constructions such as "He were not" or "It were not raining" in conversational data, but this could have been an accidental gap rather than a structural restriction, since non-contracted *not* is very rare in casual conversation. We devised two elicitation frames for regularization to *were*: (1) "If somebody asked, 'Was that you I saw yesterday?', you might say, 'No, it ____'" (to see if the form was used or avoided in direct elicitation), and (2) "If somebody asked, 'Was that you I saw yesterday?', you might say, 'No, it ____ **NOT**'" (to see if *were* could occur in non-contracted form). The responses to (1) indicated that regularization to *weren't* was not stigmatized or even particularly noticeable to island residents, since nearly everyone said *weren't* rather than *wasn't*. This information was valuable in a detailed analysis of *weren't* regularization we later conducted (Schilling-Estes and Wolfram 1994), in which we hypothesized that part of the reason this form was not in decline in the island community, as were other distinguishing dialect features, was because it was not nearly as noticeable as other island forms, for example the pronunciation of /ay/ with a raised / backed nucleus, as in the stereotypical island phrase "hoi toid" for *high tide*.

Responses to the second elicitation confirmed our hypothesis that regularization to the *were* stem was confined to contracted forms, since no one responded with "were not." Our elicitations thus yielded invaluable information on the social and structural status of one particular feature that we could not have gotten via less direct observational methods.

Our other pointed elicitation, designed to yield information on the pronunciation of *haven't*, was based on my ongoing study of the production of /z/ as [d] before nasals in contracted negative auxiliary forms in Southern English. Unfortunately, this elicitation did not yield much information on either [v] or [d] pronunciations, since many respondents replied to the elicitation frame "Have you ever seen a ghost?" with "Yes, of course I have" and proceeded to give us elaborate ghost stories! As we will see below, it is not uncommon for non-linguists to interpret structural elicitations in ways other than we might hope, since most people do not go around thinking about subtle linguistic patterns but simply try to make semantic (and social) sense of linguistic input. At least in this case, our chance use of an elicitation frame involving ghosts proved to be a happy accident, since narratives are highly sought after in variationist research, as discussed in more detail in Section 3.2.

In our Robeson County, NC, study, we became interested in a different feature we noticed in conversation and interview situations – the use of *I'm* rather than *I've* as a perfective, as in "I'm been there a long time" for "I've been there a long time." We also noted that the *I'm* form seemed also to be able to be used as part of simple past construction, but we wanted to make sure. Wolfram (1995) devised a sentence permutation task to elicit tense-marked auxiliaries that would provide more direct evidence of the tense-aspect status of *I'm* than we were able to obtain in natural conversation. The task involved having speakers make three types of changes to a number of stimulus sentences: (1) change positive to negative, (2) provide an elliptical version of the sentence via VP deletion, and (3) change declarative sentences to questions. The stimulus sentences are provided in (3.2).

(3.2)
  (a) I'm forgot to do it yesterday.
  (b) I'm went there yesterday.
  (c) I'm been there a long time.
  (d) I'm seen the toten [i.e. presage of a fateful event].

The possible permutations would be as follows, as exemplified for (a):

I didn't / haven't forgot to do it yesterday.
I'm forgot to do it yesterday, I know I did / have.
Did / have I forgot(ten) to do it yesterday?

If *I'm* can function as part of a simple past construction, we would expect *do* forms to surface in the permutations of the simple past constructions (a) and (b); but if *I'm* is always perfective, we would expect *have* in those permutations instead. Since (c) and (d) are perfective, we expect *have* in their permutations.

Because this elicitation task was quite long and involved and because it was constructed after many of our sociolinguistic interviews had already been completed, we decided to administer the task apart from the interview context. In addition, because the task is unmistakably focused on language form and seems like a test, we decided to administer the task to teenagers in an after-school tutoring program. This seemed preferable to conducting the task with adults who may not be used to tests or perhaps never contended with them, having had little formal education (as was the case with a number of our Lumbee Indian interviewees).

For the most part, the results conformed to our expectations. *Did* and *didn't* were the preferred forms for (a) and (b), while *have*, *haven't*, and *ain't* were preferred for (c) and (d). Permutations of the perfective sentences contained no instances of *did* or *didn't*, though, interestingly, there were a few cases of *am*. The fact that the (a) and (b) sentences yielded a few *haves* and not categorical *did/n't* is most likely another artifact of the elicitation situation rather than a reflection of people's genuine underlying interpretations of *I'm*. The task was highly unnatural, and respondents probably did not always know quite how to respond. In other cases, fatigue and boredom set in, and we had to halt some respondents who simply began giving the same answer to every question. Nonetheless, the results again yielded invaluable information we could only guess at through observation and analysis of natural and naturalistic conversation.

Case study: Uncovering the source of invariant *be* in Washington, DC, African American English

In the late 1960s, Ralph Fasold designed and led a foundational study of tense marking in African American English (1972). Among the features he studied was invariant *be*, particularly habitual or distributive *be*, one of the most salient markers of African American Vernacular English. Distributive *be* is an aspectual marker used to mark habitual, intermittent or ongoing action, as in "He always be on time for work" or "Sometimes my ears be itching." When non-conjugated *be* occurs without lexical items indicative of aspect (e.g. *always, sometimes*), it can be difficult to determine whether it is indeed the distributive *be* of AAVE or derives from one of two other sources – deletion of either *would* or *will*, as in "If he got a walkie-talkie, he (would) be happy" and "He (will) be here in a few minutes." In order to test whether Black working-class speakers could distinguish among the three sources of invariant *be*, Fasold designed a sentence permutation task to be administered after the conversational interview, as part of a section of elicitation tasks he cleverly titled "word games." The task consisted of a few "dummy" or practice frames, followed by the real task at hand. An excerpt showing one dummy frame and then the frames for elicitation of the underlying form of non-conjugated *be* are given in (3.3) below. Note that FW indicates a fieldworker prompt; IVee indicates possible interviewee responses.

(3.3)
(Dummy)

    FW: He can drive a motorcycle.
    IVee: I know he can.
    FW: Can what?
    IVee: Drive a motorcycle.

(a)

    FW: If he got a walkie-talkie, he be happy.
    IVee: I know he (would, do/es, will, is / are)
    (*be* derived from *would* deletion; *would* expected)

(b)

    FW: Sometimes Joseph be up there.
    IVee: I know he (do/es, will, would, is / are)
    (distributive *be*; auxiliary *do* expected)

(c)

    FW: He be in in a few minutes.
    IVee: I know he (do/es, will, would, is / are)
    (*be* derived from *will* deletion; *will* expected)

(d)

FW: Sometimes my ears be itching.
IVee: I know they (do/es, will, would, is / are)
(distributive *be*; *do/es* expected)

Only (b) and (d) are cases of distributive *be*, and so the expected auxiliary in the response is *do/es*, since this is the auxiliary for use with habitual *be* in AAVE. Since (a) derives from *would* deletion, we expect *would* to surface; likewise, since (c) derives from *will* deletion, we expect a response with *will*. For the most part, the expectations were borne out in Fasold's study, especially in (a) and (c), the *would* and *will* sentences. For (b) and (d), the responses were more varied. Fasold attributes this not to people's inability to distinguish among the various *be* forms, but rather to factors that plague elicitation tasks in general. Distributive *be* is highly stigmatized, and so respondents show a slight tendency to avoid the stigmatized form, providing *would* and *will* answers to (b) and (d) in an effort to demonstrate that they are not users of habitual *be* (even though they are). In addition, respondents will often override their intuitions in order to provide us with what they think is the "right" answer and so will provide all sorts of answers in an effort to "do well on the test." Further, there is the matter of ordering effects: a number of speakers responded with *would* to sentence (b), most likely because they had just responded with *would* to (a). Despite these issues, the results were still clear: more people responded with *do/es* to (b) and (d) than to (a) and (c), demonstrating that Black working-class speakers in DC can indeed distinguish among the different types of non-conjugated *be* in their dialect (see Fasold 1972: 172–176, and also his Appendix A for the "Auxiliary probe" word game). The results also show us that elicitations designed to yield information on the structural limitations of forms indeed form a valuable part of the variationists' sociolinguistic toolkit and yield insights we cannot always obtain via conversational or interview data alone.

Judgments of same vs. different

Another type of elicitation stems from the earliest days of linguistic anthropology but has been re-purposed to good effect in modern sociolinguistic studies of mergers in progress: judgments of pre-merger minimal pairs as "same" or "different." Some important mergers whose progress has been measured in part by such judgment tasks include the merger of /a/ and /ɔ/ (as in *cot* / *caught*), the merger of /ay/ and /oy/ in Essex, England (as in *line* / *loin*), and such conditioned mergers as /ɪ/ and /i/ before /l/ in Southwestern US varieties (as in *filled* / *field*) and /ir/ and /ɛr/ in Norwich, England (as in *beer* / *bear*). The "same / different" task can take a number of forms, ranging from the very direct to the highly obfuscated. For example, the task might involve simply playing the respondent a pre-recorded list of word pairs and having them state whether they are the same or different, playing elements of the pairs interspersed with other items and asking for definitions, or even constructing and reading to respondents elaborate stories whose interpretation depends on the listener's understanding of one or more word pairs involved in ongoing merger. The more direct methods are typically avoided, since differences between vowels in minimal pairs undergoing merger can be very subtle and it can be too easy to simply say "same" or "different" without thought or acute listening. More common is the so-called "commutation test," as described in detail in Labov (1994: 356ff). The original version of this test involves having one speaker of the dialect in question read a random list of members of a minimal pair and then later having a second participant try to identify the words. The test can be modified to be even more revealing, so that each speaker records and later attempts to identify their own productions. Sometimes the result is as expected: respondents either cannot distinguish between members of minimal pairs, indicating a merger; or they claim they can identify distinctions but do so in an unreliable way, indicating that they probably really do have a merger but are unwilling to admit to it. A third, rather unexpected, result is that respondents claim they cannot hear a difference between members of minimal pairs, but spectrographic analysis reveals that the same speakers actually *do* produce a difference. Hence, for example, Labov recorded a list of /ay/ and /oy/ words from one Essex speaker and then returned a year later to play the list to him and a couple of other residents. None of the subjects passed the test, despite the fact that there were consistent (yet subtle) acoustic differences between the vowels in the LINE vs. LOIN word classes in the recorded stimulus.

The finding that speakers can produce differences they cannot hear points to the existence of so-called near mergers, a phenomenon that has intriguing implications for the explanation of the seeming impossible "unmergers" that have from time to time occurred in linguistic history (e.g. the merger and subsequent unmerger of the MEAT and MATE word classes in English in the sixteenth and seventeenth centuries). If two different underlying representations become one, then it should be impossible to restore the original word classes as they once were. However, if what was thought to be a complete merger was in reality a *near* merger, then an unmerger is possible, since the phonetic distinction (and by implication the underlying phonological distinction) was never completely lost in the first place (Labov 1994).

3.1.3 Limitations of elicitation tasks

Despite the advantages of elicitations, whether more or less direct, those interested in how language is used in everyday life readily understand that even the best elicitations are not very natural, and people's reports of their linguistic usage may or may not match up with what they do in non-research contexts. For example, direct elicitations such as "Have you ever heard the term 'snap beans'?" can induce respondents to claim knowledge and use of features they have never heard of prior to the research situation. Less direct elicitations can be very difficult to devise, and they may yield responses other than targeted items, for example, as we saw with the indirect elicitation frame for *might could* ("When you get something done that was hard work all by yourself and your friend was standing around without helping, you say _____") reported in Bailey, Wikle, and Tillery (1997b). Another issue with even the best-designed elicitation frames is that respondents may not be consciously aware of their usage patterns or know how to express them (e.g. "How often do you use the form 'fixin' to'?"); in addition, they may purposely over- or under-report their use of particular forms. We have already seen this to be the case for stigmatized forms such as habitual *be* in AAVE. Trudgill (1972) also noted both under- and over-reporting of standard variants in Norwich, with women's self-reports reflecting higher levels of usage than their conversational data and men's self-reports reflecting lower levels. Trudgill attributes this tendency to the association, in many communities, of vernacularity with masculinity and what are often considered to be its component qualities; for example, toughness, hard-workingness, and "street smarts."

There are other problems associated with grammaticality judgments and sentence permutation tasks. No matter how you phrase your prompt, respondents are very prone to equating "grammaticality" with "standard" or "proper," not with linguistic grammaticality *per se*. And even if you are careful to use phrases like "Which is more natural to say?" (vs. "Which is grammatical?") or "Is it possible to say ...?" (vs. "Is it grammatical to say ...?"), respondents still often select the form they think is "proper," not the one they really use. In addition, as we saw with our "ghost story" elicitation above, people are usually focused on communicating via language content, not on figuring out subtleties of linguistic form, and so their responses often focus on semantic sense, pragmatic felicity, or social appropriateness.

Finally there are issues related more to the testing situation than the test items themselves. As we saw with Fasold's distributive *be* task, ordering effects may come into play, causing subsequent responses to be colored by previous ones. Fatigue or boredom may also set in as the test progresses, as we found with the Lumbee *I'm* elicitation task. However, whereas sometimes the unnaturalness of elicitation tasks leads respondents to be uncooperative, at other times their test-like nature can have the opposite effect: respondents might be more concerned with providing the "right" answer than proffering their genuine intuitions.

With careful thought, the researcher can overcome some of the limitations of the various types of elicitation tasks we have discussed. For example, we can seek to devise useful indirect elicitations rather than relying on direct ones (unless indirect frames are too unwieldy, as in the case of *might could*). We can also frame our elicitations as "games" rather than as test-like research tasks; we can avoid ever using the word "grammatical" in our prompts; and we can vary the order of elicitation items from respondent to respondent. However, we should always remain aware of possible mismatches between what people do and what they say they do; and ideally, we should never rely on elicitations alone as our sole source of data on language use.

Case study: Elicitations vs. 'real-life' language use – existential *it* in Smith Island, Maryland

As part of our study of Smith Island, Maryland, in the late 1990s and early 2000s at Georgetown University, a graduate student member of the research team, Jeff Parrott, became interested in one particular feature of the historically isolated island's distinctive dialect – the use of *it* rather than *there* as an existential, as in "It was three men outside" for "There were three men outside" (Parrott 2002). This feature is widespread in the Smith Island community, and though it is found in AAVE, it is otherwise rare in English varieties. In addition to studying the observed variable patterning of existential *it*, Parrott was interested in particular aspects of its patterning that probably would not surface in naturalistic conversation – specifically whether one could use existential *it* with both contracted and non-contracted *is* (e.g. "It's a lot of crabs in the bay"; "It is a lot of crabs in the bay"), as well as whether existential *it* could be used with both *is* and *are* in the same manner as existential *there* (e.g. "It are many crabs in the bay"; "There are many crabs in the bay"). He carefully designed a grammaticality judgment task consisting of various permutations of *it's* / *it is* and *it is* / *it are* in hopes of confirming his hypothesis that only *it's* would be grammatical. In addition, rather than administering the task to everyone as part of their sociolinguistic interview, he chose a couple residents we had already interviewed who showed a higher degree of metalinguistic awareness than other island residents (one was a college-educated writer and the other was an island schoolteacher). Despite his care in designing and administering the task, he unfortunately ran into many of the difficulties that are simply inherent in elicitation / judgment tasks, no matter how hard one tries to mask them or overcome them. For example, the issue of linguistic grammaticality vs. communicative appropriateness arose in the exchange in (3.4). Note that FW1 is Parrott, FW2 is a second fieldworker, and S1 is the Smith Islander, "Sam," the writer.

(3.4)

FW1: Okay, so this is another one like that, um. Where the register is a little high, but bear with me. So, you can say, "There are many politicians elected by Smith Islanders." That's what – okay, so I'm gonna ask you the Smith Island version. Is it possible then to say. . .

S1: Actually nobody would say that because it's not true. (laughter). . .

FW2: How about "elected by . . . the Eastern Shore"[1] or something like that?

FW1: "There are many politicians elected by Crisfielders."[2] "There are many politicians-," it doesn't matter what it says. "There are many politicians elected by Maryland." So, could a Smith Islander say, "It's many politicians elected by Crisfield?" "It's a lot of politicians elected by Crisfield."

S1: Yeah, it's just a question of, the context, uh, they'd probably be referring to, you know, a specific candidate or something like that or a specific group, uh. . .

Another difficulty arose a few minutes later, when, despite Parrott's best efforts to use words like "possible" and "natural" rather than "grammatical" or "better," Sam still could not help focusing on "proper" vs. "improper" usage and so rejected "crabs is" on that basis rather than on its possible linguistic ungrammaticality. This excerpt is given in (3.5).

---

[1] The Eastern Shore is the portion of Maryland that lies east of the Chesapeake Bay.

[2] Crisfield is a small town on Maryland's Eastern Shore and one of the main points of departure for boats going from the mainland to the island.

(3.5)

FW1:   So I'll give you pairs of sentences.
S1:   Okay.
FW1:   And tell me which one sounds more natural for Smith Island.
S1:   Okay.
FW1:   So um, "A lot of crabs is in the bay this year." Versus "A lot of crabs
       are in the bay this year."
S1:   Actually, they wouldn't do the second one, even though, the first one,
       like I said before, it would sound illiterate to the Smith Islander. "A
       lot of crabs is in the bay." They would probably – more likely they
       would probably say something closer to the second sentence
       [although they would]
FW1:   [The second one?]
S1:   Yeah. Yeah. They wouldn't use "is" like that.
FW1:   Really?
S1:   No. They don't do that here. I mean, this might sound strange, I mean
       it's not that they know how to use it properly, it's just that..
FW1:   [What about
S1:   [They know that's improper.
FW1:   Yeah, I don't – yeah. Cause you know I don't care about proper
S1:   Yeah, I know.

Finally, Parrott faced an issue in conducting his judgment tasks that had nothing to do with the task itself but rather with this community's particular communicative norms – norms he could not have known about prior to becoming familiar with the Smith Island community. While Parrott and the other members of our Smith Island research team were intrigued by the dialect's distinguishing phonological and morphosyntactic features, islanders themselves consider the most important feature of their way of talking to be a phenomenon they call "backwards talk" – namely, the pervasive use of irony, including highly creative forms that can be impossible for outsiders to interpret (e.g. using the phrase "He's barefoot!" to comment on someone's shiny new shoes). For islanders who knew we were interested in their dialect, what was uppermost in their minds was not necessarily what we were focusing on, and this led to some frustrating but ultimately amusing misfires in the existential *it* task. Thus, for example, in (3.6) below, Parrott begins the judgment task with a seemingly innocuous sentence, "It's a lot of crabs in the bay," but Sam, rather than accepting or rejecting its "naturalness," simply turns it around "backwards," to demonstrate the way a Smith Islander would normally say such a phrase in everyday conversation.

(3.6)

FW1:   And Smith Islanders can say, "It's a lot of crabs in the bay," right?
S1:   Yeah.
FW1:   Right.
S1:   "It ain't neither crab." [It ain't any crabs.]
FW1:   Huh?
S1:   However they'd say it: "It ain't neither crab."
FW1:   Mmhmm. Oh, that's right. With the backwards ...
S1:   Yep.
FW2:   It ain't neither crab.
S1:   Well, yeah.
FW1:   It ain't what?
FW2:   Oh, no! I see cause that's a lot, it ain't neither crab. That means you know it's a lot of crabs.
S1:   That's a lot of crabs.
FW2:   Ain't neither crab.

Despite, and also because of, its difficulties, the existential *it* judgment task was a valuable learning experience, enabling us to refine our understandings of how Smith Islanders really think about their community and language variety and reinforcing for us the importance of always keeping an open mind during the fieldwork experience. It served as a reminder, too, that when we go out into the field, we are no longer the "experts" we are often accustomed to being in the academic setting but rather novice students, ready to learn from the community experts around us.

3.1.4 The rapid and anonymous survey

Despite the advantages of the various types of elicitation tasks outlined above, they all suffer from the same basic problem: Because they are so highly focused on language form, they can make people selfconscious about their speech and therefore prone to skew their language away from their everyday linguistic usages. If Labov is correct that the most valuable type of speech for linguistic study is unselfconscious speech, then ideally we will observe people's speech rather than elicit it. Furthermore, we need to seek ways to observe it such that observer effects are minimized – in other words, we must try to overcome the observer's paradox.

In the course of his studies of the Lower East Side of New York City, Labov designed an ingenious way of conducting a systematic yet completely anonymous sociolinguistic survey, the rapid and anonymous survey, made famous in his study of "the social stratification of *r* in

NYC department stores" (Labov 1972c: 43–69). Most readers of this book are already familiar with this study, but it is worth outlining the data-collection methodology as a model of simplicity and profundity. Labov sought to test the observation that traditional New York City r-lessness appeared to be receding in the wake of a new prestige norm favoring r-ful pronunciations in words like *car* and *mother*, and that usage levels for the new prestige form were directly correlated with social status. He designed a survey to measure usage levels for r-fulness vs. r-lessness (r-1 and r-0) in three department stores catering to clientele in upper middle, middle, and lower socioeconomic class groups – Saks, Macy's, and S. Klein, respectively. He tested not customers but employees, reasoning that they would borrow the differential prestige of the stores where they worked, despite being of the same social class group in terms of occupation (though the Macy's employees were actually higher on the social scale in terms of earnings than the higher prestige employees of Saks).

The survey was like a traditional linguistic survey in that its speaker sample was broad and its linguistic focus highly targeted: The chief focus was on r-1 vs. r-0 and Labov sampled employees of all occupational types (e.g. floorwalkers, salespeople) and all available social groups (e.g. age, gender, race), on each floor of every store. At the same time, the survey was completely unlike traditional elicitation tasks in that respondents had no idea that their language was being studied. Labov disguised his elicitation frame as a real-life speech event – a request for information on the location of a particular category of goods. To elicit the (r) variable in two different word positions, he requested an item he knew was located on the *fourth floor*; further, to elicit a more emphatic, careful style, he asked each respondent for clarification of their original response with "Excuse me?"

With just this simple survey, Labov was able to investigate the effects of a number of social and linguistic factors on the patterning of r-l vs. r-0. The chief independent variable was the store itself (and corresponding prestige level). In this regard, the results were exactly as expected: the Saks employees had the highest levels of some or all r-1, followed by Macy's, followed by S. Klein. Stylistic variation patterned as expected, too, with employees at all stores showing more r-1 in the second, emphatic production. Intriguingly (and subsequently replicated in the large-scale quantitative study of the Lower East Side using sociolinguistic interview data), employees of mid-level prestige showed the greatest degree of stylistic variation, a pattern Labov attributed to their "linguistic insecurity" (or put more positively, their desire for upward mobility). The Macy's employees stood in contrast to those at Saks, who were secure in their status; and to those at S. Klein, who were relatively unconcerned with the social elites. Other factors Labov was able to investigate were race (with Blacks showing less r-1 than Whites), occupation type in Macy's (with floorwalkers showing more r-1 than salespeople, who in turn showed more than stockboys), floor number in Saks (with those working on the posh higher floors showing more r-1 than those on the ground floor), and age.

The results by age were more complicated than for the other social categories. Since r-1 was an incoming change, we might expect increasing usage levels among younger speakers; however, this was found to be the case only for Saks. The opposite effect was found in Macy's, where older people used more r-1, and there was no correlation between age and r-1 in S. Klein. It was only later, after he had conducted his interview-based study and found the same age-based pattern among speakers in the upper middle class, lower middle class, and working class, that Labov felt confident in his tentative explanation: it appears that r-1 had become the native form for upper-middle-class speakers and so was most prevalent in the younger speakers, who acquired the form as they grew up. However, it was not yet native to the lower middle class, and so it was chiefly older speakers with more awareness of linguistic norms beyond their immediate social circles who took up the newer prestigious form. And since r-1 was largely beyond the reach of the working class at the time of the study, there was no age-related pattern, and the general level of r-1 throughout this segment of the population was quite low.

Just as the age-based patterns uncovered in the rapid and anonymous survey were confirmed in Labov's larger interview-based survey, so too were patterns according to social class, race, and gender (with women using more r-1 than men). The rapid and anonymous survey proved to be highly advantageous in a number of regards, then: it yields accurate data on language patterning from a broad population in a short amount of time, and the effects of the research situation are completely negated. At the same time, there are a number of limitations, some of which are inherent in this type of survey methodology and others of which can be overcome with careful planning.

In conducting a rapid and anonymous survey, the researcher is inevitably limited to a very narrow bit of language, since we can only record a limited amount of linguistic data without being observed or violating research ethics and conducting surreptitious audio recordings. In addition, the social information we are able to gather is limited, since it has to be based on our impressions rather than on inquiries. So, for instance, we cannot pinpoint exact ages but can only guess at relatively wide age ranges. It is also true that our impression of native vs. non-native speaker may not always be correct, especially if we are trying to identify not only native vs. non-native English but also native vs. non-native regional dialect. And while in some cases a speaker's race may seem obvious, many people defy ready classification by surface characteristics. Furthermore, as discussed in Section 2.3.1, race / ethnicity does not seem to be a surface characteristic anyway, and so our groupings according to outward criteria will always be suspect, even in seemingly clear cases. Finally, as with all elicitation tasks, whether anonymous or not, as a rule we want to use elicitation frames that do not include the item we are seeking to elicit so as not to encourage over-reporting of usage levels for the item. In Labov's case, this was not too difficult: He simply had to be careful not to ask which *floor* an item was on but simply to ask where an item was.

Because of the limitations inherent in any rapid and anonymous survey, Labov stresses that they should only be used as preliminary or supplementary sources of data – never as the basis for an entire study. In addition, to design an effective survey appropriate to the sociolinguistic situation at hand, we need to conduct sufficient preliminary observation and investigation to determine what our relevant research question(s) will be, especially since the information obtained through a rapid and anonymous survey is necessarily extremely narrowly focused. Nonetheless, Labov and others advocate their use, especially in connection with different methods with "complementary sources of error" (Labov 1972c: 60), since they combine the benefits of focused (yet selfconscious) elicitation tasks and naturalistic (yet less systematic) observations. Or, as Labov says, "They represent a form of nonreactive experimentation in which we avoid the bias of the experimental context and the irregular interference of prestige norms but still control the behavior of subjects" (1972c: 69).

STUDENTS IN THE FIELD

Jinsok Lee devised an innovative variation on the rapid anonymous survey in order to elicit data on variation and change in deixis in Korean. His ingenious approach was to disguise his actual elicitation question within another survey context – in other words, "to hide a survey within a survey." He approached random strangers in Seoul and informed them that he was collecting data on Korean kinship terms and relationships, and asked them if they would be willing to participate. He obtained general demographic information from each of his 100 participants, who varied in age and regional background, and then asked them his questions about kinship terms. At the conclusion of his survey, he presented each participant with a choice of two thank-you gifts (two mobile phone accessories of different design and color) and asked them to select one. Their verbal selection elicited just the kind of deictic activity he was actually interested in: whether or not speakers use *ikes / ike* 'this', *cekes / cek*e 'that', or what appear to be innovative forms in this context: *yay* 'this child / kid' vs. *cyay* 'that child / kid' (with the newer forms being used to refer to all sorts of objects, not just 'kids'). Couching one survey within another could have numerous applications for eliciting sociolinguistic data, enabling collection of important demographic detail while covertly procuring targeted forms. Note also, though, that Jinsok did not lie to his participants, since he actually will use the data on kinship terms and relationships as part of another project.

3.1.5 Eliciting information on listener perception

So far, we have examined a variety of methods for eliciting information on speaker production, from sociolinguistic / dialectological surveys designed to elicit linguistic features to grammaticality judgment and sentence permutation tasks designed to elicit information on the patterning of features, including their structural limitations, to rapid and anonymous surveys, designed to elicit features while eliminating the effects of the research situation that are inherent to some extent in all overt elicitation tasks. There are also a host of methods for eliciting information on listener perceptions, including listener identification of variants, varieties, and speaker characteristics (e.g. ethnicity, sexual orientation), and listener attitudes toward the speakers who use them. There is a vast body of literature on methods and findings in listener perceptions, attitudes, and ideologies, so here we give only a very broad-brush picture of some of the main methods and offer a discussion of how information on perceptions and attitudes can be used to complement production-based studies. Readers interested in more extensive information on sociolinguistic perception and language attitude studies are referred to overview chapters by Campbell-Kibler (2010) and Drager (2010), the survey chapter by Preston (2013), and comprehensive works such as Garrett (2010).

The study of languages attitudes has a fairly long history in social psychology and a bit more recently in sociolinguistics proper. Related lines of inquiry on listener perception of varieties and variants (i.e. perceptual dialectology, sociophonetics) are more recent additions. However, one can argue that in reality the study of sociolinguistics *is* the study of language attitudes and listener perceptions, since the integral relationship between linguistic usages and social meanings and structures is necessarily mediated by people's evaluations of language (see, e.g., Campbell-Kibler 2010; Preston 2013).

Indeed, the central importance of language attitudes was overtly acknowledged in the very first sociolinguistic studies, Labov's studies of Martha's Vineyard and the Lower East Side of New York City. In the former study, Labov sought the meaning of the centralization of /ay/ and /aw/ not only in their correlation with various demographic categories but also, crucially, in individuals' positive or negative attitudes toward Martha's Vineyard. In the latter, the social evaluation of dialectal vs. standard features indicated in the quantitative patterning of stylistic variation (with fewer dialect features being used in more formal speech) was borne out in elicitation tasks testing listeners' evaluations of the various dialect features. In other words, quantitative patterns showing decreasing use of features characteristic of the New York City dialect in increasingly formal situations suggested that New Yorkers evaluated their dialect features as "inappropriate" for formal settings (and probably as "worse" than standard, formal speech as well). More direct evidence of these evaluations was obtained via perception tests in which participants rated speakers with more and less dialectal speech as more or less suitable for various types of professions, ranging from "television personality," where we would expect non-dialectal speech to be preferred, at least in the 1960s, to "factory worker," where we would expect dialectal speech to be more acceptable.

In current work in which the relationship between language and social meanings and categories is seen as co-constitutive rather than correlative, the centrality of listener perception is even stronger. If language variation has to do chiefly with speakers' proactive use of linguistic features and styles to project meanings, then speakers (and researchers) have to know a lot about how their linguistic usages will be perceived, since the social meaning of language variation is an interactive project and not a static "given." Language attitudes and listener perceptions also play a central role in language change. Linguistic innovations, for instance, are often stigmatized, but only after people have become aware of the change in the first place. Hence, changes that are below the level of consciousness spread rapidly until people become aware of them and begin to avoid them. At the same time, innovations that come into a community with positive evaluation attached to them can spread rapidly too, though the course of change will look quite different in each case. The investigation of vowel mergers in progress also typically includes a perceptual component in the form of minimal-pair distinction tasks; and as we noted above, the mismatches between perception and production have uncovered the existence of the fascinating phenomenon of the near merger. And, finally, many sociolinguists are deeply interested in language attitudes because of their concern for social justice. Negative attitudes toward language varieties and even entire languages abound, and they contribute to injustices in many arenas, from the classroom to the courtroom to the leasing office. Sociolinguists striving to combat linguistic discrimination must of course understand it before they can effectively demonstrate its existence and unfairness.

Whereas language attitudes can be directly elicited (e.g. in interviews or opinion surveys), typically they are investigated via less direct means, usually through some variant of the subjective reaction tasks devised by Lambert *et al.* (1960). These tasks involve assembling a stimulus consisting of different languages or language varieties, either a matched guise, in which one speaker produces the different guises; or a verbal guise, in which different speakers are used (Campbell-Kibler 2010: 378). Listeners are told that the different guises are produced by different individuals and are then asked to rate the speakers on various measures along a so-called semantic differential scale, involving gradations between opposite extremes of various descriptors (e.g. intelligent / unintelligent, friendly / unfriendly, honest / dishonest). Investigations over the years have shown that the scales tend to cluster along three dimensions: social status, social attractiveness, and personal integrity (though these dimensions are sometimes reduced to two: status and affect). Sometimes the adjectives chosen are based on previous studies; the researcher may also choose to elicit potentially relevant dimensions via open-ended questions in a pilot study, perhaps with focus groups (e.g. by asking participants questions such as "What do you think of this speaker?"). Care is taken to ensure that the guises are comparable to one another on every level except for the language or language variety of interest, and the researcher must control for such factors as voice quality, pitch and intonation, speech rate, and content. Such factors are of course much easier to control if a single speaker produces the various guises; however, it is extremely difficult to not only find individuals who produce the variety of guises desired, but also mask the fact that the various guises come from the same individual. Many studies therefore use voice guises rather than the stringent matched guise technique. Content can be controlled by using reading passages rather than conversational speech, but the trade-off is that reading passages sound less natural than talk, and ratings may be colored by this. Campbell-Kibler (2010: 380–381) suggests controlling for content without resorting to readings by using recorded passages from conversational speech about similar topics (e.g. childhood games). If, however, the very same content must be used, then the unnaturalness of reading can be alleviated by giving listeners a reason why the speakers are reading rather than talking; for example, perhaps they are allegedly auditioning for a job as a news anchor (Labov *et al.* 2006a, cited in Campbell-Kibler 2010: 381).

The traditional method of eliciting language attitudes is plagued by the same problems as elicitations of speech production. The tasks are unnatural, and there is no guarantee that the results are valid reflections of listeners' genuine attitudes, whether because they are unaware of their attitudes, or because they are unable or unwilling to express them, or because of issues such as fatigue, boredom, and uncooperativeness. For this reason, researchers have sought methods other than the matched guise / voice guise technique, such as so-called "commitment measures" whereby attitudes are assessed by observing behaviors (Fasold 1984: 153–158). For example, Fasold (1984: 155–158) describes how Bourhis and Giles (1976) devised a task to measure people's attitudes toward four language varieties in Wales: standard British English (RP), mildly Welsh-accented English, broad Welsh-accented English, and Welsh. The task involved two different types of audiences of theater-goers: Anglo-Welsh audiences attending films in English and bilingual audiences attending a play in Welsh. Each audience listened to a public service announcement during intermission. The Welsh audiences heard four guises (one per evening) – while the Anglo-Welsh heard all but Welsh, since they would not have understood it. Following the show, each audience was asked to fill out a questionnaire pertaining to the subject matter of the announcement, with the belief that the more people who volunteered to do so in each case, the more positively they had evaluated the guise. Among the findings were that Anglo-Welsh listeners were least responsive to broad Welsh-accented English, while the Welsh audiences were most responsive to Welsh and least respon-sive to RP. Clearly designing a "commitment measure" is an extremely difficult task, so most researchers will opt to rely on elicitation tasks, carefully designed to minimize their inherent limitations.

While it seems likely that when people assess dialects and languages they are really assessing the speaker groups associated with the various guises, this is not necessarily a given. Preston (2013) notes that research-ers often assume without testing that listeners know which dialects they are evaluating, when in reality they may not. In his work on perceptual dialectology, Preston investigates folk beliefs about dialects through such means as having people draw and label dialect regions on blank maps, or eliciting dialect attitudes from people with differing degrees of familiarity with dialect regions. Among his findings is that listeners from different areas of the US have different pictures of dialect divisions as well as different judgments about different varieties. In addition, different groups differ on whether they base their positive and negative judgments chiefly on scales of "correctness" – "incorrectness" or "pleasantness" – "unpleasantness"; in other words, they have entirely different value systems with respect to language variation, not just different evaluations. Thus, for example, speakers from Michigan, most of whom believe they speak "standard" English, give positive value to dialects they deem "correct" (including their own) and negative value to those they deem "incorrect" (especially Southern dialects). Conversely, speakers in Alabama do not concern themselves too much with "correctness" (knowing full well how devalued their Southern dialect is on this dimension) and base their positive ratings of Southern speech on "pleasantness" and their negative ratings of Northerners on "unpleasantness."

A further concern is that perhaps in evaluations of language samples as more or less "correct" or "pleasant," there is no mediating evaluation of social group membership. In other words, it is possible that linguistic features might come to stand on their own as good or bad without listeners making any (conscious) reference to the group or groups who use them, as in the universally negative associations of features like *ain't* and multiple negation (Preston 2013). Language evaluations might also be based on degree of similarity to the listener's dialect rather than the dialect itself (or its speakers); similarly, listeners have been shown to rate non-accommodating speakers lower than those who accommodate toward their audiences (e.g. Bourhis, Giles, and Lambert 1975; Willemyns, Gallois, Callan, and Pittam 1997). Other aspects of context can affect evaluations. For example, whereas non-standard dialects in general tend to be rated low on status measures but high on social and personal attractiveness, they may receive higher ratings on both measures if specifically situated in a solidarity-stressing context (e.g. school vs. home). Indeed, Campbell-Kibler (2010) and Soukup (2012) urge researchers to always specify a context for listener evaluations since, they maintain, there is no such thing as context-free evaluation; if the researcher does not provide one, listeners will imagine their own, and we cannot know what these are.

In addition to the social and contextual factors that impinge on listener evaluations of languages and dialects, we must also consider which linguistic features listeners are attending to in making evaluations and identifications. As technology becomes more advanced, it is becoming increasingly easy to devise experiments that tease out the effects of minute aspects of the speech signal on attitudes and identifications. Nowadays researchers can use computer manipulations to construct a series of guises differing along only a single dimension, whether binary (e.g. *-in'* vs. *-ing* endings) or scalar (e.g. the height of a particular vowel or length of a stop burst release). Similarly, the speech signal can be filtered to remove all segmental information, leaving only the intonational contour; or intonation can be flattened and segments can be scrambled, so that presumably one removes all effects on perception other than the segments themselves, devoid of content or context (Campbell-Kibler 2010: 381). In addition, natural speech can readily be subjected to fine-grained acoustic analysis, as another way of pinpointing exactly what listeners focus on in making the speaker and speaker-group identifications upon which evaluations often rest.

Studies involving computer analysis and manipulation of minute details of speech have yielded intriguing findings regarding listener identification of a range of speaker characteristics, including sexual identity – for example, gay, lesbian, or straight (Queen 2007; Schilling 2011) – and ethnicity. For example, Purnell, Idsardi, and Baugh (1999) found that US listeners could identify African American Vernacular English, Chicano English, and standard (White) American English based on the single word "hello," with subsequent acoustic analysis revealing cross-dialectal differences in frontness and tenseness of the /ɛ/ vowel, as well as height of the pitch peak and duration of /hɛ/. Conversely, Graff *et al.* (1986) altered the nucleus of /aU/ in the speech of an AAVE speaker from Philadelphia from naturally occurring [aʊ] to the fronter [æʊ] that correlates with White speech in Philadelphia and found that both African American and White judges misidentified the speaker as White, based solely on the alteration of this one pronunciation.

Thomas and Reaser (2004) studied listener perceptions of a genuinely "atypical" African American dialect, that spoken in coastal Hyde County, NC, which contains a number of vowel and other features characteristic of the local White dialect. As with Graff *et al.* (1986), they found that listeners indeed had difficulty identifying the ethnicity of atypical African American speakers. In addition, they subjected their stimuli to several acoustic manipulations to test the relative effects of intonation vs. segmental cues on ethnic identification, evaluating the effects of unmodified speech vs. speech which had been monotonized to remove intonational information and that which had been low-pass filtered to remove segmental information. Their results confirmed those of previous studies pointing to the importance of intonational cues in identifying African American ethnicity but also indicated that other cues are important as well. In fact, listeners' ability to identify African Americans was *less* impaired with monotonized than low-pass filtered stimuli, demonstrating the importance of segmental cues. At the same time, though, identification of African American ethnicity was improved for both monotonized and low-pass filtered stimuli that included subject pronouns that provided prosodic information that remained unaffected by filtering, thus showing that listeners also rely on intonational cues in making ethnic identifications. (See also Thomas 2002, 2011, and 2013 for comprehensive overviews of sociophonetics, including its application to perception studies.)

Findings pertaining to listener perceptions of ethnic identity have direct bearing on social issues. "Linguistic profiling" of Black vs. White ethnicity is rampant in the US, and while it can be highly accurate, as demonstrated in Purnell *et al.*'s study (1999), even a slight degree of atypicality renders it inaccurate, as shown in Graff *et al.* (1986). Identifications of ethnicity by voice alone should be treated with caution, even if used for valid purposes (e.g. narrowing a suspect pool in a well-conducted law enforcement investigation) rather than the discriminatory purposes to which it is often put (e.g. housing and job discrimination).

Researchers have also conducted intriguing studies involving how social information affects perceptions of linguistic features. For example, Strand (1999) demonstrated that listeners' beliefs about speaker gender affected their perception of /š/ vs. /s/ through playing a stimulus manipulated so that the lower-frequency [š] changed gradually to the higher frequency [s]. While the stimulus played, listeners were shown faces conforming to perceptions of stereotypical and less typical male and female faces. When listeners saw male faces, especially the stereotypical ones, the cut-off point in the perception of /š/ vs. /s/ was lower; in other words, listeners expected male voices to be lower in pitch than female, so they adjust the acoustic correlates of phonemic boundaries accordingly.

Similarly, Niedzielski (1999) showed that even variants of a single variable may be perceived differently depending on listener perceptions of who is producing the variants. She devised an experiment in which she played for two groups of Michigan listeners a Michigan speaker producing the word *house* with a centralized nucleus. (The feature is found in both Michigan and Canadian speech but is believed by Michiganders to be present only in Canadian speech.) Niedzielski then played synthesized tokens with of /aʊ/ with ultra-low, canonical, and centralized nuclei and had the listeners choose which one matched the actual centralized production they had just heard by circling the item on a form she had passed out. The twist was that one group of listeners received forms with "MICHIGAN" printed in red at the top, while the other had the word "CANADIAN." The responses of the two groups were significantly different, with most of those receiving the "Canadian" sheet correctly selecting the centralized synthesized token

but most of those with "Michigan" sheets incorrectly selecting the low
and ultra-low tokens.

   Though studies attempting to get at perceptions of individual
variables are undoubtedly fascinating, the researcher would be wise
to heed the caution of Auer (2007: 12), who points out that "the
meaning of linguistic heterogeneity does not (usually) reside in individual linguistic features but rather in constellations of such features
which are interpreted together . . . [W]e do not interpret single variables
but a gestalt-like stylistic expression" (cited in Soukup 2011: 350). It is
not certain that ever more fine-grained analyses or syntheses of speech
signals will yield ever-increasing gains in our understanding of language attitudes and speech perceptions. I would urge that attitudinal
and perceptual experiments should always be complemented with
more naturalistic data, including elicitations based on naturally produced speech excerpts, responses to questions about attitudes and
perceptions, and, best, of all, attitudinal and perceptual information
gleaned from observation. A wide variety of data types are reflective of
language attitudes, ideologies, and perceptions, including participants'
unsolicited comments and naturally occurring behaviors, such as of
course, the quantitative patterning of variation itself.

3.2   THE SOCIOLINGUISTIC INTERVIEW

The chief method of data collection for variationist sociolinguists is the
sociolinguistic interview. This section provides in-depth discussion on
interview design, as well as a historical overview of the development of
the method from its earliest formulations to the range of configur-
ations it takes in current research projects. We also consider the
advantages of the sociolinguistic interview that led to its prominence
as the premier data-collection tool of the variationist sociolinguist, as
well as an outline of critiques that have been leveled against it.

3.2.1   Situating the sociolinguistic interview

Although the sociolinguistic interview technically involves elicitation
rather than the observation of language in everyday use, in some ways
it represents a combination of both elicitation and observational techniques, combining the advantages of both while minimizing the disadvantages. Whereas the elicitations that make up sociolinguistic surveys
are quite directly focused on language and so may or may not provide
an accurate record of everyday language usage, the sociolinguistic

interview is more subtle in its elicitation procedures: the chief goal of the sociolinguistic interview is to elicit lots of talk rather than specific forms and features, and interview questions are purposefully designed to steer attention away from language itself toward topics of interest to interviewees. Thus, we are likely to obtain much more naturalistic data than with more direct elicitation techniques. At the same time, the sociolinguistic interview has a number of advantages over covert observations and recordings of completely unstructured interactions. For one, because sociolinguistic interviews involve overt elicitation and audio recording (and sometimes video recording), researchers employing them do not have to confine themselves to a narrow range of linguistic and demographic information, as with covert techniques. Conversely, sociolinguistic interviews impose limits that can actually provide advantages over recording everyday interactions or spontaneous conversations: They usually involve only a couple of participants (most typically one interviewer and one interviewee), are situated in settings conducive to relatively quiet recording, and are structured to yield maximal talk from interviewees in a minimal timeframe. Everyday interactions, on the other hand, may or may not be centered on conversation, and so our recordings may contain long stretches of silence and sporadic talk. In addition, they may be noisy; and since most everyday interactions are not simply a matter of focused one-on-one conversation, it can be difficult to separate out individual participants in multiparty interactions. Finally, we may not be able to initiate or sustain the lively conversations we seek unless we have at least a few pre-planned questions designed to inspire animated talk. For many researchers, the sociolinguistic interview strikes an ideal balance between elicitation and observational techniques, and so it is not surprising that it has long been and continues to be the primary data-gathering tool of variationist sociolinguists.

3.2.2 Structuring the sociolinguistic interview

The structure of the sociolinguistic interview depends on a loosely defined sequence of prompts designed to yield large quantities of casual, "natural" speech. Questions are grouped into modules focused on particular topics, and the modules can be re-arranged as the interview progresses to approximate the flow of natural conversation. Questions are focused on topics believed to be of fairly universal interest, as well as matters of particular interest to each community of study, and interviewees are encouraged to talk as long as they like on any topic that particularly interests them, to tell stories or narratives, and even to go off on tangents of their own. For example, Labov has long maintained that interviewees will tell particularly animated narratives and forget about the fact that they are being recorded (and so produce truly vernacular speech) if you ask them his famous "danger of death" question: "Have you ever been in a situation where you were in serious danger of being killed, where you thought to yourself, *This is it* …?" (Labov 1972c: 113).

The module-based structure of the sociolinguistic interview makes it easy to select, substitute, or re-contextualize topics in ways that fit different communities. In this way, sociolinguistic interviews can balance questions of general and community-specific interest. For example, consider the interview designs for Wolfram's (1971) study of second-generation Puerto Ricans in East Harlem, New York City, and Wolfram *et al.*'s (1999) much later studies of a very different community, the rural island community of Ocracoke, North Carolina. Both interview questionnaires include topics considered to be of general interest and highly conducive to vernacular speech; for example, games and leisure, group structure, and danger of death. Topics and questions conducive to interviewees producing animated narratives are especially important to variationist sociolinguistics, since they have long maintained that narratives are a prime site for natural, vernacular speech, a topic we return to below. In addition, the topic of childhood games is of special value, since not only is it of fairly immediate interest to children and teenagers, but it is held to be especially evocative of vernacular speech for adults. Reflection upon childhood games can cast grown-ups back in time as they produce rhymes and other word games that only sound right in the vernacular speech of their childhood.

Interestingly, the danger-of-death topic, though common to the East Harlem and Ocracoke interviews, was embedded differently in each one: In Harlem, it proceeded from a discussion of fights and accidents, while in Ocracoke it followed from a discussion of the weather. In the urban context, street fighting was common among the adolescents interviewed, and discussion of near-death experiences could be expected to naturally arise in this context. In contrast, there is no street fighting in the relatively peaceful island community. However, because it is precariously situated in the Atlantic Ocean, 20 miles off the North Carolina mainland, frequent, very dangerous storms are common, and discussions of weather and danger of death commonly go hand-in-hand. In (3.7) and (3.8) we see the modules in which the danger-of-death question is embedded in the East Harlem and Ocracoke interviews, respectively.

(3.7)

Harlem danger-of-death module
  D. Fighting and accidents
  What kinds of things do fights usually start about on the street?
  Any rules for a fair fight? (How about if someone was kicking somebody or
hitting them with a chain or lead pipe, what would you do?)
  Ever see anybody get beat up real bad? What happened?
  Do the kids around here still fight in gangs? How do these start?
  (If answered negatively, pursue why gang fights have stopped.)
  Ever been in a hospital, or automobile accident? Describe.
  How about a situation in which you thought, "Man, this is it, I'm gonna die for
sure now"? What happened?

                                      (Wolfram 1971; cited in Wolfram and Fasold 1974: 54)

(3.8)

Ocracoke danger-of-death module
  iv. Weather / danger of death

(1) What was the worst storm you've ever been in?
    (i)   What was that like?
    (ii)   Did it do much damage?
    (iii) Are the roads OK?
    (iv)   Do the roads get washed out a lot?
    (v)   What do you think should be done?

(2) Do you think you're getting more storms now than you used to?
    How come?

(3) Have you ever been in a hurricane?
    (i)   What was that like?

(4) How about shipwrecks?
    (i)   Do you remember any shipwreck stories?

(5) Have you ever been in a situation where you thought, "This is it. I'm going to
    die"?
    (i)   What was that like? Tell me about it.

Other modules are even more specific to the community under
study. For example, though clearly out of place in an interview
designed for teens in East Harlem, the Ocracoke interview included
questions about island history, tourism, and even pirates (since the
notorious Blackbeard was killed off the coast of Ocracoke). As another
example, when we designed the questionnaire for use in the ongoing
study of Language and Communication in the Washington, DC, Metropolitan Area (LCDC), housed in the Georgetown University Linguistics
Department, we included a module on transportation problems, since,

as indicated in (3.9), the DC area is one of the worst in the US in terms
of transportation difficulties. Such a module would presumably be
fairly irrelevant to teens in Harlem, since they have not yet joined the
workforce and probably do not have to worry about a daily commute,
and would of course be meaningless in Ocracoke, where there is no
such thing as a "commute" or a traffic jam.

(3.9)

Transportation module for Washington, DC
  Ever have any problems on the Metro? (the DC Metro area subway system)
  What do you think about the new rules about not eating on the Metro?
  I've heard that the daily commute here is one of the worst in the country . . .
have you found a way to get around it?

In addition to questions designed to evoke a high degree of interest and
to deflect attention away from speech itself, sociolinguistic interviews
also necessarily include questions designed to obtain basic demographic
and social information. In the US and many other Western cultural
contexts, the demographic questions can be quite straightforward
and included at the beginning of the interview, since Westerners
typically ask questions about residence, occupation, and family when
getting to know someone in everyday contexts, not just interview
situations. However, greater care must be taken in other cultures
where norms may differ. For example, it may be considered impolite
or inappropriate to ask about occupation, or to do so too early in a
social encounter.

Sometimes even seemingly innocuous demographic questions can
fail to meet IRB approval in particular cultural contexts. For example,
Sakiko Kajino, a Georgetown University student who is from Japan
but studied for a number of years in the US, was forbidden by
a university IRB in Japan from including questions about parents'
occupation in the interview she designed for her forthcoming study
of women's language in three different metropolitan locations in
Japan.

Even in Western contexts, some demographic questions are more
awkward or sensitive than others, such as questions about age (especially, traditionally, for women) or education level. So, for example, it is
common for sociolinguists to ask interviewees in vernacular speaking
communities (often of lower socioeconomic status and educational
attainment) "How many years of school did you get a chance to finish?"

Questions about social networks, patterns of contact, and orientation
to the community and its various subgroups are also important

elements of sociolinguistic interviews. For example, the East Harlem teen interview includes questions concerning "How about the guys you hang around with? In this group, is there one guy that everybody listens to? How come?" Similarly, for Ocracoke adults, we included questions such as, "Do people here get together a lot? What are some of the things they do with neighbors? Who are they friends with? What kinds of things do you do with them?" Information about islanders' general orientations to their community could be elicited with a simple, general question: "Do you think this is a good place to live? Why / why not?"

3.2.3 Stylistic variation in the sociolinguistic interview

From the outset, Labov recognized that not all interview questions would be equally conducive to obtaining casual, vernacular speech and so the conversational interview was delimited by topic and discourse type into contexts believed to be conducive to casual speech and those considered to be more careful or guarded. In order to situate genuine vernacular speech within a full range of speech styles, as well as gain valuable information on stylistic variation in its own right, the conversational portion of the interview was followed by several different subsections designed to yield increasingly careful styles: a reading passage, a word list, and a list of minimal pairs (Labov 1972c: 70–109). These sections are also often crafted to provide information on particular variables of interest. For example, in Labov's early New York City interview, there were two reading passages. The first included successive instances of each of the five variables on which the study was focused: the production of /ɔ/ as raised (the New York City variant) vs. non-raised, the production of /æ/ as raised (New York City) or non-raised, r-0 vs. r-1, and the pronunciation of initial /ð/ and /θ/ as [d] and [t] respectively. The second reading was designed to juxtapose items that form minimal pairs in standard American English but may lose distinctiveness in the New York City dialect: /e/ and /ɛ/ before /r/ (as in *Mary* / *merry*), "ng" sequences in pairs like *finger* / *singer*, and pairs such as *sauce* / *source*, which may sound quite similar when the latter item is produced with r-0. The word list was similarly focused on /r/, /æ/, and /ɔ/, while the minimal pair task focused specifically on /r/ in pairs like *sauce* / *source*, *god* / *guard*, etc.

The expected patterning of style shifting as one moves from the conversational portion of the interview to the reading passage, word lists and minimal pairs is based on the view that speech style is conditioned primarily by how much attention the interviewee is paying to speech itself rather than what they are talking about, with relatively unselfconscious speech being more casual and more non-standard and more selfconscious styles being more careful and standard. The conversational portion of the interview is designed to focus attention away from speech toward the topics of discussion and so should yield fairly casual speech, and each subsequent task increasingly focuses in on language itself. The reading passage turns people's attention toward written language, which people typically view as needing to be "correct," though there is still a storyline to distract the reader. With the word list, there is no content besides the words themselves, and with minimal pairs, the focus narrows even further to the specific feature in question, and people will presumably get very selfconscious and do their best to produce standard rather than dialectal variants.

The predictions regarding stylistic variation across the various interview tasks were often borne out in early studies, including Labov's New York City study (see Figure 3.1). Note in Figure 3.1 how, as the interview proceeds from casual (A) to careful (B) to reading passage (C) to word list (D) to minimal pair styles (D′), from left to right, speakers from a range of socioeconomic classes all use increasing levels of features of standard American English, in this case, post-vocalic r-pronunciation. Correspondingly, they use decreasing levels of stigmatized features such as r-0 (Labov 1972c: 110–121).

3.2.4 Casual vs. careful speech in the conversational interview ▪▪▪▪

While the patterning of selfconscious styles is of great interest and yields important information pertaining to questions of language variation and change, the underlying reason for obtaining a range of speech styles in the traditional interview was to elicit, and be able to identify, each interviewee's most casual, least selfconscious style – the vernacular. This focus, and the reasoning behind it, is captured in Labov's vernacular principle, re-stated here:

> The vernacular principle:
> the style which is most regular in its structure and in its relation to the evolution of language is the vernacular, in which the minimum attention is paid to speech (Labov 1972a: 112).

The main goal in conducting the sociolinguistic interview was, and often still is, to minimize attention to speech, or to overcome Labov's often-cited observer's paradox, again re-stated:

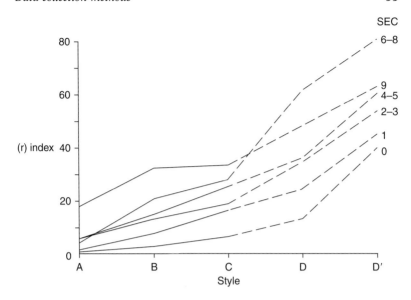

SEC scale 0–1, lower class; 2–3, working class; 4–5, 6–8, lower middle class; 9, upper middle class. A, casual speech; B, careful speech; C, reading style; D, word list; D′, minimal pairs.
3.1 Class and style stratification for postvocalic r (from Labov, William, 1968, "The reflection of social processes in linguistic structures," in Fishman, Joshua (Ed.), *Readings in the Sociology of Language*, Berlin/New York: de Gruyter, p. 244, fig. 2).

The observer's paradox:
To obtain the data most important for linguistic theory, we have to observe how people speak when they are not being observed (Labov 1972a: 113).

According to Labov (1966, 1984, 2001b), casual, vernacular speech is predicted to be found in several places throughout the interactional context of a sociolinguistic interview: (1) in speech taking place before the interview gets underway; (2) in interruptions to the interview event (perhaps to offer a cup of coffee or a beer); and (3) after the interview is over and the tape recorder put away. Casual speech is more elusive within the boundaries of the interview proper, but it can be found. In order to help locate the desired casual speech and separate out the more careful, guarded speech that also surfaces in interview interaction, Labov, working with his students at the University of Pennsylvania, devised the "decision tree" shown in Figure 3.2, which is based on eight contexts we typically find in sociolinguistic interviews (Labov 2001b: 94).

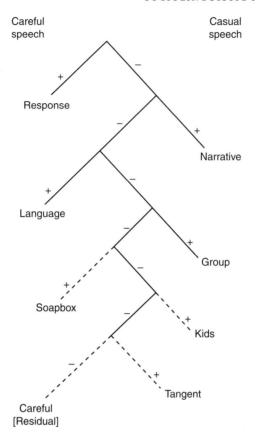

3.2 Labov's "decision tree" for delimiting casual and careful style in the sociolinguistic interview (from Labov, William, 2001, "The anatomy of style shifting," in Eckert, Penelope, and John R. Rickford (Eds.), *Style and Sociolinguistic Variation*, Cambridge/New York: Cambridge University Press, p. 94, fig. 5.1).

The four contexts on the left of the tree are predicted to yield careful, selfconscious speech, and the four on the right to yield casual, vernacular speech. The two styles at the top are the easiest to identify: response style is used in direct, matter-of-fact answers to interview questions, such as:

Q: "How long have you lived on Ocracoke?"
A: "All my life."

Narratives are readily identified according to the classic Labovian definition as containing at least two temporally ordered clauses such as the two italicized clauses in (3.10), extracted from a story about a hurricane, related by a young African American woman in Robeson County, NC, whom we call Felicia.

(3.10)

"All of a sudden we you know *we heard this thing like a train* you know. And I *looked outside* and oh lord the wind was just blowing, you know."

A full discussion of narrative structure is beyond the scope of this chapter, but in addition to temporally ordered clauses, the classic Labovian narrative may contain an orientation section situating the action; complicating action clauses; evaluations of the actions (typically found throughout the narrative); resolution of the situation presented in the story; and a coda that returns the storyteller and listeners back into the interactional present. The clauses in (3.11) are extracted from the orientation, complicating action, resolution, and coda sections of Felicia's hurricane story:

(3.11)

Orientation:
　Well, I remember um the eighty-four hurricane. Okay, we was in here, or was it um, I don't think it was this trailer. We was like the green trailer. And it was like, remember it was turned the long way? Single wide?
Complicating action:
　All of a sudden we, you know, we heard this thing like a train you know. And I looked outside and the wind was just blowing. . .
　He [Felicia's father] woke up and realized what was going on and we went over to granddaddy house. . .
　He parked it [the family car] over there, he parked it right under that tree right there. He parked it over there and all of us went into the house . . .
Resolution:
　But we ain't [didn't] die.
Coda:
　But I mean, you know, I guess, you know, it wasn't intended for us to go because everybody is entitled to their time to go.

Finally, evaluation is scattered throughout the entire hurricane narrative and cannot be neatly separated. Hence, for example, inter-mixed with the action clauses above are clauses indicative of the narrator's incredulity that her father would try to drive in a hurricane (e.g. "Toilets flying everywhere, and he gonna try to drive!"), as well as the narrator's fear of death (e.g. "I just knew we was gonna die," "I was scared to death," "I ain't never been so scared in all my life!").

As noted above, narratives are highly sought after in sociolinguistic fieldwork, since they have long been felt to be the site of speaker's least selfconscious, most vernacular speech. In telling animated narratives about personal experience, people will get so caught up in their stories that they forget all about the fact that they are being recorded or participating in a linguistic study. In addition, Labov particularly likes the danger-of-death question because not only are interviewees engrossed in their harrowing stories, but they feel compelled to convince their audience that the situation really was quite serious, and their concern for producing gripping stories outweighs any reticence they may feel about talking freely in the interview situation.

Moving down the 'casual' side of the decision tree, we find the "group," "kids," and "tangent" contexts. Group style occurs whenever the interviewee addresses third parties other than interviewers such as, for example, when a family member walks in or when the interviewee takes a phone call in the middle of the interview. This style should be relatively casual, since interviewees' norms for interacting with the people they deal with on a daily basis will typically take precedence over any effect the interview situation may be having on their normal way of speaking. The "kids" style is that associated with childhood games and other childhood matters but is considered to surface only when adult interviewees actually cast themselves back to their childhood years and speak from a child's perspective, a shift in point of view which is not always easy to identify. Finally, the "tangent" context is even more difficult to identify because it is so broad, occurring whenever an interviewee veers away from the topics introduced by the research to elaborate on topics of their own.

Moving down the careful side of the decision tree, the "language" context is also usually easy to identify and occurs whenever the topic of the interview turns to language itself, including in question modules designed specifically to directly elicit information about language forms, usages, and attitudes, usually placed near the end of the interview. We have already seen examples from the linguistic elicitation module at the end of the Ocracoke interview questionnaire, including the questions related to *weren't* regularization and our prompt for the pronunciation of *haven't* as "hadn't" ("Have you ever seen a ghost? No, I _____"), which, as we saw, failed to elicit the feature in question but succeeded as a means of obtaining animated ghost stories, many of which also involved danger of death.

Delimiting the contexts for "soapbox" style is much more difficult: This style can be considered to occur when a speaker "gets up on their soapbox" and delivers, to use Labov's words, "generalized opinions" to

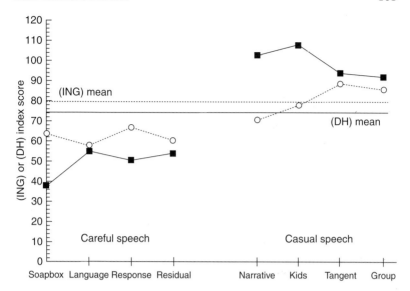

3.3 Stylistic differentiation for (dh) and (ing) for the eight categories of Labov's Decision Tree (from Labov, William, 2001, "The anatomy of style shifting," in Eckert, Penelope, and John R. Rickford (Eds.), *Style and Sociolinguistic Variation*, Cambridge/New York: Cambridge University Press, p. 104, fig.5.7).

a non-present "general audience," often using "elevated volume" and "repetitive rhetoric" (2001b: 91). For example, forceful statements of political views might be expressed on a soapbox, as might strong opinions on personal, family, community, and cultural values.

Finally, any portions of the conversational interview that cannot be grouped into any of the seven contexts discussed above (response, narrative, group, kids, tangent, language, soapbox) are best considered "careful," since, according to Labov, it is better to err on the side of caution and fail to include a bit of casual speech rather than to wrongly include careful speech in the pool of data we are going to analyze as reflective of "vernacular" language use.

After a number of years of using the eight contexts outlined above to delimit speech styles in the sociolinguistic interview, Labov and his students conducted studies to evaluate its utility. They found that the decision tree indeed seemed to be quite useful. Figure 3.3 shows results of a study of interviews with more than 180 Philadelphians (conducted during 1973–1979) of variation between [d] and [ð], as in *dis* vs. *this*, and [in] and [ɪŋ], as in *walkin'* vs. *walking*, across the eight contexts in the decision tree in Figure 3.2 (Labov 2001b: 95).

The figure shows that in all four careful contexts listed on the left, usage levels for the non-standard variants [d] and [ɪn] fall below mean levels; while in the four casual contexts, usage levels are above the mean for all but [ɪn] in the narrative context. Thus, for the most part, Labov maintains that we can fairly reliably distinguish careful from casual style in the sociolinguistic interview using these eight contexts. His findings support the basic idea that style can be arrayed along a continuum based on attention to speech, and that the various tasks comprising the traditional sociolinguistic interview provide us with just such a continuum.

3.2.5 Criticisms of the sociolinguistic interview

Despite the predictive power of the attention to speech approach to stylistic variation as operationalized in the relatively controlled Labovian sociolinguistic interview, it has been criticized on a number of grounds, for example its unidimensional focus on only one factor affecting stylistic variation and on only one continuum of stylistic variation – standard–non-standard. In addition, even if we maintain that attention to speech is indeed paramount, or at least important, we do not really know how to quantify it; and most likely there are factors other than varying amounts of attention to speech that contribute to stylistic variation even in sociolinguistic interviews designed to focus on this very factor, let alone in the myriad styles we find outside the relatively controlled interview situation. Thus, for example, we may question whether reading style lies on the same plane as spoken styles, since it is likely that people have specialized reading registers that differ in a number of ways from spoken speech, not just degree of carefulness (Macaulay 1977; Milroy 1987; Romaine 1978, 1980). Similarly, as Eckert (2001) notes, Labov's categories for separating casual from careful speech have to do not only, or even primarily, with attention to speech but also with such matters as audience (as with group vs. individual style), topic (e.g. kids), conversational control (as with tangent vs. response), and perhaps even genre (as with narrative vs. soapbox style). Finally, researchers have questioned the focus on vernacular, unselfconscious speech that underlies the attention to speech approach, arguing that there is no one single "genuine" vernacular for any one speaker, since speakers always shape their speech in some way to fit the situation or suit their purposes (e.g. Eckert 2000; Hindle 1979; Milroy and Gordon 2003: 49–51; Schilling 2013). I return to questions related to the attention to speech approach in Chapter 4.

Other criticisms of the sociolinguistic interview have to do with practical rather than theoretical matters: For one, there is the practical difficulty of reliably identifying the contexts in Labov's tree, despite his own apparent success in this regard. To aid in identifying truly vernacular speech, Labov initially advocated looking not only for interview contexts delimited by topic and discourse types, but also for particular "paralinguistic channel cues" that would indicate casual style: changes in tempo, pitch range, volume or rate of breathing, as well as the presence of laughter. However, researchers soon realized that any of these cues could just as easily be as indicative of increased nervousness and selfconsciousness as of animation and involvement, and so they quickly abandoned them as reliable markers of casual speech.

Another practical issue is designing reading passages that include the variables of interest in appropriate places without constructing a story that is so unnatural that readers greet it with incredulity (perhaps even ridicule) rather than with a relatively selfconscious attempt to produce a "good" reading. Hence, for example, whereas Labov was generally pleased with the reading passages in his New York City interview, he admits that the attempt to juxtapose the minimal pair *source / sauce* is less than elegant. The relevant excerpt from the reading passage is presented in (3.12).

(3.12)

"And what's the *source* of your information, Joseph?" She used her sweet-and-sour tone of voice, like ketchup mixed with tomato *sauce*. "Are they running submarines to the Jersey shore?" (Labov 1972c: 82)

There may also be ethical as well as practical issues associated with reading passages, since they can also cause a good bit of awkwardness for interviewees whose literacy level is not very high, or who are simply unused to reading aloud in front of an audience, much less an audio recorder. In my research experience, my colleagues and I very rarely included a reading passage as part of our sociolinguistic interview out of concern for our participants' comfort and dignity. We maintain to this day that the small gains we may have made in terms of additional information about stylistic variation would not have been worth the potential awkwardness, defensiveness, and perhaps even ill will toward us and our research project that such a face-threatening task may have engendered.

Finally, researchers have criticized the sociolinguistic interview as a speech event. Wolfson (1976) famously contended that the sociolinguistic interview is actually *less* rather than *more* natural than other types of interviews, since people expect interviews to be relatively formal and to follow a set questionnaire. Interviewees may become disconcerted and perhaps even angry when faced with an interviewer who does not follow a highly structured questionnaire and who may therefore seem unprepared for the interview. In addition, even though sociolinguistic researchers are supposed to do their best to relinquish control to interviewees, it has still been argued that there are insurmountable power asymmetries in the sociolinguistic interview. In addition to the interviewer's social role as an expert researcher, which comes with some degree of institutional authority, the interviewer also controls the turn structure and turn length within the interview, and these differences can put interviewees at a social disadvantage (see, e.g. Labov 1984; Milroy and Gordon 2003: 61–63). Further, it has been argued that the types of discourse that surface in the sociolinguistic interview are very different from those found in natural conversation, and so even if the sociolinguistic interview does yield a range of speech contexts and styles, it really does not have much to tell us about how various styles are structured in everyday speech. For example, Wolfson (1976), Schegloff (1997) and others have claimed that narratives may be quite different in sociolinguistic interviews than in non-interview conversation, perhaps more summary in nature or more focused on leading up to a final "point" that answers the interviewer's particular question. For example, an interviewee might provide quite differently constructed stories about the same near-death experience if prompted with the question "Have you ever been in a situation where you thought you were going to die?" rather than something like "Have you ever been in a bad storm?" In the former case, they may shape the story to make sure the interviewer gets the point that they really were in a life-threatening situation; in the latter, the focus may be more purely descriptive of the weather event instead of their own personal danger.

The sociolinguistic interview has other built-in limitations in terms of linguistic form. Because interviewees are relatively free to talk about anything they want to, using whatever language forms they like, the interview conversations are not likely to be pointed enough to give us sufficient information on the quantitative patterning or full structural range of many morphosyntactic features (e.g. how often will someone use multiple negatives; or how often will they use past tense negative *be*, in both non-contracted and contracted form). Even some phonological features may not occur often enough in the course of a natural conversation to enable quantitative analysis – /aw/, which is relatively rare in English, is one example. Similarly, if we are interested in interrogatives or second-person pronouns, we most likely will have to look beyond interview data, since questioners do not usually respond to interviews with questions of their own (though this is by no means unheard of); nor are interviewers usually directly addressed with "you." And despite our best efforts to make the interview event as natural and conversational as possible, respondents can still choose to avoid stigmatized forms.

Other critiques of the sociolinguistic interview as a speech event run deeper. Charles Briggs (1986) has pointed out that the very act of conducting an interview entails the imposition of hegemonic Western notions of normal, natural, and appropriate speech events, as well as the nature of language and information, onto communities we ideally would like to understand on their own terms. Thus, whereas Westerners tend to view language primarily as a vehicle for conveying information and an interview as a typical means of gathering this "objective," "factual" information, different communities and cultural groups may have quite different metacommunicative practices or different notions of how to gather information, and when to give it out. The notion of obtaining large quantities of information in a relatively short amount of time through relatively direct questions and direct answers, which may be normal and natural for Western researchers, is alien to many communities and considered to be puzzling at best and, at worst, inappropriate or rude. Even within the US, different communities have quite different norms regarding the appropriateness of direct speech. For example, in the research projects I have been involved with in rural Southeastern US communities, interactions were best proceeded by a lot of slow-paced "small talk" – that is, discussion of comfortable topics such as weather, the well-being of interlocutors' family and friends, and other details of everyday life (e.g. meals, work- and school-related events); and actual audio recording could not usually take place on initial meetings with strangers.

In their zeal for obtaining large quantities of data, even seasoned sociolinguists can become blind to the fact that interviewees have myriad interactional goals and interests, and these may not always closely match those of the interviewer – chiefly obtaining lots of naturalistic speech. So, for example, while many interviewees may fortuitously view the interview as an occasion for unselfconscious conversation and storytelling, others may view it as a performance opportunity (whether for "proper" speech, vernacular speech, or elaborate storytelling), a joke (cf. the "mock serious interview" discussed in Section 2.4 above), a grueling ordeal to finish as soon as possible, an opportunity for making money (if research participants are paid), and so on. And again, these different views can be found not only in cultures researchers consider to be quite different from their own, but even in settings whose sheer familiarity may mask potential differences in how linguistic interactions and interview events are understood.

Finally, researchers in the quantitative sociolinguistic tradition, with its emphasis on empiricism, need to bear in mind the understandings of researchers coming from more of a social constructionist point of view, such as interactional sociolinguists and linguistic anthropologists. From these perspectives, neither the form nor the content of interview speech are simple reflections of how interviewees "really" talk or how communities "really" operate but rather are joint productions of both interviewee and interviewer. For example, interviewers and interviewees who share demographic characteristics may both talk more casually (and more like one another) than interview participants who feel more distant from one another (Bell 1984). In addition, both participants can shape content, and hence understandings, for a variety of reasons, including to confirm pre-conceived expectations, to maintain conversational rapport, or to paint themselves in a positive light. Consider, for example, the following excerpt from an interview with a middle-aged Ocracoke man, "Jim," by a fieldworker who had become convinced, early in our work on Ocracoke, that the weekly poker game in which certain island men traditionally participated was a vitally important rite of passage in the island community. Notice how the fieldworker tries to steer the conversation to confirm his belief, even though Jim actually deflects the fieldworker's presuppositions rather than confirming them.

(3.13)

FW: I hear that y'all been playing poker a long time.
J: Yeah, it's just been passed right on down...
FW: Was that your grandfather's era?
J: Yeah. They're still playing. We didn't even start moving inside playing, I was playing with them – they wouldn't even let you start playing until you were about seventeen or eighteen.
FW: **Oh, so it was a privilege**.
J: And mostly when somebody'd die off you got in that group. When the old ones would die you'd get a chance to play.
FW: **It's kind of an initiation thing, huh? Some place you get initiated into being a man?**
J: We don't have the same bunch since I started playing, you know, in the last – even in the last twenty years, there was some – there's four or five that's died that used to play, the older ones.

3.2.6 Modifications of the sociolinguistic interview

Variationists have long sought to address the problematic issues raised by critics of the sociolinguistic interview, including the relative unnaturalness of the interview event, the power asymmetries it entails, and the danger of interviewers exerting more control than they perhaps realize. In light of these difficulties, sociolinguists have modified the basic sociolinguistic interview technique in various ways while still attempting to preserve its advantages in terms of amount of interviewee speech, efficiency, and sound quality.

Among the earliest modifications was moving from the one-on-one interview format to **group interviews**, with the idea that people being interviewed in peer groups would talk more with one another than with the interviewer and that the everyday interactional norms they have with peer group members would supersede any artificiality introduced by the interview event or by the relatively standard speech of the interviewer. Labov (1972b) used peer group interviews in his early studies of African American teenagers in Harlem and found that interviewer effects were minimized to such an extent that the interviewer often receded into the background while the teens talked among themselves. Other researchers have enjoyed similar success in recording teens in peer group interaction, as for example in Hewitt's (1982) study of London adolescents' use of Jamaican patois and Cheshire's (1982) study of adolescents in Reading, England. Still others have purposely designed studies to test the effects of group vs. individual interviews (Thelander 1982), and found that indeed group interviews tend to be more natural, in the sense that participants use more features of their group vernacular in peer group interactions than in on-on-one interviews with a researcher. Indeed, the effects of audience composition on interviewee speech are so striking that they led Allan Bell (1984) to formulate his audience design model for stylistic variation, which holds that speech style is primarily conditioned not by speaker self-consciousness but by to whom the speaker is talking, with direct addressees having the greatest effect on one's speech and other participants having a lesser effect. According to this model, a research participant is more likely to conform to an interviewer's relatively standard speech when directly addressing the interviewer in a one-on-one interaction, but is far less likely to do so when the interviewer is present in a group setting where most speech is directed toward the interviewee's peers.

Researchers have also sought to minimize interviewer effects and maximize use of everyday language norms by simply recording **spontaneous conversations** rather than interviews with at least a somewhat structured schedule. For example, Milroy and Milroy found that recording spontaneous conversations among groups of family and friends who often gathered together for extended visits was an excellent way of obtaining natural speech data in their studies of Belfast,

Northern Ireland, in the mid-1970s through early 1980s (e.g. Milroy and Gordon 2003: 73–76). Childs and Mallinson (2004) also had excellent results using spontaneous conversations rather than pre-set interview questionnaires in a very different setting: the small African American community in Appalachian North Carolina that is home to the "Church ladies" and "porch sitters." Although, as noted above, simply recording spontaneous interactions is not always as advantageous as we might think, in these cases the researchers were successful because they had learned through long-term participation-observation that the extended talk-centered visit was a common interactional activity in each community, and in addition they had become familiar with a range of topics likely to spark conversation in the event of a lull.

Another variant on the one-on-one interview was used by Wolfram and his research colleagues in their work in North Carolina beginning in the early 1990s (Wolfram, Hazen, and Schilling-Estes 1999). This involved **pairs of researchers** interviewing one or more interviewees. At first glance, such a tactic seems to swing the balance of power even farther toward the interviewer rather than the interviewee, but in practice we found that breaking down the one-on-one dynamic by including a third party, whether researcher or research participant, was just as effective in reshaping the "interview" into a conversation as adding extra interviewees. Indeed, using two interviewers yields some extra advantages: it divides the multiple tasks of the sociolinguistic interviewer between (or among) researchers, including keeping track of technical recording matters (e.g. is the recorder set correctly, is the speech signal being picked up well, is the battery power high?) while simultaneously paying attention to the content and flow of conversation. Furthermore, if the conversation gets stuck and one researcher cannot think of a way to re-start it, usually the other interviewer can step in with topics that get the interviewee talking again. This is especially useful since we, as sociolinguists, sometimes find ourselves inadvertently focusing on *how* people are talking rather than *what* they are saying (a common occurrence for many of us, both inside and outside the interview situation!).

STUDENTS IN THE FIELD

Interviewing in pairs can also be a useful strategy in cases where sociolinguists study a language or variety in which they have less than native-like communicative competence. Working with another fieldworker or assistant who is a native speaker can help to ensure that interviews (and interactions) are successful. In speaking of her work with a professor who is a native speaker of Brazilian Portuguese, Amelia Tseng noted, "I was nervous on first approaching the community because I was very aware that my Portuguese is not native-like. I was also nervous because the culture is new to me, and I was very worried about offending people or transgressing . . . cultural norms. [The project director] was very good at the interviews because his colloquial language makes people laugh and puts them at their ease."

It is also possible to veer away from the interview format in the other direction by having research participants make **recordings with no researcher present**. Such a technique might involve providing interviewees with audio recorders and having them record all their conversations for an extended period of time (e.g. days, weeks). For example, in Coupland's (1980) foundational study of stylistic variation outside the sociolinguistic interview context, he asked an assistant in a Cardiff travel agency to record her conversations at work for a number of days. The resultant data – taken from the fifth day of recording, after the assistant had ceased to pay much attention to the tape recorder – yielded invaluable information on a range of factors affecting stylistic variation, including audience (e.g. clients vs. co-workers who are friends), channel (telephone vs. face-to-face), and topic (work vs. non-work). Coupland's study also heralded current views of stylistic variation that focus on speaker agency in stylistic variation by demonstrating that the travel assistant shifted styles not simply in response to shifts in the conversational context but also to effect changes in her role-relations with her clients.

Interviewer-free recordings may not always be quite as valuable, especially if the context is less controlled: For example, Macaulay (2009: 33–34) reports that in gathering data for the Bergen Corpus of London Teenage Language (COLT), Stenström, Andersen, and Hasund (2002) provided teenagers with tape recorders and asked them to record for several days all conversations in which they participated. Despite this seemingly ideal set-up for obtaining natural speech, there were several problems. For one, some teenagers recorded copious quantities of data while others recorded very little. Secondly, the conversations were recorded in such a wide range of settings that they could not be said to be directly comparable with one another. For example, some students recorded conversations with friends in casual settings while others recorded classroom interactions or interactions with parents, the latter two settings of course being conducive to quite different speech than the former. Third, although we might eliminate *researcher* effects, we cannot negate *addressee* effects. In other words, participants in the COLT study did not simply talk "naturally" because they were being recorded by friends. Rather, they used a range of types of speech based on a range of situational factors and internal motivations. Indeed, the teens in this study were perhaps *more* selfconscious and performative with their friends than if they had been recorded by professional researchers with more experience in obtaining naturalistic speech data. The teenage interviewers often tried so hard to obtain interesting speech that they quite overtly manipulated their data – sometimes encouraging peers to swear on tape and sometimes soliciting arguments. Of course, professional adult sociolinguists are not immune from trying to get "good" speech at the possible expense of more naturalistic data. For example, encouraging interviewees to tell narratives about extraordinary events (e.g. near-death experiences) may yield stories that are highly performative rather than truly "vernacular," and such invitations can be every bit as manipulative as teenagers encouraging one another to "be bad" on tape.

Macaulay's discussion of Stenström *et al.*'s data-gathering methods again brings up the trade-offs inherent in relinquishing the controls built into the one-on-one sociolinguistic interview in favor of less controlled speech. The quantity, audio quality, and style of speech may be uneven in group interviews, spontaneous conversations, and unmonitored recordings made by research participants. Granted, researchers can – and should – take measures to ensure good recording quality in the first two situations, giving each conversational participant their own microphone, recording them on separate tracks or recorders, and having a stockpile of topics to introduce if conversation slows down. However, there is not much they can do to minimize the extraneous noise that often accompanies group recordings, including not only overlapping speech but other noises associated with natural interactions, for example loud laughter, rattling dishes and eating noises, and noisy comings and goings of non-participants such as children and pets. Furthermore, there is even less control when the interviewer is not present; the quality of the speech data obtained can be quite poor, and quantity of talk may be insufficient, excessive, or ill-distributed across participants, styles, and situations.

Stuart-Smith (1999) and Macaulay (2002), in their studies of language variation and change in Glasgow, implemented one ingenious variation of the traditional sociolinguistic interview. They arranged for pairs of friends to engage in conversation on their own, but in a quiet setting with high-quality recording equipment set up and activated by the researchers. The resulting data was of high quality but was also quite relaxed and casual, even among adolescents, who sometimes pose special problems for sociolinguistic research. Teenagers may be hesitant to talk with adult researchers, and it may not always be wise to send them off on their own to record whatever they see fit. Stuart-Smith and Macaulay's "interview" design also had the added advantage of yielding language forms that may be difficult to capture in researcher-directed interviews, as they are really used by teens in peer-to-peer conversation. For instance, using data from pairs of friends, Macaulay was able to collect and analyze the variable patterning of discourse markers such as *y'know* and *well* and non-standard intensifiers such as *pure* and *heavy*, as in "you pure really liked David" (Macaulay 2009: 110) and "it was heavy funny man" (2009: 112).

STUDENTS IN THE FIELD

In her sociolinguistic study of Japanese women's speech, mentioned briefly above, Sakiko Kajino conducted a number of group interviews with young women. She came up with a way to be present for the recording without also being present for the speech event. Using a 10-meter cable, she attached her microphone to a recorder located outside the room where the participants met. She could not hear or see the conversation, but she was able to monitor the quality of her recording without being too far away. (See Chapter 6, though, on potential sound quality loss when cables are too long!)

3.3 ETHNOGRAPHY / PARTICIPANT-OBSERVATION

In our discussion of data-collection methods, we have seen a range of methods from experimentation to elicitation to the combined elicitation / observation that constitutes the well-constructed sociolinguistic interview. In this section, we give further consideration to observation, with a particular focus on ethnography, or what is often called participant-observation. This mode of inquiry is defined by the complementary research goals of simultaneously developing an insider perspective while preserving a measure of outsider detachment through long-term involvement in the community of study, both as a researcher and as a participant in community activities of some sort. Because ethnographic and linguistic anthropological methods are treated fully in other texts (e.g. Duranti 1997; Saville-Troike 2003), most of the discussion in this section focuses on the integration of ethnographic methods and perspectives into sociolinguistic study. In addition to considering the practical issues involved in designing, conducting, and interpreting variation studies that incorporate an ethnographic perspective, we must also consider more fundamental theoretical issues. Chief among these is whether we as scientists wish to maintain an overarching goal of researcher objectivity, or whether we acknowledge, along with scientists in the ethnographic and anthropological traditions, that "true objectivity" is neither possible nor desirable. Again, this issue calls into question some fundamental tenets of traditional variationist sociolinguistics, namely the quest to overcome the observer's paradox, and the search for "genuine," vernacular language data.

3.3.1 The interrelation of ethnography and sociolinguistics: A long and continuing tradition

From its inception, sociolinguistics has been concerned with the interrelation between language variation and social meaning, and as a number of researchers have noted (e.g. Eckert 2000; Johnstone 2000a), understanding people from their own perspective has always been an important goal. The very first variationist sociolinguistic study, Labov's (1963) investigation of Martha's Vineyard, shows us that the patterning of centralized /ay/ and /aw/ across demographic groups (e.g. age, occupation, island location) can be explained only by appealing to local social meanings, in this case orientation toward or away from the traditional island way of life. This focus on localized meanings was downplayed in subsequent surveys of larger urban populations, which were stratified according to seemingly "objective" criteria (e.g. socioeconomic class, sex, age) in the quest for comparability across studies and the formulation of generalizable principles. However, it did not take long for the ethnographic underpinnings of sociolinguistics to resurface, and in the 1970s and 1980s researchers once again began explicitly seeking insider understandings and local meanings. Among the most important studies combining long-term participant-observation with sociolinguistic survey techniques were two studies we have already pointed to a number of times for their methodological and theoretical innovativeness: Milroy and Milroy's studies of Belfast, Northern Ireland, in the mid-1970s (J. Milroy 1981; L. Milroy 1980), and Eckert's (1989, 2000) investigation of a Detroit suburban high school in the early 1980s. Milroy and Milroy discovered through their in-depth investigations that the patterning of language variation and change in the Belfast neighborhoods they studied was better explained by individual patterns of social interaction – specifically, degree of integration into tight-knit social networks vs. looser participation in a range of networks – than by membership in wider demographic groups such as socioeconomic class. Similarly, Eckert found that teenagers' participation in sound changes affecting the Detroit area correlated more closely with local adolescent social groups (namely, the school-oriented jocks vs. urban-oriented burnouts) and practices (e.g. participation in school-sanctioned vs. rebellious extracurricular activities) than with social class.

3.3.2 Theoretical considerations: Balancing objectivity and relativity

As much as insider perspectives have always been important for sociolinguists, at times taking an ethnographic approach can feel problematic to researchers who believe their work must be grounded in detached, "objective" observation. Quantitative sociolinguists may feel torn between their mandate to overcome the observer's paradox to get at "real" language data unaffected by the research context, and their desire to immerse themselves in the community context so as to fully understand it. However, as alluded to in Section 3.2 above and discussed more fully below, there is really no such thing as linguistic data devoid of context, and it is inevitable that humans doing research on other humans will affect the research participants in some way. No matter how "neutral" we may try to remain, the people we are studying will cast us in some role and re-cast themselves accordingly, and linguistic anthropologists maintain that it is far better to figure out what our effects are than to seek to obliterate them. As Duranti notes, rather than fruitlessly seeking to overcome the observer's paradox, we need to recognize the following:

> In the social sciences, dealing with the paradox means to understand the different ways in which the presence of certain types of social actors (e.g. ethnographers) or artifacts (e.g. cameras, tape recorders, notebooks, questionnaires) play a role in the activity that is being studied, and the different kinds of transformations that each medium and technique produces (1997: 118).

In addition, people do not somehow respond in "unnatural" ways to research situations but rather draw from a host of natural interactional strategies in all their dealings with one another. As Duranti observes, "people do not usually invent social behavior, language included, out of the blue. Rather, their actions are part of a repertoire that is available to them independently of the presence of the camcorder" (1997: 118).

Furthermore, we probably should not flatter ourselves into thinking that our effect will be all that great anyway. Duranti notes that "most of the time people are too busy running their lives to change them in substantial ways because of the presence of a new gadget or a new person" (1997: 118).

And this is so not only in extended participant-observation of people's everyday activities, but even in more "artificial" research contexts. As Eckert notes in response to Wolfson's critique of the "unnaturalness" of sociolinguistic interview:

> While critics of this method have claimed that the sociolinguistic interview is not a natural speech event (Wolfson 1976), it is not clear what constitutes a "natural" speech event, and what is natural about it. If we assume speakers have a repertoire of speech events that they regularly engage in, and that other events are so strange as to elicit unnatural speech, we are working on a static view of linguistic practice. Conversations, perhaps particularly with strangers, are inventions (Eckert 2000).

Indeed, people's propensity to forget about their participation in research projects is pervasive enough to give rise to perplexing practical and ethical issues. For example, in conducting my re-study of Smith Island, Maryland, I was sometimes unsure if I had correctly identified individuals who had participated in the earlier research project because almost no one remembered having been interviewed and tape recorded 15-plus years previously. Ethical issues will be treated fully in Chapter 7, but for now I simply raise the point that since research participants are prone to background our role as researchers, the dividing line between overt and covert observation and recording gets blurred. For example, a research participant might read and sign an Informed Consent Form that explicitly states that an interview or conversation will be recorded and made available to appropriate researchers, but then halfway through the interview begin providing us with sensitive information that makes it evident to us that they have forgotten that what they are saying is being preserved (Milroy and Gordon 2003).

If we as empirical sociolinguists still feel uncomfortable involving ourselves too deeply in the research community and thereby either artificially altering the sociolinguistic setting or losing our objective ability to analyze it, we must remember that an ethnographic perspective works in two directions, requiring a balance between objectivity and subjectivity. Indeed, if we approach our researcher situations from an ethnographic perspective, we will gain *increased* analytical ability, in the sense that an insider–outsider perspective gives us a more complete, more realistic understanding of our research than either perspective alone. The first step in beginning ethnographic research is to recognize that we inevitably bring pre-conceived notions and biases with us when we enter the field. It is far better to acknowledge that we have them (even if we do not yet see what they are) than to leave them unexamined. In other words, as Duranti puts it, developing a true ethnographic perspective entails developing the following:

> (i) an ability to step back and distance oneself from one's own immediate, culturally biased reactions so to achieve an acceptable degree of "objectivity" and (ii) the propensity to achieve sufficient identification with or empathy for the member of the group in order to provide an "insiders' perspective" what anthropologists call "the **emic** view" (1997: 85).

Granted, developing these abilities is no easy task, but the results of our efforts will yield far richer rewards than simply presuming that we are already objective because of our privileged position as "expert" scientists. Indeed, when we become ethnographers, we become not so much professional scholars but new students, ready to learn from the true experts: those who are members of the communities we study.

3.3.3 Practical considerations: How to become a participant-observer

Once we recognize the value of approaching our studies from an ethnographic perspective, we then have to learn how to do this. Conducting an ethnographic study is not simply a matter of going into a community, observing diligently, and becoming as much a part of ongoing activity as possible. Conversely, it is not simply a matter of deciding what we want to study prior to entering the community then going out and studying it. Because we are seeking a dual insider–outsider perspective, ethnography involves constantly moving back and forth between immersing ourselves in the community and stepping back outside it. We consider what we observe, formulating and reformulating hypotheses, then return back to the community for more focused observations based on our ever more finely tuned hypotheses (Johnstone 2000a: 94). And while initial observations may be broad-ranging and unstructured, systematic and focused observation is crucial at some stage. Many researchers formulate heuristics, sets of things to be sure to look for, to ensure that they are not overlooking crucial aspects of the sociolinguistic situation they are seeking to understand. Such heuristics may be especially valuable in familiar cultural settings, since often the most important aspects of our daily communicative activities are simply taken for granted, presumed to be "natural," and so not subject to observation, comment, or study.

What to observe

Linguistic anthropologists, ethnographers of communication, and sociolinguists offer various guidelines to help participant-observers identify whom, what, and how to observe, in order to ensure well-rounded ethnographic understandings. For example, Saville-Troike (2003) broadly suggests observing groups (e.g. neighborhoods, social networks, communities of practice), activities and interactions (e.g. classroom interactions, interactions in a community pub or coffee shop), events (e.g. courtroom trials, marriage ceremonies, gift exchanges), and social processes (e.g. socialization, hospitalization, marginalization). In addition, she encourages looking at the following when learning about the community:

(1) background information (e.g. historical background, general description of area)
(2) material artifacts (e.g. architecture, signs, instruments of communication such as books, mobile phones)
(3) social organization (e.g. community institutions, ethnic, and class relations)
(4) legal information (e.g. language-related laws)
(5) texts (e.g. newspapers, pamphlets, local histories, official, and unofficial web sites pertaining to the community, web logs)
(6) statements indicative of "common knowledge" or common-sense beliefs (e.g. "Everybody knows…", "Everybody says…")
(7) beliefs about language use (e.g. taboos, language attitudes)
(8) the linguistic code, the last of which, of course, being one of the first things on which sociolinguists will focus their attention.

More specifically, there is Hymes' (1974) well-known SPEAKING mnemonic for conducting an ethnography of communication, in which each letter stands for a crucial aspect of community patterns, values, and beliefs pertaining to linguistic interactions and communicative systems. In brief, Hymes urges paying attention to communicative settings (including both physical and psychological setting; how participants conceptualize or "frame" their experiences); participants (e.g. speaker, hearer, and even the people or things being talked about); ends (goals and outcomes, whether community or personal, overt or covert, expected or unintended); act sequence (message form and content); key (tone, manner, or spirit; e.g. mocking, serious, perfunctory, painstaking); instrumentalities (channels or forms of speech, e.g. oral vs. written language and dialect, varieties, and registers); norms (for interaction and interpretation); and genres (traditionally recognized types with identifiable formal characteristics, e.g. myths, tales, prayers, lectures, commercials, editorials). And whereas sociolinguists will quite naturally pay close attention to such matters as physical setting, human participants, message form, and content, and of course languages, dialects, registers, and varieties, they may not initially be as primed to concern themselves with matters such as frame, ends, key, and genre – but they will most likely find their understandings to be greatly enhanced when they do.

How to observe

In addition to *what* to observe, researchers offer helpful guidelines regarding *how* to observe to ensure that the ethnographer does not miss things. For example, Erickson (1986: 144, cited in Johnstone 2000b: 95) suggests systematically altering the focus (e.g. observing different groups in different places at different times), making notes, and taking time to think immediately after each observation, trying various kinds of participation (e.g. remaining silent vs. initiating inter-action), systematically looking for discrepant cases, and including machine recording. Again, the last item is a "given" for a sociolinguist, while the others can enrich our understanding in ways we may not immediately have thought of. For example, in her high school study, Eckert entered the community with a roster of students from which she randomly selected people with whom to make initial contacts (1989, 2000). These people in turn began introducing her to their friends, enabling her to secure plenty of research participants as well as providing the information on the interrelation of language and social networks she was seeking. However, Eckert was astute enough to realize that she could not simply let herself get caught up in one or two dominant social networks. She periodically "altered the focus" by returning to her original roster and choosing new names on the list so she could also learn about them and their social groups, even though, as she admits, it would have been far more comfortable to remain with groups who had already accepted her, just as it is for high-schoolers themselves. She notes:

> the process of getting to know people developed social desire, so that like the people I was there to study, my success depended on being accepted and liked. Unlike them, I could not afford to win acceptance within one group at the expense of another. While this was not difficult to balance, I did find myself viewing individuals and groups through a perspective created by my need for approval – a perspective that would not have been appreciably different had I been a new student in the school. This is always true in fieldwork, but it is

particularly bothersome in the high school, since few of us ever overcome our own adolescent pasts. Therefore, we need to continually consult those pasts to monitor where and how we focus our attention, and to recognize our biases and blind spots (2000: 76–77).

Different levels of community participation

Sociolinguists are also familiar with different forms of participation, at least in our research interviews. We participate much more actively in one-on-one interviews than in group interviews, where we tend to recede into the background as group members' interactions with one another take precedence. Our participation can also take different forms in terms of our level of integration into the research community, which may range from **complete participation**, in which we are "able to interact competently in the native language and even perform the verbal genres one is studying" (Duranti 1997) to **passive participation**, in which our role is that of a **bystander** or **professional overhearer**. Complete participation is difficult if not impossible, unless you have been a member of the community you're studying for a good while prior to initiating your research project. And even then, once you begin researching your community, you take on something of an outsider role in addition to your longstanding role as insider, and so you are no longer simply a participant but an observer as well. In addition, we must bear in mind that for the ethnographer, communicative competence is not simply a matter of being able to produce a community's linguistic codes and genres but also, crucially, knowing how to use them appropriately – and being sanctioned to do so. So, for example, while Labov (1972b) was able to uncover the sometimes complex rules governing ritual insults among young African American boys in inner-city Harlem, New York City, he did not join in the kids' "sounding" games, since it would have been highly inappropriate (and ridiculous) for a university-educated adult White male to have attempted to do so.

Passive participation in a research community also is not as easy to achieve as we might think, since no matter how unobtrusive we may try to be, we will always have *some* role in relation to the people we are studying. In other words, we will always be something of a participant in the community, if only a **marginal participant**. In addition, there are different ways of being unobtrusive in different communities and situations, and we sometimes will not know ahead of time just what those are. For example, while it may seem that sitting quietly in a corner doing nothing will always render us unnoticeable, in some cases such behavior is very strange and so highly visible. Even in contexts familiar to Western researchers, we sometimes have to figure out what to do to blend in. For example, a student in one of my sociolinguistic field methods classes was participating in a study of a Spanish restaurant in Washington, DC, and attempted to unobtrusively observe interactions in the restaurant by simply sitting at the bar. However, she soon realized that she was the only one doing nothing, and so next time she visited the research site, she brought a small notebook with her so she could pretend to be writing in a journal – a not uncommon activity for people sitting alone in American bars. (And in fact, she ended up doing real writing in her journal – namely keeping field notes – so her tactic for rendering herself unnoticeable proved to be doubly beneficial.)

A further issue is that sometimes attempted unobtrusiveness will be seen as surreptitiousness, and it may be better for a researcher who is a stranger in a community to begin the research project by simply admitting their intrusiveness and letting themselves be the center of attention. This proved to be the case in Smith Island, where we quickly learned that it was impossible for a group of outsiders to walk around the island before or after tourists' usual visiting hours without attracting attention. Our only recourse was thus to overtly make ourselves known to local institutional leaders such as the director of the cultural and historic center, the pastor, and a schoolteacher. Luckily, these leaders willingly introduced us to a range of community members, and so we did not face the problem fieldworkers sometimes encounter of becoming too enmeshed in the networks of the leaders to enter into the community's "grassroots" networks. For example, the director of the Smith Island Cultural Center was not from the island and did not even live there, but she was able to introduce us to plenty of longstanding members of the island community.

Sociolinguistic researchers working in their field sites usually find themselves situated somewhere between passive and complete participation. We have already noted one of the chief benefits of becoming a participant-observer rather than a mere observer, namely, increased understanding of the community from its members' own perspectives. In addition, becoming a participant in the community gives us other advantages as well: it offers access to situations, people, and types of speech not afforded to complete outsiders; and it provides insight into norms and values that might aid us in collecting data and enrich our analyses. We learned through our participant-observation in the Ocracoke community, for instance, that extended after-dinner visits were common among residents in the winter months, when fishing and tourism slow down for the season. We were able to capitalize on this knowledge by participating in these visits with our audio recorders running, a very effective and less artificial means of gathering data than pre-arranged sociolinguistic interviews during daytime hours or during the summer months. And participating in community activities in Robeson County gave us access to speech genres we would not have encountered if we had only conducted sociolinguistic interviews. We were able to hear Lumbee "preacher style" when we attended one of the Lumbee churches, and oratorical and singing genres at pow-wows celebrating Lumbee Native American heritage.

However, becoming integrated into a community can bring disadvantages as well. Entering the community entails being cast in a definite role within the community, and this insider role might limit our access. For example, we found in Ocracoke that female fieldworkers who had *not* become too closely associated with established women's networks on the island were allowed – and in fact encouraged – to visit with island men at their local male-only gathering spots. Conversely, women more closely integrated into island networks never went to these places and so were not exposed to the (highly vernacular) banter that took place there.

STUDENTS IN THE FIELD

Outsider-ethnographers sometimes struggle to find a position in the community that affords opportunity for observation and participation, especially in circumstances where they are easily recognizable as "foreigners." When Cala Zubair, a White native English speaker from the US, began her study of Sinhala register formation among university students in central Sri Lanka (Zubair 2012), she had to find a way to enter a community that was initially closed to her. As we saw in Chapter 2, Cala eventually decided to focus on a group called "Raggers," who strictly adhere to Sinhala-only language practices and who view English as a threat to Sinhala identity. She had planned to conduct her interviews with Raggers in Sinhala, and she was surprised to find that they would respond to her questions only in English. After she had been working with Raggers for nearly two months, she learned that her informants had consulted with their group leaders about participating in the study, and they had been explicitly instructed to speak with her in English – as an American, English-speaking outsider, she was not to be trusted with their *hela bhasava,* "native language." But though she had difficulties getting responses in interviews, Cala had much better luck when she asked the Raggers to show her around campus and take her to their classes. She also ate meals with Raggers in the cafeteria, and was eventually invited to attend Sinhala cultural events on campus. Gradually her subjects' suspicion waned, and several of them ultimately agreed to record themselves conversing in Sinhala in her absence. By the time she left the field, Cala had not only amassed a substantial corpus of spoken Sinhala, but she had also succeeded in connecting with a group who initially saw her as an epitome of the West and all they hated. In the end, her Ragger participants came to trust her and to respect her work.

The lifelong community insider enjoys a degree of access to particular people and events that is often much greater than an outsider can achieve. Insider-researchers can use themselves as a source of factual and attitudinal information about the community, and they can readily check the validity and reliability of their observations through feedback from fellow community members. But being a "genuine" member of the community under study is not always as advantageous as it might at first seem. A longtime insider in a community may overlook community behaviors, practices, or beliefs that are so commonplace that they may be unconscious, while outsiders whose communities do not share the same communicative norms may notice the same patterns right away. As a striking *non*-linguistic example, Jermay Jamsu Reynolds, a student who moved to the US from Tibet, told me that it initially struck him as very strange that "everyone in the US wears blue pants," something few people born and raised in the US (or many other Western countries) would ever think to notice, since we are so accustomed to the ubiquity of blue jeans. (See below for more on Jermay's sociolinguistic fieldwork observations.)

Just as acquiring a role as a new participant in a community both affords and constrains access, so too does your long-term role in the community to which you "really" belong. For example, one of the members of our research team in North Carolina decided to initiate sociolinguistic study of a tri-ethnic northeastern North Carolina community into which he had married, to provide a point of comparison for our ongoing study of tri-ethnic Robeson County, in the southeastern part of the state. His insider status allowed him to fare very well in engaging White community residents in participant-observation and sociolinguistic interviews. However, his ties with a long-established White family in this very racially divided community severely limited his access to community African Americans. He eventually decided to bring in African American interviewers from outside the community, who were able to obtain quite relaxed conversational interviews.

Finally, being a genuine insider might curtail your ability to get any relatively naturalistic data at all; after all, you have long had a role in

your community that is not that of a researcher. It may strike your
longstanding friends, acquaintances, and relatives as very odd indeed if
you start behaving like a researcher, particularly if you attempt to
engage them in sociolinguistic interviews that inquire about their lives
and backgrounds – questions you obviously already know the answers
to. Typically, trained sociolinguists will avoid this by recording everyday interactions or by asking about things they really do not know
much about. However, there are many cases in which sociolinguists
hire community members to conduct interviews for them. Sometimes
this strategy is very effective in yielding highly natural speech from
interviewees, but it can also lead to quite awkward interactions, especially if, for example, the newly recruited researcher does not understand the fluid structure of the interview schedule and asks every
single question as it appears on the form. Such was the case in Smith
Island in the mid-1980s, when the sociolinguistic researcher recruited
an island teenager to help her with interviews. Some of these interviews went fairly well, especially with older relatives and neighbors
who were happy to have a chance to share old stories with a young
islander and pass down island traditions. Sometimes, though, things
did not run so smoothly, as when the teenager interviewed her father
and asked him obvious questions that caused him to get rather uncooperative, as shown in the excerpt in (3.14 below). "Debby" is the
interviewee and "Harry" is her father.

(3.14)

> D: How many children do you have?
> H: Two. Daughter and a son.
> D: What are their names and ages?
> H: **You're one of 'em**. Debby, 18. "Harry, Jr.," 15.

This resident interviewer was also the one whose strict adherence to
an interview questionnaire designed for outsiders led to the "mock
serious interview" discussed in Chapter 2, in which her cousin
embraced the artificiality of the situation by performing a "real,"
"grown-up" interview rather than talking to her as he would in everyday life.

Despite the potential drawbacks, the positive effects of interviewer familiarity, and similar demographic characteristics (e.g.
neighborhood residence, ethnicity, gender) are well known to sociolinguists, especially those involved in studying audience effects on
stylistic variation. And furthermore, the occasional awkward interview conducted by a non-linguist by no means diminishes the
important contributions of community members whose excellent

research work was invaluable, as, for example, in Labov and Harris (1986) and Graff, Labov, and Harris (1986).

STUDENTS IN THE FIELD

In addition to being an astute observer of unfamiliar cultures, Jermay Jamsu Reynolds (2012) also capitalized on his insider status as a native of a small Tibetan farming village, "Spearhead," to conduct a sociolinguistic study of the social meaning of a language change currently underway in this remote village, far removed from the urban centers or modern Western cultures that have traditionally formed the focus of variationist research. Even though he was in many ways a community "insider," Jermay recruited his brother to conduct interviews with villagers, for both logistical and deeper reasons. First, his brother still lived there, whereas travel to and extended stay in Spearhead would have been quite impracticable for Jermay. Second, Jermay determined that because he had been living and studying in the US for so long, he had acquired a degree of "outsider" status, and people would feel more comfortable with his brother, still a genuine insider. Indeed, this proved to be the case, and his brother had great success in collecting data, especially once he abandoned any efforts at using a pre-set questionnaire and just held natural conversations with his fellow villagers. Once the interview process was underway, Jermay also realized that an apparent drawback was actually a third advantage: despite his brother's high success rate in obtaining research participants, people did feel quite free to say "no" to him. In contrast, they might have felt obligated to agree to Jermay, because of his perceived heightened status as a university-educated researcher living in the US. Jermay's experience reminds us that using community members as researchers is not only advantageous because they are familiar and share demographic characteristics with other community members, but because the power differential between researcher and researched is so much smaller when both are fellow insiders in the same community.

One final very practical matter to mention is that taking an ethnographically informed approach to variationist sociolinguistic study can have emotional as well as research-related benefits. The relatively relaxed and loosely structured exploratory stages of an ethnographically informed project should serve as a much more gentle introduction to field research than immediately launching into a round of pre-planned interviews. In other words, beginning one's research with an ethnographic eye can lead not only to increased community understandings but also to increased comfort on the part of both the researcher and those being researched. After all, in our non-research lives we are more comfortable with relationships that develop organically than with roles we try to force ourselves to fit; there is no reason why things should be any different in the human relationships we form with those we are studying.

3.4 SUMMARY: COMBINING METHODS AND EMBRACING THE OBSERVER'S PARADOX

It should be evident from reading this chapter that the best sociolinguistic studies utilize a variety of data-collection techniques rather than relying exclusively on experiments, elicitations, interviews, or observations. All methods of sociolinguistic study involve observation, and since humans studying human interaction inevitably affect that interaction, even our most detached observations necessarily involve some degree of participation. At the opposite end of the spectrum, even the most ethnographically oriented variationists tend to combine observations of naturally occurring linguistic interactions with sociolinguistic interviews, and sometimes also elicitations and experiments. And even the core research tool of the sociolinguist, the sociolinguistic interview, is itself a hybrid, a "conversational interview," and we often hybridize it further by adding to it reading passages and word lists, thereby creating a sort of "style experiment," or by adding elicitations after the conversation, in order to gain more pointed information on particular features of interest or their structural limitations, than can be obtained in the connected speech that forms the bulk of the interview. A good sociolinguist is always open-minded, not only regarding the community being studied, but also regarding linguistic study itself. We should recognize that each method for gathering data on language in its social context has its strengths and purposes, as well as limitations that can only be overcome through approaching the same community (or linguistic question) from different angles.

I am not alone in stressing eclecticism in sociolinguistic research but rather echo the sentiments of the preeminent researchers in the field – researchers who indeed rose to prominence through the insightful findings they gleaned through embracing a variety of research techniques. Their work has variously combined in-depth interviews with broad-scale surveys (e.g. Milroy and Milroy in Belfast, 1975–1981), added elicitations to interviews (Fasold 1972; Wolfram, Hazen, and Schilling-Estes 1999), conducted experiments on perception along with interviews yielding data on speech production (Eckert 2000; Johnstone and Kiesling 2008; Labov 2006), or combining ethnographic participant-observation with sociolinguistic interviews (Eckert 2000; Lou 2009, 2010a, 2010b).

It has also emerged from our discussion in this chapter that no matter how much we may strive to mitigate the effects of the research situation, we can never eliminate observer effects. Very direct methods of obtaining data – for example, self-reports on language production and direct questions about language perception – have obvious effects on our data, including people's over- and under-reporting their usage levels for features as well as falsely reporting on perceptions, whether perceptions of features, mergers, or speakers / speaker groups. In addition, data obtained via less direct methods such as indirect elicitations, sentence permutation tasks, and matched guise experiments are subject to test effects such as ordering effects, participants' under- or over-cooperativeness, and the unnatural linguistic usages that may result when artificial test situations are set up.

Further, whereas sociolinguistic interviews, peer group interviews, and recordings of spontaneous conversations seemingly yield increasingly naturalistic speech, the researcher and their audio (and / or video) recording equipment is always there, and so the data are always potentially subject to effects of the research situation, whether overtly, as for example with a participant who talks into the audio recorder in an obviously performative manner, or more subtly, for example when an interviewee uses a somewhat lower percentage level of non-standard dialect features when conversing with the interviewer than when a familiar third party such as a friend or child enters the setting.

Even in modifications to the sociolinguistic interview where the linguistic researcher is not immediately present, for example with Stuart-Smith and Macaulay's pairs of peers or with people who are sent off on their own to record their interactions, researcher effects might still be felt. For example, participants in two-party peer recordings know that they are being recorded for research purposes even though the researcher is not in the room with them, and so they may alter what they say and how they say it, with the knowledge that their conversation will eventually be "overheard." In addition, people walking around with audio recorders still have to announce the presence of their recording equipment for ethical reasons; further, since they have been tasked with gathering data, they may choose to highlight, even flaunt, their role as researcher, as with the teens in the COLT study.

Finally, even if the research situation can be made to fade into the background, we can never remove addressee effects on speech – even in a rapid and anonymous survey in which participants have no idea that they are part of a study. Hence, Labov tacitly acknowledges potential effects of how he talks and who he is on the unwitting participants in his rapid and anonymous survey in New York City by noting that he is college-educated and from an r-pronouncing area (though he does not explicitly discuss what the effects might be). In addition, there are a host of other factors that inevitably shape people's speech, including some that researchers can try to control for (e.g. topic, physical setting) and others they cannot (such as how participants choose to frame the research situation, example e.g. as a casual conversation vs. a formal informational interviewer; as a serious test or as a ludicrously esoteric task whose results do not matter).

Given that linguistic usages are inevitably affected by situational and speaker-internal factors, and that speech is always being observed by some listener, whether a linguistic researcher or not, it again seems best that we adopt an anthropological / ethnographic perspective and attempt to identify and account for contextual effects, including observer effects, rather than seeking to abstract them away. In other words, it may be better to dispense with the observer's paradox rather than try to overcome it, and to admit that there is no such thing as unobserved language data and hence no such thing as one single "most important" type of language for linguistic theory (i.e. "default," "vernacular" speech devoid of observational effects) – or any one "best" method for obtaining it.

Case study: Combining data collection and analytical methods – Language and Communication in the Washington, DC, Metropolitan Area

The Linguistics Department at Georgetown University launched the Language and Communication in the Washington, DC, Metropolitan Area project (LCDC) in 2006. The project is an ongoing, large-scale sociolinguistic study seeking to describe and understand how language and social life shape one another in the diverse and changing communities that comprise the DC area. The project grew out of the Sociolinguistic Field Methods courses regularly taught in the Linguistics Department, and our growing realization of the richness of the social, historical, and linguistic environment in which all of us who live and work in the DC area are immersed.

The LCDC project aims to understand language and community from a range of perspectives, including those of variationists, discourse analysts, and linguistic anthropologists / ethnographers. We use a variety of research methods, including sociolinguistic interviews, surveys, and ethnographic participant-observation. Further, we study a range of different types of communities, including not only geographically defined neighborhoods but also people who regularly interact in social networks and communities of practice. Finally, we study language on all its levels of patterning, from minute details of phonological variation to variation in referring terms to discourse analytic studies of unfolding conversation, narratives, and ways of speaking.

Washington, DC, is a particularly interesting place to study from a variety of perspectives. As the longstanding capital of the United States, it is unique in its historical and current cultural, political, and demographic characteristics. Unlike other more "typical" cities that began as industrial centers, DC defies ready definition. It is by turn understood as the capital of the United States, the political center of the world, a majority African American city, a Southern city (or one situated on the edge of South and North), a city where "everyone is from somewhere else" and does not stay long as political tides change, and as a city benefiting from – or besieged by – efforts to transform long-standing neighborhoods of lower socioeconomic status into "gentrified" areas for middle- and upper-class newcomers. All of these definitions are emically valid, linguistically articulated, and contested truths about DC and the wider metropolitan area.

LCDC studies to date have examined how people use language to construct, convey, and challenge their various understandings of DC and their place within it. For example, we have investigated the relationship between language in Washington, DC, and the linguistic features of the US Southeast, including the *pin–pen* merger, post-vocalic *r*-lessness (Schilling and Jamsu 2010), /l/-vocalization (Nylund 2012), /u/ and /o/ fronting (Lee 2011), and /ay/ monophthongization (Jamsu, Callier, and Lee 2010). We have also examined variation in more widespread vernacular features such as word-final -*t* / -*d* deletion (Podesva 2008) and *in'* / *ing* variation (Nylund 2010) with an eye toward not only how these features are used in the DC area but what meanings they invoke in the local context.

Many of these features are also characteristic of African American Vernacular English, and we are keenly interested in the relation between Black and White speech varieties in DC, the characteristics of Washington DC African American English, and differences within DC AA(V)E, including not only across different neighborhoods, wards, and quadrants of the city (e.g. north-west vs. southeast), but also within communities and even individuals, as they use linguistic variation (including not only morphosyntactic but also prosodic and voice quality variation) to portray identities, effect stances, and position themselves in their interactional and sociocultural surroundings (Nielsen 2010; Podesva and Lee 2010). We are also extremely fortunate to have access to a body of data on DC African American English that provides rich time depth for studies of real-time change: Ralph Fasold's corpus of interviews, collected in 1968, that form the basis of his 1972 book *Tense Marking in Black English*.

Researchers working under the LCDC umbrella are also interested in the discursive construction of local identities. Because DC is continually undergoing social change and is always under public scrutiny, it is extremely important for us as sociolinguists to understand the *how*, as well as the *what*, of linguistic variation and identity construction. We find clues to the construction of Washingtonians' identities by examining oral histories of social change in disadvantaged communities (Schiffrin 2009), public discourses of neighborhood preservation and change (Modan 2007; Zubair 2008), and the ways that Washingtonians in our sociolinguistic interviews orient to topics such as gentrification of local language and AAVE (e.g. is there a "DC dialect?"), and racial diversity in local communities (Grieser 2012).

In addition, it has been very important for the participants in the LCDC project to realize and honor the fact that DC is home to a number of longstanding and emergent immigrant communities, whose experiences form an integral part of the story of Washington, DC. Work currently in progress considers the linguistic expression of the experiences of newly arrived and established Latino/as in DC (Tseng 2011) and surrounding suburbs, as well as the relation of Asian Americans and their languages and language varieties to DC-area Whites, African Americans, and Latinos (Lou 2010a, 2010b). We are also considering the complex question of what exactly constitutes "African American" language and identity in light of the growing, vibrant community of immigrants from Ethiopia.

As the project progresses, we are finding that our multiple perspectives, including variationist sociolinguistics, interactional sociolinguistics, ethnography of communication, and narrative analysis, are yielding a richer picture of language and life in Washington, DC, than we could ever hope to achieve by approaching our data through a single lens with a narrow focus.

Suggested readings

WOLFRAM, WALT AND RALPH FASOLD 1974. FIELD METHODS IN
THE STUDY OF SOCIAL DIALECTS. CHAPTER 4 IN *THE STUDY OF
SOCIAL DIALECTS IN AMERICAN ENGLISH*. ENGLEWOOD CLIFFS,
NJ: PRENTICE-HALL.

In this classic chapter by two pioneers in the field, Wolfram and Fasold
present a very useful guide to designing and conducting sociolinguistic
field studies. They cover issues ranging from sampling, stratifying the
sample by socioeconomic class (including using objective vs. subjective
measures), entering the community (including what role(s) to adopt,
how to present the project), and collecting data via various methods.
The sociolinguistic interview is described in depth, followed by discussion of group interviews, elicitation talks, reading tasks, and subjective
reaction tests. The authors also discuss ethical issues such as informed
consent and preserving confidentiality. The article is concise, accessible, and practical.

LABOV, WILLIAM 1984. FIELD METHODS OF THE PROJECT ON LINGUISTIC CHANGE AND VARIATION. IN JOHN BAUGH AND JOEL
SHERZER (EDS.), *LANGUAGE IN USE*. ENGLEWOOD CLIFFS, NJ:
PRENTICE-HALL, 28–53.

Similar to the Wolfram and Fasold chapter, this chapter presents an allecompassing overview of a full range of methods for sociolinguistic study.
There is discussion of designing and conducting the sociolinguistic interview, as well as discussion of telephone surveys, group sessions, rapid and
anonymous surveys, and field experiments (e.g. minimal pair tests for
obtaining data on mergers in progress, subjective reaction tests designed
to test people's linguistic evaluations). A key feature of this article is the
enduring advice Labov provides to researchers regarding lessening the
power asymmetry inherent in sociolinguistic inteviews between academic reseachers and (often) non-standard-speaking community
members: "The basic counter-strategy of the sociolinguistic interview is
to emphasize the position of the interviewer as a learner, in a position of
lower authority than the person he [sic] is talking to" (p. 40).

WOLFSON, NESSA 1976. SPEECH EVENTS AND NATURAL SPEECH:
SOME IMPLICATIONS FOR SOCIOLINGUISTIC METHODOLOGY.
LANGUAGE IN SOCIETY 5: 189–209.

Wolfson presents a classic critique of the sociolinguistic interview,
arguing that it is an "unnatural speech event" because it subverts

people's expectations for what interviews are supposed to be like. Far from making people comfortable, Wolfson argues that the sociolinguistic interview – with its strange emphasis on obtaining talk about anything rather than answers to specific questions, and its focus on lessening interviewer authority – actually makes interviewees uncomfortable, impatient, and even angry. Wolfson further argues that discourse types in the sociolinguistic interview (e.g. narratives) are too different from how they surface in ordinary conversation to be of real benefit in the study of language in everyday life.

BRIGGS, CHARLES L. 1986. *LEARNING HOW TO ASK: A SOCIOLINGUISTIC APPRAISAL OF THE ROLE OF THE INTERVIEW IN SOCIAL SCIENCE RESEARCH*. CAMBRIDGE UNIVERSITY PRESS.

Briggs critiques the sociolinguistic interview for deeper reasons than Wolfson, arguing that interviews of any type are uniquely Western speech events, and to impose them on non-Western cultures (and perhaps even non-mainstream Western cultures) is to assert existing hegemony concerning acceptable, expected speech events, and even the nature of language and information (e.g. the mainstream Western notion that language is a vehicle for conveying factual information and the interview is a means for efficiently obtaining such information). Briggs advocates sensitivity toward community-specific communicative norms and ways of sharing information.

CAMPBELL-KIBLER, KATHRYN 2010. SOCIOLINGUISTICS AND PERCEPTION. *LANGUAGE AND LINGUISTICS COMPASS* 4(6): 377–389.

In this comprehensive and accesssible overview article, Campbell-Kibler discusses the development of and current advances in sociolinguistic perception study. With roots in social psychological studies of language attitudes and more recent psycholinguistic and phonetic perspectives, sociolinguistic perception studies are now providing invaluable information on listener evaluation of variants, varieties, languages, and the people who use them. Studies offer ever more fine-grained anlayses of the components of linguistic evaluations and present broader perspectives on what features and their parts can and do mean to listeners and speakers. Campbell-Kibler notes that the increasing prominence of perception studies in sociolinguistics stems from technological and theoretical shifts in the field. Current sociolinguistic theories necessitate equal attention to speaker production and listener uptake, as sociolinguistic meaning is increasingly viewed as a joint production of all parties in conversation; and developments in technology now enable us to conduct detailed acoustic analysis and precise acoustic manipulations.

DURANTI, ALESSANDRO 1997. *LINGUISTIC ANTHROPOLOGY.* CAMBRIDGE UNIVERSITY PRESS. See especially Chapter 4.

This text provides an introduction to linguistic anthropology in all of its multidisciplinary scope. Of special interest for students of sociolinguistic fieldwork are Duranti's discussions of the relationship between linguistic anthropology and sociolinguistics; linguistic diversity, including linguistic varieties and repertoires; the notion of the speech community, including multilingual communities; and especially Chapter 4 on ethnographic methods. This chapter covers methods and issues in participant-observation and ethnographic interviews; and, importantly, it offers insightful discussion of the effects (or not!) of researchers, recording situations, and recording equipment on community members.

SAVILLE-TROIKE, MURIEL 2003. *THE ETHNOGRAPHY OF COMMUNICATION.* MALDEN, MA: BLACKWELL. See especially Chapter 4.

This text offers an overview of the ethnography of communication from one of the pioneers and leading practitioners in the field. Students will find Chapter 4 especially helpful, as it provides a useful overview of types of data and data-collection methods, as well as a list of various components of communicative events that can serve as a heuristic for observation in the field. Also included in the book is a comprehensive discussion of varieties of language ranging from codes, styles, and registers to dialects associated with ethnic, socioeconomic, sex, and age groups.

4   Designing research on style

As variation analysis has developed over the decades, there has been increasing interest in narrowing in from large-scale investigations of broad patterns of variation across speaker groups to investigating variation within the speech of individual speakers, as well as how individual variation coheres into personal and group speech styles and how variation unfolds in intra-individual discourse. This increasing focus on the individual stems from the recognition that patterns of language variation are not simply reflections of social meanings and group memberships. Rather, they are co-constitutive with individual, interactional, and social meanings, social categories, societal and cultural forces, and ways of thinking (i.e. attitudes, ideologies). In this, variation analysis aligns itself with the social scientific turn toward social constructionism, which holds that group behaviors and societal institutions are constituted, re-constituted, changed, and sometimes even subverted in the everyday, ongoing actions and interactions of individuals. At the same time, social constructionist views maintain that individuals do not exist in a vacuum. Their actions and interactions in turn are shaped by the individuals with whom they interact, by the groups they identify with and disassociate from, and by wide-scale and often quite enduring ideologies about social interaction, social groups, and social forces (e.g. the maintenance of a dichotomous male–female gender division).

Because individual linguistic usages and individual creativity are today seen as so important, the study of stylistic variation has now become central not only in discussions of intra-speaker variation *per se* but variation analysis more generally, since many researchers now hold that even established group and situational styles (dialects, registers) have their roots in individual agentive linguistic usages and that changes in individual and group styles are grounded in people's use of stylistic resources in unfolding linguistic interaction (Coupland 2007, Eckert 2005).

Variationist conceptualizations of stylistic variation were not always as centered on speaker agency, and there have been several distinct approaches over the decades, each necessitating different ways of designing and conducting research. This chapter presents the prominent views of stylistic variation along with the different methods for gathering data on speech style that inhere in each theoretical framework. Because our focus here must be on methods, the reader is referred to more comprehensive treatments of stylistic variation for further discussion of theoretical issues (Coupland 2007; Eckert 2000, 2005; Eckert and Rickford 2001; Jaffe 2009; Schilling 2013).

One important way in which research methods in stylistic variation differ depending on different viewpoints is in terms of how controlled our data-gathering techniques will be. In other words, will we rely on fairly controlled, perhaps even quasi-experimental studies in which, for example, we predict what conditions will affect speech style, and then manipulate those conditions to see if stylistic variation indeed patterns in predicted ways? Or will our methods be more naturalistic, such as recording naturally occurring talk to see what types of speech styles occur and then seeking explanations out of the myriad contextual factors in which naturally occurring speech is situated? As we move from older, more correlational views of the relationship between situation and style toward newer, more constructionist views, we must also consider whether we want to investigate stylistic variation as a primarily reactive phenomenon, conditioned by contextual factors such as audience, topic, and setting; or whether we can build into our studies the proactive component that researchers increasingly are coming to see as vital to stylistic variation, and so bring in less readily observable, speaker-internal considerations such as motivation and conceptualization of the speech situation.

4.1   RESEARCHING STYLE AS ATTENTION TO SPEECH

4.1.1   The attention to speech approach

We have already discussed in some detail in Chapter 3 the first variationist methods for obtaining data on a range of speech styles, namely, designing a sociolinguistic interview that comprises not only naturalistic conversation but also a range of tasks designed to increase speakers' attention to their own speech and hence yield increasingly careful, formal styles. In the conversational portion of the traditional sociolinguistic interview, interviewers seek to draw attention away from speech by encouraging interviewees to talk about topics of great interest to them. In the subsequent reading passage, speech is somewhat foregrounded but still couched in a hopefully interesting story. This is followed in turn by a word list that contains no distracting propositional context, and the interview concludes with a list of minimal pairs in which speakers' attention is drawn not just to speech itself but to the specific variables being studied (e.g. *r*-lessness). Although the conversational portion of the interview is characterized by relatively low attention to speech, we should recognize that the interviewee may still be somewhat guarded, though there are contexts where truly casual speech is predicted to surface, namely, in narratives, in discussions of childhood (from a child's perspective), and when going off on tangents.

As noted in Chapter 3, the relatively controlled sociolinguistic interview methods for gathering data on a range of styles is grounded in the attention to speech approach to stylistic variation, which holds that style is conditioned primarily by how much attention speakers pay to speech itself as they converse. Under this view, the researcher can systematically alter style by systematically adjusting attention level. It was originally held that the patterning of variation across styles would be most regular when data were aggregated within stylistic contexts and across individuals – in other words, the study of stylistic variation, just like variation according to sociodemographic factors, was thought to be fundamentally quantitative. So, for example, Labov (1972c: 70–109) shows that the aggregate patterns of stylistic variation described in his foundational sociolinguistic study of the Lower East Side of NYC are indeed mirrored in individual patterns, but the patterns begin to break down when frequencies of particular variables are too low. He illustrates with the cases of Josephine P. (age 35, Italian descent, college-educated, department store receptionist) and Doris H. (age 39, African American high school graduate), who both show predicted increases in the use of prestige variants and decreasing levels of stigmatized variants as their attention to speech increases across the interview tasks – except where their numbers of tokens are quite low.

Interestingly, too, the individuals in Labov's study mirror the aggregate in terms of both stylistic variation and social-class-based variation. Individuals in different socioeconomic class groups show the same basic patterns across speech styles but exhibit differences in index scores indicative of usage levels of standard vs. dialectal variants. This patterning is demonstrated most dramatically when

we look at individuals on extreme ends of the socioeconomic continuum, for example, Bennie N., a truck driver who completed only
one term of high school, and Miriam L., a lawyer. Bennie N.
has considerably lower use of standard variants than Miriam L. –
so much so that his highest index score for the prestigious
(r) variant, *r*-1 (i.e. *r*-pronunciation rather than *r*-lessness) is nearly
the same as Miriam L.'s lowest score. Nonetheless, each speaker's
scores for prestigious or standard variants are lowest in the most
casual speech style, and highest in word list and minimal pair styles
(with only a couple of minor exceptions).

Also of interest is the case of Steve K., discussed in Chapter 2 – the
individual who overtly stated that he refused to relinquish his NYC
dialect in favor of more standard speech. He nonetheless unconsciously
increased his usage levels for standard forms as he moved from casual
to careful to the more formal styles, just like all the other individuals
examined, and just like the aggregate pattern across the Lower East
Side. His behavior seems to illustrate the assumptions of the early
Labovian approach: that style shifting is primarily unconscious and
reactive, a function of how much attention people are paying to their
own speech. As Labov notes:

> Steve K.'s self-awareness and his set of values [i.e. his belief in not
> getting 'above his station' socially or dialectally] might prepare us to
> find a radically different pattern in the array of the variables – if we
> believed that the linguistic and social forces operating here are subject
> to conscious manipulation. But as a matter of record they are not
> (Labov 1972c: 104).

Because the most regular patterns which emerge as data are aggregated within styles and across speakers, the conclusion is drawn that
the meaning of stylistic variation lies in its quantitative patterning, not
in individual usages of particular variables. Thus, Labov maintains,

> The use of a single variant – even a highly stigmatized one such as a
> centralized diphthong in "boid" for *bird* – does not usually produce
> a strong social reaction ... It is the frequency with which Bennie
> N. uses [and others use] such forms that has social significance
> (1972c: 108).

4.1.2 Criticisms of the attention to speech approach

Labov's methods have proven to yield predictable patterns of stylistic
variation, at least in Western cultural contexts and when investigating
the patterning of variants that can be arrayed along a continuum from
vernacular / dialectal to standard. However, as noted in Chapter 3, the

attention to speech model underlying the methods has not fared as well and can be criticized on a number of grounds: its focus on only one factor affecting stylistic variation; the unidimensionality of the types of styles that can be studied (ranging from non-standard to standard but nothing beyond this); the difficulty of quantifying attention to speech and determining if indeed it is attention to speech and not some other variable serving as the primary conditioning factor in style shifting, for example audience, topic, or genre (Eckert 2001).

Furthermore, researchers have questioned the focus on vernacular, unselfconscious speech that underlies the attention to speech model for several reasons. Variationists increasingly are recognizing that people's everyday speech repertoires include a variety of selfconscious as well as unselfconscious styles; and further, selfconscious, "stylized" linguistic usages are probably becoming more commonplace as people come into increasing contact with more language, varieties, and variants (as well as their associated social meanings and norms for use) in the face of increasing mobility, globalization, and mediatization (Coupland 2007). Labov himself admits that the attention to speech model was never intended to be applied to speech beyond the sociolinguistic interview. However, even within the interview, selfconscious speech is more prevalent than we might like to think. Interviewees can – and do – conceptualize interviews as occasions for display, perhaps of identities they wish to project, dialects they want to perform (Schilling-Estes 1998), or even entire genres or styles, as we saw with the "mock serious interview" discussed in Chapter 2.

Even narratives, which traditionally have been held to be most conducive to yielding vernacular speech, are very often performative rather than "natural"; and in addition they are often replete with quoted speech (Tannen 1989) in which interviewees might "put on" the voices of others (often exaggerated stereotypes of these voices), hence abandoning their "own" vernacular voice. To illustrate, let us consider a couple of narratives drawn from our studies of Robeson County, North Carolina. The first was excerpted in (3.11) and comes from an interview with "Felicia," a young African American woman in Robeson County, North Carolina. By way of contextualization, the interview was conducted by two fieldworkers, "Alex," a young African American man with family connections in Robeson County, and "Lou," a young Lumbee Indian man who is friends with Alex and knows Felicia from their having grown up in the same area. The story is presented in full in (4.1). Felicia's grammatical dialectal features are indicated in bold.

(4.1)

Felicia's hurricane story

A: Do you remember any hurricane or storms or anything around here?
F: Well, I remember um the eighty-four hurricane. Okay, **we was in here**, or was it um, I don't think it was this trailer. **We was** like the green trailer. And it was like, remember it was turned the long way? Single wide? Okay well **we was** in the middle room. Alright and . . . I was like in the upper room, I had my own room, Ronald and Donald had the middle room. And mama and them had the um back room. But for some reason daddy was in our room asleep, and mama was in there watching TV, and I was in my room. All of a sudden we you know we heard this thing like a train you know. And I looked outside and oh lord the wind was just blowing, you know, and the outside toilets and stuff was all up in the air. Okay and you know, it was like boards flying everywhere, and it was like a red, red whirl just coming. And daddy was asleep, oh lord. I was like, "Daddy wake up wake up wake up wake up!" Then when he finally woke up, **he gonna** try to drive to **granddaddy house.** Toilets flying everywhere and then **he gonna** try to drive! I said, "Oh, Lord!" I said, "We gone, Lord!" I was just like lord I just knew we was gonna die. **But we ain't die.** He was trying to hold the car like this right here. But he parked it over there, he parked it right under that tree right there, as you're coming into **granddaddy yard** right on that side. He parked it over there and all of us went in the house. I was scared to death.
A: Was Ronald and Donald born then?
F: Mmhmm. You know they was hollering: "Aaaahh!"
A: So he put all y'all in the car. And drove over there.
F: We had I think it was the brown Pontiac too at the time. It was that brown Pontiac Bonneville. We had that car at the time. Mama after we finally woke him up, he woke up and realized what was going on and we went over **granddaddy house.** And I was scared to death. Lord, I ain't never been that scared in all my life, I'm sorry. I was really scared, I'm serious. I mean because I was like, I said, "Oh, Lord!" I said, "**I just know you gonna take me**, I ain't even lived my life, Jesus! I ain't even ready, Lord!" But I mean you know I guess you know it wasn't intended for us to go because everybody is entitled to their time to go.

At first glance, Felicia's hurricane story seems to be an excellent example of a narrative that produces natural, vernacular speech, since it is replete with features of African American Vernacular English, including regularization of past *be* to *was* ("We was in here"), copula deletion ("I just know you gonna take me"), and possessive -*s* absence ("He gonna try to drive to granddaddy house").

However, the second narrative from Robeson County, in (4.2), is not as clearly reflective of the storyteller's "genuine" speech. It was told by Alex and occurred during the sociolinguistic interview he conducted with his friend Lou, an "interview" that really involved equal conversational contributions from both participants. The story has to do with

Alex's first night in the university dormitory and an argument he had with his White friend "Frank." Note that monophthongal vs. diphthongal variants of /ay/ are indicated in parentheses where appropriate. Monophthongal /ay/ in pre-voiced contexts is characteristic of AAVE, while diphthongal /ay/ is characteristic of White speech.

(4.2)

Conga line story
And one n- I'll tell you what happened the first night [naɪt]. We got here, my – the first night [naɪt] we stayed here Frank came over to the room and he said, "Yeah, because we had some guys [gaɪz] stay over here last year, and uh, what we're gonna do is, uh, make a line [laɪn], a conga line [laɪn] from your room to my [maː] room, you know, and, uh, we're just gonna party all night [naɪt]." And I looked – I looked him straight in the eye [aː], I said, "Not in my [maɪ] room, you won't." I said, "Now if you want to make a conga line [laːn] that's fine [faːn], but it's gonna be out of here by ten o'clock." And after that Frank wouldn't never mess with me no more after that. He wouldn't never mess with me more no more after that.

In this narrative, not only does Alex produce what seems to be his "own" vernacular, but he also performs the voice of his White friend, including some features of Frank's dialect such as increased use of diphthongal /ay/ (e.g. "We're just gonna party all night [naɪt]"). However, in addition to performing Frank's voice, in a way we can say that Alex is also performing his "own" dialect, especially when he quotes himself (e.g. "Now if you want to make a conga line [laːn] that's fine [faːn]"). And really, the same can be said for Felicia, since her narrative is also very performative and rich with self-quotation (e.g. "Daddy wake up wake up wake up wake up!", "Oh, Lord! ... I just know you gonna take me, I ain't even lived my life, Jesus! I ain't even ready, Lord!"). Thus even when speakers use their "own" voices in narratives, they may be putting them on for effect, not just allowing a "default" speech style to surface. Furthermore, it is a short step from performance to hyper-performance, or "dialect stylization," to use Coupland's (2001a) term. We see, then, that narratives cannot always be readily classified as vernacular and unselfconscious.

Finally, no matter how seemingly unselfconscious a stretch of speech may be, we can question whether there really is any such thing as an individual's single "genuine" vernacular – a default style unaffected by any contextual factors – since people always shape their speech to fit the situation at hand and suit their various purposes, even when they are not feeling very selfconscious (Eckert 2000; Hindle 1979; Milroy and Gordon 2003; Schilling-Estes 2008).

Indeed, sociolinguists increasingly are coming to see all speech as selfconscious to a degree and stylistic variation as a primary means for the creative performance of personal identity, interpersonal relations, and social categories and meanings. These newer views are, of course, dramatically different from early variationist conceptualizations of stylistic variation as primarily reflective of the demographic categories and responsive to the speech situations in which speakers find themselves – or into which they are placed by sociolinguistic researchers. However, this is not to say that speakers (or researchers) can completely disregard established associations between linguistic and social meaning as they shape their speech styles and identities; rather, interactants necessarily draw on these associations to help craft new meanings, a matter discussed in more detail in the sections that follow.

The attention to speech approach imposes a number of limitations in terms of the types of styles and stylistic variants it can encompass, the contexts in which it can be applied, and the explanations it can provide. In response, researchers have developed theoretical and methodological alternatives to analyzing stylistic variation that permit a fuller picture of the array of styles, stylistic variants, and stylistic meanings that surface in everyday life – and in research contexts such as the sociolinguistic interview – which as discussed in Chapter 3 above, is no less "natural" than non-research interactions, but simply different.

4.2 RESEARCHING STYLE AS AUDIENCE DESIGN

4.2.1 Bell's audience design approach

Another very important model for stylistic variation is Allan Bell's (1984) audience design approach, which holds that style shifting is conditioned primarily by one's audience: speakers exhibit linguistic convergence when they wish to associate with listeners, and divergence when they wish to distance themselves. This model ameliorates a number of the limitations of the attention to speech approach. Although the model may at first glance appear to be just as unidimensional as the attention to speech approach, with one unitary conditioning factor ("attention") being replaced by another ("audience"), Bell's conceptualization of audience is in fact multifaceted. Bell goes beyond simply the addressee, or person being directly addressed, to consider the effects of other types of audience members on speech style: auditors, or ratified participants in the interaction who are not being directly addressed; overhearers, non-participants known to be within hearing distance of the conversational participants; and eavesdroppers, non-participants whose presence is not known but may be suspected.

Important also is the fact that this approach can be applied to real-world contexts as well as research interviews. In fact, Bell developed the model based in part on his studies of radio announcers in New Zealand. He found that their styles shifted between dialectal New Zealand English and "proper" British English, or RP, based on whether they were reading the news on stations broadcasting to lower status or higher status audiences.

In addition, under Bell's audience design approach, we do not have to confine ourselves to variants arrayed along a standard–non-standard continuum. We can consider speaker alignment with addressees in terms of features with a range of meanings, including both group-associational and interactional meanings. For example, whereas a speaker might indeed use more standard speech when talking with a relatively standard-speaking addressee (as in the case of a sociolinguistic interview), they might also (or instead) increase their usage levels for features associated with other addressee attributes (e.g. demographic factors such as region, socioeconomic class, ethnicity, or personality traits such as friendliness, enthusiasm).

Further, the audience design approach recognizes not only audience but also topic effects, though topic is held to be derivative of audience. In other words, speakers switch styles when talking about different topics because they associate the different topics with different audiences. So, for instance, an interviewee who becomes more standard when talking about education is considered to be doing so because they associate the topic with teachers and other educational authorities they would have talked with while in school.

Finally, the audience design approach adds a very important component to variationist views of stylistic variation in its recognition of both unconscious, reactive style shifts (as in Steve K.'s unwitting shifts toward more standard speech in response to more formal interview tasks) and conscious, proactive shifts that speakers agentively employ to alter the speech context in some way. In this, Bell's approach echoes the findings of a classic study by Blom and Gumperz (1972) investigating the use of local vs. wider standard varieties in Hemnesberget, a village in Northern Norway. They found that speakers typically employed reactive or responsive style shifting, whether based on audience (e.g. shifting into more standard style when outsiders entered a locals-only conversation) or topic (e.g. shifting into more dialectal speech when shifting from business to personal topics). At other times, however, they engaged in initiative style shifting to inject a new flavor into the conversation (e.g. shifting into dialectal speech in the middle of a business discussion to add local color, or shifting into standard speech with local friends to clinch an argument by demonstrating authoritativeness).

In his initial conceptualization of style as audience design, Bell held that most style shifts were responsive. Even apparently initiative shifts were considered responsive in the sense that the shifts were tailored toward non-present audiences ("referees") whom the speaker called to mind as they sought to alter relations with present audience members. In more recent formulations (e.g. Bell 2001), initiative, agentive shifts are considered to be just as important as responsive ones, though speakers cannot simply decide for themselves that they will use particular linguistic features to inject certain meanings into ongoing talk. Rather, according to Bell, they must draw on longstanding associations between linguistic variants and speaker groups and / or situations. Hence, speakers in Hemnesberget who wish to sound authoritative draw on forms already associated with authoritative language (i.e. standard forms), while those who wish to highlight localness use forms that they know carry these connotations (i.e. dialectal features). As we shall see, the importance of speaker agency has only increased as the study of stylistic variation has continued to develop; however, we should be careful, along with Bell, to remember that linguistic structure and speaker agency go hand-in-hand. Even as speakers creatively craft styles and meanings in unfolding interactions, they must necessarily recruit meanings from a set of longstanding linguistic–social associations and enduring interactional, societal, and cultural behaviors and beliefs.

4.2.2 Conducting research on style under an audience design-based view

Given that the audience design approach to stylistic variation is intended to be broadly applicable to a range of speech contexts, we can study audience and referee effects on style using a variety of types of data and an assortment of methods ranging from the quasi-experimental to the naturalistic. If we seek control, we have some choices, since in addition to purposely designing speech events in which we control for all possible influences on stylistic variation besides audience, we can also find real-world situations that serve almost as ready-made experiments in the effects of audience design. Bell's study of New Zealand radio announcers is a perfect example of the latter. He was able to find a context in which speakers at two radio stations addressed different audiences with different expectations for appropriate radio speech – namely, a higher status audience who expected RP and a lower status audience who appreciated a local New Zealand flavor. In addition, the two stations employed the same newsreaders reading the exact same content, and so the situation offered control over potential non-audience effects such as topic and individual dialectal / stylistic norms. If, on the other hand, the news content were more variable, we might worry that the different usage levels for RP vs. New Zealand variants with the two different audiences might be due to the different topics that were talked about (e.g. perhaps more local matters for the lower status audience and more global matters for the higher status audience) and not due to audience *per se*. Similarly, if the news were read by one group of announcers on one station and another group on the other, then we might worry that the differing usage levels for RP vs. New Zealand variants might be due to group differences rather than stylistic effects, with the announcers for the high-status station typically using more RP-oriented speech no matter who they were talking to and the announcers for the lower status station typically using more local speech norms.

It is also possible to capitalize on research settings designed chiefly for other purposes in order to test the effects of audience on stylistic variation. In particular, though the sociolinguistic interview was designed primarily to yield vernacular speech and secondarily to test the effects of attention to speech on style, it can also be a fruitful context for information on audience effects. Labov himself acknowledges audience-based effects on interview speech when he notes that style shifting occurs when interviewees switch from addressing the interviewer to directly addressing third parties who enter the one-on-one interview situation (e.g. kids or friends who walk in, a friend or relative who telephones during the interview). However, he characterizes the shifted speech simply as more "vernacular," not necessarily as tailored toward the new audience member (Labov 1972c: 89–90). Similarly, as we discussed in Chapter 3, sociolinguistic researchers have long recognized that there are stylistic differences between one-on-one interviews and peer group interviews in which interviewees tend to talk more to one another than to the interviewer (again, characterized as more "vernacular"). Data from peer group vs. individual interviews has even been used to quantitatively demonstrate that addressee effects are indeed greater than auditor effects, as Bell's model predicts. Interviewees show a greater degree of shifting between peer group interviews and interviews with the interviewer alone than between peer group speech with no interview present and peer group speech when the interviewer is present as an auditor (e.g. Bickerton 1980; Douglas-Cowie 1978; Thelander 1982).

We can also test for audience effects by purposely manipulating the "audience" variable in the sociolinguistic interview. Here we present two case studies that illustrate possible research designs, as well as the valuable insights such style experiments can yield. In addition, these studies demonstrate that there are trade-offs between researcher control and naturalness of the speech event, as well as limitations to the amount of control the researcher can exert over human subjects with human agency.

4.2.3 Case studies: Experiments in audience design

"Foxy Boston" with Black and White interviewers

Rickford and McNair-Knox (1994) designed a study in which a teenage African American female, "Foxy Boston," from the lower-class multi-ethnic neighborhood of East Palo Alto, California, was interviewed at four different time periods by two different interviewees with different social and linguistic characteristics. The first three interviews were conducted by the second author, Faye, an African American female linguist, and her daughter, roughly the same age as Foxy, in 1986, 1988, and 1990. The final interview was conducted by Beth, a 25-year-old White Stanford University graduate student. Based on the two latest interviews, Rickford and McNair-Knox demonstrate that for three of the four AAVE features studied, Foxy indeed shows higher usage levels when speaking with the African American addressee than with the White interviewer. Thus, they are able to provide empirical confirmation for Bell's model, though with the caveat that Faye and Foxy's usage levels for the features studied are not exact matches. Instead, it seems that Foxy accommodates not simply to the speech of her audience, but also to personal attributes like ethnicity and familiarity, an issue we return to below.

But Rickford and McNair-Knox's findings also partly disconfirm Bell's model, in that they find more topic-based variation within each of Foxy's two later interviews than variation across the two interviews. They nonetheless conclude that audience effects are still more important in the long run, since Foxy overall shows higher usage levels for vernacular features with Faye than with Beth.

A further very important finding is that although Foxy's style shifts may appear to be reactive responses to her different audiences, in reality she can actively *choose* whether to accommodate to Faye or not. This is evidenced in the 1988 interview, in which Foxy's usage levels for the features examined when talking with Faye are quite low, indeed not significantly different from her usage levels in her later interview with the White interviewer, Beth. Rickford and McNair-Knox offer as explanation the fact that at this time in her life, Foxy had been attending a predominantly White school outside her community for a year and so had been exposed to both White language norms and prejudices against African Americans and their dialect, and perhaps she temporarily minimized her use of AAVE features as a result. Further, there are other factors besides audience for which Rickford and McNair-Knox did not control. The 1988 interview was the only one of the four conducted in Faye's home rather than Foxy's, the tone was not as relaxed, and Foxy did not seem cooperative. In this interview, Foxy may have been purposefully dissociating from Faye in her linguistic usages, rather than simply unconsciously shifting toward the White linguistic norms she had been exposed to over the past year.

In their nuanced explanation for Foxy's non-accommodative style in the 1988 interview, Rickford and McNair-Knox foreshadow current approaches to stylistic variation. In addition to external, fairly readily observable factors such as audience, topic, and setting, these approaches point to factors internal to speakers (e.g. Foxy's uncooperative stance; Foxy's desire to project a less "African American" identity), as possible explanations for style shifting, and particularly for initiative shifting, which by definition does not correlate with any readily observable shifts in the speech situation.

Rickford and McNair-Knox's study also shows us that designing a study that attempts to isolate the effects of audience on stylistic variation is not easy. We cannot always fully control external factors contextualizing the interview situation and, more importantly, we are unable to control the internal factors motivating speakers themselves. Whereas three out of four of the interviews with Foxy held most external contextual factors constant, the 1988 interview was in a different setting than the other three (the interviewer's home rather than the interviewee's). Furthermore, participants' ages could not possibly be held constant, and with different ages come different life experiences and different attitudes toward language and ethnicity, among many other matters. Even more problematically, even if the four interviews with Foxy had all been conducted in the same setting over a much shorter time span, the interviewers still could not have exerted complete control over how Foxy chose to position herself with respect to her interlocutors, or what facets of identity she chose to foreground via her linguistic usages. Even in the course of a single interview, it is likely that Foxy highlights different aspects of her identity at different times, depending on such matters as topic and production format (e.g. whether she is speaking her "own" or another's words; see Goffman 1981). So, for example, she shows dramatically higher usage levels for AAVE features when talking about sex (i.e. "wives and slamming partners") than when talking about college and career plans, with both the African American and White interviewers. This is in part because the latter topic is associated with more standard language and the former with her friends and their non-standard usages; in part because she is far more interested in the topic of sex; and in part because, in talking about sex, she gives lots of direct quotes from her friends, whom she presents as speaking vernacular AAVE rather than standard English.

Testing the effects of gender and ethnicity on audience design

Another intriguing case study is Bell and Johnson's (1997) study of audience effects on usage levels for several discourse features associated with various demographic groups in New Zealand. Similar to Rickford and McNair-Knox, Bell and Johnson's study involved conducting a series of interviews, though in a more experimental and controlled manner.

Bell and Johnson varied both interviewee and interviewer, along both ethnic and gender lines. The experiment involved four interviewees, a Maori man, a Maori woman, a Pakeha (White) man, and a Pakeha woman. Each of the participants was interviewed three times, by interviewers of matching and non-matching ethnicity and gender (e.g. the Maori man was interviewed by a Maori man, a Pakeha man, and a Maori woman), with only the least matched pair excluded (e.g. the Maori man was not interviewed by a Pakeha woman). All other factors were kept as constant as possible, including age, setting, and even questions asked – the same interview questionnaire was used for each interview, in order to minimize topic-based variation. This is an unusual fieldwork design and one clearly tailored to a very specific research question: "What is the effect of like vs. unlike audience demographics on stylistic variation?" It obviously would not be the most effective method for gathering naturalistic speech data for more general variationist purposes. (Consider, for example, the artificiality of being asked the exact same set of interview questions three different times.)

Bell and Johnson's experiment is also unusual in that the variants studied are not the typical phonological and morphosyntactic features that form the backbone of variationist research. Rather, they focus on a set of discourse features that serve, they maintain, as "addressee-oriented pragmatic markers," namely, *y'know* (e.g. "they're losing ... the real meaning of it, y'know"), tag questions (e.g. "It's hot in here, isn't it?", the *eh* particle ("It's becoming a bit of a business now, eh?"), and high rising terminal intonation on declaratives. In addition to serving the pragmatic function of drawing audience attention and bringing the listener into the conversation, several of the features also have group-associational meanings. In the New Zealand context at the time of the interviews, *eh* was associated with Maori men and high rising terminals with Pakeha women. A quantitative analysis of the use of these features by interviewees reveals patterns indicative of "classic audience design," namely, increased use by interviewees of features associated with each of their different audiences. Hence, the Maori man uses the most *eh* with the Maori male interviewer (as well as the most *eh* of all the interviewees), while the Pakeha woman shows the highest usage levels for high rising terminals with the female rather than male interviewers (and the highest usage levels in general for this feature).

Importantly, not only do Bell and Johnson measure the interviewees' usage levels for the features in question, but they also quantify those of the interviewers. This interest in interviews as two-party conversations (and not just occasions for gathering speech from interviewees of interest) brings the study of stylistic variation into closer alignment with qualitative approaches to sociolinguistics that focus on conversational interactions rather than aggregate, quantitative patterns of phonological and morphosyntactic variables. In addition, Bell and Johnson have helped set the stage for current approaches to stylistic variation that focus on how style unfolds in interaction and that recognize that style and its meanings are dialogic, not the monologic productions of interviewees alone.

Bell and Johnson find that the interviewers' speech shows patterns that seem to run counter to the expectations of audience design. The interviewers use more *eh* than the interviewees, including interviewees who neither use much *eh* themselves nor would be expected to do so based on their demographic characteristics. So, for example, while the Maori man not surprisingly receives the most *eh*, the Pakeha woman receives almost as many – even though she never uses the feature. In their explanation for this patterning, Bell and Johnson again pre-figure current views of stylistic variation. They suggest that the interviewers are using *eh* not because of its group-associational meanings (again, it is associated mostly with Maori men) but because of its interactional meaning, as a device to draw co-participants into conversation. It is the interviewers' job to elicit talk, and using more *eh* is one strategy for doing so. And such strategies are most needed with the Pakeha woman interviewee, since she is the most reticent speaker. Bell and Johnson sum up their realization that single features can serve multiple purposes in conversation thus:

> While we have presented our analysis here largely in terms of demographic characteristics, accommodation to one's audience is in fact much wider than that. It includes speakers making active use of the resources of their speech community in order to accomplish their conversational purposes, in this case a successful interview (Bell and Johnson 1997: 15).

In other words, speakers use linguistic stylistic resources not only for their group-associational meanings but for their interactional meanings as well. In addition to merely reacting to their listener's actual or expected speech, speakers utilize stylistic resources in interaction to actively take up stances such as "interestedness" or "involvement" and to project character attributes such as "friendly and encouraging listener" – all of which are important for interviewers who wish to successfully keep talk flowing.

A final way in which the Bell and Johnson study heralds newer approaches to stylistic variation is in its combined quantitative and qualitative approach. While the researchers do indeed examine aggregate usage levels for the features under study, they also investigate where the features occur in each unfolding conversation and consider what their syntagmatic patterning may suggest about their stylistic meanings. Their conclusions are tentative but suggestive of interesting avenues for research that are eagerly taken up in current variationist studies of style: whereas *y'know* is relatively evenly distributed throughout each conversation, perhaps because of its "relative lack of social [i.e. group] associations" (1997: 17), it does seem to cluster a bit in areas of discomfort (e.g. when the topics of gender and ethnicity are raised). Furthermore, the *eh* particle, which does have strong associations with the Maori demographic, occurs more with Maori-related topics.

Bell and Johnson's study thus demonstrates that valuable information about audience effects on stylistic variation can be gained through quite controlled study designs, including not only information on the patterning of variants across different audiences but also on the meanings of the variants used. Thus, whereas the researchers expected their participants to shape their speech according to audience demographics, they found that features were also used to effect stances and display character attributes.

In addition, Bell and Johnson's study teaches us a valuable lesson about researcher control. Although they tried to control for every major influence on stylistic variation besides audience, unexpected factors still intervened. Hence, for example, the Pakeha female was more reticent than the others, and this hesitancy induced increased usage by the interviewees of features conducive to conversational flow (e.g. *eh*). Conversely, it seems that discomfort with the interview situation had rather an opposite effect on the Pakeha male interviewer. Impressionistically, and as evidenced by such extralinguistic features as lots of nervous giggling, the Pakeha male interviewer was quite uncomfortable during his interview with the Maori man. But rather than let his nervousness lead to reticence, he instead hyper-accommodated to the Maori man, using even more of the *eh* particle than the Maori man himself. In contrast, he used absolutely no *eh* when interviewing another Pakeha male. Thus, no matter how hard we try, we cannot control for everything, and although we may be able to screen out a speaker who just does not talk much, no matter who she is talking to, there does not seem to be much we can do about a speaker who feels perfectly comfortable in some situations but less so in others. This suggests, first, that as valuable as control may be, we must always be on the lookout for unexpected influences on the variation we observe; and second, that perhaps seeking control which is bound to remain ultimately elusive is not as desirable as it might seem at first glance, given the trade-off, mentioned above, between researcher control and naturalness of speech.

Luckily, under the audience design framework, we do not have to confine ourselves to experimental or sociolinguistic interview settings, since the model is intended to be applicable to stylistic variation as it occurs in everyday life. In an early study in which audience effects figure prominently (briefly outlined in Chapter 3), Coupland (1980) investigated stylistic variation by asking an assistant in a travel agency in Cardiff, Wales, to record herself and her interlocutors throughout several normal workdays. Coupland found that not only did the assistant shift styles based on who she was talking with (co-workers / friends in her own office, clients, agents from other offices), she also shifted according to topic (work vs. non-work) as well as channel (in-person vs. telephone). Thus, besides providing quantitative demonstration of the audience effects on speech style we all impressionistically observe in everyday life, Coupland also showed that when we expand our investigations beyond audience (and perhaps topic as well), we may discover other factors (e.g. channel) that also impinge on stylistic variation. In addition, there is no shortage of initiative shifts in either sociolinguistic interviews or in everyday life. Hence, the travel assistant shifted not only across audiences, topics, and channels, but also within situations in which all these factors remained constant, in order to effect situational change. For example, when talking on the phone with a client who is a bit unhappy with the travel options she proposes, Sue gradually shifts toward the dialectal speech of her client as part of her attempt to appear helpful and friendly rather than adversarial.

4.2.4 Theoretical questions associated with the audience design model

In the preceding discussion we have outlined the main advantages of the audience design approach to stylistic variation over attention to speech-based approaches, in terms of both theory and method. In addition, we have pointed to several key theoretical questions. One central question is, if indeed speakers design their speech styles primarily for their audiences, what exactly is it about their audiences that inspires them to shape their styles as they do: addressees' actual speech patterns, the speech patterns we might expect based on demographic characteristics, or other personal characteristics of audience members?

Although speakers do seem to accommodate in part to their interlocutors' speech, they do not tend to fully accommodate, in the sense of exactly matching their interlocutors' usage levels for all speech features, as demonstrated in interviewee speech by Rickford and McNair-Knox, as noted above, and in interviewer speech by Trudgill (1981). Further, it seems that the audience's personal characteristics are even more important than their speech *per se*, in that speakers often accommodate toward the expected linguistic usages of interlocutors rather than their actual speech patterns – so much so, in fact, that in studies such as Bell and Johnson's, the different audiences (i.e. interviewers) were selected based not on their speech patterns but on their demographic characteristics. In addition, we have seen that speakers adjust their speech for interactional effects in addition to audience demographics. Thus, the interviewers in Bell and Johnson's study show high usage levels for features conducive to audience rapport no matter who they are talking to or which demographic factors the features are associated with, because their primary goal is to get their interlocutors to talk, not to show solidarity in terms of common ethnic or gender group membership. Conversely, in Rickford and McNair-Knox's study, though Foxy adjusts her speech according to her interviewers' demographic characteristics when she wants to, she also adjusts away from them when she is not feeling particularly cooperative.

The question of what specifically speakers accommodate to in accommodating toward their audiences raises three related questions.

First, are the meanings of stylistic variables primarily group-associational, or do interactional meanings hold sway? Second, is stylistic variation primarily reactive (whether to audience, topic, or other factors such as channel or setting), or is it chiefly proactive, given that speakers often call upon both the group-associational and interactional meanings of linguistic features to effect situational changes? (Recall Foxy's low usage levels of AAVE features with Faye despite their group-associational meanings, and the New Zealand interviewers' high usage levels of the rapport-building particle *eh* with interviewees who use little or none of this feature themselves.) And finally, is accommodation toward one's audience the only way, or the best way, to gain audience rapport, or is purposeful linguistic distancing sometimes what is needed to achieve psychological closeness?

With regard to the first question, we have seen that both group-associational and interactional meanings can come into play, at least with discourse-level features such as *eh*, *y'know*, and high rising terminal intonation. As we shall see below in our discussion of current views on stylistic variation, researchers in recent years have come to believe that even phonological and morphosyntactic variants whose meanings initially appeared to derive solely from their group associations also have interactional meanings, and indeed, the interactional meanings may hold primacy. In other words, a feature becomes firmly associated with a particular group only when the stances and character attributes it indexes (i.e. points to) in interaction come to be associated with the group in question. So, for example, it is argued that the use of a variable feature such as the use of *-in'* for *-ing* in verbs like *walkin'* and *talkin'* is not associated with social groups such as "working class" or "men" or "US Southerners" simply because these groups have high usage levels for the *-in'* variant. Instead, the variant takes on group-associational meanings only indirectly, when its interactional meanings (e.g. hardworkingness, masculinity, being down to earth) come to be associated with particular social class, gender, and regional groups. Of course, we cannot discount group-associational meanings once they arise, since these meanings too become available for exploitation in interaction. Thus, whereas the interviewers in Bell and Johnson's study in general seem to rely on the interactional meaning of *eh* as a device for encouraging interlocutor interaction, they still show the highest usage levels for *eh* in their interviews with the Maori man, thereby showing that the feature's group-associational meanings are important as well. We will have more to say on group-associational vs. interactional meanings in the discussion of speaker design approaches to stylistic variation.

The issue of whether stylistic variation is primarily reactive or proactive has been important now for decades, and over the years researchers have moved away from "Fordist" (Rampton 1999) conceptualizations of speakers as automata whose linguistic productions are largely unconscious, automatic correlates of their "social address" (Eckert and McConnell-Ginet 1992) and the contextual situations in which they find themselves. Instead, variationists increasingly view speakers as agentive, creative individuals who use linguistic variation to shape themselves and their situations every bit as much as (perhaps more than) they are shaped by the structures and forces around them.

For all his early emphasis on the primacy of responsive style shifts, Bell was an early precursor to current views embracing speaker creativity, and this emphasis on agency has only grown since Bell's original and revised formulations of the audience design model. Even in the earliest investigations of stylistic variation in everyday life (e.g. Coupland 1980), we saw that some style shifts cannot be accounted for by any readily observable shifts in external situational factors such as audience, topic, channel, etc. And furthermore, even in controlled research situations, we have seen that participants can take control from researchers and initiate style shifts that have little or nothing to do with the different audiences presented to them. For example, Foxy uses more AAVE than expected when talking with the White interviewer about a topic that really excites her (wives and slamming partners) and less AAVE than expected when she does not feel like being interviewed or being closely associated with her African American ethnicity. Similarly, the interviewers in Bell and Johnson's research go against what is expected of them by using lots of *eh* with interlocutors who do not use it themselves, or by using even more *eh* with the Maori male interviewee than he uses himself, out of nervous hyper-accommodation.

Finally, there is the question of whether linguistic convergence is the only or best way to achieve psychological convergence with one's interlocutors, or whether sometimes linguistic divergence might be the best means toward achieving increased closeness with one's audience. We have already seen that the interviewers in Bell and Johnson's study indeed seek increased closeness with the hesitant interviewee by using the rapport-building *eh* particle, a feature the interviewee herself never once uses. In addition, they also linguistically diverge from her by talking more than she does, in an attempt to get her to start talking more as well. And in Bell's early studies of New Zealand radio announcers, the newsreaders who use more RP variants for the upper-class audience are not actually converging with their audience's speech, since the upper-class New Zealanders who listen to the station are actually speakers of New Zealand English and not RP. Rather, the announcers are conforming to the audience's *expectations* – in this case, expectations for what constitutes "proper" broadcast speech.

Another classic study we can point to in this regard is Trudgill's (1983) study of the pronunciations of British pop singers from the 1950s to the 1980s. In particular, Trudgill takes an in-depth look at the Beatles 1963–1971, noting that in their early years, when they were mostly performing for audiences in the UK, the Beatles made heavy use of American pronunciations such as *r*-pronunciation and intervocalic /t/ flapping, because audiences throughout the world held American pop music in highest esteem. In the Beatles' later years, they used more British pronunciations, because, thanks in large part to their own tremendous success, everyone now wanted to hear British pop music, including Americans.

In other cases, it is *unexpected* speech patterns that win audience favor, as with drag queens who juxtapose normally disparate styles (e.g. stereotypical AAVE, White women's English, and gay male English) to ensure successful performances (Barrett 1995), or teens who "cross" out of their "own" language varieties into out-group varieties to establish rapport with in-group friends. For example, Bucholtz (1999) and Cutler (1999) show how White teens in the US use features of AAVE to project character traits associated with African American street culture but desirable among their (White) peer groups (e.g. toughness, "coolness"), while Rampton (1995) shows how multiracial teens in the south Midlands of England and in London selfconsciously cross in and out of Stylized Asian English (SAE), a performative variety characterized by exaggerated use of stereotypical features of South Asian English, to accomplish various social ends, including effecting a stance of resistance against adult authority that wins them favor with their teenage peers.

There is really nothing incompatible between the audience design model and the fact that psychological convergence is often achieved through linguistic divergence, whether from one's audience or even from one's "own" speech. The model does not adamantly insist that speakers' language must converge with audience's actual speech patterns; rather, "convergence" is more broadly defined to include speech associated with audience demographic characteristics, as well as with other demographic groups, character traits, and interactional meanings that the audience may look upon favorably (as with classic "referee design"). In addition, the audience design model has its roots in Speech Accommodation Theory, a social psychological framework later reworked into Communication Accommodation Theory, the latter of which holds that there are indeed many ways of increasing closeness with audience members besides linguistic convergence (e.g. Giles, Coupland, and Coupland 1991).

4.3 CURRENT APPROACHES TO STYLISTIC VARIATION

4.3.1 From first to second to "third wave" studies

Following Eckert (2005) it has become current among variationists to conceptualize variation analysis in terms of "three waves" of study.[1] First wave studies are those that investigate quantitative correlations between demographic factors (e.g. socioeconomic class, gender, ethnicity, age) and patterns of language variation, for example Labov's (1966) classic study of the Lower East Side of New York City. These correlations, in turn, form the basis of the social meaning of linguistic variation. In other words, if particular features such as standard pronunciations correlate with membership in higher socioeconomic groups and with women, then people can pick up on these associations, whether less or more consciously. For example, features associated with social class groups might become **markers** used to indicate more or less formal speech, with speakers perhaps little aware of exactly how they are varying their linguistic usages but obviously aware of their group-associational meanings on some level. In addition, features can become **stereotypes** of which people are quite consciously aware and about which they make overt commentary. For the most part though, speakers employ linguistic usages quite unconsciously, using the variants associated with the various groups to which they belong, because they were surrounded by these features as they acquired their native language and dialect.

First wave studies go hand-in-hand with the attention to speech approach to stylistic variation. Stylistic variation, like other social group-based patterns of variation, is thought to be largely unconscious and reactive, and the meaning of stylistic variation to reside in its quantitative patterning. In other words, speakers can make stylistic meaning only by varying frequency levels for particular features. A single occurrence of a feature, even a highly noticeable one, means very little, and even features that do show quantitative patterning but

[1] An update of Eckert's widely circulated (2005) manuscript will be published just as this book goes to press. Readers are encouraged to consult her most recent discussion, which refines and develops claims made in her original argument (see Eckert 2012a).

occur only at a relatively low rate tend to disrupt rather than conform to the regular patterning of variation across speech styles.

Second wave studies are those in which social categories and the potential social meanings of linguistic variables are no longer pre-determined and imposed from above but rather discovered from below, via ethnographic study of locally important social and linguistic meanings. Again, the classic example is Eckert's (2000) study of a Detroit-area high school, in which she finds that variation correlates more closely with social groups that are relevant to the teens ("jocks" and "burnouts") than with socioeconomic class. In addition, the meanings of the variables studied, mostly those associated with the Northern Cities Vowel Shift, do not have to do simply with regionality (e.g. residence in the US Inland North) or standard vs. non-standard speech. Instead they reflect locally important matters such as orientation toward or away from the high school and the mainstream social norms and aspirations it embodies.

Despite the seemingly revolutionary nature of Eckert's work, she is quick to point out that in reality the ethnographic perspective was present at the inception of variationist sociolinguistics, in Labov's (1963) groundbreaking Martha's Vineyard study. As we have already discussed, Labov did not rely solely on global social categories such as age and ethnicity to explain the unexpected rise of centralized /ay/ and /aw/ in the island community. Crucially, his analysis focused also on locally relevant social groups (e.g. fishermen vs. non-fishermen, residence in the rural vs. less rural end of the island) and local social meanings – especially positive, negative, or neutral orientations toward the local Martha's Vineyard community. And indeed, it turns out that it is this last, attitudinal, factor rather than any objective demographic criterion, that most closely correlates with usage levels for centralized vs. non-centralized /ay/ and /aw/ and imbues centralization with its meaning. The centralized (and historically older) variants have come to symbolize the local, traditional way of life: they are used most by those who most value the local community and the continued maintenance of its traditional maritime way of life in the face of a growing tourism industry that threatens to overwhelm it.

In a way, we can say that the audience design model for stylistic variation is a natural correlate of the second wave approach to variation analysis (e.g. Soukup 2011). With audience design, the focus shifts from the quantitative patterning of pre-imposed stylistic meanings (chiefly standard / formal vs. non-standard / informal) in pre-determined speech situations (i.e. the sociolinguistic interview), to the patterning of variation in local interactions with specific types of audience members. Audience design also admits a wider range of stylistic meanings, including group-associational, interactional, and / or identificational; and speakers may use features to identify with or dissociate from certain groups, to take up particular stances with respect to interlocutors and topics, or to project particular facets of identity. Further, whereas the audience design approach initially focused on responsive rather than initiative shifts, we begin to see that speakers can agentively employ linguistic features to effect situational changes. Just as with second wave studies more broadly, we see that people use variants not simply because of where they happen to find themselves, demographically speaking (e.g. on Martha's Vineyard), but because their speech styles enable them to stake out particular types of meanings and identities (e.g. as an islander who values traditional island life).

The developments that took place as we move from first to second wave studies culminate in so-called "third wave" studies, in which the main focus is now on the social meaning of linguistic variants rather than on correlations between variants and social groups, whether in terms of speakers' social group memberships or those of their audiences. In addition, much research now seems to suggest that the interactional meanings of variants hold primacy over group-associational meanings, so that variants first take their meanings from stances and projected character traits and only later get associated with the social groups who most often use those stances, traits, and associated variants. Hence, as noted above, the use of *-in'* for *-ing* in words like *walkin'* or *talkin'* may index "working class," but only because it has often been used in interaction to project characteristics associated with members of this social group such as hardworkingness, being down to earth, and not "putting on airs." On a broader scale, the use of non-standard vs. standard variants more generally can carry group-associational meanings such as "working class," "male," or "Southern regionality" because again the many variants comprising "non-standard" style carry interactional and identificational associations such as hardworkingness, toughness, honesty, straightforwardness (on the positive side), and / or uneducatedness and sloppiness – associations often called forth by (or thrust upon) the particular groups with whom the features then become associated. In other words, third wave approaches may seem to take so-called second-order indexical meaning – that is, the meanings associated with stances and character traits (Ochs 1992) – to be primary, while group-associational meanings (first-order indexical meanings) are considered derivative, not central as they used to be in first and second wave studies.

Because current approaches to stylistic variation focus on "stance," the reader should be aware that this term defies ready definition and is sometimes used differently by different researchers. For some, stance is primarily centered around the speaker's relationship to the content of talk, including source of knowledge, type of knowledge, and resultant certainty about and commitment to that which they are talking about (e.g. Schiffrin 2006: 208–211). For our purposes, we follow researchers such as Kiesling (2009: 172–173) and take a slightly broader view of stance as encompassing both relationship to talk (epistemic stance) and relationship to interlocutors (interpersonal stance). As Kiesling (2009) points out, the two are often interrelated; for example, those who position themselves as subordinate (interpersonal stance) might also project uncertainty (epistemic stance), while a confident conversational leader (interpersonal stance) will project more certainty (epistemic stance).[2] When we speak of affecting stances and projecting "character traits," the latter can be taken to be more directly tied to the project of *personal* identity vis-à-vis the more *interpersonal* connotations of stance *per se*.

Because the projection of stances and personality traits are often held to be primary in current views of stylistic variation, the focus of study has shifted from investigating the aggregate patterning of variation across speaker groups and styles (whether defined in terms of formality / attention to speech or audience and topic) to examining how variants are used in unfolding discourse. In addition, researchers on stylistic variation also stress the importance of investigating how variants co-occur and cohere into individual speech styles. Other developments include the investigation of a wider range of linguistic features, for example lexical, discoursal, and prosodic. In addition, rather than focusing chiefly on features indexing change, third wave researchers also take an interest in features characterized by longstanding, stable, and widespread variation.

The inclusion of variables common to many speaker groups has led to the finding that although many of these features seem to share core meanings across communities, these meanings may become instantiated as quite different localized meanings in different communities. For example, in Chapter 1, we saw how one such variable, word-final /t/

---

[2] The interpersonal side of stance is sometimes separated out as part of "positioning" though, again, the term can mean different things to different researchers. For a concise presentation of the interrelation between stance and positioning (as well as the related notion of "footing"), the reader is referred to Schiffrin (2006: 208–211). For more detailed discussions of these notions, the reader should consult works focusing on positioning theory (e.g. Davies and Harré 1990) stance (e.g. Du Bois 2007; Jaffe 2009; Ochs 1992) and footing (e.g. Goffman 1974, 1981).

release (vs. the unreleased variant) carries common meanings in the US such as intelligence, carefulness, and precision. However, various facets of these meanings can be highlighted or downplayed by different groups, and subsequently quite different group-associational meanings can arise in different groups as well. Hence, Orthodox Jewish men may capitalize on the association of released /t/ with educatedness (e.g. Benor 2001), while gay men may use the feature to project extreme precision and "prissiness" (Podesva 2007). Eckert refers to the constellation of related meanings associated with a variant as its "indexical field" (2008). This fluid conceptualization of the interrelation between linguistic variation and social meaning contrasts with older approaches that tended to focus on more unitary meanings, or at least meanings lying along a single unidimensional plane. For example, released /t/, if studied at all, would have been seen as a marker of standardness, formality, higher social class, and perhaps female gender, but not much beyond this.

Stable variables common across varieties, such as released vs. unrealized /t/ or -*in'* vs. -*ing*, may seem to be below speakers' conscious awareness – but this is not to say that they are absent from the quite conscious deployment of "standard," "educated," "precise," or "prissy" styles. Indeed, another hallmark of recent approaches to stylistic variation is their explicit interest in selfconscious styles and selfconsciously employed features in addition to the unmonitored "vernacular" speech that has held primacy throughout the decades of variationist sociolinguistic study. There are a number of reasons for this widening of focus. For one, researchers have come to recognize that selfconscious styles are by no means unusual or merely an artifact of the linguistic research situation. In fact they are commonplace in people's everyday linguistic practices, as well as in portions of the sociolinguistic interview that have long been held to be the most *un*selfconscious – namely, narratives. In addition, despite Labov's assertion, articulated in his vernacular principle, that "the most systematic style is that used when the minimum attention is paid to speech" (Labov 1972a: 118), performative speech has been shown to be regularly patterned as well. For example, in Schilling-Estes (1998), I examine the speech of a resident of Ocracoke, North Carolina, in several different stylistic contexts, including when he is having a fairly relaxed conversation in a sociolinguistic interview, when the interview is interrupted by several of his brothers, and when he puts on an exaggerated performance of the Ocracoke dialect. In particular, I focus on the production of /ay/ with a raised / backed nucleus, a quintessential stereotype of the Ocracoke or "hoi toider" [high tider] dialect. The analysis shows that while this

speaker indeed shows a bit of scatter in the acoustic placement of his
performative /ay/ tokens, he also has some fairly high standard devi-
ations in his other two styles as well. Further, quantitative analysis
reveals that this speaker shows the same basic ordering of linguistic
constraints for raised /ay/ in both performative and non-performative
contexts. This finding is particularly surprising, given that the
ordering of constraints affecting raised /ay/ is quite unusual (and
seemingly phonologically unnatural) in Ocracoke, with raising
favored in pre-voiced contexts, as in [tɔɪd] 'tide' rather than in pre-
voiceless contexts (e.g. [tɔɪt] or [tʌɪt] 'tight'), as in other North American dialects, including Canadian English and Tidewater Virginia
English.

Finally, traditional variation analysis asserts that unselfconscious,
vernacular speech is not only systematic in a synchronic sense but also
provides the clearest insight into ongoing patterns of change. But more
recent approaches have pointed to the importance of individual
performativity – and indeed highly performative, noticeable individuals – in processes of language change: When shaping their ways of
speaking, people orient toward noticeable people and their speech
patterns rather than simply unconsciously adopting forms to which
they pay little attention (Eckert 2000; Johnstone 1996).

Because third wave approaches to sociolinguistic variation focus on
speaker agentivity and creativity in local interactional contexts, they
have also been referred to as "speaker design" approaches. However, it
is crucial that, in our zeal for investigating agentivity, we do not
neglect the structural side of the equation. Just as speakers shape
personal, interpersonal, social, and cultural identities, attitudes, and
ideologies through their linguistic usages, so too are their linguistic
usages shaped by societal structures, norms, and beliefs. We have
already noted that when particular speaker groups repeatedly use
linguistic features to index particular interactional meanings, the
group-associational meanings that arise in turn become available for
interactional purposes. In other words, a feature such as -in' for -ing
that is initially used to index attributes and stances like hardworkingness and informality can later come to be used in interaction to index
"working class" as well, once it has become associated with this social
group. And on an even broader scale, social groups are implicated in
social orders and ideologies about social order, so that when a person
performs their working-class identity, they are situating themselves
within an entire socioeconomic hierarchy. Indeed, speakers very often
reinforce this hierarchy through their stylistic usages, even if elements
of their linguistic performance sometimes work to resist or undermine

it. Similarly, performing a fairly traditional male or female identity implicates us in a longstanding and deep-seated hegemonic gender order, complete with its deep-seated inequities. And further, as we saw in Barrett's (1995) study of Texas drag queens described in Chapter 2, even if we purposely craft non-traditional identities, we must nonetheless use existing linguistic resources to express them, since no one will understand our new meanings unless we shape them out of familiar materials. This means that even our innovations draw on longstanding associations with traditional social groups and / or types (often stereotypes).

Early variationists have been criticized for stressing the importance of socioeconomic class above all else in shaping patterns of linguistic variation. But we cannot escape the overarching importance of the larger political economy, no matter how locally we focus our studies. For example, Eckert (2005) points out that the interrelation between language and identity in Martha's Vineyard was not simply a local matter of whether or not one felt positively about the island community. It was also inextricably tied to wider scale political and economic forces that worked to undermine localized small-scale fishing and farming economies in favor of larger business conglomerates. In their patterns of variation, then, islanders showed their resistance to these larger forces, as well as related attempts to turn "traditional" communities into quaint tourist commodities. Similarly, the kids in the Detroit-area high school did not create their "jock" and "burnout" identities in the vacuum of one small high school; rather, these identities are intricately intertwined with a wider socioeconomic class order that works to keep privileged classes in power and lower classes removed from mainstream power structures. Thus, the jocks who orient toward the high school and anticipate later success in mainstream society typically come from families who have enjoyed mainstream success. Conversely, in their orientation away from high school norms, the burnouts are also orienting away from mainstream "success" and toward the same types of localized, working-class lives led by their families and neighbors.

4.3.2 Research methods for third wave studies

Because the focus of third wave or speaker-design-based approaches to stylistic variation is on speaker creativity, we would expect the main source of data to be naturally occurring interactions rather than controlled experiments. In addition, we would expect interpretations to emerge organically from the data instead of from pre-determined factors presumed to affect stylistic variation (e.g. attention to speech, audience composition) or pre-set meanings of stylistic variables (e.g. formality / standardness, convergence with audience demographics). Many third wave studies do focus on naturally occurring interactions – with "natural" being taken to mean not only everyday, "mundane" interactions, but also overtly performative speech events such as media performances of radio announcers (Coupland 2001a), television personalities (Sclafani 2009), and politicians (Cutillas-Espinosa, Hernández-Campoy, and Schilling-Estes 2010; Podesva, Jamsu, Callier, and Heitman forthcoming). However, there is still plenty of room for researcher control. For instance, we might still use sociolinguistic interviews as our chief method of data collection, but rather than using them only to obtain aggregate data on the patterning of variation and its conditioning factors, we can study them as interactions, investigating how variables are used in the course of unfolding discourse and extrapolating from this their probable interactional meanings. Further, a large portion of third wave study is focused on listener perception, in recognition of the fact that the social meaning of language variation depends not only on what speakers wish to convey but crucially also on how listeners interpret what they say. As discussed in Chapter 3, perception studies are often quite experimental, and technological advances allow for ever more fine-grained control over minute elements of the speech signals upon which judges base their perceptions of features, styles, and speakers.

Third wave studies focus relatively narrowly on unfolding interactions and individual features, and even specific components of features, such as the duration of stop burst releases or hertz values of ultra high-pitched falsetto speech (Podesva 2004, 2007). At the same time, these approaches are also broad, since, as just noted, they incorporate both perception and production data. In addition, they may encompass a wide range of features, including not only linguistic features but also other elements of style such as clothing, make-up, posture, and gesture (Bucholtz 1999, 2011; Eckert 1998, 2000). Further, they may make use of types of data not traditionally used in linguistic or sociolinguistic studies, in order to adduce independent evidence for indexical meaning other than correlations between linguistic usages and speaker groups. Such studies might include, for example, historical research on linguistic features, social groups, and social meanings in the community of study; interviews and discussions with study participants about local social and linguistic meanings; and case studies of individuals and their life histories (e.g. Johnstone and Kiesling 2008: 11).

Let us examine in detail several illustrative third wave or speaker design studies, each using a different data type, focusing on different elements of style, and examining different types and facets of individual, interpersonal, and group identity.

4.3.3 Case studies in speaker design

Studying speaker design in natural speech: Heath's use of falsetto to construct a "diva" personality

Podesva's (2007) case study of one individual's use of falsetto speech in three different interactional contexts provides an excellent example of a third wave approach to stylistic variation in natural speech. For this study, Podesva asked a friend, Heath, a young male medical student who is openly gay, to record himself in a wide variety of settings. From these, Podesva chose three situations for analysis: a barbecue with four close friends to whom Heath is out; a phone conversation between Heath and his father, again to whom Heath is out but with whom the topic of sexuality is not often discussed; and a meeting with an older White male patient who does not know Heath's sexual orientation. Podesva conducts quantitative analyses of frequency of use, overall height, range, and duration of falsetto utterances in each of the three contexts. He also presents a qualitative analysis of how the feature occurs in discourse in an attempt to arrive at what meaning(s) falsetto carries for Heath and, by extension, other speakers and speaker groups who stylistically employ it. Quantitatively speaking, Heath uses falsetto most frequently in the barbecue setting, less frequently on the phone with his father, and least often in the patient meeting. Further, his falsetto in the barbecue setting is also of longer duration and has a higher maximum pitch and greater pitch range.

Qualitatively, we see that Heath uses falsetto at the barbecue event for a range of discourse purposes but always with a core meaning of "expressiveness" (e.g. he uses falsetto when yelling, expressing surprise or excitement, and offering opinionated evaluations). In addition, when we examine the topics where falsetto occurs in the barbecue discourse (e.g. when talking about clothing, hair, and other topics related to appearance and non-linguistic style) and the other elements of linguistic meaning with which it occurs (e.g. epistemic certainty), we see how Heath tailors the general expressive meaning of falsetto. The feature plays an important part in his construction of a particular type of persona: that of a "diva," or, roughly speaking, a flamboyant individual who takes "center stage," is highly image conscious, and expresses strong opinions, often negative ones.

There is some indication that Heath is also using falsetto to project a "gay identity." For example, the high-pitched expressiveness he

projects is stereotypical of gay speech, while inexpressiveness is stereotypical of heterosexual male speech and heteronormative masculinity.
However, Podesva cautions that identities are not monolithic but
rather multifaceted. If Heath is indeed projecting any type of group
identity in addition to individual persona, it is a particular type of gay
identity (e.g. flamboyantly gay), not simply "gay" *per se*. And although
Heath is indeed a flamboyant diva in the causal barbecue setting with
his close friends, he projects very different identities to his father and
to his patients – further evidence that identities are dynamic, not
static.

Podesva's study has several key elements that make it an exemplary
third wave study. First, it moves beyond traditional phonological and
morphosyntactic variables to examine a linguistic feature not often
treated in studies of sociolinguistic variation. Second, it combines both
quantitative and qualitative methods to better arrive at the social
meanings of linguistic variation. Third, it treats interactional meaning
as central and group-associational meaning as secondary; and, fourth,
it views identity as a process, unfolding in different ways across and
within interactional contexts, not as a fixed product of one's demographic address.

Stylistic variation, persona display, and social critique in performance
speech: Radio personalities and the 'stereotypical' Welsh

Coupland (2001a) exemplifies the complex relationship between linguistic variants, performance, and individual and cultural identities in
his study of an interaction between a radio talk show host and a regular
guest on the show. The show has a fairly wide audience all over Wales
but also in bordering areas of England, and the host frequently draws
on ideas of "real" or "authentic" Welshness in the different segments.
Although the segment discussed in the article, referred to as *Today in*
History, is framed as a dialogic interaction about a historical figure, the
audience knows that it is a staged interaction. Coupland suggests that
this performative arena allows the two participants to perform the
complex idea of "Welsh authenticity" on several levels. The two
speakers variably use phonetic variants associated with two dialects –
"posh" RP, and "working-class" South Wales dialect. In particular, the
realization of the vowels (ou) and (ei) as either diphthongal (RP) or
monophthongal (South Wales English) forms part of the discursive
construction of an "authentic" Welsh voice. So, in a stretch of speech
referencing literary criticism and famous authors, the speakers use
diphthongal forms in utterances which report the majority (critical)
opinion of an author, and style shift to the monophthongal forms

when expressing dissent from the praise Ernest Hemingway has received as "the greatest author since Shakespeare." The dissent and resistance to cultural elitism and dominance is, crucially, a stance very strongly associated with "authentic" Welsh identity in the romanti-cized images of working-class Wales. However, because the two speakers are so obviously *performing* "authenticity" rather than simply presenting themselves as authentic, they are able to distance them-selves from essentialized images of what it means to be Welsh; in other words, they simultaneously highlight what the stereotypes are (through obvious parody), while at the same time critiquing them (metaparody).

As with the Podesva study, Coupland's study exemplifies speaker design approaches to stylistic variation in its focus on how features are used in unfolding discourse to create a stylized persona. In this case, though, the speakers are overtly performing for media audiences, and they are not attempting to project their "real" selves or "real" views but rather attempting to display obviously overblown caricatures to critique cultural stereotypes.

Constructing identity in the sociolinguistic interview: Ethnic and interpersonal alignment in Robeson County, NC

Schilling-Estes (2004) provides an example of how a sociolinguistic interview interaction can be used to illuminate how people use stylistic resources in speaker design. In this study, I examine how linguistic features are used in unfolding discourse in an interview from our Roberson County study. The interviewer is Alex, a young African American man with family connections in Robeson County, and Lou, a Lumbee Indian who is Alex's friend. The two use linguistic variation, whether in terms of usage levels for particular variants (e.g. *r*-lessness), or strategic features deployed at certain key points in the talk (e.g. repetition of each others' morphosyntactic structures or lexical con-tent, use or non-use of familiar direct address forms) to variously position themselves in relation to one another and to the ethnic group to which each "belongs." Their positioning is in part dependent on what they are talking about. Hence, for example, early in the interview, when the two talk about race relations in Robeson County, they indi-cate affiliation with their "own" ethnic groups and dissociation from each other's through divergent usage levels for *r*-lessness, a feature often associated with African American English. Their divergent ethnic affiliations are also constructed and indicated in the referring terms they use to refer to ethnic groups (e.g. "*my* people," "*your* [Black people's] ideas"). Later, in talking about common friends at the

university they both attend, their levels or *r*-lessness are more congruent, which helps them foreground their interpersonal connections and
background their ethnic differences, along with other features such as
frequent use of friendly nicknames.

However, topic alone does not tell the whole story, and the two
interlocutors also position themselves differently depending on how
they align themselves with what they are talking about. Later in the
interview, they return to the topic of race relations, but this time on a
more global level. Their distant stance toward race relations enables
them to maintain close connection with one another as well as dissociation from ethnic division. Again, their alignments are effected
through congruent levels of *r*-lessness and through the use of such
discourse-level features as referring terms indicative of distance from
personal ethnic affiliation. (For example, Alex refers to African Americans in general as "Blacks" rather than "my people.")

Just as personal, interpersonal, and group identities are shown to be
malleable and multifaceted, so too does the study reveal that the social
meanings of linguistic variants are dynamic and multiplex. For
example, the feature of *r*-lessness is variously associated with African
American English, current vernacular Southern American English, and
a historic "posh" Southern accent. At the same time, converging vs.
diverging usage levels for the feature carry their own meanings related
to interpersonal alignment.

My study is thus illustrative of speaker design approaches to stylistic
variation in its focus on how features are used in unfolding discourse to
shape and project identities and stances, as well as the various meanings that can be associated with what at first glance appear to be
unitary variants.

4.3.4 Cautions regarding third wave studies

Despite the many insights that have come out of so-called third wave
studies of sociolinguistic variation – which are, by definition, studies of
stylistic variation – the beginning researcher is urged to venture into
the waters with caution. It is easy to get caught up in the interactional
moment and forget that much as we want to celebrate speaker agentivity and creativity, we are all bound by structures and norms, and we
cannot create meaningful styles out of the blue but rather must draw
on pre-existing associations between linguistic usages and social meanings (whether interactional, group-associational, or both) in order for
our listeners to garner interpretations from our linguistic productions.
And although on the one hand we can view all linguistic usages as
agentive (in the sense that even with seemingly reactive stylistic usages

we must *choose* to be reactive rather than initiative), on the other hand, it does not seem intuitively correct that all speakers in all conversational interactions are purposely and consciously projecting and crafting stances and identities. Many (indeed, perhaps most) of our stylistic moves are relatively unconscious, sometimes to the point of seeming automatic, as attention to speech-based approaches would hold. And as much as we may strive for agentive stylistic choices, our creativity is restricted by the necessary limitations of our linguistic repertoires – even in an age of ever-increasing exposure to a wide array of languages, language varieties, and linguistic variants and their associated social meanings.

And even if we are aware of and can control our usage of particular forms we wish to use in a creative way, there is still the issue of listener uptake. Just because I may use a feature to effect a particular stance (e.g. perhaps I use Pittsburgh [a:] for /aw/ to project "localness" in the Pittsburgh context) does not mean that my hearers will perceive my intended meaning (e.g. perhaps my listeners will perceive [a:] as "incorrect" or "sloppy" rather than "local"; Johnstone and Kiesling 2008).

In order to conduct a solid third wave study, it is necessary to consider the inevitable interplay between agency and structure, between the initiative and the (at least relatively) responsive, between creativity and linguistic limitations, and between speaker intention and listener understanding. In this vein, I again stress to the reader that *our fullest understandings are gained when we approach our linguistic questions from a range of perspectives.* I therefore urge the application of complementary methods such as investigating the qualitative patterning of linguistic variation in discourse against the backdrop of the large-scale quantitative patterning of features; or, conversely, augmenting studies focused on big-picture patterns with ethnographic and / or discoursal investigation of what these patterns actually mean to the speakers who use them. Podesva's (2007) exemplary case study of Heath's use of falsetto in three interactional contexts is set against the backdrop of previous studies of voice quality differences across languages, dialects, and speaker groups (e.g. males vs. females; gay vs. straight males), thus situating Heath's individual usages within larger stylistic and social contexts. Conversely, the impetus for my study of Alex's and Lou's use of features on various linguistic levels to forge and display interpersonal and group alignment actually grew out of my puzzlement over the fact that we could not get a clear picture of the large-scale patterning of *r*-lessness across ethnic groups in Robeson County. (No wonder, considering how multifaceted and dynamic its meaning potential turned out to be when examined in unfolding talk!)

Another angle to be further explored is the discourse analytic investigation of listener uptake in addition to speaker moves. Hence, for example, Nielsen (2010) draws upon positioning theory (Harré and Langenhove 1999) to show that a teenage African American ("Michael") has more prominent falsetto (i.e. of higher pitch, wider range, and longer duration) when he is engaged in so-called "forced self-positioning" (i.e. responding to how his interviewer positions him) than "deliberative self-positioning" (i.e. projecting his own personal identity and point of view). Nielsen argues that this is perhaps because his interviewer often positions him wrongly (in Michael's view), and Michael responds to the interviewer's "incorrect" uptake of what he is trying to say by using heightened falsetto as part of the projection of an indignant stance.

Just as linguistic variables derive their meanings from both local interactional usages and wider scale patterns, from both speaker production and listener perception, so too are they only meaningful in the context of other variables – in other words, as part of individual and group styles. As tempted as we might be to focus on individual variables and variants, and even *parts* of individual features, now that we have the computational means to do so, we would be wise to recall Auer's caution, repeated here from Chapter 2: "the meaning of linguistic heterogeneity does not (usually) reside in individual linguistic features but rather in constellations of such features which are interpreted together ... [W]e do not interpret single variables but a gestalt-like stylistic expression" (2007: 12, cited in Soukup 2011). Thus, for example, while a feature like /t/ release might carry generalized meanings associated with clarity and precision, the specific meanings it indexes for a particular speaker group or particular individual come about only through its co-occurrence with other stylistic features in a given context. Released /t/ may index "educatedness" when it co-occurs with *-ing* (as in *working* rather than *workin'*) in the speech of Orthodox Jews, but "prissiness" when it co-occurs with falsetto in the speech of a gay man who often projects a flamboyant "diva" style.

And despite our best computational efforts, we cannot tease apart the exact contribution of each minute aspect of style to the sum total of the meanings that style conveys, since the meanings of linguistic variables are relational, not atomistic. For example, can we really talk about the meaning of intonational contour minus segmental information when in reality the two never (or only rarely) occur separately? Conversely, it seems even more questionable to talk about the meaning of scrambled segments, devoid of content or intonational contour, since we are *never* exposed to such signals outside of highly artificial research contexts.

Case study: Investigating styles as clusters of variants – the development of stylistic variation in African American children and adolescents

At the same time that technological advances make possible the increasingly detailed investigation of speakers' productions of individual features and parts of features, as well as sophisticated manipulation of the components of speech in tests of listeners' perceptions, computational statistical techniques also allow for increasingly robust examinations of styles in their true fullness, as composed of multiple co-occurring features. For example, Wolfram, Van Hofwegen, Renn, and Kohn (2011) conducted a uniquely comprehensive longitudinal study of the development of African American English in children and adolescents involving seventy African Americans in their first 17 years and forty-four linguistic features. As part of this study, they investigated patterns of variation between AAE and Standard American English in formal and informal contexts as the study participants aged, thus providing a rare look at the acquisition of stylistic variation (Renn and Terry 2009; Van Hofwegen 2012; Wolfram *et al.* 2011). The study design was quite controlled, and data were gathered in contexts purposely designed to yield relatively formal and informal speech, with "formality" and "informality" being defined rather broadly, as having to do with the effects of audience, topic, and task on how much attention kids paid to speech itself rather than the content of talk, hence combining the various views regarding stylistic variation outlined above. The data-gathering situations were also tailored to age. Younger children (grades 1–2) were recorded in conversation with their mothers (informal speech), and children in grade 2 were also interviewed by strangers (formal speech). In the other two grade levels examined with respect to stylistic variation, grade 6 and grade 8, each child was recorded with a friend recruited into the study at grade 6, in both free talk / discussion of topics of interest (informal speech) and in producing two speeches for simulated adult audiences (formal speech). Results indicated one of two patterns of the development of stylistic variation: (1) a general increase in amount of variation between formal and informal styles with increasing age, and (2) an increase in stylistic proficiency between grades 1–2 and grade 6, followed by a decrease in grade 8. The latter pattern is particularly intriguing for views of stylistic variation focused on speaker agency, since, as Wolfram *et al.* note: "It seems unlikely that speakers exhibiting their peak in Grade 6 lose the ability to shift in Grade 8; instead, there is probably a choice not to utilize their full range of shifting capability during this period" (2011). Explanations for kids' stylistic choices are likely to be complex and most likely fully revealed only through combining quantitative study with qualitative investigations of unfolding interactions; nonetheless, quantitative investigation of the degree of linguistic similarly within conversational dyads reveals some intriguing patterns suggestive of speaker motivations. For example, girls were highly accommodating to one another in dyads at all three time points, whereas boys were only weakly accommodating in pairs at grade 6 and not at all at grade 8, suggesting that perhaps girls develop accommodative skills earlier than boys and / or apply such skills more consistently (Van Hofwegen 2012).

Wolfram *et al.*'s (2011) study thus makes a number of important contributions to the unfolding study of stylistic variation. For one, it provides time depth. In addition, it provides breadth in terms of number of features examined, thereby serving as an important corrective to studies that sometimes downplay the composite nature of speech styles in their focus on the details of individual components. Furthermore, the study adds to our toolkit of data-collection methods by demonstrating the efficacy of "role playing" (e.g. composing speeches for pretend audiences) for collecting data from a range of styles. Finally, Wolfram *et al.*'s (2011) results demonstrate the pervasiveness of speaker creativity, showing that agentivity can come through even in highly quantitative studies investigating multiple speakers, multiple time points, and multiple variables, when we might expect such studies to indicate only straightforward correlations between speech styles and pre-set contexts (e.g. free talk vs. speeches; cf. the conversational vs. reading portions of the traditional sociolinguistic interview).

As a final concern in thinking about third wave studies, even when we do bring individual variants into their stylistic settings and conceptualize variants as pointing to broad fields of meanings that only gain specificity in their stylistic [and interactional] contexts, sometimes the notion of "indexical field" breaks down, too, since some variants defy association with a single core meaning, however general it may be. One obvious illustration is *r*-lessness, since it carries oppositional rather than related meanings in British-based varieties of English, where it is considered standard, vs. American-based dialects, where it is stigmatized, or at least heard as "marked" (by region or ethnicity) rather than standard. We also saw above that *r*-lessness even carries different meanings within single dialects and individual speakers. For example, Lou, the Lumbee Indian from Robeson County, uses *r*-lessness not only to indicate alignment with or dissociation from his African American interloctutor via convergent vs. divergent usage levels, but he also capitalizes on the feature's various group-associational meanings to index both vernacularity and upper-class status, at different points in the interview, calling upon the feature's current associations with non-standardness as well as its historic association with "posh" Southern US speech.

As exciting as it may be to feel that we are getting to the heart of the social meaning of linguistic variation by uncovering the meaning (fields) of each individual variant in an individual or group style, it is perhaps a bit too easy to get sucked under by the "third wave." We might do well to occasionally step back from the water's edge and remember that variants, by classic definition, can have no social meaning apart from those which are (initially) *arbitrarily* given by language users, and so variants need not have related meanings across speech even though they sometimes, perhaps even often, do. In other words, if we as linguists start believing that a variant like released /t/ "naturally" connotes precision because it is fully pronounced, we are guilty of the same "iconization" (Irvine 2001) of the arbitrary link between linguistic form and social meaning that non-linguists routinely engage in when, for example, equating slow rate of speech with slowness of speakers' mental processes, hypo-articulation (e.g. word-final consonant cluster reduction in words like *des'* for *desk*) with sloppiness, or paradigm regularization (e.g. *myself, yourself, hisself*) with uneducatedness. Released /t/ may indeed connote "precision" in word-final position in American English, but it sounds artificial and affected in flapping contexts (e.g. *letter, water*); conversely, in British English fully articulated /t/ is "proper" in *letter* and *water*, but so is hypo-articulated /r/ in these very same words.

Eckert suggests that we might look to "more abstract aspects of variables such as fortition-lenition, hypo-hyperarticulation, or the differential stylistic potential of different phonetic classes" as important carriers of social meaning in linguistic variation (2008: 472). But even if we broaden our scope and begin to address phonetic processes as carriers of social meaning, we are still dealing with iconization, not "natural" associations between articulatory settings and sociolinguistic meanings: hypo-articulate *r*-lessness can go hand-in-hand with hyper-articulate /t/ to create a precise, clear, educated style, while hyperarticulations like fricative stopping in words like *this* and *that* is arbitrarily considered imprecise, unclear, and uneducated. Other features with widespread social connotations, for example the production of verbal *-ing* as *-ing* rather than *-in'*, have nothing to do with either hyper- or hypo-articulation (since all that is involved in the case of *-ing* is backness of articulation, not pronouncing a /g/, though we must grant that *-ing* is at least believed to be more fully articulated than *-in'* by non-linguists.

The idea that certain phonetic resources have special iconic potential is a fascinating one, and it certainly bears further investigation. However, we must remember that the social meaning of linguistic variation is at heart social, not linguistic, and variants and varieties can only take on the social evaluations we give them. And because linguistic features do not have inherent social meanings, we want to be cautious in re-ordering first- and second-order indexical meaning, since it is unclear from where socially meaningful features would originally derive their interactional meanings if not from association with speaker groups who use them. As Labov so aptly noted decades ago, "if a certain group of speakers uses a particular variant, then the social values attributed to that group will be transferred to that linguistic variant" (1972c: 251).

Asserting the primacy of speakers over linguistic material in no way undermines third wave approaches but rather strengthens them, since current approaches to stylistic variation, above all, focus on how speakers make meanings, not on how linguistic forms somehow inherently convey meanings apart from those who speak them. And in this, even the most seemingly radical third wave approaches stay rooted in classic variation analysis, since the whole point of sociolinguistics is that language and social life are intricately interconnected, and we can never fully understand language without investigating how and why people use it as they do.

4.4 SUMMARY

In sum, we have seen that how one designs research on stylistic variation depends very much on one's theoretical viewpoint. If stylistic variation is taken to be primarily reactive, dependent on situational factors such as formality, audience composition, and topic, then we can design research tasks in which we seek to control for the factor(s) of interest and subsequently test their effects on amount and type of stylistic variation. For example, we can (arguably) test the effects of attention to speech by subjecting interviewees to tasks of increasing formality (conversational interview, reading passage, word list), or test the effects of audience design by having different interviewers interview a single interviewee, a single interviewer interview an interviewee alone and in a peer group, or different interviewers interview different interviewees, all carefully chosen so that factors other than the audience characteristics of interest (e.g. ethnicity, gender) are controlled for as much as possible. In addition, we can capitalize on naturally occurring situations where the factors of interest just happen to be controlled (as with Bell's study of New Zealand radio announcers who read the exact same news content to different audiences).

If, on the other hand, we hold stylistic variation to be a proactive resource that speakers use to alter the situation at hand by taking up particular stances, projecting particular character attributes or personas, and purposefully aligning with or distancing themselves from various speaker groups, a wider range of data and methods are available to us. Indeed, we *should* use complementary approaches and speech data as we seek subtle speaker-internal motivations for stylistic variation (as opposed to its more readily observable situational correlates). For example, we can study naturally occurring everyday events (as in Podesva's 2007 study of Heath), naturally occurring mediated performances (as in Coupland's 2001a study of the radio announcer), or sociolinguistic interviews (as in Schilling-Estes' 2004 study of the interview interaction between Alex and Lou). In addition, we can combine quantitative methods, which aggregate patterns of variation across stylistic contexts and speakers groups, with qualitative ones, which illuminate how variants are used as discourse unfolds. Further, we can supplement studies of speaker design with investigations of listener perception. These studies in turn may have various methodological slants, for example an experimental perspective rooted in the tradition of language attitude studies (e.g. Campbell-Kibler 2010) or a more discourse-analytic perspective, for example interactional sociolinguistics as informed by positioning theory (Nielsen 2010). Finally, we can broaden the data field even further by incorporating investigation into community, individual, and linguistic history; interviews and discussions with study participants regarding what they themselves feel is personally, socially, and linguistically meaningful; and an examination of the extralinguistic elements of style in which linguistic style is always embedded (e.g. clothing, make-up, hairstyle, physical stance).

Choosing data and methods for a third wave investigation of style is not as simple, then, as it might seem at first glance. Third wave approaches are not a matter of "anything goes." In reality, when we

are tasked with uncovering not just *how* variants pattern across different situational contexts, but also *why* they do so, then we become
involved in rigorous interpretive work that requires a very careful
selection of a range of types of data and methods. We must ensure
that our analyses of speaker intentions and listener apprehension are
as valid as possible, given that we have now moved beyond the realm of
the directly observable to the psychological, interactional, and ideo-
logical workings behind the linguistic patterns we see.

Suggested readings

LABOV, WILLIAM 1972. THE ISOLATION OF CONTEXTUAL STYLES.
CHAPTER 3 IN WILLIAM, LABOV, *SOCIOLINGUISTIC PATTERNS*.
PHILADELPHIA: UNIVERSITY OF PENNSYLVANIA PRESS.

This chapter outlines Labov's Attention to Speech approach to stylistic
variation and describes the various styles that we can expect to encounter in a sociolinguistic interview, ranging from casual and careful styles
in the conversational portion of the interview to styles that surface in
interview tasks purposely designed to yield increasingly careful speech:
reading passages, word lists, and minimal pair lists. It is here that
Labov also provides clear evidence of the orderly patterning of stylistic
variation when data from individuals and contexts are aggregated;
here, too, is his demonstration of the shared linguistic norms that
unite the New York City speech community despite widely differing
usage levels for dialect features.

BELL, ALLAN 1984. LANGUAGE STYLE AS AUDIENCE DESIGN.
LANGUAGE IN SOCIETY 13: 145–204.

This article revolutionized the study of stylistic variation by presenting
a new approach in which style is viewed as conditioned primarily by
audience design rather than by attention to speech. The effects of
audience on speech style have been empirically demonstrated in a
number of subsequent studies (both inside and outside the sociolinguistic interview context) and continue to be considered of central
importance. In recent years, Bell (2001) has updated his model to give
more consideration to proactive as well as reactive style shifts, at the
same time judiciously maintaining that stylistic creativity can never
exist apart from pre-existing associations between linguistic forms and
social meanings.

ECKERT, PENELOPE 2012. THREE WAVES OF VARIATION STUDY:
THE EMERGENCE OF MEANING IN THE STUDY OF VARIATION.
ANNUAL REVIEW OF ANTHROPOLOGY 41: 87–100.

In this highly influential article, Eckert presents the progression of variation study as "three waves," the latter of which is focused on how linguistic variables get their meanings in unfolding interaction. This approach thus elevates "style" from its somewhat subordinate status in early sociolinguistics (where its study was viewed primarily as a means of identifying "genuine," vernacular speech) to the spotlight of variation analysis. Numerous students and other researchers have adopted Eckert's "third wave" approach, though Eckert is careful in her article to stress that the "three waves" were never really separate and that variation study has always been vitally concerned with social meaning, beginning with Labov's foundational study of the social meaning of centralized diphthongs on Martha's Vineyard.

COUPLAND, NIKOLAS 2007. *STYLE: LANGUAGE VARIATION AND IDENTITY*. NEW YORK: CAMBRIDGE UNIVERSITY PRESS.

Coupland's book is a brilliant excursus into how viewing style as "speaker design" – that is, as primarily concerned with projecting and shaping individual identities and interpersonal relations – can lead us to re-think in exciting new ways traditional variationist notions about the connections between linguistic variation and various facets of social identity, including socioeconomic class, place, ethnicity, and gender and sex. Coupland also discusses the importance of investigating highly selfconscious styles rather than limiting ourselves to speech we believe to be unselfconscious, and he demonstrates the importance of selfconscious "stylizations" in individual and group identity performance, as well as in individual, social, and linguistic change.

COUPLAND, NIKOLAS 2001. LANGUAGE, SITUATION AND THE RELATIONAL SELF. IN PENELOPE ECKERT AND JOHN RICKFORD (EDS.), *STYLE AND SOCIOLINGUISTIC VARIATION*. CAMBRIDGE UNIVERSITY PRESS, 185–210.

Coupland (2001b) provides a succinct encapsulation of his views on style and how stylistic variation has grown in importance as variation study has developed. The growing interest in style is not only due to developments in the field, but to social developments as well – notably people's increasing contact with and awareness of stylistic, dialectal, and language variation, whether through face-to-face or mediated contact.

ECKERT, PENELOPE AND JOHN R. RICKFORD 2001. STYLE AND SOCIAL MEANING. IN PENELOPE ECKERT AND JOHN R. RICKFORD (EDS.), *STYLE AND SOCIOLINGUISTIC VARIATION*. CAMBRIDGE UNIVERSITY PRESS, 119–126.

This edited volume brings together a wide range of views on stylistic variation (and related critiques), including not only variationist approaches but also anthropological views, functionally centered, and psychologically oriented approaches. The volume includes influential chapters by Judith Irvine ("Style as distinctiveness"), Penelope Eckert ("Style and social meaning," a precursor to her "three waves" approach), and Douglas Finegan and Edward Biber, who view social class variation as derivative of functionally based register variation rather than seeing class-based variation as primary. Also included are updated discussion and critique of Labov's Attention to Speech approach, Bell's reworking of his 1984 audience design model, and, as noted above, Coupland's speaker-identity centered views on stylistic variation.

5   In the field: Finding contacts, finding a place

We have seen in the preceding chapters that conducting a sound sociolinguistic study involves many stages of careful planning: defining your community of study (including what counts as a "community" in the first place); deciding how to sample and stratify the population; and designing data-collection instruments, whether sociolinguistic interviews, structured observations, surveys, experiments, or some combination of data-gathering tools. Further, since sociolinguistic studies generally require some level of ethnographic involvement, planning and conducting the study almost always involve going back and forth between pre-determined definitions and designs and new understandings about what and how to study, gleaned from ongoing participant-observation in the community of study.

Because the best sociolinguistic studies aim to situate their perspectives within the community rather than standing apart, most sociolinguists will introduce themselves into the community fairly early in the research process, most likely in the early phases of the project design. And while research design may seem daunting to the new sociolinguistic researcher, the most difficult step in any sociolinguistic study is almost certainly entering the community for the first time. However, as with other aspects of the research process, your entry into the community can be greatly facilitated with a bit of careful forethought, and with a mind open to the inevitable surprises that you will encounter in the field.

5.1   INITIAL CONTACTS

5.1.1   Introducing yourself and your project to the community

Of course you want your initial entry into the community to feel natural, and you may be able to start getting to know the community and its members simply by showing up and talking with people. But

177

there comes a point in even the most organically unfolding relationship between researcher and research participant in which you simply have to describe who you "really" are and what your research is about. In other words, in order to proceed with your studies you will have to admit that you are in the community as a researcher; otherwise, you will be guilty of participating in community life for hidden purposes and thus violating the most basic ethical protocols of social science. (See Chapter 7 for in-depth discussion of fieldwork ethics.) This should not be taken as simply a stumbling block, another barrier to overcoming the observer's paradox: instead it can actually be seen as a step toward increasing research participants' (and researchers') comfort level. Community members need to place you in some role or another, and it can be quite difficult to figure out where to place an "unobtrusive" stranger who does not say much about who they are or what they are doing.

When you introduce the "observer" side of yourself and the nature of your project, you cannot help but foreground your "outsider" status, even if only to a small degree. But in case you are worried that highlighting your status as a researcher will permanently exclude you from achieving any sort of insider status, recall that the "observer" half of your participant-observer status is usually of very little importance to your research participants (see Section 3.3 above), since, as Duranti (1997: 118) so aptly notes, "people are too busy running their own lives to change them in substantial ways" for you. And when they do adjust themselves to you, they do so in natural ways that most likely foreground familiar participant roles. For example, if you enter the community via the well-known "friend-of-a-friend" method (see below for more details), community members will tend to keep this role uppermost in their minds, even after you introduce your research role.

So in very practical terms, how do sociolinguistic researchers introduce themselves and their studies to the communities they wish to study? This is one of the questions I am asked most frequently by students and other researchers seeking information on how to design and conduct a field study, and it is a pivotal one indeed. Your first introduction can set the tone for your whole study and cast you into a role that will follow you throughout the course of your research. The key here is honesty. We are all obliged as ethical researchers to provide honest information about our researcher identities and our research purposes (and methods) to those we wish to study. At the same time, though, we are not obliged to provide the excruciating details of our often esoteric sociolinguistic interests to people who probably honestly do not care too much about them. Researcher and research participant alike have multifaceted identities and play many roles in different spheres, in different interactions, and even in the course of a single unfolding interaction. There is no need for us to provide detailed information on all aspects of our life for our research purposes, since our research lives are typically focused on only a few facets of who we are.

In short, as in our non-research lives, honest and general introductions are better than overly detained descriptions. More detail may be needed later, depending in part on the terms of your IRB approval, especially when community members become active participants in permanent recordings, analyses, and write-ups of project results. However, when initially introducing our research, and indeed periodically throughout the progress of the research project, brief summaries are best. Indeed, when we take the trouble to prepare clear and streamlined introductions that get to the heart of who we are, what we hope to accomplish, and what we would like participants' roles to be, we are actually doing community members a favor. Well-rehearsed and concise introductions are far easier on our participants than if we insist that they listen to and / or read through pages of detailed information on the social, cultural, and linguistic information we hope to uncover and the technicalities of exactly how we hope to do so.

By way of illustration, let us consider a few examples. In Chapter 3, we presented a detailed description of the Language and Communication in the Washington, DC, Metropolitan Area project (LCDC), an ongoing sociolinguistic study directed by faculty in the Georgetown University Linguistics Department. Each semester, students in appropriate classes conduct research that furthers the study, and each time they enter the field, they must introduce themselves and the research project. At first glance, this may not seem too difficult, since the study has been going on for some time, and a number of descriptions of the project are already available in articles and conference presentations, in the Project Background and Plan of Study sections of our IRB Protocol, and in the Informed Consent Form which the IRB requires all study participants to sign, indicating that they understand their role in our research project, including potential benefits and risks, as well as the steps we will take to ensure their anonymity. However, these descriptions are too detailed for immediate introductory purposes. The students work in a range of types of communities in the DC area and approach their studies from a range of perspectives (both professional and personal), so each student must craft an individually tailored introduction (or perhaps even several introductions, for different segments of the community), rather than enter the field with a "one-size-fits-all" introductory statement. Consider, for example, how the level of detail and the focus of study change in the descriptions in the case study below. These are excerpted from (5.1) the official Plan of Study intended for scholarly audiences; (5.2) the Informed Consent Form that provides a full description of the project to study participants (the vast majority of whom are not academics); and (5.3) the basic introductory statements used by individual graduate student researchers. These descriptions show significant differences, including wording differences indicated in italics (added here for emphasis), though they all proceed from the same general starting point.

Case study: From full description to brief introductions in the LCDC research project

(5.1)
Language and Communication in the Washington, DC, Metropolitan Area IRB Protocol (excerpts):

Propose of project:
To study linguistic variants of speech (including sounds, structures, meanings, discourse practices) that help reveal how people project and construct identities in their neighborhoods, communities, and city or suburb.

Plan of study:
The goal of this project is to conduct a large-scale sociolinguistic study of the Washington DC community, i.e. to study how people in the Washington DC Metropolitan Area talk. The study grows out of the Sociolinguistic Field Methods course we regularly teach each year in the Linguistics Department and has now grown to encompass faculty and graduate students working in other Georgetown Sociolinguistics classes, as well as related sociolinguistics projects in the DC area ... We plan to continue conducting interviews and surveys, and to add ethnographic–linguistic study as well ... to gain an increasingly full picture of the myriad interrelations between language and personal, interpersonal, and group (e.g. ethnic, gender) identity as manifested in the Washington, DC, Metro Area.

Because dialect studies of phonological variation are being partially supplanted by a discursive focus on ways of speaking and acting in a variety of media and modalities, our study seeks to strike a balance between these two extremes by examining several different features of language structure and use among people who share a geographical space (a neighborhood) *but may have come to that space through widely different pasts...*

In addition to eliciting well-known language features that differentiate Northern vs. Southern dialects (e.g. the merger of the vowels in the words 'pin' and 'pen'; the pronunciation of 'greasy' or 'greazy'), we examine variation in more local practices, such as calling Washington DC 'the district,' 'DC' or 'the city' and pronouncing Glover Park to rhyme with either 'lover' or 'clover', a difference that is said to correlate with length of time in the area ...

On the more discursive end of the features of language we study, we pay special attention to narratives. Narratives have several advantages: (1) they are

a well-known site for 'casual' speech; (2) they encourage highly stylized
language performance (e.g. through expressive phonology, direct quotes,
dialect adaptation), an increasingly important speech style that has recently
been suggested to be equally indicative of vernacular style as the well-known
Labovian casual style; (3) because narratives are a genre that recapitulates and
performs the past, they provide a site for language practices whose deictic
center is partially displaced from the 'current' world to be centered in the world
of the past experience . . .

(5.2)
LCDC Informed Consent Form (excerpts):
   INTRODUCTION
   You are invited to consider participating in a research study *to investigate life
in different Washington DC area neighborhoods, including how people in
different neighborhoods talk and communicate with one another.* This form will
describe the purpose and nature of the research, its possible risks and benefits,
other options available to you, and your rights as a participant in the study.
Please take whatever time you need to discuss the study with your family and
friends, or anyone else you wish to. The decision to participate, or not to
participate, is yours. If you decide to participate, please be sure to sign and date
the last page of this form.
   WHY IS THIS RESEARCH STUDY BEING DONE?
   The study is being done to learn about life in the Washington DC area. We
are interested in how contemporary life here compares with other places and
earlier times. More specifically, we are interested in people's everyday
experiences, for example, how people find jobs and get to their jobs; where they
interact with friends, acquaintances, co-workers, and neighbors; how they use
local resources; how they communicate and use language with one another. The
study will contribute to general knowledge of how people communicate with
one another in large cities and their surroundings.

(5.3)
LCDC individual student introductions, LING 571: Sociolinguistic Field
Methods; Spring 2010, Spring 2011:
   Spoken introductions, Spring 2011:
   "*We are students* exploring the U Street area and we are interested in learning
more about the neighborhood and the people that live here."
   "Hello, Sir. My name is XX. You may have seen my colleague YY and me
around here at the [community] center or at the pavilion over the past few
weeks. *We are students at Georgetown University* and we are very interested
in language and communication here in the Washington DC area. We are
specifically interested in how language and communication are related to
society. For example, perhaps for someone that has just moved to this area
from El Salvador, it is very difficult to learn English, and so it is difficult to
find a job or get access to opportunities. We would like to understand this
issue more, and that is why we come here to the center. We enjoy talking with
you and hearing your stories, and hearing about the difficulties you face. We
also like hearing about how this center works, and we are interested in trying
to recommend ways to increase the opportunities you have here to find work
and improve your life."

> **Written / email introductions, Spring 2010:**
> "Hello! My name is XX and *I'm a graduate student at Georgetown
> University*. I'm looking for Americans of Latino heritage to discuss their
> experiences working on Capitol Hill. The ultimate purpose of this study is
> a preliminary look at interaction in different communities of practice on
> Capitol Hill."
> "My name is XX and *I am currently a graduate student in the Linguistics
> Department at Georgetown University*, and recently a resident of the Del Rey
> neighborhood. I am fascinated by the small business community of Del Rey and
> am interested in pursuing a relationship with YY [a particular small business] as
> part of a semester project which will focus on the small business as a
> community wherein the residents of Del Rey come to socialize, relax, learn, etc.
> During my visits to YY, I've observed the interactions between your staff and
> customers. I find this aspect of your establishment an exciting and worthwhile
> research pursuit and would like to explore it further. Additionally, I feel that my
> research could be beneficial to the understanding, health, and continued success
> of YY and am fully amenable to sharing my findings with you."

Notice that in the LCDC IRB Protocol (5.1), linguistic study is foregrounded, including specific features and types of language to be
studied (e.g. phonological variants, narratives, vowel mergers, expressive phonology, deixis). In the Informed Consent Form (5.2), the terms
"linguistic" and "sociolinguistic" are replaced with less technical terms
("talk," "communicate," "language"), and the linguistic aspect of our
study is embedded within our larger interest in social life. Finally, the
individual introductions (5.3) are usually only a couple sentences in
length, and the student researchers tend to foreground the "student"
aspect of their identities, rather than the details of the research project.

As we will discuss in more detail below, "student" is an excellent role
for a sociolinguistic researcher on a number of levels. For one, it
naturally highlights one's status as a learner rather than an expert,
and so practically automatically minimizes potential power differen-
tials between the researcher and the non-academics who usually make
up our research communities. In addition, many people from a variety
of walks of life can identify with the "student" role and its rigors, and
they will often be much more cooperative with students working on
what they conceive of as a "school project" than with professors they
think of as either intimidating, incomprehensible, irrelevant, or some
combination of the three.

Of course, if you are not a university student, you cannot introduce
yourself as one; however, non-students can usually come up with some
sort of introduction that minimizes participants' trepidation. For
example, professors can introduce themselves as a "researcher,"

"teacher," or, better yet, someone who "teaches" at X university (with the latter description minimizing the prominence of the "teacher" facet of the researcher's identity). Further, as discussed in more detail below, once you enter the community, you really should think of yourself as a "student," in the field to learn about community life and language, not to impose your "expert" academic understandings.

Finally, in reference to the above examples, note that a couple of the student introductions stated not only why the project was of interest to them as researchers, but also how it might benefit the research community. As will be discussed in detail in Chapter 7, sociolinguists have long believed in giving back to the communities who provide the data that advances their studies (and careers) – indeed, many engage in particular research projects because they have identified a language-related problem in need of sociolinguistically informed solutions.

5.1.2 Making initial contacts

As you are deciding how to introduce yourself and your project, you will also have to think about when you will first discuss your research, and with whom. Often, researchers will enter the community for preliminary ethnographic observation prior to talking directly with anyone about their research project. In some communities, though, your presence will be too obtrusive to go unnoticed or unremarked upon, and you may have to introduce yourself and your study right away. As mentioned in Chapter 3, this was the case in our research in Smith Island, Maryland, where unfamiliar non-residents almost never visited for periods longer than a couple hours in the mid-afternoon. Our presence on the scene outside those hours demanded explanation. On the opposite side of the spectrum, in some cases the researcher can remain unobtrusive for quite some time. For example, you can usually conduct extend informal observation of a crowded, multiethnic city neighborhood without being noticed; in addition, a community insider will have been making observations about their community for as long as they have lived there and can begin making observations focused on research questions for years before they actually plan and launch a structured project.

If you are able to be in the community for a while before introducing your research goals, then it will probably be natural for you to start talking about your research with people you have already gotten to know. However, if you need to introduce your research right away, you will have to introduce yourself to strangers. This task is made much easier if you enter the community through a common contact – through a "friend of a friend." In my research experience, I have learned that acquaintances who know people in the research community of interest are often surprisingly easy to find. Working or studying at a university brings you into contact with people from diverse geographic and social spaces: students and faculty often come from all over, while staff may be drawn primarily from local communities. Our entry into the first field site in which I worked, Ocracoke, North Carolina, was greatly facilitated by a faculty member at North Carolina State University whose best friend was a well-connected islander who subsequently introduced us to his various social networks. We initially entered the Robeson County Lumbee and African American communities through a Lumbee student who was from the area, and through an African American student who had family in the community. In initiating my re-study of Smith Island, Maryland, I did not think I knew anyone there, and so I got up my nerve to make a cold call to the Smith Island Cultural Center. The person who answered the phone referred me to one of center's directors, who unfortunately was not from the island but heartily agreed to introduce me into the community. To my surprise, when the director and I landed on the island and entered the Cultural Center, I realized that the person I had initially called was a high school classmate of mine who had married into an island family, and so I had an islander contact after all! Even more surprisingly, I learned soon thereafter that I had another contact in the small island community, a member of a longstanding island family with whom I had attended university for a couple years.

Entering a community through official channels raises some important issues. Sociolinguists typically advocate entering the community from the bottom up – through "regular" people with no particular leadership status – rather than through community institutions and leaders. This principle is grounded in the assumption that leaders are often not integrated into the community's central, "grassroots" networks and indeed may be cast in something of an outsider or even oppositional role (a sort of "them" vs. "us" relationship). In addition, leaders may try to steer you toward who they view as the "right" people rather than toward those you wish to get to know. For example, they may want you to meet people of higher socioeconomic and educational status, while your focus might be on working-class people with strong local dialect and dense local social networks.

However, in my research experience I have found that entry into an unfamiliar community is often facilitated by institutions and leaders who are used to acting as "brokers" between the community and the outside world. Meeting with leaders does not have to preclude meeting others in a diverse range of community networks, especially if we do not simply allow a particular leader to guide our selection of individuals but rather keep our eyes and ears open to a wide range of contacts. In addition, I have learned that a particularly valuable type of contact is the "unofficial leader" or "community leader" – an individual who holds leadership status by virtue of the esteem in which the community holds them rather than by authority conferred by official title and / or position. My initial contact on Smith Island was an "official" leader, who introduced me in turn to a key unofficial leader, one of the island schoolteachers. The teacher turned out to be indispensible in introducing me to a host of islander residents – in particular the teenagers from whom I most needed data (since I was conducting a re-study that depended on adding the next youngest generation to a study conducted 15+ years earlier) and with whom I admittedly was most nervous about talking. Similarly, in Robeson County, we benefited from the help of a man regarded as an important Lumbee elder, even though he had no official leadership status of any sort. He introduced us to people we never could have met on our own, including highly vernacular elderly Lumbee who never interacted with strangers.

Not only can the participation of official and unofficial leaders prove to be beneficial; in some communities, it is an outright necessity. For example, if you are interested in obtaining relaxed, natural speech from children or adolescents in a particular school, you will absolutely have to enter their community through school officials, since unknown adults who approach children asking them for information about their lives will certainly be stopped by the adults responsible for their well-being – or even by law enforcement officers. Even Penelope Eckert, who conducted one of the most ethnographically sensitive sociolinguistic studies to date, began her work on language and social life in a Detroit-area high school, not by approaching the teenagers who were the focus of her research, but by addressing a teachers' meeting. Eventually she was able to distance herself from the adult authorities in the school, but it was not easy. She had to forego her initial plan to attend students' classes, since the classroom teachers were too prone to regard her as a fellow authority. Eckert knew she needed to downplay this aspect of her role and highlight her role as a learner in order to earn the teens' trust – a task she managed admirably.

Other cases may not be as clear-cut in terms of whether or not you need to enter a community via official channels. When I first began working in Smith Island I contacted the researcher who had done the initial study in the mid-1980s and asked her the same question we are pondering now: should I enter the community through official channels and risk being steered toward marginal or unrepresentative community members, or could I simply start visiting "regular" islanders and make my way through their social networks? The researcher adamantly insisted that I absolutely had to talk with the island pastor (another unofficial leader) before I spoke with anyone else, or I would be in violation of all local protocols for how a stranger respectfully enters the island community. Worried because I had in fact already talked with a couple islanders, I dutifully contacted the pastor, expecting to be chastised for my insensitive behavior. However, when I explained my situation, he simply laughed and said, "Don't worry about me! Things aren't like that anymore, and you can talk to whoever you want." Thus I was reminded again that you have to get to know each community individually in order to know how to introduce yourself and to whom – and you may have to re-educate yourself as the community changes.

There is a further problem with excluding officials from fieldwork contacts. The prescription against their participation rests on an implicit belief that some community members are less "authentic" than others by virtue of their wider contacts, higher socioeconomic status, and, most likely, greater command of the standard language. The preference for "authentic" or "pure" people, communities, and language varieties – those that are supposedly relatively free from outside influences – is a holdover from traditional dialectological studies that aimed to paint a picture of historical forms before they faded away. Those studies focused their data-gathering efforts on non-mobile, older, rural males, who presumably were the least linguistically innovative and had the least contact with outside influences, including the standardizing influences of education. As Milroy and Gordon (2003: 16–19) note, modern sociolinguistics has expanded the focus to include community members of a range of socioeconomic classes, educational levels, and patterns of contact. Nonetheless, the old roots are still visible. For example, as thoughtfully discussed in Bucholtz (2003) and Eckert (2003), the investigation of African American English has mostly comprised the study of African American *Vernacular* English, especially as represented in its "purest" form by inner-city teen boys who are highly locally oriented and quite far removed from standard (White) American English. Similarly, while also the subject of much sociolinguistic study, women have been seen as less "authentic" than men because they often have wider contacts and tend to orient toward wider language norms rather than localized linguistic forms, though as we saw in Chapter 2, gender-based patterns for language variation can differ widely across communities and community subgroups. Finally, we have already discussed at length the problems with privileging vernacular, unselfconscious speech over more selfconscious styles, and there is no inherent reason to exclude community members who are not as "vernacular" as others from our studies, particularly if we do not believe in the notion of "default," "decontextualized" speech anyway.

Hence, entering the community through leaders is sometimes necessary or at least useful on a practical level. In addition, working with leaders also reminds us that all communities are heterogeneous, made up of individuals who belong to various social networks. Some may be central to the community we have decided to study, and others may be marginal but nonetheless relevant (and in addition central to other communities). Unless we are explicitly studying a single social network within a community, we probably do want to move beyond the networks of our initial contacts in the community. This does not mean, however, that we should automatically discount our first contacts as somehow less "authentic" than those we may make later, as we become more deeply immersed in the community and gain access to more localized individuals who do not interact as readily with outsiders.

STUDENTS IN THE FIELD

A number of my students over the years have entered their communities of study via "official" channels and branched from there to successful interact with "ordinary" community members as well. Sakiko Kajino, studying Japanese university women's language in three urban centers in Japan, had to gain access to women's universities through official channels, since their security is quite strict. She conducted Internet research about the universities of interest, located professors who might be interested in her project, and emailed them with information about her project. The professors readily agreed to help her, though one university required IRB permission, as we saw in Chapter 2 above. The professors who gave her permission introduced her to several students, and from there she was able to go through student networks to find participants. She also found participants by visiting students during club activities, as well as bravely approaching strangers in the cafeteria. Though this last approach to entering a community is often quite difficult, Sakiko found that people readily agreed to participate in her study as long as she prefaced her request with general conversation about the university, the neighborhood, and other topics of particular interest to the university women, such as shopping and favorite actors.

Sometimes community entry via official channels is less purposeful but nonetheless beneficial. Jackie Jia Lou began her studies of Washington DC's Chinatown (Lou 2009, 2010a, 2010b), by conducting unobtrusive ethnographic observations in the neighborhood, including attending a Chinese New Year's Parade. During the parade, she tried wandering around and taking pictures, but it was so cold that she followed a line of people streaming into a building. This building turned out to be the Chinatown Community Cultural Center, an institution that Jackie had not known about prior to walking in. By very lucky coincidence, as she stood in the building, she found herself next to a very important unofficial leader, the "mayor" of Chinatown and the chairperson of the Chinatown Steering Committee. He warmly welcomed Jackie to volunteer at the Center and agreed to be interviewed right away. Her volunteer work at the center as an ESL teacher proved to be crucial to her community entry and enabled her to get to know and interview a number of "ordinary" community members, many of them elderly. Not only did her participants from the Center welcome her study, but they also welcomed her into their lives and their homes, providing her with delicious home-cooked food in addition to invaluable data. Jackie was especially touched by their generosity, given that they were socially, economically, and linguistically disadvantaged within the DC context, and it could not have been financially easy for them to host their student researcher so open-handedly.

Of course, sociolinguists over the years have had valid reasons for suggesting that we enter our research communities through unofficial rather than official channels, and there are indeed problems associated with making contacts from the "top down" rather than from the "bottom up." For one, leaders are used to taking charge and to viewing themselves as experts, and they may formulate their own notions of how we should conduct our studies, some of which will run counter to our study design and principles for sound sociolinguistic fieldwork. In such cases, we will have to figure out a way to diplomatically continue with our own plans rather than adopting theirs (unless, of course, we realize that some of their ideas will be better suited to the community of study).

My best example of the problem of a community authority assuming the role of research authority comes again from my Smith Island re-study. Recall that I first entered the community through a non-islander who held a leadership role with the Smith Island Cultural Center, an organization dedicated to preserving the island's cultural heritage through such efforts as running an island museum, organizing events highlighting island activities such as boat races and dinners composed of traditional island foods, and, yes, assisting researchers. My contact was eager to help me by introducing me to islanders and even went so far as to arrange a couple of initial interviews for me, for which I was deeply grateful. However, she took things a bit farther, and this led to a bit of awkwardness. In addition to providing me with introductions and contacts, she also decided to provide me with a tape recorder, microphone, and a quiet, nearly empty room in the Cultural Center in which to conduct my interviews, with me seated on one side of a table, the interviewee on the other side, and the tape recorder sitting prominently in the middle. Clearly, she had interpreted "interview" in the way that most non-sociolinguists would, and she arranged for a formal setting for what she perceived to be a formal event. Unfortunately, the setting was not conducive at all to a successful *sociolinguistic* interview: The Center consisted of a fairly new, stylishly designed building housing a small museum, and it contrasted sharply with the older houses, small businesses, and gathering places that stood nearby. In addition, the Center was visited chiefly by tourists rather than islanders, and it was not a natural place for island residents to come to have relaxed conversations. Further, there were a host of practical issues: the Center was an echoing wooden building with terrible acoustics, and the tape recorder and microphone the director offered fell far short of the specifications needed to obtain the high-quality audio recordings necessary for sociolinguistic analysis.

So what did I do? I first and foremost profusely thanked the director for her help, and then proceeded to politely inform her that I had brought my own recording equipment with me but would certainly keep hers in mind, if a back up was needed. In addition, I did indeed conduct my first couple interviews in the Center, though in an open area that was far more welcoming than the little room that she had set aside. Later, my students and I also conducted interviews outside the Center, on the steps or porch, a location that offered somewhat better acoustics – except for noise from passersby, birds, and the occasional auto – and improved upon our interviewees' comfort, since the periphery of the Cultural Center served as a sort of liminal space between residents' own territory and that associated with the outside world.

The other main problem with making your way into the community through official channels is one we have already mentioned: unless you are careful, you may become enmeshed in leaders' social networks, which may be viewed as "other" by the majority of community members. In addition, communities are not monolithic, and there are often different subcommunities, or perhaps even rival factions, with different leaders. If you enter the community through one leader, you may find yourself limited to only one subcommunity, especially if relationships among the various subgroups are strained or hostile. Accidentally associating yourself with one faction can be a particular danger if you do not know ahead of time that different factions exist.

This is exactly what happened to us in Robeson County. We knew going in that there were sharp divisions among the three local ethnic groups, the Whites, Blacks, and Lumbee Indians. However, we did not know until we had been working with the Lumbee for some time that there were factions within the Lumbee community – factions divided over issues such as who "counts" as "real Lumbee" and how best to work with dominant (White) society to achieve full Federal recognition (still unfortunately an elusive goal for the Lumbee). Fortunately for us, by the time we realized that there were different Lumbee subgroups, with quite different opinions, we had met such a variety of people, including recognized officials, unofficial community leaders, well-liked individuals, and people who simply kept to themselves and did not care about political questions, that we were not relegated to one "camp" or the other. And we were lucky to find several participants whose orientations and connections helped us navigate internal group boundaries. One of our initial contacts, the tribal elder mentioned above, seemed to transcend intra-Lumbee dividing lines and was respected by all. Another of our key contacts was so well connected among the Lumbee through friendship and family ties that, once we had befriended him, we were able to obtain numerous research participants simply by mentioning his name. Indeed, even a recalcitrant interviewee who had hung up on us when we "cold called" her subsequently gave us a very friendly welcome into her home when our well-connected friend called her and told her we were coming over to record her.

The risk of being funneled into one particular network is not confined to researchers who enter the community through officials. It is an ever-present danger for any fieldworker, since it is very natural to make new acquaintances via old ones, whether your initial contacts are community leaders or "regular citizens." Thus, in entering the community, you need a plan for systematically and sensitively stepping outside the networks of your initial contacts (unless, again, your goal is to research only a single social network rather than a community comprising multiple networks). Sometimes, too, stepping outside your initial network of contacts can result in surprising new directions for your research, as Cala Zubair found when she ventured outside the group of Sri Lankan English majors and began to interact with the Raggers, who became the center of her research.

All in all, in thinking about who to approach when entering the community, in my experience there is no single "best" type of initial contact. Anyone can help you, from titled officials to unofficial leaders to those with many connections to those who keep to themselves. The key is to recognize that different communities call for different approaches; and no matter who helps you out initially, you will almost always want to move beyond their immediate social circles to achieve a more representative sample of the various subgroups that make up your community of study.

5.2   FINDING PARTICIPANTS

Once you have made your initial entry in the community, you will need to branch out and find study participants. Sometimes this will be accomplished by seeking people who fit various social categories you have determined to be important in the community and relevant to your study purposes (e.g. people of different age, socioeconomic and gender groups). At other times, you may be more interested in the interrelation between linguistic and social meaning across local social networks and communities of practice that you can only uncover as your research proceeds. Regardless of whether you have opted for a judgment sample or a more network-based approach, one of the best methods for finding study participants is the tried and true "friend of a friend" or "snowball" technique made famous by Milroy and Milroy in their studies of Belfast in the late 1970s–early 1980s and subsequently utilized in countless studies to great effect. Clearly, if you are interested in who interacts with whom, it makes sense to let each participant guide you to the next one, for example by asking questions about local networks in the course of your interview (e.g. "Who are some of your neighbors?"; "Who are some of the guys you hang around with?") or asking each participant if they know anyone else who might be willing to participate in the study. However, there is nothing to preclude your also using a snowball technique to fill the cells in a judgment sample, since you can also tell participants you would like to talk with people who meet various social criteria. (For instance, you could ask an elderly man if he has any children or grandchildren who might take part in your study, or you could ask a woman if she knows any men who might be participants, perhaps a spouse or other male relative.)

The multifaceted value of the snowball technique and the "friend-of-a-friend" role in which this approach casts you is discussed in detail by Leslie Milroy and her colleagues (L. Milroy 1980; Milroy and Gordon 2003), and we will not repeat everything here but will reinforce a few key points. Making contacts as a friend of a friend in the research setting works so well because it is a natural and important role in everyday life: we all feel more comfortable meeting people with whom we share an acquaintance or friend than we do meeting complete strangers, and often instant trust is conferred upon a new acquaintance when we know they are friends with a person we already know and trust. At the same time, being a friend of a friend involves "reciprocal rights and obligation" (Milroy and Gordon 2003: 75), and once you are accepted into a community as a friend of a friend, you will be expected to give something in return for people's trust. Friends of friends are expected to help one another, whether through providing goods and services such as small gifts, transportation, or lending a sympathetic ear (Labov 1984), or, in the case of the sociolinguistic researcher, using one's expertise to provide language-related help to the community. Such help can be relatively minor; for example, creating an amusing dictionary of dialect lexical items (Locklear, Wolfram, Schilling-Estes, and Dannenberg 1996), or quite major, such as assisting in a court case involving language or dialect discrimination, as in the Ann Arbor case of the 1970s (Labov 2001a). (See Chapter 7 for more on sociolinguists returning linguistic favors to the community.) In the course of my studies, I and my colleagues have engaged in a range of activities in our "friends of friends" capacity, from simply being active listeners during interviews to giving community members our business (e.g. by staying in locally owned hotels and eating at locally owned restaurants), to developing and conducting dialect awareness curricula for local schoolchildren (again, see Chapter 7 for more details). And while it is vital for beginning researchers to realize their obligation to the research participants who let them into their lives, it is also important to bear in mind that very often what is most important is simply being there as a new friend.

As personally and professionally rewarding as working your way through a community as a friend of a friend can be, we should stress again that if your goal is to obtain a picture of language and social life in the community in general, you will need to ensure that you do not get so enmeshed in any one network that you forget about other groups or find yourself unable to enter them. It is easy to get caught up in a single network. As we heard from Eckert in Chapter 3, once you get to know people, you develop "social desire" (2000: 76–77), and you find yourself not only needing to be accepted for research purposes but wanting to be liked as a friend. Once you have made your way into one friendship network, you feel comfortable, and it becomes difficult to move beyond this network and begin all over again the awkward process of introducing yourself to strangers and hoping that they too will accept you. In order to guard against the very natural tendency to let yourself stay in a comfortable place and thereby obtaining a skewed sample, it is useful to follow Eckert's lead and devise a means of ensuring that you will move between networks *before* you get comfortable with any of them, for example by constructing in advance a random sample of community members and periodically returning to this list to enter new networks.

Of course, you can guard even further against the "silo effect" of the social network (Eckert 2000: 77) by attempting to fill your quota with participants drawn solely from a random list or by opportunity. If you adopt the latter approach, you will need to find good methods and good locations for recruiting participants. In my own and my students' experience, we have learned that finding people who are willing to listen to your introduction and subsequently agree to participate in your project is much easier in areas where people are not too busy, where they are sitting and not in motion, and where they are not already actively engaged in talk. Hence, for example, it will likely be more fruitful to approach someone relaxing on their front porch than walking purposefully down the street, or people who are sitting companionably together on park bench rather than a couple engaged in earnest conversation in a restaurant. Another method is to encourage participants to seek you out, perhaps by posting or distributing recruitment flyers, or situating yourself at a table in a community gathering place with a sign inviting people to approach and learn about your study.

But relying solely on fortuitous circumstances or on random samples has its difficulties. Though you may achieve a more representative sample of the community this way, since you are not limited to any particular network or group, your relations with participants are likely to be a good deal less comfortable at first. You will be a stranger to everyone you encounter, and you will need to re-introduce yourself repeatedly, as well as spend a lot of time gaining the trust of each new participant. Further, it can be quite unnatural *not* to let participants introduce you to their friends, especially in a small community. Indeed, refusing recommendations for study participants could prove detrimental to your relations with the community. Many sociolinguistic researchers, myself included, have learned that often we have to interview people who do not fit our study criteria (e.g. non-natives to the community), acknowledging to ourselves that any time "wasted" in conducting these extraneous interviews is really time well invested in maintaining good community relations.

5.3 THE ROLE OF THE FIELDWORKER

5.3.1 The role of the fieldworker in the community ▬▬▬▬▬▬▬

As you enter the community, you cast yourself and are cast by others into a particular role. There are a couple different aspects to your role in the community. The first concerns your **level of involvement**. We have already discussed this to an extent in Chapter 3, in our discussion of whether or not you will choose to be a participant-observer or, to the extent that it is even possible, more of an "objective" outside observer. Beyond that, we discussed different forms of participation, ranging from the complete participation that is usually reserved for longtime members of the community, to more marginal forms of participation that you will more likely have access to as an outsider-researcher. In addition to your role in a **research** sense, there is the question of how involved you will be in a more **humanistic** sense – in giving back to the community. We will discuss this more fully in Chapter 7, but for now we can simply mention a few different levels of humanistic involvement outlined in Cameron *et al.* (1993): ethics, advocacy, and empowerment. Every researcher must at least be ethical in their dealings with research participants, and some researchers (though not many sociolinguists) maintain that an ethical yet relatively detached stance is best, so that you affect the community as little as possible; and when you are finished with your research community, you should aim to leave it in largely the same state in which you found it. Increasingly, though, sociolinguists are following other social scientists in realizing that human researchers cannot help but impact their human subjects, to some degree or other. Therefore, it is best to actively seek a positive impact, whether in ways that help the community (advocacy), or in ways that help the community help themselves (empowerment). So, for example, in conducting research on African Americans of lower socio-economic status in a large US city, I could plan simply to conduct observations and interviews in an ethical manner, serving briefly as a sympathetic ear to those from whom I learn and gather data. Or I could add an advocacy component to my community involvement and intervene on behalf of the community where issues of dialect discrimination come into play, perhaps by teaching schoolchildren about the regular patterning of dialect differences (e.g. Wolfram, Adger, and Christian 1999) or exposing dialect-related housing discrimination (e.g. Baugh 2003). And I could go a step further and work with community members to equip them to actively combat dialect discrimination, perhaps by training teachers and speech pathologists to distinguish legitimate dialect differences from deficits in language development (Adger and Schilling-Estes 2003; Wolfram, Adger, and Christian 1999). We will have more to say on ways the researcher can give back to the community in Chapter 7, but for now you should at least consider that your research and human involvement with the community can take myriad forms and that objective detachment is not always best and probably not even possible.

Another aspect of your role in the community has to do with **who you are**. As discussed above, your sociolinguistic research will almost inevitably involve an ethnographic component. Hence, your goal is to take on a dual role as an outside observer and inside participant – and somehow figure out the right balance between the two. You may worry about how you will ever manage to work your way into a community, but if you can begin as a **friend of a friend**, you might find it much easier than you had imagined. When you enter the community in this manner, most community members will put your "friend" role at the forefront, often even forgetting about your "researcher" role. And while you certainly do not want your researcher status to get in the way of good community relations or good language data, the ethical researcher should realize that there is also a risky aspect to gaining instant trust. A crucial aspect of conducting ethical research involves obtaining from community members informed consent to participate in your research project. Indeed, Informed Consent Forms are usually mandated by IRBs. However, when people forget you are researching them, it is no longer clear whether their "informed" consent is still actually informed or not. If you sense that your researcher role has receded too far and participants begin revealing information that is too personal, or potentially damaging to themselves or others, you may even have to consider whether you should publish your research proceedings. This is particularly troubling if the potentially harmful information is audio recorded. For this reason, researchers often include a clause in their Informed Consent Forms informing research participants that they have the right to rescind part or all of their data, at any point during the study or thereafter. In addition, researchers may choose to stop an audio recording in progress if they sense that the informant is beginning to reveal things they will regret later, or at least remind the informant at the end of the interview of what they said and ask them if they still want their entire conversation to be on record.

The researchers in Milroy and Milroy's Belfast project faced the issue of having their role as friends supersede their researcher roles. This was especially clear in the comfortable speech of group conversations, whose participants would often enter after recording had begun – thereby rendering it questionable whether they even realized they were being recorded. The researchers adopted the policy of overtly stating that recording was beginning at the outset of each recording session but did not interrupt recordings each time someone new came in. However, they always kept their (then much more obtrusive) recording equipment in plain sight and had a standing agreement that they would erase any material from the recordings that participants wished. Nonetheless, participant comfort level remained extremely high, and indeed, as Milroy and Gordon note, most often it was the researchers rather than community members who erased recorded information due to discomfort (2003: 81–83).

STUDENTS IN THE FIELD

On the opposite end of the spectrum from having your role of outside research fade too far into the background, sometimes no matter what we do, we simply cannot shake off our "outsider" status. In her study of Indexicality and Sociolocation in a Bangladeshi Market, Jen McFadden (2011) knew from the outset that she as a White middle-class female student from the US would enter the community as an obvious outsider. However, she was not quite so prepared for her outsider status to remain as prominent or to last as long as it did (the entire duration of her study, really), or for the enormous impact her role as a foreign, even "exotic," researcher had on her data and her study. She collected most of her data in the marketplace of one neighborhood in Dhaka, Rajabajar, spending much of her time recording interactions in the dry goods shop of her key contact in the community, Shah Alom. No matter how much time she spent in the shop, she found that people spoke inordinately frequently to or about her rather than about "natural, everyday" matters. After quite some time, Jen finally realized that the "unnatural" interactions she was recording were actually quite valuable data that would lead to important insights about linguistic meanings and social understandings. In other words, rather than continuing to fight her obtrusiveness and perpetual outsider status, she learned to embrace it as she gathered and analyzed her data rather than discount her role in the research process. As she puts it, "The interactions that I had with Bengalis *were* authentic. They were unusual, but they were authentic. And once I realized that similar semiotic principles were at work [in her interactions with Bengalis and their interactions with each other], I began to value and even prize my data: hours and hours of conversation between a *bideshi* 'foreigner' and the native informants to whom that foreigner was socially and semiotically accountable." Jen also notes that whereas she was never unobtrusive in the Rajabajar community, she was in the long run warmly embraced and became quite close to Shah Alom and a number of other vendors and patrons of the marketplace where she had spent so much time.[1]

Along with the trust you gain as a friend of a friend (and increased responsibility to maintain ethicality) is a **lessening of the power asymmetry** that inheres in the relationship between the researcher, usually someone with an advanced education who is affiliated with an authoritative research institution, and the community, whose members are often rather far removed from mainstream power structures. Beginning with Labov's earliest works, sociolinguistic researchers have recognized and sought to minimize potential power differences between themselves and their research participants both for humanistic, ethical reasons and for the purpose of obtaining more natural, relaxed language data. Labov (1984) and others have stressed that, in addition to highlighting your role as "friend," one of the best ways to minimize power differences is to **foreground your role as a learner** rather than expert. This can be done at every step of the research project, from how you introduce yourself to the community and to each new research participant, to how you design, frame, and conduct your sociolinguistic interviews (see Section 5.3.2 below), to how you comport yourself in the community in general, sometimes involving very simple matters. For example, sometimes simply dressing differently or carrying your equipment and paperwork in a less obtrusive way can make you seem much less like an expert researcher and more like a potential new friend who just wants to learn about people. At one point in our research in Ocracoke, we needed to re-visit people we had already interviewed, in order to see if they would agree to be part of a documentary on language variation that we wished to produce. Volunteers were required to sign a quite legalistic permission form. Most of the research team fared very well and managed to secure willing permissions from nearly everyone. However, one researcher reported that he was sometimes met with suspicion and resistance. We soon realized that this was simply because he was dressed too "formally" – his carefully ironed and neatly tailored clothes were out of place in this community, and he carried his paperwork in an official-looking briefcase rather than in a casual shoulder bag or a dog-eared folder, like the

[1] Note that Shah Alom is not a pseudonym; Jen McFadden's research participants wished for their real names to be used in write-ups and discussions of her research project, and I here follow her in honoring this request.

rest of us. Appearance matters in the field – right down to the recording equipment itself, as I learned in this and subsequent research projects. I had gone out of my way to purchase protective cases for my expensive recording equipment, but the cases drew attention to themselves and made my equipment seem terribly "high-tech." I soon switched to carrying my tape recorder, tapes, etc., in a nondescript shoulder bag padded with clothing or towels, so that I could preserve my status as a friend and student in addition to protecting my expensive equipment.

Altering your appearance or comportment to conform to community norms is not always a simple matter and can raise sticky ethical questions. Above, I stressed that honesty in your relationship with the community has to take precedence over attempts to fit in, but sometimes in order to fit in you may feel the need – or even be required – to change yourself in ways that feel unnatural or perhaps even wrong to you. You may feel like you are putting on a role that is not "you" – participating in activities that you would not normally take part in, or appearing to conform to beliefs and values you do not really hold (or to which you may even be opposed). Behaving in ways that are not typical for you may be easy in some circumstances and difficult in others, and you may be surprised to find yourself wrestling with choices that at first seemed fairly minor. For example, altering your dress is usually a simple matter, but sometimes even this can feel alien and even wrong. Janet Fuller (1997), in her fieldwork in two Mennonite communities in South Carolina, had to wear conservative dresses in order to conform to the communities' very traditional gender roles. In one sense, this was a straightforward matter of changing clothes before entering the field – but at the same time, it was very difficult for Fuller, a progressive feminist, to adopt an appearance that, for her, represented women's traditional subjugation. On the other side of the coin, some researchers have had to pretend to be *less* conservative than they really are. For example, an important bonding activity in Ocracoke was going to the local pub to socialize and drink beer. And while this felt natural and comfortable to most members of the fieldwork team, the team leader, Walt Wolfram, felt quite awkward socializing in this setting because he did not normally drink or hang out in bars. But he recognized that his participation in this activity was an important part of his integration into local social networks – and he did not want to risk appearing too uptight or too "good" for the local community. Plus, he found that it was easy to hang out at the pub without actually having to imbibe, since he was so jovial that no one noticed whether he was drinking or not.

STUDENTS IN THE FIELD

Mark Watson conducted a fascinating study of similarities and differences in Cuban Spanish as spoken in Cuba vs. Miami, Florida, focusing in particular on lexical recognition and language attitudes (Watson 2006). Because he had strong ties to a family in Cuba – and because he can speak Cuban Spanish like a native even though he is a native English speaker – he did not find it too difficult to integrate himself into local networks in Cuba. However, actually obtaining consent to conduct and record interviews was a bit more of a challenge, because unfortunately people in Cuba have to be wary even of their neighbors, since everyone is technically obligated by the government to report any "anti-communist" activity they observe. Luckily, Watson found an easy fix for this seemingly insurmountable problem; as he put it, "If you give food and alcohol, you get a line out the door" of people willingly offering themselves as research participants. In many (probably most) cultures, sharing food and drink is a tremendously important bonding experience, and this is no different in the research context. As Watson found, sometimes the researcher has to be the one doing the offering. Conversely, in Jackie Lou's Chinatown study, she was the recipient of the community's hospitality. Often, too, the exchange is mutual, as in the Ocracoke pub, where everyone joins together to enjoy drinking with friends.

Even more difficult than deciding whether or not to alter your appearance or activities is the issue of what to do if you are directly questioned about deep-seated beliefs (e.g. religion, human rights, politics), and your beliefs do not conform to those of the community, or at least the individual who is asking. There is no one "right" answer to this question, and each researcher will have to find their own solution and to discover for themselves a comfortable balance between being true to themselves and fitting into the community. My colleagues and I have found it helpful to remember that our dual role as both outsiders and insiders gives us some flexibility. It is often possible to give polite yet noncommittal responses to uncomfortable questions; and sometimes, depending on the individuals and cultural views involved, we have engaged in lively yet respectful (and often enjoyable) debates.

We have to remember that our relationships in the research setting are still *human* relationships; and dealing with people whose beliefs and actions do not conform to our own is a part of our everyday lives in addition to our research lives. In other words, we already have ways of handling interactions with such people, and our usual comportment may carry over just fine into the research setting. In my case, I am not a confrontational person, and I tend to adopt a noncommittal stance in both research and "real-life" settings when faced with questions about potentially charged subjects such as politics and religion, so that no one knows my real views, nor do I directly challenge anyone else's. Once when I was fairly directly asked by a Lumbee Indian in Robeson County if I was a "born again" Christian (she asked me, "Have you been saved?"), I replied with a question to her: "That's very important to you, isn't it?" She proceeded to answer my question at great length, and our friendly relations continued unimpeded. Indeed, in both my research and non-research life, I have found that answering a question with a question is a good strategy to use when confronted with uncomfortable queries: it "protects" me and at the same time affords people an opportunity to talk more about themselves, a natural propensity (in some cultures, at least) that fieldworkers can use to the mutual advantage of both researcher and research participant.

But others may have fewer qualms about challenging people. In another community in which my colleagues and I conducted research, one of the student researchers was a fervent proponent of recycling. At the time of our research, the community had no recycling facilities, since this was not yet an important issue for them. Most of the fieldwork team conceded to local norms and regretfully threw away recyclable materials rather than confront community residents with the issue. However, this student insisted on carrying all of his (and many of our) recyclables home with him, and was happy to tell local residents what he was doing and why – and to urge them to initiate recycling efforts of their own. His efforts had not met with success by the time we concluded the data-gathering phase of our project, but by the same token, he had not angered or alienated anyone. Indeed, he was a source of amusement to community residents who thought he was a bit crazy for lugging used bottles, cans, and bags home with him.

Sometimes, though, the differences between our views and those of our research communities can be grave ones. We have had potential researchers refuse to work in communities they viewed as too sexist or racist for them to tolerate. And on occasion, we have sadly learned that the people we want to research simply will not tolerate us – not just because of aspects of ourselves that we could change or adjust, but because of characteristics that are fundamentally inalterable. For example, in one tri-ethnic community we studied, we learned that African American male researchers were regarded with suspicion and even hostility when they visited predominantly White and Indian neighborhoods. In what I regard as a very sage move, the leader of our fieldwork team, Walt Wolfram, discussed the situation with the fieldworkers involved and told them that it was their choice whether they wished to continue trying to work in these neighborhoods. He stressed that he would support them regardless of any hindrance their presence might be to the research project. The fieldworkers actually chose to shift their focus to predominantly African American neighborhoods, but I too would have supported their continued efforts with the other ethnic groups, as I would to this day, in my position as a director of the Language and Communication in Washington DC project, situated in another multiethnic area.

Interestingly, it was not only these fieldworkers' ethnicity that made some community members uncomfortable but also their sex. We have found over the years, along with researchers in quite different communities (e.g. Milroy and Milroy in Belfast), that in much of the Western world women are more trusted as fieldworkers, probably because they are viewed as less threatening than men. Age, too, can work for or against you, sometimes in unexpected ways. For example, in beginning her research with adolescents, Eckert suspected that her adult status would be difficult to overcome as she worked to earn the trust of the teenagers she wanted to study. But she found that her age was actually an asset in the field, since she represented to the teens a very different kind of adult: one who would listen to them rather than simply tell them what to do (and what not to do). She describes the unique relationship of the adult ethnographer–sociolinguist to younger research participants thus:

> if adult status can pose problems for the researcher, it can also provide an opportunity, because to the extent that kids are locked into power asymmetries with adults, many are starved for new kinds of relationships with adults. Most of kids' waking hours are spent in school, and since they are generally excluded from the workplace and other adult spheres, they have few opportunities to develop more equal relationships with adults. An ethnographer has the opportunity to offer another kind of relationship, as someone who is interested in kids on their own terms, wants to listen to them, does not want to change them, and is not part of the local authority structure (Eckert 2000: 71).

In addition to race, sex, and age, other aspects of yourself that you cannot alter during the course of a fieldwork project include disabled or non-disabled status, native vs. non-native linguistic competence, and audiological status. And these matters, too, can have a profound impact on access, trust, and the amount and quality of your data. For example, Lucas, Bailey, and Valli note in their groundbreaking work on Sociolinguistic Variation in American Sign Language that Deaf ASL signers are very sensitive to the audiological and ethnic status of their interlocutors, and they will radically adjust their signing to bring it closer to what they believe to be the preference of their interlocutor (2001: 39–40). In communicating with a hearing person, they may switch rapidly between ASL and signed English. Researcher effects on ASL are compounded by the fact that, in Lucas *et al.*'s words, "The study of sign languages requires more intrusive methods of observation than the study of spoken languages. That is, video cameras and the small size of many closely knit Deaf communities magnifies the effects of the Observer's Paradox" (2001: 49–50). A further complication is that, despite increasing awareness of and respect for the linguistic value and cultural worth of ASL and other signed languages, many potential study participants still hold quite different beliefs and feel that the patterned variation that is found in ASL, as in all natural languages, is merely "lazy" signing (p. 39). Lucas and her colleagues worked to minimize researcher effects in their study of Deaf communities in seven sites across the US by entering these communities through respected contact persons, videotaping groups with no research present, and matching interviewees with deaf interviewers of like ethnicity.

STUDENTS IN THE FIELD

In conducting a study of language and identity among people with visible, mobility-related disabilities in the Washington, DC, area, Leslie Cochrane, an able-bodied researcher, sought to gain the acceptance of research participants by adopting a slightly different role than we have so far advocated. We have been stressing that researchers should stress their role as "learners." In Leslie's case, however, she entered the community as one of the "wise" – Goffman's (1963) term for someone who does not belong to a (stigmatized) group but has become personally or professionally identified with it. Leslie's identifications came from her close friendship with a person with a physical disability. In initiating contacts with strangers as well as when conducting recordings, she deliberately talked about her friend (with her permission), thereby demonstrating her own personal knowledge of and experience with physical disabilities. Leslie further gained people's trust by introducing topics and vocabulary that also indicated familiarity with disability. Despite her "wise" status, however, Leslie nonetheless positioned herself as a student with a lot to learn. Her study reminds us that, while we need to be open-minded learners when entering a community, it also pays to "do our homework" prior to engaging in fieldwork – an issue noted in Chapter 2, where we discussed in detail the fieldwork planning stages.

Other student projects illustrate the effects of level of linguistic competence in the language of the community of study. For example, Sheena Shah conducted interviews with Gujarati heritage language learners in Gujarati communities in the UK, Singapore, and South Africa. She reported that "Speaking the language helped a ton (and also being a heritage speaker did too – as the participants could identify more easily with me)." Conversely, Jen McFadden experienced a somewhat opposite effect in her studies in Bangladesh. Although she found it frustrating to have limited competence in Bangla, she also found that one of the reasons people were willing to participate in her project was because they were quite pleased that a foreigner was making such an effort to speak their language and wanted to help her learn. And sociolinguists must be concerned not only with linguistic competence but also (perhaps especially) communicative competence, as Cala Zubair found when she tried to interview her Sri Lankan Ragger informants in Sinhala and they responded in English.

We see, then, that earning community trust is not a simple matter of being like or acting like members of the community of study, whether demographically, behaviorally, or ideologically. Often, likeness works in your favor, but there are many situations in which difference does not pose a problem or can even be capitalized upon, for example when community members go out of their way to help a hapless young outsider to learn their ways (and maybe even their language).

We noted above that along with earning community trust comes the assumption of increased responsibility. As Eckert notes in reference to her work with students:

> I have been surprised by the relative unimportance of age differences in my work both in Belten High and in my current work with even elementary school kids. I have been both pleased (for myself) and dismayed (for the kids) by the swiftness with which even the most skeptical ones have told me things that could have been extremely damaging to them (2000: 71–72).

In other words, the relationships we form with research participants can be richly rewarding, but they also carry the potential to be hurtful, much like our close relationships in our non-research lives. Conversely, to conclude this section on a very practical note, members of the community we are researching can be harmful to us, and not only emotionally or in terms of our research careers (e.g. people may reject our advances and refuse to participate in our study), but, quite frankly, physically as well. Some communities and neighborhoods are dangerous, and you may not even know where potential trouble spots are if you are a stranger to the area or the culture. Thus, while I wrote above in favor of allowing members of my research team in Washington to conduct research in whatever neighborhoods they want, regardless of potential difficulties, I really have to add a caveat to that statement: Washington, DC, is a large US city, and it is dangerous. I always caution students conducting research here to be aware of this unfortunate fact, and to look out for their safety in addition to exciting new research material when setting out on their fieldwork adventures.

5.3.2 The role of the fieldworker in the interview ▬▬▬▬▬▬▬▬▬

We have just discussed how to find the right role for yourself in the
research community, in terms of your level of involvement with the
community, how you present yourself to the community, and how
the community responds to who you are. It also is important to think
specifically about your role in more specific fieldwork tasks, especially
the research interview. As with the researcher–researched relationship
more generally, the interviewer–interviewee relationship entails power
asymmetries that we need to work against if we hope to establish good
relations with our participants and obtain relaxed speech data. In a
typical interview, the interviewer controls the event, asking questions
and directing the flow of talk. The sociolinguistic interview, in contrast,
is designed to limit the interviewer's control and to maximize the
interviewee's. It is composed of questions designed to prompt the interviewee to take over the conversation, going off on tangents and producing lengthy narratives. In addition, interviewers are taught to ask open-
ended questions, to follow up on topics interviewees seem particularly
interested in (and letting other topics drop), and in general to give
interviewees plenty of space to elaborate on tangents and narratives
rather than adhering to a strict interview schedule. For example, in
(5.4) Wolfram and Fasold cite the exchange, from a sociolinguistic
interview conducted as part of Shuy, Wolfram, and Riley's (1968)
groundbreaking sociolinguistic study of Detroit, Michican, as a good
example of an interviewer following up on the interviewee's interests:

(5.4)

Fieldworker:	Do you play marbles?
Informant:	Yes, I have 197 marbles right now.
Fieldworker:	Oh, tell me about them. How'd you get them? What are the different ones called?
	(Shuy, Wolfram, and Riley 1968: 117; cited in Wolfram and Fasold 1974: 51)

Conversely, in (5.5) they provide an example where an interviewer let
slip a good opportunity for extended talk by not following up when
they could have:

(5.5)

Fieldworker:	Did you ever play hide and seek?
Informant:	Yes, I played that a lot.
Fieldworker:	What other games did you play?
	(Shuy, Wolfram, and Riley 1968: 118; cited in Wolfram and Fasold 1974: 52)

Some researchers (e.g. Milroy and Gordon 2003; Wolfson 1976) have suggested that reversing the roles associated with the typical interview, by allowing the interviewee to take control from the interviewer, may not always work very well, since people who are not sociolinguists come to the interview with pre-set notions about what the "interview" speech event is supposed to be like, and sociolinguists who attempt to alter this frame and let the interviewee take control may be met with confusion or even anger. For example, Wolfson (1976: 196) reports on an interview in which the interviewer attempted to elicit some narratives by telling a story of his own. The interviewee, rather than respond with another narrative, tried to bring the interview back on track – to put the interviewer back into his "proper" role as questioner by interrupting with the exchange in (5.6):

(5.6)

Subj:	"Now what's the story?"
Int:	"What's the story?"
Subj:	"Yeah, what type questions – are you all set up now?"
Int:	"Well, we'll continue with what we've got. Well, I've just got some more, you know."

However, most of us find that our efforts to minimize our control over our interviews are generally met with success. This is especially true when the person we are interviewing has some sort of power over us, by virtue of their social status. Hence, older people and men will often more readily take control of the interview situation than younger people and women. However, as Eckert found in her high school and elementary school studies and I have found in communities as diverse as Smith Island and Washington, DC, even teenagers and children can take over when talking with adult interviewers. Every interviewee, no matter what their social position relative to the interviewer, holds power in the sense that they hold the knowledge about themselves and their communities that we are seeking. Successful fieldworkers will continually strive to emphasize their role as learner and the role of the research participant as expert.

Interviewees can also exert power by taking over what is often considered to be the powerful discourse role – namely, that of questioner. And when interviewees do turn the tables and start asking questions of us, we may find that not only is their interactional power heightened, but so is the relaxedness of their speech, since increased control can lead to increased comfort. Consider the excerpts in (5.7) and (5.8) below, drawn from the last ten minutes of an interview with an 18-year-old Ocracoke male, "Billy," conducted in 1993 by a graduate student at North Carolina State University, "Charlie." In the first excerpt, Charlie is clearly in the role of questioner, while Billy is the answerer. In the second one, Billy takes over as questioner and begins asking Charlie why he is interviewing people in the first place. In each excerpt, questions are in bold.

(5.7)

C: **You have, uh, you see many people come through doing what I'm doing?**
B: Mmmm...
C: **Talking about speech?**
B: Once in a while. Most of 'em come here through the school ... come down here for the school, to have a ... to have a program about it and everything. It ain't- ain't very often many people come down here.
C: **Did you have one of them, programs?**
B: Yeah, I had a ... We had two people coming in when I was in school.
C: **What'd they tell you?**
B: Uh, just they're down here, you know, wanted to- mostly basically teaching us how to make things that ... somebody from somewheres else made or something, you know? Just ... trying to get our accent down. They made a movie ... Can't remember the name of it, made a movie ... based on- on Ocracoke? And they showed like two or three scenes of Ocracoke, they was supposed to be living on the Outer Banks or something but ... they come down here and got a real whole lot of time for dialect and everything.

(5.8)

B: **So wait. Is this like ... school project, right?**
C: Yeah. It's my Master's thesis.
B: **You go any other places besides here or just-**
C: I'm doing here.
B: **Just here? You get to choose, or they assign you?**
C: Well, see ... I- the guy that- my- my boss- my thesis director ... is uh, it's just me and, and, you know, like this thing ... (Searches for project description form) It's uh ... (Whispers: Wow, where the hell is that?) It's um ... Five others of us, we're working on it. We were in a class this semester. Supposed to be a-
B: **Just that list that had them names on it?**
C: Yeah.
B: I think you put a piece of paper over top of it or something.
C: I did?
B: It was right on top, cause you got me to [read it].
C: [That one, yeah.]
B: Yeah, that's it.
C: And, uh, we're working on a class ... with that guy Walt Wolfram. And uh ... this is the- you know, we're pretty much the only people doing this right now, on- you know, here. [We- well, there's one other guy.]

B: [Are there's- there more of you here?]
C: Not now.
B: Oh, okay.
C: Just me.

Impressionistically, Billy's speech in the two excerpts sounds quite similar and fairly relaxed. (Though both participant's contributions may read as rather stilted, they are actually simply talking slowly and calmly). However, a quick quantitative analysis of a single dialect feature, the stopping of the voiced interdental fricative in words like *this* and *those*, in the 10-minute section from which the two excerpts are taken indicates a difference between Billy's "answering" style and his "asking" style. When Billy is in the role of questioner, he has 74% [d] (14/19), including in a brief section where he initiates a couple jokes by asking questions. In contrast, his /θ/-stopping when he is being questioned by Charlie is much lower, at 28% (12/43).

Hence, it can indeed be very productive to try to turn the usual interviewer–interviewee relationship on its head in the sociolinguistic interview, both in terms of stressing the powerful components of the interviewee's social role as expert and encouraging the interviewee to take conversational control in the interview interaction.

However, sociolinguistic interviews can be very individual in character. As we saw above, sometimes interviewers' attempts to relinquish control can backfire, resulting in the interviewee's insistence that the interviewer stop wasting time and return to the questionnaire. Conversely, we have even found that interviewers who *do* stick closely to the interview schedule, despite their training to do otherwise, sometimes still obtain long stretches of interviewee speech – even when they abruptly cut off topics of obvious interest to interviewees in order to make sure they cover all the topics on the questionnaire. One example comes from the interview from which the "hurricane story" in Chapter 4 was drawn. The interview was part of our study of Robeson County, North Carolina: the interviewer is "Alex," a young African American man, and the interviewee is "Felicia," a young African American woman. The interview begins with a lengthy discussion of racial tension, violence, fighting, and drugs in the Robeson County area. Just as Felicia begins talking about the personal impact of drug-related issues in her life, relating a short narrative about two friends who were killed over drugs, the interviewer very abruptly changes the subject to the completely unrelated topic of childhood games (a standard module in the traditional sociolinguistic interview, as discussed in Chapter 3). Rather than show any confusion or annoyance, the interviewee readily switches gears and proceeds to talk about her childhood in a light-hearted tone, cheerfully reminiscing about making "mudcakes" and singing in church. The excerpt in (5.9) illustrates:

(5.9)

A:	Now, um, now the Indians would tell you something different man. They would say drugs in the Indian community is worse than in the Black community.
F:	But I really don't know cause I haven't really been around drugs, drug community. I don't know. I know there are people around here who sell drugs because I just lost two friends in November over drugs.
A:	Really?
F:	One of the guys I mean we was real close we was at a point that we was gonna talk.
A:	Um hm
F:	I mean he wasn't selling drugs he was- his friend- Okay. The guy that he was with, he- his sister pregnant, they were gonna go riding, then another guy, they went with his sister, killed them because of drugs, they went back to his girlfriend house, killed his girlfriend cause she knew too much. All because of drugs.
→A:	**Now I got a question for you, I'm gonna change the subject a little bit.**
F:	Okay.
A:	Um, what kind of games and stuff did you play as a little girl?
F:	Me?
A:	Yeah.
F:	What did I play? Mudcakes, patty cakes.
A:	That is the second time I've heard that: mudcakes.
F:	I don't know I mean, God. I mean mostly I was like in church singing and stuff.
A:	Um hm
F:	I wasn't really really into stuff like that, maybe make a little seesaw outside or something.

Felicia's comfort with whatever topics are raised, no matter how suddenly, is probably due to several factors: For one, she was already acquainted with Alex and his family long before the interview took place. In addition, she probably did not see herself as any less powerful than Alex, since both were of the same age, ethnicity, and approximate socioeconomic class. Further, she simply had a lot to say on many topics, and so it did not bother her to change subjects quickly, in response to Alex's abrupt topic shifts.

Another example, also from Robeson County, comes from an interview between two men of quite similar demographic characteristics: young White men born and raised in North Carolina. "Robby" is the interviewer, and "Johnny" is the interviewee. In this interview, Robby not only switches abruptly from topic to topic, but he also rather "blindly" follows the interview questionnaire, asking all the questions, in exactly the order in which they appear, regardless of whether particular modules are likely to appeal to Johnny, who spends the bulk of his leisure time hunting, fishing, and engaging in other outdoor and social activities typical of young people in his rural community – not philosophizing about life and human relationships. The excerpt in (5.10) shows how Robby cuts short a topic usually of great interest to young people (favorite movies) to ask the "next" question in the interview, even though the question was intended mostly for somewhat older people, or at least those who are married. Nonetheless, Johnny gives a detailed response and seems to be quite interested in the unlikely and sudden new topic.

(5.10)

R:	**How about movies? What's one of your favorite movies?**
J:	I like those action movies, the violence, I guess, I don't know. I like that, uh, Last Boy Scout, and those kind of movies. I like Lethal Weapon and stuff like that.
R:	Gets you right on the edge of your seat.
J:	Yeah, I don't like those old boring movies.
→R:	**What kind of advice would you give to somebody who's getting married?**
J:	I'd just, I'd tell them to, just to make sure you know they're doing the right thing and to uh, I guess always be honest to each other, you know. I guess that's the main thing.
R:	What do you think makes a marriage work?
J:	I guess again honesty would work uh, you know, always be honest to each other, you know. Along with honesty comes you know the faithful part and just make sure you don't take each other for granted I guess. Just always- And don't let it be, you know, even though you start having kids and stuff, you kind of tend to get away from each other, like the husband and wife. I guess always set aside some time for yourself or something.

[Discussion of Marriage and Dating continues.]

Here, too, we attribute Johnny's comfort in producing long stretches of speech to the two participants' very similar characteristics and symmetrical relations. In addition, we must credit another factor we do not have too much control over: while most of us can (and should) effect a non-threatening and pleasant demeanor in the fieldwork situation, and demonstrate interest in what our interviewees have to tell us, some people are simply naturally more personable than others. In this case, the interviewer was a natural at winning friends and getting people to open up to him, in both research and non-research settings.

So while it may not be disastrous to plow forward with your interview schedule exactly as it is laid out, we still advocate being flexible and being sensitive to interviewees' interests. After all, we cannot interview only those who already feel comfortable with us, or only those who will quickly feel at ease. In fact we will usually be interviewing strangers and people with quite different social characteristics and interests than our own. Those of us who are not blessed with a natural gift for encouraging people to talk will probably want to stick with tried and true methods for encouraging interviewee conversation: designing questions to be interesting to interviewees, following up on those questions that yield promising responses, and allowing space for interviewees to elaborate on the things they want to talk about.

In addition, researchers have advocated that interviewers should talk as little as possible in interview interactions, making their questions as short as possible, delivering them fluently, and proffering backchannels visually rather than verbally (e.g. nodding one's head in agreement rather than saying "uh-huh" or "yeah" to indicate active listenership). However, the interview is an exchange, not a one-way street, and most interviewees will feel a lot more like talking (and a lot more like they are participating in a friendly conversation rather than a formal interview) if the interviewer contributes to the conversation, too. It is very natural for both parties in a conversation to contribute equally, and much more natural for both rather than one to ask questions. We should not worry, then, if we sometimes find ourselves talking at length during our interviews – as long as we remember that we cannot take over the conversation. Nor should we fear that an interview has gotten too far out of our hands if the interviewee asks us some questions. Of course, conducting interviews in which both interviewer and interviewee provide relatively equal amounts of talk will be more time-consuming, since we cannot just leave with half as much data from the interviewee as we would have gotten if the interview were more one-sided. Transcribing and analyzing more dyadic conversations may be more time-consuming and possibly somewhat frustrating as well, since our interest is typically the interviewee's speech and not our own. But we are more likely to get the sort of data we really want, since conversational interviews to which all participants contribute equally are more conducive to yielding naturalistic speech. Remember, too, that interviews are always joint productions by all participants, and so we should not focus only on our interviewees anyway, but should also pay attention to our own contributions and how they shape the data, no matter how far we may try to recede into the background.

There are a number of sound and tested methods for designing and conducting sociolinguistic interviews that yield large quantities of naturalistic speech from interviewees. But, at the most basic level, the key to a good sociolinguistic interview is flexibility. We must be prepared to adapt to individual circumstances. This can involve designing different types of interviews and interview questions for different communities; or it can involve conducting sociolinguistic interviews "by the book" or departing from typical methods, when individual relationships and personalities warrant. Adaptability can also involve reversing the power asymmetry that inheres in the "typical" interview by stressing the interviewee's social and interactional power, or it can involve offering our own stories and discussions in exchange for the interviewee's conversational contributions.

We have touched on some researchers' negativity regarding the seeming "unnaturalness" of a speech event that is part interview and part conversation. We should bear in mind, though, that both interviewees and interviewers are quick to frame sociolinguistic interviews as natural speech events of various sorts. In addition, the interview is framed and re-framed as it progresses, so that what might start out feeling like a "formal interview" will shift into a "friendly conversation," perhaps punctuated with various performative events, for example narratives, dialect performances, and soapbox "speeches."

STUDENTS IN THE FIELD

Over the years, I have tried stress to students the importance of maintaining flexibility during the fieldwork process, and we have seen a number of examples of such flexibility in the case studies above. In her work on women's language variation in Japan, Sakiko Kajino was required by a Japanese IRB to amend her interviews to exclude questions about parents' occupations. Jermay Jamsu Reynolds' brother abandoned the interview altogether in favor of recording naturally occurring conversations between him and his fellow villagers in Spearhead, Tibet. Like Jermay, Jen McFadden found it was useless to attempt interviews or prepared topics in the marketplace and instead recorded spontaneous conversations. Many of these interactions centered around *her*, and the resulting data required her to take a slightly different approach to the indexical activity she was interested in. And Cala Zubair altered the entire focus of her research project: she had initially intended to study how Sri Lankan students orient themselves toward and define boundaries between Sinhala and English in relation to government policies, but ended up focusing on one group who orient themselves in total opposition to English and to the students who willingly learn it.

Despite their flexibility, there have been a few regrets as well. For example, Sakiko Kajino determined that her interviews were too long, with a 10-minute warm-up and 30 minutes for each of three different

topic areas, and participants grew tired and untalkative by the end.
Mark Watson felt that despite the relaxed setting for his interviews in
Cuba, the interviews themselves were not open-ended enough, since he
asked a lot of set questions about level of recognition for a number of
vocabulary words, with very little time left for open-ended discussion,
resulting in a dissertation that was more quantitative and less anec-
dotal and personal than he would have liked. Nonetheless, everyone
just mentioned adjusted to the unexpected issues they encountered in
the field and conducted successful research projects, both in terms of
sociolinguistic data and insight gained, and also in terms of establishing and maintaining good community relations.

5.4 SUMMARY

In this chapter, we have explored a host of practical, theoretical,
ethical, and even emotional issues that arise when the researcher
actually enters the field and begins making contacts, finding participants, and gathering data. Throughout, we have stressed that there
really are no "best" strategies for entering and engaging with the
research community. Rather, researchers need to remain sensitive,
open-minded, and flexible, whether in terms of how they introduce
themselves and their projects, who they introduce themselves to first,
how they move beyond their initial contacts to expand their networks,
how they get people to agree to particulate in their studies, and how
they manage to record good data.

There are many ways of making contacts, forging networks, and
engaging people in naturalistic conversation, and sociolinguists should
not be as fearful as we often are that we may not be able to find
research participants who are willing to talk with us, or to us, or to
talk freely and naturally. Indeed, as Labov notes in his classic (1972a)
article on linguistic methodologies, most people are actually very
appreciative when someone takes the initiative to strike up a conversation, and they are even more appreciative when that someone wants to
listen. And while there are many potential trouble spots along the way,
once we sit down to record willing participants, there is actually very
little that the conscientious sociolinguist can do to cause a sociolinguistic interview to go horribly awry. As Walt Wolfram (p.c.) notes, people
in many cultures like to talk about themselves – so much so that many
will pay psychiatrists and psychologists quite a bit of money for an
hour's worth of listening – and they are usually more than happy to
talk to sociolinguists for free.

Suggested readings ▬▬▬▬▬▬▬▬▬▬▬▬▬▬▬▬▬

MILROY, LESLEY 1980. *LANGUAGE AND SOCIAL NETWORKS*. OXFORD: BLACKWELL. See also Milroy and Gordon 2003, Chapters 2 and 5.

In this foundational book, Milroy brings social network analysis and one of its key components, the "friend of a friend," to the study of sociolinguistics. Milroy explains that the friend of a friend (i.e. second-order network contact) plays a key role in social interactions, in social network study, and in sociolinguistic study more generally. Indeed, one of the most effective methods for entering the research community and building one's network of study participants has proven to be the friend-of-a-friend method, in which the researcher makes community contacts by proceeding from initial contacts to their friends, to the friends of these friends, and so on and so on, capitalizing on a natural "snowball" effect. The book also demonstrates the value of social network analysis in offering explanation for patterns of linguistic conservatism and innovativeness. Milroy and Gordon (2003) provides a succinct treatment of the friend-of-a-friend approach to sampling and to social-network-based analyses of language variation and change in relevant sections (e.g. Chapters 2 and 5).

ECKERT, PENELOPE 2000. *LINGUISTIC VARIATION AS SOCIAL PRACTICE*. MALDEN, MA: BLACKWELL. See especially Chapter 3.

In this pathbreaking book, Eckert demonstrates the importance of enriching variation study by incorporating ethnographic understandings of local social groups, practices, and ideologies rather than simply relying on global demographic categories and investigating their correlations with patterns of language variation and change. Of particular interest for our purposes is Chapter 3, in which Eckert presents a detailed and highly personal account of her ethnographic and sociolinguistic study methods. While upholding the value of the friend-of-a-friend method, Eckert cautions that it is in fact a bit too easy to get caught up in a network once one enters it, and if we hope to gain a full picture of a community comprised of more than one network, we need to periodically step outside each social network to find participants in other networks. Eckert also provides invaluable advice on working in the school setting and with adolescents, with whom we must take special care to guard their trust.

LABOV, WILLIAM 1984. FIELD METHODS OF THE PROJECT ON LINGUISTIC CHANGE AND VARIATION. IN JOHN BAUGH AND JOEL

SHERZER (EDS.), *LANGUAGE IN USE*. ENGLEWOOD CLIFFS, NJ: PRENTICE-HALL, 28–53.

In addition to offering a comprehensive view of a range of sociolinguistic field methods, this article also discusses how to make initial contacts in the community. Labov notes that there is no "one-size-fits-all" formula; instead, different channels will be effective in different communities. (For example, it may be easier to enter middle-class communities through people connected with community institutions but to enter working-class communities through unofficial channels, such as people who happen to be socializing outside.) This article also provides timeless advice on the role of the reseacher in the sociolinguistic interview, as researchers are urged to foreground their role as learners and that of their research participants as experts in the ways of the community they have come to study.

CAMERON, DEBORAH, ELIZABETH FRAZER, PENELOPE HARVEY, BEN RAMPTON, AND KAY RICHARDSON (EDS.) 1992. *RESEARCHING LANGUAGE: ISSUES OF POWER AND METHOD*. LONDON: ROUTLEDGE. See especially the Introduction.

In the introduction to this thought-provoking volume focusing on issues of power and ethics in fieldwork in the social sciences, the editors present the convincing argument that, since humans doing research on human subjects cannot help but affect our research participants in some way, we should move beyond maintaining an"objective," detached stance toward active involvement in the community to help achieve positive effects. In particular, the editors argue for moving beyond basic ethical treatment toward a position of advocacy (i.e. working *for* the research community) and, ideally, empowerment (i.e. working *with* communities to help members achieve their own goals). Cameron *et al.*'s principles align with sociolinguistic principles for community involvment, namely Labov's Princple of Error Correction and Principle of the Debt Incurred, and Wolfram's Principle of Linguistic Gratuity.

LUCAS, CEIL, ROBERT BAYLEY, AND CLAYTON VALLI 2001. *SOCIOLINGUISTIC VARIATION IN AMERICAN SIGN LANGUAGE*. WASHINGTON, DC: GALLAUDET UNIVERSITY. See especially Chapter 2.

This groundbreaking work is the first comprehensive study of American Sign Language from a variationist sociolinguistic perspective. The book is fascinating not only in its presentation of the history and current patterning of variation in ASL but also its thoughtful discussion of research methods, including both general issues and those unique to studies of ASL and signed languages. In particular, the authors discuss the impact of researcher demographics on the language data obtained, including sex, age, and especially ethnicity and audiological status, as well as the effects of necessarily more obtrusive (video) recording methods.

6 Recording and record-keeping

There are many steps that lead up to recording language data as part of your sociolinguistic study – conceptualizing and designing the study, conducting background research on and ethnographic observation of the community, making your initial entry into the community, and, finally, getting people to agree to participate in your study. At this point, after going through all the time and effort to set things up so that you can now begin making permanent records of language and communication in your community of study, you need to be confident about making excellent recordings. There are few things more disappointing than returning from a sociolinguistic interview, especially one that seemed to go really well, only to realize that you cannot use it because the sound quality is too poor – or even worse, that you failed to record anything at all. To ensure that this does not happen to you, the first half of this chapter is devoted to a discussion of the technical specifications for recording equipment (based on the unchanging physics of speech, not passing fads in technology) and a summary of recording techniques that have been proven to yield high-quality recordings in the field environment. In the second part of the chapter, we discuss how to organize and store your data and information about your data (metadata) in such a way that you can readily find what you need and analyze it efficiently. Finally, we address issues of data security and privacy protection.

Because this book is focused on sociolinguistic field methods for variationists, Section 6.1 focuses primarily on equipment and techniques for audio recording sociolinguistic interviews. However, we also briefly touch on recording for sociolinguistic surveys via telephone or the Internet, recording stimuli for language attitude and perception tests, recording peer interactions set up by the researcher but with no interviewer present, and recording naturally occurring interactions, including recordings made by the researcher and those made by participants themselves as they go about the course of their daily lives. We will also briefly discuss video recording, though in-depth discussion of specifications and techniques for video recording are beyond the scope of this book.

Section 6.2 presents general guidelines regarding how to store and catalog sociolinguistic interview data and associated metadata, including sociolinguistically relevant information on interview participants and summary information on the quality and content of individual interviews. We also touch on other types of records that you may need to keep track of, including ethnographic field notes, recordings of everyday interactions, and written information on who you meet in the field, including contact information for current and potential participants. We take you step-by-step through the process of planning your systems for storing data and metadata prior to entering the field (including both digital and hard copy records), keeping track of data in the field, and finally, ensuring appropriate access to and security of data once it has been gathered, cataloged, and neatly stored.

While indeed it is necessary for you and members of your research team (and possibly authorized researchers at other institutions) to have ready access to your data, you will need to ensure that access beyond legitimate research purposes is restricted. Occasionally, IRBs (and your own ethical standards) allow access to identifying information from consenting participants when such access is deemed necessary and non-harmful. As a rule, though, you will need to strictly limit (and often prohibit) access to confidential and identifying information stored in your records or on your recordings themselves. Nowadays, many sociolinguistic researchers use online data storage and management systems to ensure easy access by all members of their research team. However, as you should be aware, the Internet is public space unless it is carefully password protected to ensure that the easy accessibility it can afford does not lead to breaches of confidentiality.

6.1 RECORDING EQUIPMENT AND TECHNIQUES

Choosing and correctly using audio and video recording equipment is one of the most daunting yet crucial aspects of conducting sociolinguistic research. In the sections that follow, I present some guidelines for choosing recording equipment and employing it effectively in the field.

6.1.1 Recording equipment

Because technologies change so rapidly, I do not give recommendations for specific equipment but instead present general specifications that digital recording equipment will always have to meet, no matter what form it takes. I also describe a number of recording techniques that have proven to be effective in the field situation. Requirements can be complex, especially for microphones; and it is also very important to appropriately match microphones to recorders. Detailed discussion of all the technicalities involved is well beyond the scope of this book.

Here I first present a summary of some basic specifications, and then provide some general discussion. Recommended sources of more detailed information are given at the end of this chapter.

Box 6.1 Minimum specifications for recording equipment

Your audio recorder should have the following features:

- sampling rate: **44.1 kHz**
- frequency response: **20–20,000 Hz**
- quantization rate (or resolution): **16-bit**
- dynamic range: **30–40 dB**
- recording format: **uncompressed** (e.g. PCM); file type: **WAV or AIFF**

Look for an external microphone that has these features:

- **condenser or electret style**, if field circumstances and budget allow
- **unidirectional (cardioid) or omnidirectional**, depending on field circumstances and application
- frequency response / range: c. **20–20,000 Hz +/– 2 dB**
- if possible, **low impedence (below 600 ohms)**; low impedence microphones usually have a separate balanced XLR cable
- for a high impedance microphone (usually has a built-in cable and ¼ inch (6.33 mm) connector), make sure the cable is less than 5 meters long

AVOID the following:

- recorders using only lossy, compressed formats (e.g. MP3, WMA, QuickTime)
- internal or built-in microphones
- cables that are longer than 5 meters or have unbalanced ¼ inch (6.33 mm) phone jacks
- plug adapters (e.g. ¼ inch (6.33 mm) to ⅛ inch (3.5 mm) or vice versa)

Audio recorders

Nowadays, virtually all audio field recording is conducted using digital recorders. Digital audio recorders offer many advantages over analog recorders (e.g. reel-to-reel tape recorders, cassette tape recorders), one of the most important being that only with digital recordings can one make absolutely perfect copies, with no loss of fidelity (if done correctly). As we will see below, periodically copying your audio files to new media is an essential component of successful long-term data storage.

Digital recordings also allow for a greater dynamic range (i.e. range between quiet and loud sounds) and introduce less noise due strictly to the mechanics of the recording equipment and process. But while analog recorders capture sound in waves, just as it is produced, digital recorders cannot capture continuous waves. They can only "sample" discrete portions of the wave. Sound waves comprise different frequencies (pitches), and a digital recorder must be able to sample portions of these waves rapidly enough that all frequencies relevant to human speech are captured. In addition to capturing many "slices" of the sound wave as it moves through time, digital recorders must be able to approximate the smooth curve of the sound wave on the height axis, enabling the full range of loudness and softness (dynamic range) of human speech to be captured as well. These basic requirements give rise to a couple of basic specifications for audio recorders that will yield sound of the excellent quality needed for sociolinguistic research.

Recording specifications
- sampling rate: 44.1 kHz
- frequency response: 20–20,000 Hz

Sampling rate refers to the number of portions of the sound wave that your recorder will capture in each second of speech. It is expressed in hertz (Hz), meaning "cycles per second," or more commonly kilohertz (kHz), thousands of cycles per second. Research in phonetics and acoustics has established that the range of frequencies young, healthy human ears can hear extends from about 20 to about 20,000 Hz (20 kHz). In order to achieve this **frequency response**, a digital recorder must sample at twice this rate (in order to capture the full periodicity of the wave at each frequency). This is why audio CDs, which have extremely high sound quality, are sampled at 44.1 kHz. The range where useful speech information lies is considerably smaller (ranging from 50 to 8,000 Hz, perhaps up to 10,000 Hz); so sampling at 22 kHz is theoretically adequate for human speech. The only advantage to sampling at the lower rate is that it generates smaller files, enabling you to save storage space on your recorder, storage card, and / or computer hard drive. But digital storage is no longer at the premium that it used to be, and since it is now easy to find audio recorders with sampling rates of 44.1 kHz that are both highly portable and quite inexpensive, there is really no reason to purchase equipment incapable of sampling at the rate of the music CD standard.

- quantization rate: at least 16-bit
- dynamic range: 30–40 dB

Quantization rate refers to the number of values into which the height (amplitude) of the speech sound waveform can be divided during sampling. Higher rates produce a smoother curve that more closely approximates the shape of the actual continuous sound wave, and lower rates provide more jagged signals of lesser fidelity. Quantization introduces quantization noise, an extraneous waveform that is the result of the inevitable difference between the continuous curve of the actual sound wave and the discrete samples of the digital signal, and the higher the quantization rate, the lower the quantization noise level will be. Quantization is basically the same thing as **resolution**, a term you may be more likely to find when researching equipment specifications. The number of **bits** (binary digits) determines how many possible values the height of the waveform can be divided into, since computers store all information as 1s and 0s and all numbers as binary numbers. Further technicalities are not important here; what is important for field recording purposes is that as the number of bits increases, the number of values increases exponentially, so that whereas 8-bit quantization (borderline acceptable but not necessary in this day and age) allows for 256 amplitude values, 16-bit quantization allows for 65,536 values. The only reason you would employ a quantization rate lower than 16-bit would be to save space and, again, this is becoming increasingly unnecessary since digital storage space is now so inexpensive and compact. Another related term you may come across is **bit-rate**, expressed in kilobits per second (kbps). This refers to how many bits are used each second to represent the signal. This can be calculated for uncompressed audio (see below) by multiplying the sampling rate by the quantization rate (or resolution) by the number of channels; hence the bit-rate for sound recorded at a 44.1 kHz sampling rate with 16-bit resolution and two channels would have a bit-rate of 1,411 kbps. An adequate quantization rate ensures that the full **dynamic range** between loud and soft sounds (typically 40 dB) will be captured in the recorded signal.

Technicalities aside, all you have to know when choosing an audio recorder (or adjusting its settings, if applicable) is that you need a **sampling rate of at 44.1 kHz**, and a **quantization rate / resolution of at least 16-bit**, specifications which ensure a **frequency response of 20–20,000 Hz, and an amplitude response of 30–40 dB**. In many ways, selecting and / or setting your audio recorder is like buying and driving a car: you do not have to know how it works, but you do have to ensure that it is built to appropriate specifications for performance and safety, as well as how to adjust its settings (e.g. mirrors, seat placement; sampling rate, quantization rate) prior to driving.

Recording formats In addition to the specifications above, there is one other very important consideration in selecting and using your audio recorder, and this involves ensuring that you can record in **uncompressed audio format**. Uncompressed recordings capture as much of the original signal as possible (given the sampling rate, quantization rate, frequency rate, and dynamic range), with no loss of information. The most common lossless uncompressed format is known as PCM (pulse code modulation), and this is typically used with WAV and AIFF file types. When choosing your recorder, you want to make sure that it will record one of these two file types. WAV is more common and is compatible with acoustic analysis software such as the popular freeware program PRAAT (Boersma and Weenink 2012; Plichta no date). The WAV file type is also compatible with many sound editors and sound file management systems (e.g. iTunes). In short, **recording in the WAV file type is an excellent way to go.**

Compressed formats, on the other hand, are generally "lossy" – which means that they eliminate some redundancies and other elements from the original signal in order to reduce file size. And while there are a few compression formats that involve no loss of information (e.g. FLAC, MLP), most popular formats are lossy, including MP3 (MPEG-1 Audio Layer-III, from the Moving Pictures Experts Group), MPEG-AAC (Advanced Audio Coding, sometimes called MP4), Quick-Time, RealAudio, and WMA (Windows Media Audio). **You will want to take great care that you do not purchase a recorder that records solely in one of these compressed formats.**

WAV files are of course much bigger than compressed file formats such as MP3 – consider, for example, that a commercially produced music CD which uses uncompressed data usually holds about 10–15 songs, but we can burn hundreds of songs in MP3 format onto a CD with the same storage capacity. And it is true that most of us can detect no difference in quality between the uncompressed files of commercially produced music CDs and the compressed songs we listen to on our MP3 players – especially given that great care is taken to "lose" only information that is irrelevant or redundant in terms of what we hear. However, the key word is "hear": Compression (also called encoding) is based on perception, not the actual acoustic properties of the sound signal. (Indeed, when developers of compressed audio formats create and upgrade their products, they rely not on acoustic measurements but on the feedback of trained listeners.) But although impressionistically good quality is fine for entertainment and other non-linguistic purposes (e.g. recording voice memos, business meetings, etc.), it is insufficient for linguistic analysis, especially acoustic phonetic analysis. No matter what type of analysis you are performing, you want the sharpest audio signal you can get. And even if you do not intend to perform acoustic phonetic analysis of your data initially, members of your research team or other interested scholars may eventually wish to do so. It would be a shame if they were unable to use the data simply because you were unaware of specifications and formats for optimal sound quality, or because you chose to save a bit of space or money. In conducting your sociolinguistic fieldwork, you will be presented with once-in-a-lifetime opportunities to record invaluable speech data. **I cannot stress enough that you should take full advantage of these opportunities while you have them, by investing in high-quality audio recording equipment**. You cannot put a price tag on your field recordings; do not skimp on the price tag of your recording equipment.

Microphones

Just as important as the audio recording device in making excellent quality voice recordings is a microphone that meets appropriate specifications. Most audio recorders come with built-in microphones, and it can be tempting to use these for their convenience and unobtrusiveness – but you should train yourself to ignore that temptation from the outset. **ALWAYS use an external microphone so that you can control overall quality, particular specifications for particular needs, and microphone placement**.

Microphone specifications Microphone specifications are similar to audio recording specifications, in that again you need to be concerned with **dynamic range** and **frequency response**. Dynamic range again refers to the amplitude range (or the "loudness") the microphone will pick up. It is limited at the lower end by the internal noise made by the microphone itself (self-noise) and at the higher end by distortion, or clipping, when signals that are too loud for the microphone are simply clipped off when they are recorded. The internal noise generated by the microphone should be much lower (about 15 dB lower) than the level of the softest voice sounds that will be produced, while the upper limit of the sound the microphone picks up should be equal to or higher than the loudest voice sounds.

Frequency response has to do not only with capturing a range of frequencies but with accurately capturing the intensity of frequencies across a particular frequency spectrum. Ideally, we would like frequency response to be completely accurate, or have a **flat frequency response**, across the specified range – but no microphone has a perfectly flat frequency response, and some frequencies will be exaggerated while others will be attenuated. Most microphone specifications will list a frequency response that ranges between two figures (ideally 20–20,000 Hz for speech), with a tolerance for exaggerated / attenuated frequencies expressed in decibels (dBs); however, these specifications do not indicate where in the spectrum the response will be less than flat, nor how smooth or abrupt the exaggerations or attenuations in amplitude may be at particular frequencies. Neither dynamic range nor frequency response are absolutes; they can be affected by type of microphone, microphone directionality, and microphone placement.

Another microphone specification to consider is **impedance**. Impedance, measured in ohms, is a highly technical issue but in general has to do with the degree to which a circuit impedes the flow of an alternating current, such as an audio signal. **Low impedance is better than high.** The chief disadvantage of high impedance microphones is that when attached to cables of more than 5 to 10 meters (c. 16–32 feet) in length, they tend to lose high frequencies. Generally, low impedance is considered to be less than 600 ohms, medium impedance is from 600 to 10,000 ohms, and high impedance is greater than 10,000 ohms. Often, microphones with built-in cables and ¼ inch (6.33 mm) connectors are high impedance, and those with a separate balanced XLR cable are low impedance (see below for more on connectors), though, as always, you will want to check the equipment specifications to be sure.

Transducer type There are two basic types of microphones, differentiated by the type of transducer they use; that is, how they convert acoustic pressures into an electrical signal. **Dynamic microphones** produce electric signals through electromagnetic induction, while condenser microphones rely on capacitance change. Again, the technical details of the inner workings of microphones are not important for your immediate fieldwork purposes. However, you should understand the best uses for each type of microphone, including the advantages and disadvantages of each.

Good dynamic microphones have the advantages for field researchers of being relatively inexpensive and durable; in addition, unlike condenser microphones, dynamic microphones do not need an external power supply. Conversely, dynamic microphones are less sensitive than condenser microphones; they have lower dynamic ranges and do not respond as well to sharp, quick sounds and minute changes in voice intensity (Plichta no date).

Condenser microphones can be subdivided into two types: **condenser** and **electret**, with the difference being in the power source: Condenser microphones use externally applied voltage and so require power from a battery or external source (so-called "phantom power"), and electret microphones have permanent voltage built in. Overall, condenser and electret microphones produce much better recordings than dynamic microphones. They are more sensitive, and they can be very small and portable. In addition, whereas condenser microphones are generally more expensive than dynamic ones, electret microphones are now affordable and ubiquitous, used in many lavalier (lapel) and headset microphones for professional recording as well as in everyday equipment such as mobile phones and computers. The other primary disadvantage of condenser microphones is that they can be less durable than dynamic microphones, an important consideration in many field situations. Overall, though, the consensus among phoneticians and acousticians seems to be that you should try to use condenser microphones if possible, depending on your purposes, field circumstances, and budget.

Directionality Microphone directionality, or polar pattern, refers to the direction(s) from which the microphone will pick up sound. The basic directionalities are unidirectional (often "cardioid"), omnidirectional, bidirectional, and shotgun. **Unidirectional microphones** can be advantageous for sociolinguistic fieldwork in that most of the sound they pick up comes from in front of the microphone (usually by holding the microphone tip parallel to the speaker's lips, sometimes at a perpendicular angle), while noise coming from other directions (e.g. unwanted background noise) is minimized. The most common type of unidirectional microphone is the so-called **cardioid microphone**, so named because sound is picked up in something of a heart-shaped pattern, with the greatest degree of sensitivity at the front of the microphone, some sensitivity extending 90 degrees to each side, and theoretically no sound pick up at the back of the microphone.

There are a couple of issues to bear in mind with unidirectional microphones. One is that they are especially sensitive to how close they are placed to the speaker's mouth and are subject to the so-called proximity effect – that is, the boosting of lower frequencies when placed too close to the mouth. Some manufacturers have built-in compensation for the proximity effect, but unfortunately most do not specify the optimal distance at which the compensatory effects work best. See below for more on microphone placement.

Another issue regarding unidirectional microphones is that, as discussed in previous chapters in this book, there is increasing recognition in sociolinguistics of the dialogic nature of the sociolinguistic interview. Ideally, we will want to consider not only interviewees' productions but also how the interviewer helps shape the interviewee's speech; and this means examining recording and examining both sides of ongoing talk. For example, we may ask how the interviewer phrases questions, how they respond to interviewee's utterances, how much control they take over topic shifts, and so on. Directional microphones are designed to minimize the relatively weak speech signal produced by those not sitting directly in front of the microphone, and the signal is further weakened if they are seated farther away than the interviewee. Luckily, in my experience, I have not found cardioid microphones to be terribly limiting in this regard, especially if they are not placed extremely close to the interviewee's lips. However, focused directionality does become a bigger problem if you are conducting multiparty interviews or recording spontaneous conversations among a number of participants.

The other directional pattern common in the sociolinguistic fieldwork situation is the **omnidirectional microphone**. As the name implies, this type of microphone is theoretically equally sensitive around its full 360 degree circumference and so is well suited for multiparty interviews and conversations. Omnidirectional microphones are also advantageous in that they do not suffer from a proximity effect. However, you should be aware that omnidirectionality is only ensured up to a certain frequency limit, with microphones of smaller circumference having higher frequency limits than those of larger circumference. Unfortunately, though, microphones that are too small will yield a high noise level, so there is a trade-off between size and sensitivity. Another issue with omnidirectional microphones is that they also pick up background noise from all directions, which can be a problem in certain recording settings. Lavalier (lapel) microphones are often omnidirectional, as are the built-in microphones on audio recorders (which, recall, you should *never* use).

Sociolinguists do not tend to use bidirectional or "shotgun" micro-phones. Both of these have two narrowly focused areas of sensitivity to the front and rear of the microphone – too narrow for most field conditions, where speaker placement cannot be completely controlled or held perfectly constant. (You may be familiar with shotgun micro-phones from television and film sets, where the microphone is moved along with the actor to keep constant the relative placement of micro-phone and speaker.)

Stand-mounted vs. "speaker-mounted" microphones Other micro-phone options have been hinted at above. Will your microphone be mounted on a stand (e.g. at a table), clipped to the speaker's lapel or other piece of clothing close to the mouth (lavalier microphone), or mounted to a headset for extreme proximity to the mouth? Because head-mounted and lavalier microphones are much closer to the mouth, they pick up a stronger speech signal, and so they are advantageous over table-mounted microphones in this regard. At the same time, though, microphones that are close-mounted need to have the capabil-ity to pick up the stronger speech signals without distortion while at the same time minimizing the amount of non-speech noise. In other words, headset and lavalier microphones must have a higher (more stringent) signal-to-noise ratio (SNR) than tabletop microphones placed farther from the mouth. (This is not to say that the SNR becomes unimportant when the microphone is relatively far from the mouth, since clearly, too much extraneous noise will ruin any recording.)

In my experience, I have used both tabletop and lavalier micro-phones and do not strongly recommend one over the other, though many sociolinguists recommend lavalier or headset microphones. Some interviewees may feel that microphones they have to wear are more obtrusive than those placed a bit farther away. Conversely, others may feel that a relatively large stand-mounted microphone is more of an interference than a tiny clip-on microphone that cannot even be seen unless the interviewee purposely looks down at it. I and my fellow researchers have had good luck using a tabletop microphone without a stand. This is a trade-off that is typically *not* recommended, since microphones placed on hard surfaces will pick up reverberations that can wreak havoc on recording quality. However, you can buffer the reverberations by placing the microphone on soft material such as a pile of papers. In this way, we avoid the invasiveness of attaching microphones to people as well as the awkwardness occasioned by having them stare straight into a stand-mounted microphone. A more technically advanced alternative to our makeshift tabletop microphone is to use a microphone that is actually designed to be placed directly onto the table's surface – namely, a so-called "boundary" microphone that has been engineered so that when it is placed on a surface (boundary), the reflections from that surface are not sensed. Boundary microphones are often marketed as "conference microphones"; as with any equipment you buy, you need to ensure that microphones (and recorders) designed for non-linguistic purposes meet our particular specifications for high-quality voice recording in various field conditions.

One final note regarding microphone choice is whether or not you can use wireless microphones in sociolinguistic fieldwork. At the time of writing this book, they are not yet recommended (see, e.g. Plichta no date); however, you should keep abreast of developments in this area, since obviously wireless technology is advancing by leaps and bounds.

Other recording devices

Video recorders As sociolinguists place increasing emphasis on how language variation unfolds in interaction rather than simply how it patterns after it has been produced, they are paying more attention to unfolding context as well as linguistic content. In this regard, it is becoming more common for sociolinguistics to record information on both video and audio channels. In addition, sociolinguistic research on sign languages necessitates video recording. Clearly, researchers who plan on making video recordings need to become just as familiar with video equipment specifications and recording techniques as sociolinguists traditionally have had to be with audio recording specifications, technologies, and techniques. Because this book is focused mainly on the audio recording of sociolinguistic interviews (and a few related speech events), we will not delve into a full discussion of video recording. However, since most sociolinguistic purposes necessitate that video recordings be accompanied by high-quality audio, we will devote just a bit of space to the matter of ensuring that high-quality video is not marred by a less than acceptable audio track.

At first glance, it may seem that assuring high-quality audio in a video recording situation is a simple matter of ensuring that your video camera meets the same audio specifications as audio recorders demand. Video cameras listing appropriate specifications for their audio recorders (i.e. sampling rate, quantization rate, frequency response, dynamic range) are not difficult to find and can be reasonably inexpensive. But just as you are cautioned not to use the built-in microphone on even the best audio recorder, experts also caution against simply using the one built into your video camera, since the internal microphones in consumer-grade video recorders do not meet our minimal recording specifications (e.g. Plichta no date).

Plichta notes that there are basically two ways to ensure high-quality audio when making video recordings. The first is to record with your video camera (and its internal microphone) while simultaneously recording an audio track using a separate audio recorder microphone that meets your recording quality specifications. When you have finished recording, you can use video and audio editing software to replace the audio recorded on the video camera with the separate audio track. Synchronizing the audio and video can be done using high-tech (and expensive) equipment, or it can be done in a simple, old-fashioned way. If you have the resources, you can invest in digital video and audio recorders with time-codes that can be synched to one another. If you do not have equipment capable of time-coding, you can use a digital time-code slate (a separate piece of equipment which may be expensive) or simply an old-fashioned, Hollywood-style clapperboard slate, which essentially makes a loud, abrupt sound that you then use to align your audio and video. (Minimal technology is required here – even making a loud hand clap will work.)

Another option for obtaining good quality audio on your video recordings is to hook a single external microphone to both an audio and video recorder. With this method, there is no need to synch audio and video; however, you need to be aware that audio quality will suffer if the external microphone is not properly matched to the video camera.

STUDENTS IN THE FIELD

In preparation for her dissertation study on how multilingual children negotiate linguistic identity development, Corinne Seals conducted a pilot study of heritage language learners of Russian and Ukrainian in a partially immersive multilingual school in Oregon (Seals under review). Part of her multifaceted data-collection process involved recording classroom interactions. She used a stationary video camera to capture whole-class interactions. At the same time, she recorded small-group interaction with audio recorders placed on tables at which each student group was seated. Her video recordings provided important information on students' linguistic usages, as well as movements, gestures, and expressions. However, the students' whole-class behaviors told only part of the story; and Seals found that sometimes children exhibited behaviors for their small groups that they would never perform in front of the entire classroom, or within teacher eye- or earshot. For example, one child who almost never spoke in front of the entire class produced large quantities of (quite aggressive) talk "behind the teacher's back." Corinne's use of audio as well as video recording thus not only provided high-quality audio data that

> the video camera would not be able to capture, but also gave her multiple perspectives that enabled her to get a fuller picture of students' identity displays than would have been possible using either channel alone – or only a single audio recorder in addition to the single video camera.

Laptop computers Many sociolinguistic researchers use laptop computers to record in the field. If you go this route, you should ensure that you have a high-quality sound card (which should not be a problem with any relatively up-to-date computer) and microphone. A tabletop USB microphone is a good option. You should also be aware that unless your computer is entirely solid-state (i.e. uses flash memory rather than a mechanical hard drive), it will generate noise that may be unacceptable, depending on the computer and microphone used. Another potential problem with using your laptop as a recording device is that unlike dedicated audio recording devices, the computer does not automatically save the audio file when you stop the recording. And while having to hit "save," name your audio file, and assign it a location is not a problem under normal conditions, it could be disastrous if you are somehow interrupted during the save process, whether due to computer malfunction or external circumstances. Another issue that makes me wary of recommending using your laptop as a recording device is that it seems rather obtrusive compared to today's portable digital audio recorders. Its presence may lend something of a business-like tone to what could otherwise be a friendly, casual interview. Formality will also be augmented if you simply place your computer in its "normal" position – that is, with the screen directly in front of you (and hence, of course, the back facing the interviewee), effectively establishing a physical barrier between you and your interviewee. Further, open laptops connote divided attention, and even though they are increasingly common in both work and leisure settings, you will have to ensure that you maintain eye contact with your interviewee and not your computer screen – and of course keep your focus on the interview and avoid the multitasking that often goes hand-in-hand with laptop use.

Recording long distance In the above discussion, we have presumed that you will actually be physically present in the field setting and will be conducting interviews face-to-face. While in-person interviews are best in terms of sound quality and interactional quality, there may be times when you need to conduct interviews long distance. Usually, long-distance interviews will be a supplemental part of your research; for example, you might conduct follow-up interviews with research participants after you return home from the field. At other times, however, long-distance interviews may be an integral part of your study, or even your only source of data. For example, large-scale sociolinguistic surveys such as the TELSUR on which the Atlas of North American English (ANAE) is based, can only practicably be conducted via phone (Labov, Ash, and Boberg 2006b). Other studies may involve focused populations in several geographically disparate areas, for example Sheena Shah's research on language and identity among heritage Gujarati speakers in London, Singapore, and South Africa, mentioned in Chapter 5. As discussed in a bit more detail below, audio quality necessarily suffers when recording long distance. Nonetheless, careful researchers can still obtain data of sufficient quality for sociolinguistic analysis.

No matter what the geographic scope of your study is, and no matter what method you use for gathering language recordings (whether in person or long distance), sociolinguistic research always involves something of a trade-off between optimal sound quality and optimal interactional quality. And while some researchers may view lessened sound quality as a serious limitation, we must also bear in mind that data gathered under perfect recording conditions (i.e. in a phonetics laboratory) is quite limited in its own way, in terms of what it can tell us regarding language use in everyday settings.

Traditional land-line telephones Unfortunately, no matter what recording equipment you have at your disposal, recording via traditional land-line phones is always less than optimal, chiefly due to the limited frequency range allowed by the phone system: about 300–4,000 Hz. Compare this to the 20–20,000 Hz range of a professional-grade, research-quality audio recorder, and you can readily see why land-line phones are considered poor recording environments. Luckily, most of the human speech signal lies below 4,000 Hz, which is why telephone voices typically sound reasonably close to in-person speech. As long as you use high-quality recording equipment (e.g. use a sampling rate of at least 8,000 Hz; ensure an appropriate, low-noise connection to the telephone), telephone recordings can yield a good deal of useful linguistic information – even acoustic phonetic information, as the success of the ANAE project amply demonstrates.

Internet phone Another option for making long-distance recordings is to use a computer and an Internet phone service. This is an excellent choice in terms of cost; and because Internet phone services use digital rather than analog signals, they are not inherently limited to the narrow frequency range of traditional phones. In addition, Internet phone programs now often offer the opportunity for video chat, which can be helpful in enabling interlocutors to have a degree of "face-to-face" interaction.

This is not to say that all Internet phone services are better than traditional land-line phones – indeed, they can be worse and are also often less reliable than traditional phone services. For example, heavy Internet traffic can result in a choppy or clipped voice signal, or worse, unpredictable signal dropping. The bandwidth required for video in particular makes connections notoriously unstable for many Internet users. And, of course, power outages will halt Internet phone conversations, so it is wise to invest in a Universal Power Source (which also keeps your computer powered up during outages) if you are planning to rely heavily on Internet phone recordings.

The wide array of choice in Internet phone service is of course advantageous, since it enables you to shop around for one that meets your audio specifications; at the same time, the sheer number of options can be quite daunting. It is beyond the scope of this book to make specific technology recommendations, but the pragmatic reader will likely find established Internet phone services to be more reliable than smaller or newer services, both in the short term (i.e. ensuring a clear and steady signal during a particular phone conversation) and in the long term (i.e. ensuring that the service provider will not go out of business halfway through your research project).

STUDENTS IN THE FIELD

Internet phone programs like Skype can be enormously helpful in reaching far-flung communities, but they can also present logistical challenges. In her study of heritage Gujarati speakers in diaspora communities in London, Singapore, and South Africa, Sheena Shah first attempted to pilot her interviews in the latter two locations using Skype. Scheduling the interviews proved to be difficult because of the time differences (she would try to conduct interviews in the middle of the night so as to reach respondents at times that were convenient for them), and she found that there were a great many last-minute cancellations. In addition, the Internet was not always very reliable in South Africa, adding a further layer of complication. Sheena thus decided to travel to all three locations to conduct her interviews the "old-fashioned way," and found that she had much more success, in terms of rate of participation, audio quality, and interactional quality, when she simply conducted her interviews face-to-face. Interestingly, Sheena also switched from long-distance to in-person methods for another aspect of her study, administering Gujarati language tests to participants. Originally, she had asked her mother, who is more proficient in Gujarati, to administer the tests by phone, but again, due to time zone and technical issues, Sheena later recorded her mother's prompts and took the audio with her on her research trips to administer the tests in person. Sheena's experiences teach us that even in an age of ever-increasing technological advances aiding long-distance communication, there is sometimes (often) no substitute for face-to-face human contact.

Mobile phones A final phone technology to consider is of course the now ubiquitous mobile phone. Today's smart phones theoretically can be used as audio (and video) recorders for both long-distance and in-person interviews, since they have built-in recording devices in addition to their phone capabilities. However, as with any recorder, the specifications must be checked, and even if the recorder itself meets your specifications, the built-in microphone almost certainly will not. If you are planning to use your mobile phone as a recorder in the field, you will need to attach a high-quality external microphone. Again, full discussion of specific equipment is beyond our scope, but as one example, the various Macintosh portable devices (iPhones, iPods, and iPads) will work very well as audio recorders since they feature a 44.1 kHz sampling rate with 16-bit quantization. However, the sampling rate of the built-in microphone is at the time of this writing only 8 kHz, which reduces the upper limit of sound frequency that can be recorded to 4 kHz – rendering these high-tech devices no better than traditional land-line phones.

Other equipment, supplies, and software

In selecting your recording equipment, it can be easy to focus on the major elements, recorder and microphone, and neglect the apparently minor accessories that are equally essential to obtaining high-quality voice (and video) recordings. This includes connectors, memory cards, batteries, adapters, and software for transferring data from the recording device to the computer. I cannot stress strongly enough how important it is to obtain – and check – all of these items prior to entering the field and prior to each interview. The best pieces of equipment in the world are useless if they cannot be appropriately connected to one another, if they are not adequately powered, if their storage capacity is filled up, or if the data cannot be transferred to a central data storage repository. I strongly recommend that you make a checklist of all equipment and supplies necessary for field recordings and that you refer to this list each time you set out to record. Or better yet, using your checklist, prepare and pack all equipment and supplies for their next use as soon as possible after each recording event. You never know when a recording opportunity might arise, and you do not want to miss your chance because you took too long to get your equipment together or you forgot to take something vital to a successful recording. A sample checklist is given in Box 6.3 below.

Connectors Clearly, since you will almost certainly have more than one piece of equipment, appropriate connectors are crucial, including between the recorder and microphone and between the recording device and the computer onto which you transfer your audio data. And while it is of course necessary that connectors fit the slots available on the relevant equipment, there are other issues. For example, impedance-balanced cables connecting the microphone and recorder are better than unbalanced cables; in addition, XLR (typically 3-pin) cables are better than other types such as ¼ inch (6.33 mm) or ⅛ inch (3.5 mm) mini jacks, though not all recorders and microphones allow for XLR connectors. Be especially careful to avoid microphones with ¼ inch unbalanced phone jacks; these are very common on consumer-grade equipment. And you should resist the temptation to rig connections that are not really intended on a particular device (e.g. using a ¼–⅛ inch (6.33–3.5 mm) adaptor): these changes may be easy enough to implement, but they significantly degrade recording quality.

Data storage All recording devices come with built-in storage, and many also allow for additional removable storage such as compact flash memory cards. If additional storage is an option, it is always recommended. High-quality audio files are quite large, and sociolinguistic interviews are long (usually at least one hour each). Many commercially available voice recorders of otherwise high quality have limited built-in storage capacity, since they are typically intended for business and personal use (e.g. making short voice memos) rather than linguistic research purposes. When checking recording equipment for its storage capability, you should figure that every minute of recording (WAV file, 44.1 kHz sampling rate, 16-bit quantization) will take up 10 megabytes of storage space. Many voice recorders offer the option of different (i.e. lower quality) recording settings to allow for increased storage space, but as we have already discussed, you should avoid the temptation to record in compressed file formats (e.g. MP3) or at a lower sampling rate. Whether or not you rely on built-in memory or use removable storage, or both, you should **transfer your audio files from the recording device to the fieldwork computer as soon after each recording session as possible,** to avoid both running out of storage space and accidental erasure. (The files can later be uploaded to a central data repository upon returning from the field.) Of course, if you are recording directly onto a computer, you will not face a transfer issue while still in the field. No matter what recording device you use, though, **you should always make at least two copies of each audio file**, ideally on two separate storage devices, possibly even different types of media (e.g. computer hard drive, flash drive, CD), **as soon as possible after you record each file. Do NOT wait until you return from the field to make back-up copies!** See Section 6.2 below for more on managing data in the field and back at home.

Batteries Of all the items you take with you into the field, none is easier to pack – and easier to overlook – than ample batteries of appropriate types. You may be tempted to "travel light" with regard to batteries, to save space, weight and money; however, there are few more important investments you can make than an adequate battery supply. Rechargeable batteries are very useful – but only in situations where you will be able to plug in the charger – so you should never rely on these alone but should also carry regular batteries as well. In addition, you should never presume you can buy batteries in the fieldwork setting. Even in relatively un-"exotic" locales, you may find that certain sizes are hard to find, or you may find stores stocked only with batteries of dubious vintage. Another very useful but little-known item you can carry with you is a battery tester. These are very inexpensive and easy to use, and end up saving both money and heartache, since you can use them to ensure that your battery supply contains only batteries with most of their charge remaining. And as we noted above, many microphones require batteries, which can be especially easy to overlook – it may not be obvious that the microphone even has a battery compartment, let alone that the battery should be tested frequently. If your microphone uses a battery, make sure you know its size and type, and remember to check its performance before each use.

STUDENTS IN THE FIELD

Having back-up equipment on hand can be invaluable, as Sheena Shah learned in her study of diaspora Gujarati speakers: "My computer power cord stopped working while I was in Singapore. Luckily I was able to get this sorted out fairly quickly (in two days – thankfully this happened in Singapore and not in South Africa, where it would have taken much longer to get it fixed!), but it meant that I had to reschedule a few interviews, as I did not have enough battery left on my computer. Lesson learned: carry extra computer equipment when collecting data abroad!"

Software for audio file transfer, editing, and analysis The final issue to consider when lining up your recording equipment and supplies is that of software. Before you enter the field, you need to ensure that you have – and know how to use – the correct software for transferring data from your audio recorder to the field computer. It is also helpful if you are familiar with the software you will later use for editing and analysis, but as long as you can record and transfer files in formats appropriate for later digital signal processing, it is not imperative that you learn how to perform such processing before heading into the field. Again, we stress recording and transferring only uncompressed files (most likely WAV). And once recorded, original files should never be converted to compressed formats – though you may choose to make compressed *copies*, for reference purposes. Conversely, you cannot improve quality by converting a file recorded in a lossy compressed format (e.g. WMA, MP3) to an uncompressed file type (e.g. WAV), since elements of the original signal that are lost during recording cannot later be recovered. However, if for some reason you do find it necessary to produce original recordings of lossy format – perhaps an unexpected interview opportunity arises and you have access only to a recorder with limited capabilities – you *will* need to convert the compressed recordings to uncompressed format (i.e. un-encode them) in order to digitally edit and / or analyze them.

Clearly, if you are going to conduct acoustic phonetic analysis, you will also need sound analysis software. Most sociolinguists today use PRAAT (Boersma and Weenink 2012), a free open-source software program for sound editing, analysis, and recording. PRAAT reads both WAV and MP3 files though, again, you want to avoid lossy compressed formats such as MP3 if at all possible. Additionally, you should **never use adulterated files for acoustic analysis**. Acoustic analysis software incorporates at least basic digital audio editing capabilities, since you must be able to cut your data into very short segments to perform acoustic phonetic analysis. You may decide to use additional sound editing tools, such as noise reduction, volume maximization, and volume equalization across tracks, for purposes other than acoustic phonetic analysis. These can be especially useful for preparing clips of your data for presentations: you can make short, clear clips of equal volume that have been cut from different interviews recorded at different volume levels. We cannot make specific recommendations for particular software here, but you should be aware that most free or inexpensive programs involve so-called "destructive" editing – meaning the changes you make are applied right away and are irreversible. No matter what program you use, you should **always work from** copies rather than originals when performing digital audio editing, to ensure that the unadulterated file will always survive.

Box 6.2 Protecting your recordings

- transfer your audio file from the recording device to a computer as soon as possible
- make at least two copies of each audio file and store each in a different place
- never use adulterated files for analysis
- always conduct digital editing and analysis on copies rather than originals

---

6.1.2 Recording techniques

Once you have assembled all your recording equipment and supplies, you need to learn how to use your technology for optimal results in the field. Field conditions are not always ideal, and you must cultivate and maintain good relations with people as well as with your technology. Because you need to be concerned with ensuring interviewee comfort and interactional naturalness, you may worry about the obtrusiveness of the setup process, which entails not only preparing and arranging your high-quality equipment, but also physically positioning participants for best results. As long as you are prepared, practiced, and confident, though, most people do not mind if you temporarily step into the "expert" role in setting up the interview situation – and of course you will do your best to let this role recede once the recording is underway. After all, it is a waste of everyone's time to participate in an interview than ends up being of poor quality, so it is in everyone's best interest to help set things up properly to ensure this does not happen. Preparing for a good interview is a lot like setting the scene for professional photographs: Subjects do not typically mind having themselves and their surroundings "manipulated" by the photographer, because they know the results will be much better if they listen to the expert while the stage is being set.

Practicing prior to entering the field

Some people learn best by trial and error, and others read instructions, but no matter what your learning style, I strongly recommend the latter in familiarizing yourself with recording equipment and techniques – you do not want to waste time on bad practice recordings when you could be making good recordings out in the field. A vital part of the learning process involves practice – and by practice I *do not* mean making a two-second test recording of your own voice. You need to try conducting practice interviews in various settings, using various equipment set-ups and settings. Recruit a friend to act as your interviewee and bring a notebook to keep track of what you learn, and devote some time to experimentation. Try recording indoors in both quiet and noisy locations, as well as in various outdoor spots. Try different microphone placements and set-ups. Does it really work to use a tabletop microphone that is not mounted on a stand, as I suggest above? What seems to be the optimal distance between the microphone and your practice interviewee, and how does their voice sound – and your voice – when the microphone is placed directly in front of the interviewee vs. sideways between the two of you? If you have more than one microphone, try them all out. How does an omnidirectional lavalier microphone sound (and feel to the inter-viewee) compared with a cardioid tabletop microphone?

If your recorder has different settings, you should also experiment with these. Many good recorders allow you to adjust the recording level and include a display showing you when the level is optimal, too low to register, or too high (resulting in a clipped signal). You can usually find a good setting a few minutes into the interview and can keep it there, but you should also periodically monitor the recording level throughout the course of the interview. Discreetly checking your equipment takes a bit of practice, since you do not want recording worries to distract you from listening to your interviewee, or even to let them think that you are distracted.

As we noted above, there are a couple of recording settings you should *not* alter. One is sampling rate, sometimes called "voice quality" on consumer-grade equipment: If your recorder offers you a choice, set it to 44.1 kHz (i.e. "high quality") and leave it there. Similarly, if your recorder offers a choice of recording formats, you know what to do: set it to WAV or AIFF (or other uncompressed format) and keep it there. As a general rule, you should set your equipment to record in mono, not in stereo, unless you will be recording more than one speaker.

As you make your practice recordings, you should periodically stop them and play them back to make sure things sound fairly good. Do not be dismayed if they do not sound crystal clear, because most built-in speakers on recorders are not of particularly great quality them-selves. The real test of your recording quality will come when you transfer your practice recordings to your computer, which you should do before going out and getting real interviews. Once your practice audio files are on your computer, you can then play them back through your computer, ideally using decent auxiliary / external speakers. In addition, you should see how your sound waves look using your sound editing and / or analysis software. If you are not yet well versed in looking at sound waves, you can ask for help from an experienced sociolinguistic researcher or phonetician; or you can consult the numerous books and Internet resources on the subject. Not every sociolinguist has acoustic analysis as their current research goal, but as we have briefly discussed already, excellent quality recordings are desirable for *all* types of close analysis of language features, whether they are sound segments, supra-segmental features, morphosyntactic structures, lexical items or con-nected discourse. And acoustic phonetic analysis may turn out to be something you (or a colleague) might wish to pursue later. So regardless of the particular direction of your research, you should ensure that you know how to make recordings of superior quality,

STUDENTS IN THE FIELD

The importance of familiarizing yourself with your equipment cannot be understated, as Jen McFadden discovered in her ethnographic study of Bengali speech in an urban marketplace in Dhaka, Bangladesh. In discussing her fieldwork later, she remarked, "I made a lot of dumb mistakes with the recorder. I had a solid-state digital recorder that made decent recordings, but it had fiddly little buttons and if I did not have the 'lock' key set, it was very easy to turn off by mistake. It also went through a charge very quickly, so it might shut off prematurely, before I had ended a session at the market. I'd go home thinking I'd captured a really wonderful interaction, and then I'd try to save my files and discover that I'd only gotten the first hour of the conversation. Brownouts and power surges made it difficult or impossible to recharge the recorder between some sessions . . . I had a lot of frustrations with my lack of technological savvy."

Data collection is often subject to these kinds of frustrations – there is no shortage of missed opportunities or technological failures in the field. Jen learned the hard way that practice and foresight can help to avert these circumstances, but she also learned to accept that technological mishaps are part of fieldwork. After all, there's no point to getting overly distressed about the "conversations that got away." Instead, that energy can be used to plan better for the next time.

Out in the field

Once you have become familiar with your equipment and conducted a number of successful practice runs, you are ready to make your real recordings. Again, make sure you take all equipment and connectors into the field, as well as an ample supply of batteries and memory cards.

Box 6.3 Recording equipment checklist

It is helpful to double-check your equipment against a master checklist every time you head out into the field. Use the one provided here, or make your own.

- recorder (with fresh batteries or a fully charged rechargeable battery)
- microphone(s)
- microphone power supply (batteries or external power source)
- extra fully charged batteries
- battery tester
- cables / connectors
- power cords
- removable storage media (flash drives, etc.)
- labels for storage media
- pens
- field notebook

Location, location, location Once you have gotten people to agree to be recorded, you can then make arrangements to make the recordings. Obviously you will need to arrange a mutually agreeable day and time, and then comes the somewhat trickier matter of arranging a location. The recording location is very important and often involves a balancing act between interviewee comfort and your recording needs. Researchers often make recordings in interviewees' homes, since they offer privacy and quiet and course familiarity to the interviewee. However, this is not a setting guaranteed to be successful with all interviewees or in all communities. Not everyone is comfortable with holding a one-on-one meeting with a stranger or near-stranger in a private space, or welcoming a stranger into their private space; furthermore, such an interaction might be culturally quite inappropriate as well. And even if a private one-on-one meeting would be welcome, some people may not have their own private residence, while others may be unable to arrange for a temporary quiet space and time within the home. In addition, you too may prefer a less private location than a personal residence, for your own comfort and safety. Unfortunately, public locations tend also to be noisy ones.

If a quiet home is likely to be available, a good strategy for potentially getting yourself invited is to meet with the research participant in a public place at least once prior to making any recordings, in the hopes that once they get to know you, they will feel comfortable having you come to their home for the actual recording. And even if no invitation results, the eventual interview should still be more comfortable, no matter where it is held. A preliminary visit or two will ensure that you and your interviewee(s) will not be complete strangers when you make the recording. When planning and scheduling with your interviewee, you should be forthright in stating your needs: You need a quiet location to ensure excellent audio quality, and you want to avoid distractions so that you can give your interviewee your full attention. Once interviewees know what suits you best, they will work with you to accommodate your needs, presumably without sacrificing their own too greatly. Remember, too, that once the interview is underway, you can step back from your leadership role to accommodate to the interviewee and the topics they want to talk to you about.

It is much trickier to find quiet locations outside of private homes, but again, your research participants can be a big help in this regard, since they know the community better than you. Perhaps certain outdoor locations or indoor spots such as restaurants and cafes are relatively quiet during particular days and hours. Or perhaps community members might help you gain access to meeting rooms and other fairly private places in public buildings such as libraries or community centers. It may even be an acceptable option to record in an interviewee's office, though you want to be careful that the conversational interview does not become too formal, through association with the relatively formal setting of the interviewee's workplace. As noted in Chapter 2, a good compromise location between public and private is a front or back porch: The porch is private and familiar, just like the indoor portions of the interviewee's home; at the same time, though, it is not quite as sacrosanct as the indoors itself. Occasional foot and vehicle traffic may make the interviewee feel less secluded (and hence safer with a relative stranger) than if they were indoors and out of view. A trade-off here, of course, is that there could be too much traffic, increasing noise level and potential interruptions.

Though some sociolinguists urge against outdoor recordings, we have had good luck with these, as long as the location is chosen with care. In addition to passing people and motor vehicles, you want to avoid other obvious sources of noise such as lawn equipment, construction equipment, and children's playgroups. You should also be aware of less obvious ambient noises such as wind and birdsong, which we tend to filter out of our consciousness. And indoor locations, as quiet as they may seem, sometimes have even more sources of noise that is hidden to our ears but picked up all too clearly by audio recorders. Among the acoustic "traps" you should avoid are computers and related electronic equipment, fluorescent lights, appliances (especially refrigerators), aquariums, and ticking clocks. In other cases, noises can be silenced. For example, you should politely ask interviewees to turn off televisions and radios, again stressing that you want to be able to focus on what they are saying without distraction. Negotiating noisy fans and air conditioners may be a trickier issue, as we found when conducting fieldwork in Robeson County, North Carolina, in the heat of the summer. In one case, we interviewed two elderly Lumbee Indians in a home with a window air conditioning unit. We were too worried about the effects of the heat on their health (not to mention their comfort) to ask them to turn off the appliance, so we decided to treat the interview as a preliminary and then planned to return at a later, cooler date to record a full interview.

In addition to electronics and other appliances, you should avoid rooms with only or mostly hard surfaces, since they produce too many reverberations, resulting in a recording full of echoes. This is one of the reasons outdoor recordings can actually be quite good, since you are not confined by hard walls and ceilings. When recording indoors, you should try to find rooms with carpet or other attenuating surfaces such as wall hangings, curtains, etc.

Unfortunately, the most comfortable locations for participants may be the least likely to produce acceptable acoustics. All of what we have just outlined regarding indoor noises adds up to the fact that the worst room for recording in most homes (at least in modern, Western society) is the kitchen – the very room in which many people feel most comfortable. Thus, we strongly urge you to do your best to convince interviewees to move into a "softer" room like the living room, perhaps after a preliminary period in the kitchen to help set a comfortable tone. Another unfortunate trade-off between recording quality and interviewee comfort is found in coffee shops: as pleasant as they are for so many of us, they are *very* loud. Not only do you have to contend with customers chatting at other tables and baristas calling out orders, but you are faced with the practically incessant high-volume noise of the espresso machine. When attempting to set up or shift interview locations, you will fare best if you simply state your needs rather than try to come up with some sort of ruse for suggesting a different locale. After all, it is not just you who benefits when a recording is successful.

Positioning participants and microphones Unless your particular equipment states otherwise (e.g. directional microphones with built-in compensation for proximity effects), a good general recommendation for maximizing speech signal and minimizing extraneous noise is to place stand-mounted microphones 30 cm (c. 12 inches) from the front of the interviewee's mouth and head-mounted microphones no more than 5 cm (2 inches) to the side of the mouth. Remember, the closer the microphone is placed to the mouth, the higher its SNR needs to be (i.e. you need a very high-quality microphone for very close placement to the mouth), though of course no equipment used in sociolinguistic fieldwork can have an unacceptably low SNR. Also consider your microphone's directionality: A unidirectional microphone placed close in front of an interviewee's mouth may not be the best choice for capturing the true dialogicality of the sociolinguistic interview, since your voice may be muted (or even practically inaudible). My research team and I have found cardioid microphones to perform fairly well in picking up both interviewee and interviewer voices. Omnidirectional microphones will be best for group interviews (and peer group interactions with no interviewer present), though you could use a unidirectional microphone with all participants situated on the same side. (This may feel interactionally awkward, however, since groups of friends in conversation will tend to sit in a more circular arrangement.) In group interviews, participants ideally will be placed so that those with softer voices will be closer to the microphone and those with louder ones will be situated a bit farther away. Of course, this may not always work out in practice, since the closest friends may opt to sit closest together; but again, you can assert your expert status and ask for a particular seating arrangement. Explain your reasons in unoffensive terms, and if your relationship with your fieldwork participants allows for good-natured teasing, a little humor can help, too. (For example, you might say something like, "Now, we all know that John talks louder than the rest of us, so let's put him over here, so all of us can be heard.") If you are not "authorized" to tease, "John's" peers very often will be, and you can let them do the teasing for you, by simply asking the group members to position themselves so their volume levels will be equalized.

Though a well-placed microphone and well-placed participants can yield a good quality group recording, if you are recording more than one interviewee, you will ideally want to make a multi-track recording. This is because though your ear is an expert in distinguishing voices coming from different speakers (and you have your eyes to aid you when you are present at the interaction), a single-track recorder cannot do so. Similar-sounding voices will be difficult to tell apart later during transcription and analysis, and it will be impossible to separate overlapping speakers from one another. High-quality multi-track recorders can be quite expensive, though you can probably obtain a decent four-track recorder for a reasonable amount of money. Another option requiring less specialized equipment is to have each participant in the group interview use their own small digital recorder and lavalier microphone lightweight headset. To help maintain recording quality, you can set up each recorder yourself, turn it on, then set the "hold" button to prevent accidental changes by participants. After the recording session, you can synch the different audio recorders with a clapper board or simply a loud clap, as with synching a separate audio and video recording (see Plichta no date).

"Minor" issues in making recordings Finally, just as with your prac-tice recordings, you must remember to stay attuned to the "little" things that can ruin an otherwise perfectly designed recording situ-ation. Insofar as possible during a busy day of interviewing, you should check batteries and battery levels prior to each recording session and ensure that all connecting cables are correctly and securely in place. Many microphones have an "on" switch, so do not forget to use it. Once the recording is underway, make sure you monitor it as it progresses. Many recorders enable you to monitor recording level with indicator lights, and some have battery level indicators as well. In addition, do not be shy about briefly stopping your recording after a few minutes to double-check that everything seems fine. Again, this may seem obtru-sive, but interviewees will appreciate a conscientious researcher who wants to ensure that their voices are faithfully captured, even if it causes a few minutes of awkwardness. A simple strategy for perform-ing a recording check is to begin each recording by stating the date, location, perhaps the project name (e.g. LCDC study), and the names of the interviewee(s) and interviewer. You can then stop the recorder before the conversation begins, explain that you need to check to ensure that all is working well, play the file back, and then resume recording on a more conversational footing. This technique also serves another important purpose: it creates a record of the basic metadata associated with the interview that can never accidentally be separated from the interview. The same data entered on a paper form (as in a label or in an Interview Report Form) could be lost, misplaced, or attached to the wrong interview; and even in electronic databases where metadata is associated with each interview via database pro-gramming tags, the information could theoretically become corrupted. Beginning each interview recording with the "who, what, and where" helps to insure that this information is never lost. (Of course, including participants' real names on audio recordings raises important confidentiality issues, and great care will have to be taken to ensure that access to original files with people's names is appropriately limited; see in Section 6.3 below.)

Box 6.4 Recording: Some tips for success

- Do an inventory each time you go into the field.
- Practice making recordings and adjusting settings in various locations, and check the sound periodically.
- Set your sampling rate (44.1 kHz) and recording format (WAV), then leave these settings alone.
- Schedule preliminary visits before recording.
- Identify a recording location conducive to good sound quality: try to avoid kitchens, coffee shops, and other locations with too much ambient noise.
- Ask to turn off TVs and radios.
- Position interviewees appropriately for the type of interaction and type of microphone(s) used.
- Ensure the interviewee's comfort.
- Check positions of "hold" buttons, operations of "record" buttons, etc.
- Place stand-mounted microphones 30 cm (12 inches) from speaker's mouth, and lavalier (lapel) microphones no more than 5 cm (2 inches) from speaker's mouth.
- In the absence of a stand, place a tabletop microphone on top of a stack of papers or a folded cloth to limit surface echoes.
- Begin each recording with a spoken "stamp" that records time, date, setting, participants, etc.
- After recording this tag, listen to it to check that your setup is functioning properly.
- Make a single loud handclap at the beginning of the session to use for synchronizing tracks or editing later.
- Reschedule if the current setting is not conducive to successful recording.

Audio quality vs. interactional quality I have strongly urged that you exercise your expert and leadership role in that crucial portion of your sociolinguistic research project that involves setting up the recording situation. However, as I have already admitted, sometimes you simply have to make compromises. For example, an interviewee may insist on being recorded in a setting that is likely to yield poor sound quality (e.g.

a kitchen, a coffee shop), or you as the researcher may not have the heart to optimize recording conditions at the expense of interviewee comfort. Or there simply may not be any locations in the community of study where you can reasonably conduct recordings in a quiet atmosphere, especially nowadays, as increasing noise levels are coupled with growing suspicion of strangers. A good solution in many cases is to do what we did in the case of the elderly Lumbee Indians who we felt could not do without their air conditoner: Conduct a cursory interview under less-than-ideal conditions, then suggest a follow-up interview in a better location. Even interviewees who were originally reluctant to follow your suggestions for recording location are likely to relent once they realize (hopefully!) that the interview was not the uncomfortable event they may have anticipated but on the contrary was perhaps even enjoyable.

Sometimes, too, you will find yourself making less-than-optimal recordings even when it is not possible or necessary to follow up, in the interest of maintaining good community relations. After all, while you do have to maintain some control over your pool of participants and your recording conditions, you do not want to gain a reputation for being too controlling, or for ignoring suggestions that community members believe to be truly helpful. I used to worry that conducting "extra" interviews under poor acoustic conditions or with participants who did not meet the research criteria was a waste of time – but I have come to realize that, within reason, they are not. Just as recording in "real-life" field conditions is a balancing act between recording quality and "naturalness" of the speech data, it also involves a balance between treating people as research "subjects" to be interviewed as methodically and efficiently as possible, and treating them as human beings who deserve your time, patience, and listening ear – especially considering the generosity they have shown you by agreeing to participate in your study.

6.1.3 Recording beyond the sociolinguistic interview

In addition to recording sociolinguistic interviews in natural(istic) field settings, sociolinguists also often make other types of recordings, all of which involve their own issues of audio quality, "naturalness" vs. artificiality of speech, interviewee comfort, and researcher-community relations. We have touched on long-distance interviews and survey recordings and noted that sometimes wide geographic scope necessitates sacrifices in terms of audio quality and interactional quality. In what follows, we briefly touch on issues in making laboratory recordings for sociolinguistic purposes, recording peer interactions in a controlled setting, and sending participants off to make recordings of their everyday interactions, with minimal researcher control over setting, situation, etc.

Exercising control: Laboratory and related recordings

When making recordings in a laboratory setting (for example, to use as stimuli for language attitude and perception studies), you will have much more control over sound quality than when recording in the field. Ideally, you will use a sound-attenuated room that is as free of external and internal ambient noise as possible. You can also use high-quality USB microphones that record directly onto laboratory computers, thereby circumnavigating the issue of having to transfer data from a recording device to the computer. Further, the speaker and the microphone can be positioned exactly as you want them, and you can use more obtrusive – and expensive – equipment (e.g. headset microphones) than will be comfortable or practicable in the field. In addition, you can play recordings back immediately to check for quality (perhaps through headphones so speakers do not have to hear their own voices on tape), then re-record right away if you are not satisfied. In the field, you have to wait until the end of an hour-plus interview (or even the end of the fieldwork day) to see if you actually have the recordings you want. Finally, the lab allows you to control not only for quality but for content as well. Laboratory recordings made for studies of perceptions and attitudes almost always consist of readings that have been contrived by the researcher to place particular speech segments in linguistic environments of interest. Researchers can also ensure that lab-recorded stimuli are as free as possible of any value-laden content that might skew judgment tasks away from language itself and toward what speakers are talking about.

Of course, making laboratory recordings for sociolinguistic purposes involves just as much of a trade-off as conducting recordings in the field: this time we achieve optimal recording quality at the expense of naturalness rather than vice versa. However, it is by no means essential to record stimuli for language attitude and perception studies under ideal lab conditions – in fact you may wish to more directly access attitudes toward language in more naturalistic settings. In this case, you might draw stimulus sentences or tokens from sociolinguistic interviews. In addition, as we have already discussed, you may choose to sacrifice some of the control afforded by pre-designed reading passages by having speakers talk more freely. Ideally you will want to control for topic by having them all talk about the same subject matter if recording in the lab, or by selecting passages from sociolinguistic interviews on similar topic areas (typically something relatively innocuous such as childhood games, though sometimes you may chose more "charged" content for your research purposes, for example discussions of ethnic group relations, gender relations, etc.).

Relinquishing control: Removing yourself from the recording situation

At the opposite end of the spectrum from the linguistics lab in terms of controlled recording conditions is the case of making recordings with no interviewer present. Often, you can exert a good bit of initial control by arranging the recording situation yourself, choosing the location, positioning participants in groups or pairs (Macaulay 2002; Stuart-Smith 1999), and placing, preparing, and turning on the recording equipment. If you decide to send participants off to make their own recordings, then you can still ensure that optimal equipment is used and that participants are trained in optimal recording techniques (e.g. microphone placement, recorder settings). Further, you can control for setting by requesting that participants record only in one particular place (e.g. the workplace, as in Coupland's [1980] study; see Chapter 3 for more detail) or only with particular kinds of audiences (e.g. interactions with clients and co-workers). However, since sociolinguists, especially those interested in stylistic variation, are very often interested in how people speak across the full spectrum of their everyday interactions, they may seek recordings that are rather less controlled. Unmonitored recordings can cause difficulties not only in terms of sound quality (e.g. noisy vs. quiet environments) but also in terms of speech quality / type. For example, as cited in Macaulay (2009: 33–34) and discussed above in Chapter 3, the teenagers who were solicited to gather data for the Bergen Corpus of London Teenage Language (COLT) recorded speech in such widely different settings (e.g. casual conversation with friends, classroom interactions) that the data across the different situations could not be said to be directly comparable (Stenström, Andersen, and Hasund 2002). In addition, several over-enthusiastic young participants overtly manipulated their "natural" data by encouraging friends to swear or by trying to start arguments.

Again, there is no single best solution for gathering sociolinguistic data that is of optimal quality in terms of both sound and speech. However, as top-quality recording equipment gets smaller and easier to use, it is becoming ever more possible for professionals and amateurs alike to make high-quality recordings across a variety of situations, from the "artificial" linguistics laboratory setting to everyday interactions recorded with no researcher in sight. Furthermore, as we have discussed periodically in this text, there are many sociolinguists who believe that there is no such thing as an "artificial" speech situation anyway: Every situation and event has something to tell us about how people respond to and shape their surroundings through language variation.

6.2 RECORD-KEEPING AND DATA MANAGEMENT

6.2.1 Pre-planning

Planning the database

As you begin to gather data, you will quickly realize that you risk losing track of recordings and associated metadata regarding participant and interview characteristics unless you devise a database for storing and cataloging all of your information. Ideally, you should begin designing your storage system as you design your project, since once you are in the field gathering field notes, interviews, and other recorded interactions, you will want to be able to put each bit of information in its proper place as soon as possible. Waiting to organize your data until you have some "down time" in the field (or worse, waiting until the conclusion of the data-gathering phase) can be risky, and you will waste a lot of time sifting through unorganized information. Immediate cataloging ensures that you will not lose data and that your memory will be fresh enough to add field notes and summary information before the details of your observations and interactions begin to fade away.

What to store At a minimum, you can use a readily available spreadsheet or database program for organizing, storing, searching, and sorting the metadata associated with each participant and interview. Audio and video files and documents associated with participants and interviews, such as electronic transcript files, Informed Consent Forms, and project protocols (e.g. recording instructions, transcription protocols, interview questionnaires) can then be stored in separate, clearly labeled computer folders whose location is referenced in your database spreadsheet. Another very important document is the Interview Report Form, a short form outlining basic information about each interview for quick reference purposes. Interview Report Forms and their importance are discussed in more detail below.

Ideally, you will want to use a storage system that is a bit more specialized than a spreadsheet or series of spreadsheets, so that the various types of information – audio data, transcript, interview summary information, and interview / participant metadata – are automatically cross-referenced. In other words, if you search through your list of interview metadata and find a particular interview you wish to examine, you should not have to go to a separate location to retrieve the audio file, transcript, and interview summary information but should let your database program do the work and bring up all files associated with the interview automatically. Database programming can quickly become rather complicated, even for small projects, so ideally you should try to budget some of your resources to hire or assign someone with database expertise to serve as your Database Administrator (unless of course you have such expertise yourself). Once the database is set up and populated with your data, maintaining, revising, and upgrading are usually easy matters for a specialist, so if you invest in good design from the outset, keeping your data organized should not be a continual drain or your resources. Sometimes, you will even be lucky enough to find a student who will build your database for free, because they are interested in your project or are in search of a project for a class or thesis project. We have encountered just such luck during the course of our LCDC project and have benefited greatly from the help of a computational linguistics student, Stephen Kunath.

Where to store things One very early consideration as you plan your data management system is where to store everything – on a private computer, a dedicated hard drive, the Internet, digital media such as CDs or DVDs, magnetic tape, and / or hard copies of relevant documents such as Informed Consent Forms and transcripts. No matter where you choose to store your data, it is strongly recommended that you store everything in more than one format, with the possible exception of documents containing participants' identifying information, which you may elect to store in hard copy format alone, or in a separate database to which only the project director has access.

One useful and practicable idea is to set up a password-protected Internet-based data management and storage system (thereby enabling easy access by authorized users) while maintaining a dedicated, password-protected hard drive as a back up. In addition, audio and video files can be stored on securely housed CDs / DVDs, providing a bit of reassuring "physicality." However, **you should never use CDs as your sole storage medium**, since they have proven to be disappointingly degradable. If you do use CDs, you will ideally use archival quality CDs and marking pens (for labeling). There are a number of sources that provide specifications for these materials. Your university library is a good place to start.

Storing and re-storing: A note on data preservation and migration
As we have discussed, digital audio still has a major advantage over
older analog formats in that it can be transferred to new media without
loss of signal or addition of noise. The disadvantage, however, is that
many researchers who collect audio data do not realize that digital data
too must be periodically renewed, just as with analog tapes. You need
to be aware that in the long run *no* audio storage medium is permanent, and all data, even digital data, must be preserved as well as stored.
Preservation entails, among other considerations, regular monitoring
to ensure file integrity, as well as periodic migration of data to new
media. (For detailed information on pressing needs in digital [and
analog] sound preservation, including the crucial need for migration
and integrity checks rather than simple static storage, see the National
Recording Preservation Board report titled *The State of Recorded Sound
Preservation in the United States: A National Legacy at Risk in the Digital Age*
[Bamberger and Brylawski 2010].) Ideally, audio data preservation
would be an automated and integrated process – but today such a
scenario remains beyond the technical and financial means of most
institutions housing audio files, let alone those of a single sociolinguistic researcher or research team.

    For your immediate purposes, you should at least ensure that you
make recordings of appropriate audio quality and store them in an
uncompressed file format (e.g. WAV, AIFF) in at least two locations, at
least one of which should be a dedicated hard drive. Preservation needs
will be much easier to address in the future if you are able to start from
this solid foundation. In addition, you are probably already in the habit
of regularly migrating data to new media, for example transferring
files from floppy disks to CDs to flash drives; burning analog cassettes
onto CDs; and transferring computer files from outdated computers
and applications to new ones. To establish at least the rudiments of
"automatic" preservation, you could plan to migrate your fieldwork
data every time you upgrade to a new computer – usually around every
three years or so. (See Bird and Simons 2003 for a definitive discussion
of data storage and preservation in linguistics; see Kendall 2008, 2013
on sociolinguistic data more specifically.)

Tools for data transcription, extraction, and analysis As your project
progresses, you may want to add tools for transcribing and extracting
data that draw data directly from your database and allow you to work
from within your own data management system rather than toggling
back and forth between separate applications. A detailed discussion of
data transcription and analysis is beyond the scope of a book focused

on data collection. Tagliamonte (2006a: 53–63) offers some excellent general guidelines for transcription and points out the importance of devising and abiding by consistent conventions that render your data most useful for *future* research, not just your own, as well as the importance of budgeting lots of time for this task, and perhaps money as well, so that you can farm out the work among a team of people rather than taking on this onerous task alone. Tagliamonte also discusses several basic yet very valuable tools for data extraction and at least preliminary analysis: **indexers** to produce an alphabetical listing of each word in a given interview transcript (or perhaps the entire transcript database) along with the number of words of each type and total number of words; **concordancers** to produce alphabetical listings of each word in context; and tools that produce lists of selected forms in the contexts in which they occur (e.g. **kwic**, Key Words in Context) (2006a: 64–67). Various versions of these tools are readily available as commercial and open-source software, and it is convenient (but not imperative) to incorporate them into your data management system.

Case study: Simple tools for insightful analyses

While the simple listings provided by indexes and concordances may not at first glance seem very important or revealing, Tagliamonte notes that sometimes simply knowing which words are most frequent is indeed of great sociolinguistic interest, especially if we see increases or decreases for particular forms as we move from older to younger speakers, a pattern suggestive of change in progress. For example, using relevant corpora from her studies of York English and Toronto English (1998, 2006b) and a simple indexing tool, Tagliamonte found that whereas discourse marker *like* represented only 0.09 percent of the total number of words for speakers aged 60 and older in the British Isles in 1997; in Toronto English in 2003, it made up a full 4 percent of the total number of words for young speakers aged 10–19, a difference strongly indicative of a huge increase in the use of discourse marker *like* in recent decades among English speakers in disparate geographic locations across the globe. Interestingly, Tagliamonte also compared the frequency of discourse marker *like* against the two most common words in the English language, *and* and *the*, for young speakers in Toronto in 2003 and found that many of these young speakers actually use more *like* than the other two words, a fascinating development indeed.

For more sophisticated searches, you will eventually want to annotate your data for grammatical information such as part of speech, and perhaps even phonological information as well – for example, tagging all instances of particular phonological word classes (e.g. PRY, PRIZE, PRICE; see Wells 1982). You can also tag for semantic, discourse, and pragmatic analysis purposes (e.g. speech act type, speech act form). It is becoming ever more feasible to conduct sophisticated linguistic tagging through automated means. However, you will want to take care to ensure that any pre-existing machine taggers you use have been tested for accuracy and will probably want to conduct tests yourself, to ensure that the taggers you use work well with your particular data.

Finally, as you continue building your data storage and management system, you may also find it useful to incorporate tools for coding tokens of linguistic variables. Following standard variationist proced-ure, tokens would be coded for their variable realization and for lin-guistic and extralinguistic factors relevant to particular variables and research questions. Tools for this kind of coding are not commonplace, however, and they must be built from scratch, or borrowed and adapted from sociolinguists willing to share the fruits of their labors. An excellent example of a data storage, management, and analysis system that *does* incorporate coding tools is the Sociolinguistic Archive and Analysis Project (SLAAP), a collaborative initiative between the North Carolina Language and Life Project (North Carolina State Univer-sity Linguistics Department) and the North Carolina State University Libraries, designed by Tyler Kendall (Kendall 2007). Among the variable features that SLAAP enables researchers to code for are post-vocalic *r*-lessness (e.g. [faː] for *far*), velar nasal fronting ("workin'" for *working*), third-person singular *-s* absence (e.g. "He go to school"), and *was / were* leveling (e.g. "They was home"; "It weren't me").

More on interview and project metadata

As you build your basic database for storing interview and project data and metadata, you need to think carefully about which bits of infor-mation about each recording and each participant (including both interviewees and interviewers) you will want to store, and then con-struct your database so that each piece of information is its own field. Remember also that some interviews will have more than one inter-viewee and maybe even more than one interviewer. Conversely, a single interviewee may participate in more than one interview, and individual interviewers are quite likely to do so. Therefore, you should devise a way to store and relate information pertaining to each participant with the information associated with each interview. Again, this is where a good database program, and programmer, will serve you well, since spreadsheet programs quickly become unwieldy in this regard.

You must also think about how you will keep interviewees' real names, contact information, and other identifying details confidential without losing track of the information in case you need to contact participants again in the future. Each interviewee's real name should be kept only on the original Interview Report Form associated with each interview (see below) and on their Informed Consent Form (which necessarily includes the real name because it includes the participant's signature). These forms can be stored separately from the project database in a secure location (physical, digital, or both) accessible only to project directors, or stored in the database in fields requiring an additional layer of password protection so that only project directors can gain access. Project directors can discuss storage of identifying information in secure online locations with their IRB, or they can simply keep confidential information out of shared spaces altogether. At the same time, no matter how innocuous you may think that non-identifying and / or anonymized information may be (e.g. interview transcripts with real names replaced by pseudonyms), you should ensure that your entire project database is password protected, whether it resides on a single computer, on a shared network, or on the Internet. Passwords should be given only to members of your research team (and possibly researchers from other institutions who have been carefully vetted), and these passwords should periodically expire, so that those no longer working on the project no longer have access to the data. Issues of confidentiality and access to data are discussed a bit more in Section 6.3.

For database programming purposes, each interview and participant (interviewers as well as interviewees) will need to be assigned a unique identifying number. For human purposes, you will also want to assign meaningful codes, for example OCR-002 for Ocracoke interview #2, or OCR-025 M54 for Ocracoke speaker #25, a 54-year-old male. Codes are essential not only for database management but for anonymizing your data. Tagliamonte (2006a) recommends that you use pseudonyms rather than numerical or alphabetic codes, since the former are easier to remember and give more life to interview excerpts used in presentations and publications. She also suggests that you devise a principled system for assigning pseudonyms rather than using random or fanciful names. She recommends keeping original initials and substituting ethnically and community-appropriate pseudonyms for participants' real names. For example, an Ocracoke Islander named Rex O'Neal could be given the pseudonym Ronald O'Hara, or you could even preserve his original last name, given that O'Neal is a very common last name in the Ocracoke community. The file that associates codes with real names should of course be very securely protected.

Generally, there is no problem with preserving interviewers' real names. In fact, as we will see below, access to researchers' real names can be crucial if we realize at some point after the interview has been conducted and catalogued that we need additional information that was not originally entered into the database.

While most fields in your interview database will contain information about interviewees, we strongly recommend that you also include at least basic demographic information about your interviewers. As we keep stressing, but as is still often forgotten in sociolinguistic research, interviews are dialogic, and interviewers play a big role in shaping the interview interaction, as we discussed in Chapter 4 on stylistic variation, and particularly Section 4.2 on audience design. We may see this dialogicality reflected in the way participants use phonological and morphosyntactic features, or we may find it in dimensions of interaction, such as participants' framing of the interview and the sub-events within it; their stances and identity projections; and their treatments (and elaborations) of interview topics.

Box 6.5 Don't forget the interviewer!

We ourselves have been guilty of neglecting the interviewer in favor of the interviewee in building the database for the Language and Communication in the Washington, DC, area (LCDC) project at Georgetown University. This oversight came to our attention thanks to a student who astutely remembered that interviews are co-constructions, not monologues in which interviewees present "genuine," unfiltered pictures of themselves and their communities using their "real" language varieties. The student wanted to investigate whether interviewer ethnicity impacted topics discussed by African American interviewees in the LCDC database – in particular whether White interviewers had more of a propensity than African American interviewers to raise and / or encourage topics centered on the negative stereotypes often associated with African Americans in the US (e.g. violence, drug use, poverty, etc.). However, this proved to be more difficult than we had originally anticipated. We had been so focused on interviewee speech and which of their characteristics might shape their speech that we included plenty of information on interviewees. In contrast, the only information we had about the interviewers were names alone, not even basic demographic information such as age, gender, or ethnicity. Luckily, because the project directors and other department faculty have been closely involved with the project since its inception, we were able to scroll through the interview metadata and identify the African American interviewers and so help the student find relevant interviews for her project. However, this potentially very important project would have to have been abandoned at the outset if we did not personally remember who all the interviewers were, or if the student had come along, say, 10 years from now, and the original project directions were no longer associated with the project. This taught us a valuable lesson about keeping better records on *all* interview participants, and we pass that lesson along to you now. This incident also reminded us once again that data collection and corpus building are iterative processes and, inevitably, plans, classificational schemes, and even research questions change shape as our projects progress.

The interviewee information you will want to keep track of will be based in large part on your study design and research questions. For example, did you select a particular population stratified by ethnicity, gender, age, and / or socioeconomic class as roughly defined by occupation and education? If so, you will want to include a field for each bit of demographic information. Researchers typically also keep track of information on where interviewees grew up (and so presumably acquired their vernacular speech patterns; but see Chapter 4 for criticism of the notion of "default," vernacular speech), as well as where else they have lived, in order to glean information on patterns of language and dialect contact. In situations where language and dialect contact or multilingualism will be of special importance, you may need to keep a record of more specific information on participants' linguistic backgrounds, for example native language(s), second languages (and when they were acquired), and information on amount and type of exposure to various languages and language varieties (e.g. through so many years of schooling in a particular language or so many years of living in a particular country or region). If you are doing more of a social network-type study or if you are taking a community-of-practice-based approach, you will still want to keep a record of each participant's basic demographic information. You might also include additional fields that identify participants' social networks, such as a Network Strength Score (L. Milroy 1980), as measured by a carefully considered formula you devised when designing your study; or perhaps you might use a dedicated field to identify those participants who interact in networks or communities of practice.

As with designing and stratifying the research sample more generally, database design becomes more complicated if you take the view that linguistic and social variation do not simply co-vary but rather co-constitute one another. We have come up against this issue in our LCDC project. Among our research questions, we are interested in how people use language to create and shape ethnic identity. Ironically, though, in choosing interviews to examine in detail for our in-depth investigation of this matter, we select speakers based on the pre-determined ethnic labels we gave them when entering them into our database (or which they perhaps gave themselves during interview discussion). We then examine how they use linguistic variation to project different types and facets of identity as they talk about different topics or position themselves differently with respect to their inter-locutors, wider social groups, and institution, or to what they are talking about. In other words, at the same time that we have pre-classified each interviewee as belonging to a particular ethnicity, we examine their ethnicity as an ongoing *project*, not a static *product*. We acknowledge this glaring inconsistency in our ways of thinking about ethnicity, but we have not yet determined whether it would be practicable to re-classify speakers according to more subtle ethnic identity categories, or to dispense with ethnic categories altogether. It strikes us as unwieldy to *not* keep track of interviewees' basic demographic information; otherwise, we would be faced with a long list of participants about whom we know nothing until we listen to each individual interview. Further, our interviewees also make sweeping categorizations (about themselves and others), and people do orient to familiar societal institutions, linguistic and other, even as they variously re-position themselves in interaction.

6.2.2 In the field

When you move into the fieldwork phase of your study, you of course begin to actually record your data. Usually, data will be recorded and stored in a temporary location and then transferred to central reposi-tories – either the project database that will be shared by the research team, or secure, non-shared sites accessible only to project directors (whether electronic or physical, e.g. locked file cabinets). For reasons outlined above, in most situations audio and video files will be recorded on specialized equipment rather than directly into a computer. In addition, even in today's electronic age, other types of data are typically recorded first on paper and then later transferred to electronic form, such as field notes, Informed Consent Forms, Interview Report Forms, and participant contact information. Below, we discuss how to keep track of each of these types of data while in the field, to make sure nothing is lost prior to transfer and, concurrently, that information that should *not* be shared does not make its way into the central project database.

Field notes

Because ethnographic participant-observation is so much a part of sociolinguistic field research, ethnographic field notes will almost certainly be a component of the data you will collect in the field. As noted in Chapter 3, full discussion of ethnographic methods is beyond the scope of a book focused on variationist sociolinguistics, but we here offer some basics regarding taking and keeping track of ethnographic field notes. Bernard (2006) notes that there are several different types of field notes, including "diary" notes, which are typically kept private rather than transferred to a central repository; and field notes "proper" – that is, notes concerning research methods, observations, and at least preliminary analyses. Diary notes are personal expressions of perceptions and feelings, including feelings about one's relationships with community members. They provide a necessary outlet for researchers engaged in the typically very emotional process of ethnographic fieldwork. At the same time, they constitute a useful analytical tool in that they raise researchers' awareness of their own perspectives and how these may shape their data, observations, and analyses. For example, you may find that you are a more active participant in an interview you conduct first thing in the morning, after a good night's sleep, than one you conduct at the end of an exhausting day spent trying to meet new people – and that your increased involvement in interviews may either help or hinder your efforts to get relaxed speech data. There may be days when, despite all your attempts to be receptive to your community and its norms, you may feel especially like an outsider. On those days, practically every behavior you observe may seem alien to you and so perhaps an object of disfavor – but at the same time, when you are feeling "left out," you may be especially attuned to patterns that you might otherwise take for granted as "normal," "natural" behavior. Because researchers need a private space into which they can pour their emotions and immediate reactions, diary notes are best left private, to be kept as the confidential property of each field researcher. If these notes end up informing observation and analysis, the information will find its way into shared space, whether as part of the methodological and analytical field notes that get uploaded to the project database or hard drive space, or as part of later write-ups of the ethnographic and sociolinguistic analysis.

More formal field notes, on the other hand, can become part of the project database if community members are given pseudonyms. Bernard (2006) advises researchers to make jottings throughout each day and to set aside time at the end of each day for writing more thorough notes. Even in today's digital age, most field notes are still initially handwritten in notebooks rather than typed into a computer, in part because paper still feels "friendlier" for many people, and also because you can write fieldnotes in a much wider range of situations than those in which you can open up your computer and start word-processing, for example during recording sessions, and throughout the course of your daily observations and interactions in the community, as you think of ideas to pursue or questions to ask, or in order to take down contact and demographic info as you meet people. Bernard advocates making many short notes – typically one per day, clearly labeled by date, rather than one long running document which you will later have to sift through to find a particular day's observations. And while the researcher may be tempted to try and use every waking moment in the field for actual participantobservation and data collection rather than for reflection and writing, it is strongly advised that you do set aside at least a short time every evening for writing field notes, since your perceptions will never be as fresh as they are while you are still in the field.

Because you will be recording such invaluable information, great care must be taken to ensure that you do not lose your field notes prior to adding them to the project database. One way to provide some back up if you are working as a team is to designate one laptop computer as the central repository for data collection until it can be more securely stored at the home institution. And both teams and individuals should get in the habit of saving field notes in at least two locations, perhaps a personal laptop and a flash drive, or perhaps even in both electronic and paper form. Granted, paper can become unwieldy in the field, and most people do not own or wish to carry portable printers. However, paper provides an invaluable back up should electronic systems fail, and even in our ever more "paperless" age (and at the risk of sounding environmentally unfriendly), Bernard notes that "trees are a renewable resource" (2006: 395), but your fresh perceptions from the field are not. A third method of transfer from personal laptops to a central database is to upload daily over the Internet. However, this will not be possible in field locations with sporadic or no Internet coverage, and if it is adopted as fieldwork practice, great care will have to be taken to ensure that data cannot be accessed by unauthorized persons during the uploading process. In the interest of simplicity and keeping things streamlined, I personally feel quite comfortable with keeping field notes in the field (in two places, one of which most likely will be on paper), and both of which should be labeled in accordance with explicit protocols (consistent across the fieldwork team) and then immediately transferring them to the project database upon my return.

Although the focus here is on managing field notes, not their content, we should at least note in passing that, following Bernard (2006), most of the "field notes proper" that you take in the field will concern methodology and description, including methods for interacting with the particular groups you are studying, and descriptions of behaviors, norms, and processes from both your own and community members' perspectives. You will learn a great deal about how to comport yourself in the field from instances in which you act inappropriately in the cultural setting at hand – as, for example, in the case of my fellow researcher in Ocracoke Island, who was too "formally" dressed for island norms (discussed in Chapter 5 above); or for all of us on the Robeson County, NC, research team who did not realize the strength of the racial boundaries separating the three area ethnic groups until we had accidentally sent a couple of African American males into a Lumbee Indian community, where it quickly became apparent that such racial mixing was not only culturally inappropriate but actually potentially dangerous. And though you may sometimes feel ashamed to share your fieldwork mistakes with your research team, you should always remember that there is no learning without error, and that what feels to you like an embarrassing (or even stupid) gaffe can serve as an excellent teaching tool for field researchers on human behavior across a range of disciplines. For all these reasons, we encourage including "field notes proper" in the project database, even though they can contain information that may feel almost as personal as that contained in your "diary" notes. Methodological, observational, and analytical field notes are just as important as more personal ones, and some of our most valuable insights and preliminary analyses come to us while we are immersed in the field situation.

Interview Report Forms

Interview Report Forms provide a quick overview of basic demographic and other information on interviewees (and ideally also interviewers), as well as a brief description of the interview that includes such information as location, recording equipment used, sound quality, interactional quality (e.g. uncomfortable, lively), informational quality, significant dialectal and other linguistic features, and notes on any particularly interesting or important sections of the interview and where in the recording they are located (e.g. 32:35). Also useful are notes on the interviewee's family, friendship, and occupational networks, as well as how the interviewee was met and recruited. Researchers should fill out a report form as soon as possible after each interview, whether in electronic or paper form, and forms should of course be entered into the project database (in the field and back at home) as soon as possible. Original forms with identifying information should be maintained in a location with severely restricted access; anonymized forms can go into an area of the database available to all authorized researchers on the project. As an example, the LCDC Interview Report Form is shown in Figure 6.1.

STUDENTS IN THE FIELD

Anastasia Nylund has been an instrumental member of the LCDC project team for some time. She has conducted fieldwork as well as analyses of the interrelation between language variation, ethnicity, and residents' sense of "place" (Nylund 2010, 2011, 2012). In discussing her work, Ana points to the crucial importance of not only filling out an Interview Report Form, but also listening to the interview as soon as possible after it has taken place. She notes, "One thing that I've found really added depth to my field observations was taking the time to listen to an interview soon after doing it, checking with my notes . . . and really taking the time to form a picture of the interview encounter in my mind. Often this is when nascent analysis starts appearing!"

Contact information

In addition to diary notes and methodological, descriptive, and analytical notes, you are encouraged to keep a daily log of planned activities and actual activities (Bernard 2006). Again, this log is mostly for personal purposes and will probably find its way into the project database (or other permanent record) only indirectly, as your recollections of people you interacted with and activities you observed and took part in inform

Interviewer name(s):

Date/time of interview:

Location of interview:

Name of interviewee:

Pseudonym for interviewee:

Age and/or birthdate:

Ethnicity:

Current residence:

Time spent in DC area:

Childhood residence(s):

Occupation:

Education:

Recording equipment (recorder and microphone):

Brief description of interview, including sound quality, interactional quality (e.g. uncomfortable, lively), informational quality, interesting dialectal and other linguistic features. If there are any particularly interesting or important sections, please indicate where in interview these are (e.g. halfway through, 32.35 minutes into the recording)

Other potential interviewees mentioned by this interviewee:

Any other information you feel is relevant for future research:

6.1 Interview Report Form for the Language and Communication in the Washington, DC, Metropolitan Area (LCDC) project.

your analyses and write-ups. However, one essential part of your daily log should be prepared for direct submission to project directors (or your own permanent storage area, if you are working alone), and this is a record of contact information for each community member you meet, and in what context, regardless of whether or not they actually end up participating in the study. Some information will be rather general (e.g. "Bill Jones, owner of General Store, seems to be there in the early morning hours"), while other contacts may provide you with specific name and address information. You can record this information as you receive it, in a log book you carry around with you, though it should then be integrated into an alphabetized database at the end of each day, so that information on specific contacts can later be easily retrieved when needed. **Your field contact record is extremely important but also extremely sensitive, so you should take great care to prevent unauthorized access.** If you are supervising other researchers, you must decide how long each researcher can keep their contact information for purposes of follow-up visits and interviews, and you should make sure you collect all contact information (and any copies) at the completion of the research project. Once the contact information is gathered, it should *not* be stored anywhere in the project database that is accessible to the project team in general. Rather, this information should be housed either in the central database with an extra layer of password protection, ensuring access only by project directors (and authorized database administrators), or in a completely separate database stored on project directors' personal password-protected computers (and / or in paper form, in project directors' locked file cabinets).

Keeping track of recordings in the field

As noted above, your database system will include a place to store actual audio and video files, which ideally will be linked to the metadata associated with each file. In the field, you should have a password-protected computer set up with a folder structure that mirrors that of your home database system, as well as a file labeling system that will be consistently followed. For immediate purposes, labels can include pseudonyms or initials of interviewees without numbers, though eventually each interview will have a unique identifying number and code, and you may wish to wait to devise your coding scheme after you have been in field for awhile and have a better sense of a scheme that works well with your particular community, sample, stratificational categories, etc. You may elect to have one field computer to which every member of the research team transfers audio / video files following each interview (or at the end of each day); or researchers on a team may initially store the data on their own computers, taking care to ensure that labeling and storage protocols are consistent.

All audio and video recordings should be transferred as soon as possible from the recording device to the appropriate computer location. Immediately thereafter, **files should be copied to at least two other storage media**, for example CD / DVD, flash drive, portable hard drive. Media that can be password protected are of course strongly preferred, and again, you should *never* store data only on CDs, since they have proven to be disappointingly degradable despite their reassuring "physicality" vis-à-vis disembodied digital files. If you do elect to store *back ups* of files on CDs, you should use one CD per interview and label each clearly and consistently.

6.2.3 Fine-tuning your database

As we have discussed repeatedly in this book, research design involves interplay between pre-planning and making discoveries in the field that may alter your plans. You may enter the field planning to study the patterning of language variation according to certain wide-scale demographic characteristics, but then discover locally important categories that may be equally or more important and so need to be added as metadata in your project database (e.g. jocks and burnouts, or Lumbee subcommunities in addition to undifferentiated ethnic categories such as Lumbee Indian, White, and African American). Conversely, you may realize that certain information you thought would be important actually has no bearing either socially or linguistically (e.g. church membership in Ocracoke, NC). You can remove fields from your database if you realize you do not really need them; however, you might wish to leave them in, in order to keep as rich a record as possibly of the sociolinguistic landscape, for the benefit of future researchers who may have other questions.

As noted above, as your field project progresses, you will want to attach other information to each interview record. For example, you will probably include transcription files as you produce them, and you may want to keep a record of which linguistic features have been analyzed in each interview.

6.3 PRESERVING CONFIDENTIALITY

Throughout the second half of this chapter, we have stressed that in storing your data you need to achieve an acceptable balance between allowing access and maintaining confidentiality. Here we sum up our suggestions regarding what types of data to store in what types of locations and who should have access to each. If your project is a team effort, we recommend that all anonymized and otherwise non-identifying data and metadata associated with the project be stored in a password-protected Internet (or Intranet) data management system to which all authorized researchers have access for the duration of their involvement with the project. This information includes *copies* of audio files with interviewees' names edited out, interviewee information (as identified by pseudonym or code), interviewer information, interview information, transcripts (also identified by pseudonym or code), project forms, and protocols. You may also elect to include field notes "proper" (see above) in your shared database, provided pseudonyms can reasonably be substituted for identifying information. Great care should also be taken to protect the confidentiality of video data, since editing out identifying information will very likely render the videos less than fully useful, perhaps not useful at all, and it is a dangerous practice for non-anonymized video files to be uploaded to Internet space. In addition, video files are even larger than audio files, and having researchers access them via remote download will probably prove to be cumbersome anyway, in terms of download time and storage space the downloaded files will take up on individual computers. (And further, once researchers download files with identifying information, you have no control over their security.) Hence, we recommend that video files be kept out of Internet and Intranet space and instead be stored on a central hard drive. This should *not* be the same hard drive as the dedicated drive housing *all* project information, for reasons outlined below.

The central repository for all project data (with the exception of diary-style field notes) should be a dedicated hard drive that is password protected to allow access only by project directors and authorized database administrators. **No one else should have access to this drive**, since increased access entails increased risk of compromising data and database programming. In addition to all the non-confidential pieces of information listed above, the secure hard drive will also contain confidential information, including original audio and video files with identifying information intact. You may also elect to store here the only other files that necessarily contain identifying information: Interview Report Forms, Informed Consent Forms, the database containing participant contact information, and unedited descriptive and analytical field notes. Alternatively you might choose to store forms, field notes, and contact information on project directors' personal computers; in addition, forms and field notes can be kept solely in paper form, in a locked file cabinet. In submitting your request for Institutional Review Board approval for your project, you will have to specify in detail where you will store the various types of information associated with your project, and your IRB will let you know if centralized, password-protected storage of confidential information is acceptable or not. A further possibility is to store files with identifying information in shared Internet or Intranet project space with an extra layer of password protection; however, this is a less secure option.

6.4 SUMMARY

As stated at the outset of this chapter, recording and managing your recorded data from the field is one of the most important yet initially most daunting aspects of sociolinguistic fieldwork. In the above I have outlined specifications for achieving optimal audio recording quality and also touched on some considerations for video recording as well. I have also emphasized that recording in field situations necessarily involves some sacrifice in audio quality in order to maximize interactional quality – and quality of community relations more generally. Conversely, when recording under optimal conditions for audio quality (i.e. in a phonetics laboratory), there is inevitable sacrifice in terms of the information that can be gained on how language is actually used in everyday life.

When it comes to storing and managing data, there are balancing acts to be performed as well, including balancing simplicity of design and use of your data management system with sophistication of storage, search, analysis, and long-term preservation capabilities – and, perhaps most important of all, balancing accessibility and confidentiality. As researchers, we are of course eager to advance the field by sharing our data as well as our findings; however, we have to exercise great caution to ensure that we do not let our linguistic zeal overrun the obligation we have to our research participants to keep their personal information out of the spotlight. As with every step in the fieldwork process, and as we will see in sharp relief in this book's final chapter, our human interactions with our human subjects are always more important than our academic gain, and we should gladly sacrifice widespread data access to ensure ethical research practices and respectful treatment of the community members who are, in reality, our research partners.

Suggested readings

PLICHTA, BARTŁOMIEJ. AKUSTYK WEBSITE no date
HTTP://BARTUS.ORG/AKUSTYK

This all-inclusive and continually updated website provides free speech analysis and synthesis software, detailed information on recording specifications and techniques, equipment reviews and recommendations, and tutorials and online seminars. It is *the* single most comprehensive source for information on recording equipment and techniques.

JOHNSON, KEITH 2012. *ACOUSTIC AND AUDITORY PHONETICS*, 3RD EDN. MALDEN, MA: WILEY-BLACKWELL.

This is an indispensible guide to acoustic and auditory phonetics, the physics of speech, and their implications for audio recording. The reader is referred especially to Chapter 2 on Digital Signal Processing.

LADEFOGED, PETER AND KEITH JOHNSON 2010. *A COURSE IN PHONETICS* (WITH CD-ROM), 6TH EDN. LONDON: WADSWORTH.

This update of Ladefoged's classic work (1993) is an invaluable instructional guide to articulatory and acoustic phonetics. The CD-ROM contains audio files of numerous English varieties and nearly 100 languages, as well as exercises in articulatory and acoustic phonetics. The clear, concise discussion of acoustic phonetics is an invaluable overview that the reader will return to repeatedly for reference.

TAGLIAMONTE, SALI 2006. *ANALYSING SOCIOLINGUISTIC VARI-ATION*. CAMBRIDGE UNIVERSITY PRESS. See especially Chapters 2, 3, and 4.

Tagliamonte's practical guide to conducting a sociolinguistic variation study from beginning to end includes extremely helpful chapters on collecting and managing data. Also included is an especially useful section on transcription.

KENDALL, TYLER 2013. DATA IN THE STUDY OF LANGUAGE VARIATION AND CHANGE. IN J.K. CHAMBERS AND NATALIE SCHILLING (EDS.), *THE HANDBOOK OF LANGUAGE VARIATION AND CHANGE*. 2ND EDN. MALDEN, MA: BLACKWELL.

Kendall provides a comprehensive and thoughtful treatment of issues in sociolinguistic data collection, organization, storage, preservation, annotation, and coding. Included are discussions of the nature of "data" in sociolinguistics, the composition of a sociolinguistic "corpus," data access and sharing, and the various types of metadata and annotation associated with sociolinguistic databases / corpora. Kendall illustrates his points using examples from several important large-scale sociolinguistic studies.

BIRD, STEVEN AND GARY SIMONS 2003. SEVEN DIMENSIONS OF
PORTABILITY FOR LANGUAGE DOCUMENTATION AND DESCRIP-
TION. *LANGUAGE* 79(3): 557–582.

This definitive treatment of data management in linguistics discusses
in detail the problems that the transformation from analog to digital
technologies have created in terms of the storage, management, preservation, and sharing of language data, despite the fact that such
technologies have of course been of great benefit. The authors note
that unless best practices are developed and followed in terms of
content, format, discovery, access, citation, preservation, and rights,
digital data collections will be (and indeed already often are) lost,
whether through the inability of scholars and communities to find,
understand, and utilize them; the physical degradation of storage
media; or the recurring obsolescence of digital technologies. The
authors discuss highly promising efforts by the Open Language Arch-
ives Community (OLAC) to work with endangered language communities to identify and implement community-agreed best practices, and
they provide their own recommendations for moving toward general
best practices in data management in linguistics.

7 Giving back to the community

This book has taken us on a long journey through sociolinguistic field-work. Along the way, we have considered not only practical and theoretical matters but also relational and ethical issues. When we conduct research with and about human communities, we necessarily interact with those communities. In other words, we as sociolinguistic researchers are not simply observers but, some extent, participants as well. Because participant-observer status entails a dual insider–outsider perspective, we have to think about just how far "inside" the community we should go – that is, how involved we should become with our research communities and in what ways. Clearly, we must engage in at least **ethical involvement**. That is, we should ensure that people's privacy is protected, that no one comes to harm, and that our research participants are compensated for any inconvenience and discomfort they may experience as a result of taking part in our research project. However, most sociolinguists maintain that we should involve ourselves more fully than this, adopting a position of **advocacy**, in which we actively seek ways to work *for* the community of study rather than simply conducting research *on* them, or a position of **empowerment**, in which we actively work *with* community members to help them help themselves (Cameron, Frazer, Harvey, Rampton, and Richardson 1992).

Sociolinguists believe in community involvement for a number of important reasons. For one, when people agree to participate in our studies, they give us a lot, including their time, their voices, their thoughts, and even expression of their innermost hopes and desires. In addition, we gain a lot from our research participants – not just valuable linguistic and sociolinguistic knowledge, but also practical and personal gain in the form of degrees, jobs, career advancement, and possibly even (limited) fame. We owe our research participants at least *something* in return. Further, since we often enter the community and gain valuable contacts through capitalizing on being a friend of a friend, we need to remember that this position confers obligations as well as rights (Milroy and Gordon 2003: 75–78). It would be unfair and unethical for us to simply pose as someone in this important position, and it is our obligation to participate in both the "give" and the "take" that being a friend of a friend entails. Friends of friends are important precisely because they do things for one another, and the value of these connections breaks down if we abuse our position by capitalizing on a friend's name solely for our own gain.

Finally, sociolinguists believe in giving back to the community because the communities we study are often in need of help. Although sociolinguists are of course interested in communities of all social and economic strata, many of us are interested in minority communities whose language varieties differ from widespread standard dialects. And all too often, these communities are cast aside by the majority, not only linguistically but socially, economically, and educationally. Often the non-standard linguistic practices that excite us as linguists are seen by non-linguists as "evidence" of minority groups' supposed "inferiority." Linguists can and should challenge these assumptions and injustices when we encounter them, in whatever way we can.

Hence, there are a number of important reasons for sociolinguistic researchers to commit to giving back to the communities who have generously shared their language, their social networks, their stories, and their time in order to provide us with data. At the same time, as in all human relationships, commitment does not yield straightforward rewards for the researcher and the research community but can raise tricky ethical and practical issues of its own, and we need to be aware of these as well as the joys of community involvement. In what follows, I outline a number of forms community involvement can take, the issues that can surface, and the rich benefits that can result. I illustrate my points with examples, but unfortunately (or fortunately!) I cannot in the space allotted do justice to all of the humanistic efforts in which sociolinguists have been so tirelessly involved from the beginnings of sociolinguistics to the present day.

7.1 OPERATIONALIZING ADVOCACY: LABOV'S PRINCIPLES FOR COMMUNITY INVOLVEMENT AND THEIR IMPLEMENTATION

Since the very inception of the field, sociolinguists have worked to apply the knowledge they gain from their research communities for the betterment of these communities, and often for the betterment of society more generally. These efforts are based on fundamental ethical tenets of accountability and involvement, which Labov (1982) articulated as follows:

The Principle of Error Correction

A scientist who becomes aware of a widespread idea or social practice with important consequences that is invalidated by his [sic] own data is obligated to bring this error to the attention of the widest possible audience (p. 172).

The Principle of the Debt Incurred

An investigator who has obtained data from members of a speech community has an obligation to use the knowledge based on that data for the benefit of the community, when it has need of it (p. 173).

As conscientious scientists, we are obligated to let non-linguists know that they are wrong in believing non-standard dialects to be illogical and ill-formed. Linguistic scientific research has shown from the inception of sociolinguistics that *all* dialects are systematic and fully formed, regardless of whether they are seen as standard or non-standard, and regardless of whether they are socially esteemed or disparaged. Hence, it is vital for sociolinguists to speak out in specific cases involving mis-perception of the nature of language variation, as well as against linguistic misperceptions being perpetuated more widely. We are also obligated not only to speak out against these misperceptions, but to actively work to *undo* them – to correct the injuries that they have inflicted, to prevent further harm, and to protect the communities and speakers who suffer from them. As we will see, these principles underlie a number of influential initiatives undertaken by sociolinguists, some of which have far-reaching consequences indeed.

7.1.1   Sociolinguistics and education

Labov himself has spent his entire career combating linguistic discrimination in the US. Since the 1960s, he has worked to convince educators, courts, and the general public that the non-standard dialects whose structures he has studied so thoroughly over the decades are at least as linguistically systematic as standard English, and that the speakers of these non-standard varieties are equally capable of skill-fully expressing complex thoughts and ideas. His efforts have included important and widely published articles such as "The Logic of Non-standard English" (1969), educational materials designed to help non-standard-speaking children overcome difficulties in learning to read in a non-native dialect (i.e. standard English), and court testimony per-taining to dialect discrimination.

At the same time that variationist sociolinguists were beginning their systematic study of non-standard dialects in the 1960s, some educational psychologists were putting forward the view that African American Vernacular English and other non-standard dialects represented "restricted codes" rather than fully fledged language varieties. Proponents of this view argued that speakers of restricted codes suffered a "linguistic deficit" that prohibited them from conveying (and perhaps even from thinking) fully formed, logical ideas (Bernstein 1961, 1972; Williamson-Ige 1984). Labov and other sociolinguists reacted against this erroneous view by demonstrating that the linguistic usages of speakers of AAVE were dialect *differences*, not deficiencies. Equally importantly, linguists demonstrated that although the differences may slow children's progress in school if they are ignored or disparaged by educators, they do *not* connote any sort of linguistic or cognitive deficiency on the part of speakers.

One of Labov's most important contributions to educational advocacy was his court testimony in the now-famous Ann Arbor case of 1979. In this case, parents of fifteen African American children successfully brought suit in Federal court against the Martin Luther King Elementary School, the Ann Arbor School District, and the Michigan Board of Education. The suit found fault with educational authorities' failure to take into account the barriers to academic progress posed by the differing structure of, and disparaging attitudes toward, the children's home dialect (Labov 1982; Smitherman 1981).

Despite the success of the Ann Arbor case decades ago, however, misperceptions about AAVE and other non-standard dialects continue to abound in the educational arena today. Sociolinguists have had to keep working to try to inform educators, parents, students, and the general public about the true nature of dialect variation, as well as to ameliorate poor educational outcomes related to dialect differences and how they are viewed. (See, e.g., Wolfram, Adger, and Christian 1999; Wolfram, Reaser, and Vaughn 2008.) In 1996, a public furor arose over a policy approved by the Oakland Unified School District Board of Education that was in essence exactly what the presiding judge in the Ann Arbor case had mandated nearly twenty years earlier as a corrective to the dialect discrimination taking place in the Martin Luther King School – namely, that AAVE (which the Oakland School Board called Ebonics) must be recognized as a legitimate language variety, and that educators must start from a basis of knowledge of and respect for this dialect as they work toward helping AAVE-speaking students achieve mastery of standard English. The media seized on this news, and it was widely publicized, usually in a distorted version in which it was claimed that Oakland schools would now be teaching children Ebonics rather than standard English. Parents, educators, and public figures, including a number of prominent African Americans, vehemently spoke out against the Oakland policy.

Fortunately, sociolinguists were ready to speak out, too, and they proactively put forward correct interpretations of the Oakland School Board policy as well as accurate information about AAVE and other non-standard dialects and their speakers. A few media sources were astute enough to realize that they should talk with language specialists and not just celebrities, and linguists' voices were heard countering the non-experts that labeled Ebonics as "broken English." One notable example of an expert voice cutting through the cacophony of public opinion is John Rickford's (1997a) "Suite for ebony and phonics," which appeared in the popular science magazine *Discover*. In addition, the media picked up statements made in academic venues, including the Linguistic Society of America's "Resolution on the Oakland 'Ebonics' Issue," passed in January 1997, which affirmed, among other linguistic and sociolinguistic truths, that:

> The variety known as "Ebonics," "African American vernacular English" AAVE, and "Vernacular Black English" and by other names is systematic and rule-governed like all natural speech varieties. In fact, all human linguistic systems – spoken, signed, and written – are fundamentally regular. The systematic and expressive nature of the grammar and pronunciation patterns of the African American vernacular has been established by numerous scientific studies over the past thirty years. Characterizations of Ebonics as "slang," "mutant," "lazy," "defective," "ungrammatical," or "broken English" are incorrect and demeaning.

In addition to speaking out in public and academic venues, Rickford and others sociolinguists have also followed in Labov's footsteps by developing materials for teachers and schoolchildren to more directly help combat dialect prejudice and educational difficulties caused by dialect difference. For example, John Rickford and Angela Rickford (1995) have been proponents of dialect readers, in which children whose home dialects differ from standard English are first presented with reading material in their native dialects and gradually transitioned into reading standard English. From a slightly different angle, Wolfram has for decades developed and taught dialect awareness curricula in which students (and their teachers) learn about the linguistic and cultural value of non-standard dialects. Wolfram has also been working for nearly two decades on a broader scale to effect policy changes that will make the study of language variation a part of the standard curriculum for grade-school students in North Carolina public schools.

To their great credit, Labov, Wolfram, Rickford, and other pioneers of sociolinguistics have passed down their zeal for educational improvement to their students. Outreach efforts continue in the form of dialect awareness curricula developed by sociolinguists such as Kirk Hazen, Anne H. Charity Hudley, Anne Lobeck, Christine Mallinson, Jeffrey Reaser, and Julie Sweetland, as well as in studies of the effects of such programs (Reaser 2006). Today's sociolinguists continue with efforts to inform educators and parents through teacher training workshops and publications aimed at disseminating knowledge about linguistic and dialect diversity and its educational impact to teachers, educational administrators, policy makers, and the general public (Wolfram and Reaser forthcoming; Wolfram, Reaser, and Vaughn 2008).

As Labov's second principle for community involvement reminds us, we are obligated to use our linguistic knowledge to help communities when needed, because the communities we study help us so much in advancing our field of study and our own careers. Part of the reason linguists like Labov have worked so hard to improve educational outcomes for native speakers of AAVE is that we have learned a tremendous amount from speakers of this variety. The knowledge we have gained is not limited to AAVE itself, but includes insights into dialect variation more generally. For example, we now know that dialects can vary in terms of integral structural matters such as tense and aspect systems in addition to more surface-level phonological and lexical variation. AAVE has given us important insights into dialect history and formation, including the fact that features arising from original language contact situation(s) may be retained in language varieties, as they appear to be in AAVE. Researchers have also learned a great deal from AAVE about attitudes toward dialect variation and their consequences in social life. For example, since the Ann Arbor decision, it has been acknowledged that negative attitudes toward AAVE are actually a bigger obstacle to AAVE-speaking children's educational progress than are the structural differences between AAVE and standard English *per se* (Rickford 1997b: 178). Further, there is no denying that the careers of many of the founders and leading figures of modern sociolinguists, including William Labov, Roger W. Shuy, Walt Wolfram, Ralph W. Fasold, John R. Rickford, and others, were launched and advanced via their studies of AAVE.

7.1.2 Sociolinguistics and housing discrimination

Just as minority populations who speak non-standard dialects are subject to education discrimination, they also often face discrimination in a number of other arenas, including housing. In the US, denying housing on the basis of race is illegal but sadly often still practiced.

As John Baugh has dramatically demonstrated, housing discrimination is often grounded in language and dialect discrimination, or what he terms **linguistic profiling**. In other words, realtors and landlords do not wait to see housing applicants in person before denying admission to "exclusive" (i.e. wealthy, White) neighborhoods, but rather begin weeding out "undesirable" people of color based solely on the voices they hear in telephone inquiries. Baugh found this out firsthand, when he was looking for housing in the very wealthy and predominantly White community of Palo Alto, California. Following the usual procedure for seeking housing in the US, Baugh made a number of phone calls to realtors, using the dialect he usually uses for business purposes, standard English, to set up appointments to come view prospective homes. However, on several occasions, when he showed up for his appointment, he was abruptly told that the house in question was no longer available and surmised that the realtors' sudden denials had to do with the fact that they had believed him to be a White man based on his voice but then realized their mistake in person (he is, in fact, Black). Being a scientist and staunch advocate of equal rights, Baugh decided to put his unfortunate experience to good use. He conducted an experiment in which he made numerous phone calls to landlords in five Palo Alto-area neighborhoods using the three different dialects he commands – standard English, African American English, and Chicano English – to see if the dialect discrimination he suspected really was being practiced. Sadly, his hypothesis was confirmed, and he obtained significantly different results regarding housing availability depending on which dialect or "guise" he used, with results being most stark in the most exclusive neighborhoods. Baugh published his findings in a range of venues (Baugh 2003; Purnell, Idsardi, and Baugh 1999), and worked with the National Fair Housing Alliance to produce a series of public interest advertisements alerting African Americans and Latinos to be wary of housing discrimination linguistic profiling and to report it to authorities when it does occur.

Baugh's findings and their wide publicity clearly have huge potential to benefit minorities who suffer from housing discrimination. In addition, as Labov (2008) and Rickford (1997b) note, working to ameliorate housing discrimination will in the long run aid efforts to improve educational outcomes for minorities whose home language differs from that of the classroom: Dialect-related educational problems are inextricably linked to housing discrimination and segregation, since members of minority populations who come into little contact with more privileged communities have little direct exposure to the privileged language variety and hence have more difficulty in learning the standard in the schoolroom. Further, as Labov (2008), Rickford (1997b) and others point out, the discrimination that begins in the home neighborhood and continues into the classroom then spirals into high dropout rates from school, decreased access to legitimate employment, and increased crime and imprisonment. See, for example, Matsuda (1991) and Lippi-Green (1994) for work on occupational discrimination, Gumperz (1982) and Butters (2000) on courtroom discrimination, and Rickford (1997b: 173–175) for further discussion of these issues. Together these factors create a feedback loop of poor living and family conditions that work along with societal disparagement to disadvantage children from the outset.

Also implicated in this cycle are media portrayals of disenfranchised peoples and their languages and dialects, including not only distorted media portrayals of breaking "linguistic news," such as the Oakland Ebonics controversy, but more pervasive and so perhaps more unconsciously accepted forms of cultural and linguistic devaluation. For example, sociolinguist Otto Santa Ana, in his analyses of mass media representations of Latinos, has exposed the anti-Latino slant of various media outlets, including nationally televised news programs and talk shows, as well as a disturbing *lack* of coverage of issues impacting Latino communities. In addition, he has investigated how even the "good-natured," humorous banter of talk show hosts can in reality serve as a powerful force for creating and sustaining political hierarchies and anti-minority sentiment (Santa Ana 2002, 2009, forthcoming, 2013). If sociolinguists working against institutional discrimination can effect even a small change in any one of these myriad areas of linguistic and cultural disparagement and discrimination, they can help break a very vicious cycle indeed. Even efforts that start out as seemingly modest ones (e.g. developing and teaching a dialect awareness unit in a community school) can contribute to important change.

7.1.3 Sociolinguists and the law

In addition to using their expert knowledge to help combat education and housing discrimination, whether in the public media, in the classroom, or in the courtroom, sociolinguists have also applied their knowledge in the legal arena more generally. They have served as expert witnesses in an array of cases involving language variation and interpretation of discourse. They have documented and described power inequities in courtroom discourse, some of which are rooted in the legal system itself and others of which have to do with language and dialect variation, such as matters of interpretation and *mis*interpretation of non-English languages in US courts. They have also worked more generally to assist and educate legal and law enforcement professionals, as well as the general public, in matters related to language and the law – that is, forensic linguistics. For example, sociolinguists Roger W. Shuy and Ronald R. Butters have been involved in numerous criminal and civil cases in which they applied their expertise in linguistic variation and discourse analysis to such matters as author identification (e.g. regionality of authors of anonymous ransom notes, ages of suspected perpetrators chatting online with children); determination of whether language crimes such as bribery and solicitation had indeed been committed; and trademark and copyright disputes. In terms of education on forensic linguistics, examples include workshops presented by me and my colleague James R. Fitzgerald to linguists and sociolinguists to law enforcement agencies (e.g. presentations on linguistics, sociolinguistics, and forensic linguistic for the US Federal Bureau of Investigation and the Royal Canadian Mounted Police); publications such as Shuy's numerous books on forensic linguistics (e.g. 1996, 1998, 2005); and the development and implementation of entire programs of study in forensic linguistics (e.g. Hofstra University's Master of Arts in Forensic Linguistics, designed and headed by linguist Robert A. Leonard, and the University of York's Master of Science in Forensic Speech Science, whose faculty includes sociolinguists Paul Foulkes and Dominic Watt).

7.2   FROM ADVOCACY TO EMPOWERMENT: WOLFRAM'S PRINCIPLE OF LINGUISTIC GRATUITY AND ITS IMPLEMENTATION IN INFORMAL EDUCATION

In addition to their important work in institutional settings, sociolinguists have also worked to disseminate information on language variation and dialect diversity more generally, in a range of informal educational venues. A pioneer in this regard is Walt Wolfram, who, together with colleagues and students, has developed a vast array of materials designed to promote dialect awareness (e.g. Wolfram 2013a). His outreach efforts over the decades have taken many forms, ranging from dialect vocabulary booklets and audio CDs of community stories, to museum displays and video documentaries highlighting local dialects. Titles include *The Ocracoke Brogue* (Blanton and Waters 1996), *Indian by Birth: The Lumbee Dialect* (Hutcheson 2001), *Mountain Talk* (Hutcheson 2004), and *Voices of North Carolina*, a documentary about dialect variation across the entire state (Hutcheson 2005).

Wolfram and his team have also worked with community members to produce documentaries and other materials that focus on cultural and historical aspects of the communities in which they have conducted research. For example, films like *Celebrating Princeville* (Hutcheson 2003) and *Celebrating Muzel Bryant* (Grimes 2004), commemorate local history and the lives of prominent community members.

Wolfram's informal educational materials move beyond Labov's principles for community involvement in that they encourage sociolinguists to proactively seek ways to help the community rather than simply reacting to visible need. The rationale behind this more active engagement is encapsulated in Wolfram's Principle of Linguistic Gratuity:

> Investigators who have obtained linguistic data from members of a speech community should actively pursue positive ways in which they can return linguistic favors to the community (Wolfram 1993: 227).

In moving from a reactive stance to a proactive one, Wolfram has also extended the advocacy position embodied in Labov's principles to one of empowerment: community members are key collaborators in developing outreach and educational projects. Wolfram and his colleagues work closely with community leaders to plan their video documentaries, which show local personalities speaking for themselves in their own words. When narrators are required, locals lend their voices. Productions are screened for community members prior to releasing them to wider audiences. Community members have also been involved in helping design (and re-design) museum displays about local dialects, writing dictionaries of dialect lexical items (Locklear *et al.* 1996), and telling narratives for us to include in CDs of community stories.

While working toward empowerment can be richly rewarding to both community members and researchers, it also forces some complications to the forefront – complications that are much easier to avoid or ignore if we remain more distant from our research communities. First, there is the issue of what exactly power is and who holds it. For example, is it inevitably the case that power must flow from the researcher to the research community, or is it not also true that community members hold power of their own, even if not the institutional and academic power of the university researcher? In previous chapters, we have talked about the researcher's position as both "expert" and "learner," since community members hold the knowledge we seek to gain from our fieldwork ventures. In addition, it is community members, not researchers, who have the power to grant access to the people, places, and events we want to observe and analyze. And further, if we work with community members in producing outreach products, they may very well decide that they do not like what we have produced and subsequently seek to alter it – or veto it altogether.

I was involved for a number of years with Wolfram's community outreach projects in North Carolina. Early in our work there, we discovered how the results of community advocacy and empowerment can unexpectedly turn out to be at odds with researchers' intentions and community expectations. We were invited by the Linguistic Society of America to create a display on the Ocracoke dialect for an exhibit showcasing projects funded by the National Science Foundation (whose support we gratefully acknowledge to this day). We worked diligently with a professional designer to create what we believed to be an attractive and effective display. Following the event in Washington, DC, we decided to donate the display to the Ocracoke Historical Preservation Society museum, and they seemingly gratefully accepted. However, soon after the display had been donated, we walked into the museum and saw that the Preservation Society had dismantled our carefully crafted free-standing display and tacked various panels from the exhibit onto existing museum walls. We were at first dismayed and felt that the artistic integrity of display had been compromised. However, we soon realized that the incident was a valuable learning experience: Once we gave the display to the community, it became *their* display, not ours, and we needed to either accept this new ownership or demand the return of the display. Naturally, we conceded to community needs since, after all, our intent was to help them, not impose our will on them; and no real harm had been done. Things could have been trickier, however, if in addition to altering the aesthetics of the display, the Preservation Society had also changed the content so that the Ocracoke dialect and its regular linguistic patterning were misrepresented. In that case, we would have felt obligated to negotiate rather than concede, following the Principle of Error Correction and our commitment to disseminating accurate knowledge about language variation.

Another case in which community powers came up against our own did not turn out quite so well, and this case demonstrates a greater peril than simply aesthetic differences. We had learned from the earlier Ocracoke museum display incident that community members might have different ideas regarding the representation of their community and language variety than we do. While making a video documentary of the dialect of a small community to the south of Ocracoke,

North Carolina, we decided that we should screen a rough cut at a community meeting prior to going into final production. The rough cut was indeed met with disapproval by community members, who felt it was too flashy for their more conservative tastes and values. Unfortunately, the producers we worked with refused to alter it, a decision that not only halted our community outreach efforts in the community but practically stopped our research efforts there as well.

Since this incident, we have trodden more carefully and worked to bring our interests and those of community members into alignment. But accommodating community members' perspectives raises a number of issues of its own. For one, what if the views community members espouse do not accord with what we view as linguistic or social accuracy? For example, in *Mountain Talk,* a documentary on North Carolina Appalachian English (Hutcheson 2004), there was no narrator and hence no one to "correct" community members' discussion of their dialect as "Shakespearean English." Wolfram *et al.* (2008) maintain that this issue is relatively minor, since what linguists and non-linguists actually mean by "Shakespearean English" is very likely different. The linguistic definition is the scholarly one – the historical form of English spoken from roughly 1500 to 1800 (i.e. Early Modern English). However, the non-linguist's definition is broader and can be applied to current dialects that contain relic features, not only to English as it existed during Shakespeare's day. However, sometimes non-technical labels can be less innocuous, and no conscientious linguist would allow community members' descriptions of non-standard dialects as "bad English" to stand without accompanying commentary correcting this dangerous misinformation.

Another issue that arises when we try to ensure that our outreach products please both researchers and community members (and when working *with* rather than simply *for* communities more generally) is the fact that communities are not monolithic. A portrayal that pleases one person or group could very well anger another. Hence, for example, when we produced a video documentary on the community and dialect of the Lumbee Indians, we had to work very carefully to balance the views of two factious groups who were actually in litigation over the right to represent the Lumbee tribe. We solved the issue in this case by steering clear of highly contentious matters in the video content, and by ensuring that people from both factions were included as spokespeople.

The question of which viewpoint(s) to represent is by no means confined to this particular community. It arises any time researchers produce outreach products – and indeed it crops up in the very conduct of research itself since, as we have learned, researching a community involves sampling the community, and we have to ensure that our sample is balanced and representative if we are to obtain as full a sociolinguistic picture as possible.

We must also consider a third issue: is it, in fact, always desirable to help empower the communities we research? Labov raised this question early in his research career, noting that "many linguists gather data from the rich and powerful, rather than the poor and oppressed ... [A]re these linguists obligated to protect the privileges of the upper classes if these privileges are menaced?" (1982: 173). His answer has been to work from a somewhat circumscribed position on advocacy and empowerment, focusing on sharing linguistic knowledge for community benefit rather than on empowering one's research communities *per se*. This position seems satisfying on both scientific and humanistic levels, since sharing accurate knowledge about the patterning of language and dialect variation will never actually increase the societal power of those who already hold it (since their language varieties are already held in high esteem). In the long run, dissemination of accurate information will always be of benefit, even if longstanding power relations are unsettled, since we as scientists believe that knowledge is valuable for its own sake, even (perhaps especially) when increased knowledge casts new light on unquestioned assumptions that underpin societal structures and belief systems.

7.3 PASSING THE TORCH: STUDENTS GIVING BACK

The examples we have considered so far in this chapter show sociolinguists working in circumstances where they are making large-scale differences in communities and in society at large. These efforts at outreach, education, and social justice are of inestimable value – but "giving back" to research communities does not have to be grand in scope or vast in scale in order to make a difference. Small-scale community involvements may affect a smaller number of people, but they may do so more directly, and they may be more deeply appreciated.

Cala Zubair became involved with the Sri Lankan community in Washington, DC, early in her research, and she participated in a group called Educate Lanka, whose goal is to send textbooks and classroom supplies to rural Sri Lankan schools. One of the founders of Educate Lanka was instrumental in Cala's early work, and in exchange for his assistance, she became involved in his fundraising efforts. In her subsequent trips to the field for data collection, Cala hand-delivered donations to rural schools in the area where she worked. She also became a mentor and advisor for Sri Lankan students who aspire to study in the US, and she volunteered to tutor two students preparing for their A-level college entrance exams in English.

Jackie Lou Jia also gave back through teaching. She began her field-work by volunteering at the Washington, DC, Chinatown Community Cultural Center, where she taught beginning ESL classes. She also occasionally provided simultaneous interpretation for meetings between government agencies and neighborhood residents. Her con-nections with the Center gave her a "place" in the community and put her in immediate contact with potential participants; but these oppor-tunities also provided her with a way of "giving back" from the moment she entered the field. But like many fieldworkers, Jackie had to confront the uncomfortable circumstances of being unable to do "enough" for the participants in her study. She notes:

> For me [the volunteer activities] highlighted the incongruence between the shiny bilingual landscape and the struggling monolingual Chinese residents. Sometimes I felt quite helpless. Most of my students were in their sixties or beyond, of similar age as my own parents or grandparents, but they were struggling to learn English to adapt to the changing linguistic environment. It was sad to accept the fact that the subject of my research [the linguistic landscape of Chinatown] could not really help them much.

Even when it seems difficult or impossible to find ways to improve the lives of our participants, students can often find ways to share their knowledge (linguistic, cultural, or otherwise) in ways that benefit the community. Sakiko Kajino gave talks to Japanese university students about studying abroad and about her intercultural experiences as a student in the US. Similarly, Jen McFadden spoke at an orientation session for departing Bangladeshi Fulbright scholars, advising them of some of the cultural and academic differences they could expect from graduate studies in the US.

Sometimes "giving back" can simply be a matter of appropriately expressing thanks. Many of the students who conducted research abroad gave their participants small gifts as tokens of appreciation: postcards, photographs, souvenir trinkets, inexpensive jewelry, recorded collections of songs. These kinds of gifts are often received with a degree of appreciation that is much greater than the monetary value of the gift might suggest. They are, after all, tangible reminders of the "field encounters" that brought researcher and participant together, and of the social connection that they now share.

For some participants and communities, research itself can be an important contribution, since it can shine a public spotlight on social issues that might otherwise receive little or no attention in the wider world. Jason Sanderson's Breton participants voiced a hope that his work, written for and presented to English audiences, would raise international awareness of Brittany's social and linguistic issues. When Leslie Cochrane undertook her study of identity, narrative, and disability, her participants expressed a concern that their community be portrayed accurately and sensitively. She has regarded that as one of her primary responsibilities, and when she presents her research, it is always couched in an understanding of disability as a socially constructed and mediated experience, rather than a product of physical impairment. In addition, she notes, "I try to ensure that the stories I use in each presentation reflect the tellers' experiences in everyday life, including, but not limited to, accessibility issues."

Giving back can also be the primary impetus for a study. Jermay Jamsu Reynold's sociolinguistic studies of his home village (and indeed his graduate studies in linguistics more generally) grew out of his interest in and work on gathering oral literature in Tibetan communities and his desire to help these communities in some way. His sociolinguistic work is a way of giving back because, he notes, "it sheds light on language change in the village, and some of these insights will be useful for language revitalization in Tibetan areas."

And finally, sometimes interaction in and of itself is a meaningful and rewarding way to be involved with a community, and it can spark unparalleled moments of recognition and understanding. Like Jackie Lou, Jen McFadden felt underequipped to help the community she studied – a group of poor Bangladeshi market vendors and their customers. But, as she later noted:

> Many Rajabajar participants – indeed, Bengalis wherever we traveled – expressed delight that any foreigner would take the trouble to learn their language. Upon hearing me or my husband issue a greeting in Bangla – something as simple as *kemon achen,* "how are you" – Bangladeshis would often say *dhonnobad,* a message of appreciation far more literal and pragmatically elevated than its English equivalent "thank you". So in some way, I suppose, learning Bangla and being curious about Bangladeshi life was something that my participants valued for its own sake ... In a lot of ways, I felt like the main way I was "giving back" to the community was just by showing interest in their lives and by allowing them to take an interest in mine.
> I suppose that's not usually what researchers mean when they talk about "giving back" ... but in general it seemed that it meant a lot to everyday lower class Bangladeshis to have the opportunity to talk at length with me. That good will was something that never failed to move me.

Knowing when, how, and what to "give back" is not necessarily straightforward, nor is it always easy. We have seen a number of examples throughout this book where the views of researcher and researched do not align, or where communities resist, reshape, or refuse our efforts at involvement. But we are obligated to do what we can to repay the generosity of our participants in whatever form we can, whether that involves reshaping educational policy, producing a video documentary, or simply being a friend who is there to listen.

7.4 SUMMARY

In conclusion, we must return once more to the questions we raised earlier in this chapter and wrestled with in prior sections of this book: is it possible for researchers to truly gain genuine, accurate, objective knowledge about our world, and especially about human society? We researchers are still human, after all, and in our pursuit of ethnographic goals, we want to represent the perspectives of our research communities at the same time as we present our "expert" views from the academy. Does this mean that our work is always necessarily subjective, and if so, does it discount the value of what we do? I argue that subjectivity, while inevitable, is not necessarily a flaw: it is part of all human activity, to some degree, and it is part of what makes fieldwork so rich and so rewarding.

We must also consider our own institutionally privileged positions as researchers and scholars. Although we have questioned whether "power" is always a one-way street, we must ask ourselves whether, in sharing what we believe to be scientific "truths," we may actually be imposing highly culturally specific (and arguably elitist) beliefs: beliefs about the nature of knowledge, for example, and the privileging of scientific, "expert" knowledge over organic community-based ways of knowing. Clearly, these are complex questions that cannot be answered in the space of a single chapter or single book, or by a single researcher such as myself, but they must be confronted as we think about our level of involvement in our research communities. And while all of us are committed to our studies and the validity and value of their results, some of us may choose to step more lightly than those who proactively disseminate expert linguistic knowledge in the communities they study. And this moderation is, I think, perfectly acceptable. While I would agree with Labov, Wolfram, and a host of others that we must indeed find some way of giving back to the communities we study, for all the reasons outlined above, I would also stress that each individual researcher must find their own comfort level. Not all of us have the time, resources, or energy – let alone the courage – to initiate large-scale dialect awareness programs or to step onto the witness stand in a court of law. We should each give back to our research communities in ways that work best for us and for them. Even the smallest return can be a valuable one, as many of the examples of student involvement show. Many people have immediate needs that have nothing to do with increasing their linguistic knowledge – for example, help with childcare, transportation, or a home improvement project. Further, sometimes the biggest gift we can give is simply our friendship and our listening ear. After all, listening to people talk in everyday life, about their experiences and beliefs, their joys and their troubles, is at the heart of sociolinguistic study and always will be, just as talking with and listening to each other lies at the heart of social life and human experience more generally.

STUDENTS IN THE FIELD

In reflecting on the value of her own fieldwork, Jen McFadden notes, "The rewards for me were actually most profound on a personal level rather than on a linguistic or scholarly one. That is, I valued the relationships and understandings that arose through my fieldwork more than any particular bit of data that came out of it (and I did turn up some great data!). It wasn't until I left Dhaka, though, that I realized how much my participants meant to me – and how much I'd come to mean to them. On the day of my departure, at about 4:30 in the morning, I had arranged a taxi to pick me up at my front gate. I had already said goodbye to the market men a few days before, and had given them all small parting gifts – photographs, postcards, new sarongs. So when my husband and I went down to meet the cab, we were deeply moved to find Shah Alom, Caca, and Zia – three of my participants – waiting to see us safely off. It was a very tearful goodbye for all of us, and as we boarded our taxi, my friends held their hands over their hearts and waved solemnly as we drove away. That image has become a sort of symbol for me of what my fieldwork was like – painful and profound – and what it was ultimately about: the interactional work required to produce a moment of understanding and connection between people who have little or nothing in common."

Suggested readings

LABOV, WILLIAM 1969. THE LOGIC OF NON-STANDARD ENGLISH. IN JAMES E. ALATIS (ED.), *GEORGETOWN MONOGRAPH ON LANGUAGES AND LINGUISTICS* 22. WASHINGTON, DC: GEORGETOWN UNIVERSITY PRESS, 1–44.

In this foundational article, Labov presents convincing evidence and argument against the mistaken yet sadly widespread notion that speakers of African American Vernacular English are linguistically deficient. Rather, as Labov eloquently demonstrates, AAVE is as systematic as standard English, as well as an equally rich, if not even richer, communicative resource.

LABOV, WILLIAM 1982. OBJECTIVITY AND COMMITMENT IN LINGUISTIC SCIENCE: THE CASE OF THE BLACK ENGLISH TRIAL IN ANN ARBOR. *LANGUAGE IN SOCIETY* 11: 165–202.

Labov demonstrates in this important article how linguists' commitment to ameliorating language- and race-based discrimination led not only to an invaluable social contribution (the ruling in favor of the African American plaintiffs in the Ann Arbor case) but also to momentous scientific outcomes, as linguists' zeal for demonstrating to the public the systematicity of African American Vernacular English led them to work together to make new discoveries about this unique linguistic system. This article also presents Labov's highly influential principles for linguists' involvement in research communities: The Principle of Error Correction and The Principle of the Debt Incurred.

RICKFORD, JOHN R. 1997. UNEQUAL PARTNERSHIP: SOCIOLINGUISTICS AND THE AFRICAN AMERICAN SPEECH COMMUNITY. *LANGUAGE IN SOCIETY* 26(2): 161–197.

In this article, Rickford outlines the many contributions to linguistics gained from working with African American communities and argues that while sociolinguists have indeed made important contributions to these communities, they have not yet done enough. He urges that service in return should be a general principle and practice in sociolinguistics, with some specific goals for service being the introduction of more African Americans into linguistics and increased efforts by linguists to ensure linguistic equality in courts, workplaces, and schools.

WOLFRAM, WALT, JEFFREY REASER, AND CHARLOTTE VAUGHN 2008. OPERATIONALIZING LINGUISTIC GRATUITY: FROM PRINCIPLE TO PRACTICE. *LANGUAGE AND LINGUISTICS COMPASS* 2(6): 1109–1134.

WOLFRAM, WALT 2013a. COMMUNITY COMMITMENT AND RESPONSIBILITY. *THE HANDBOOK OF LANGUAGE VARIATION AND CHANGE*. 2ND EDN. MALDEN, MA: WILEY-BLACKWELL.

In these contributions, Wolfram and his colleagues illustrate the myriad ways that they have given back to numerous research communities and to society in general, following Wolfram's (1993) Principle of Linguistic Gratuity, which urges linguists to proactively seek ways to return linguistic favors. Wolfram *et al.* note that although there are a number of tricky issues associated with community involvement, the positive benefits to both communities and committed researchers far outweigh the difficulties.

References

Adger, Carolyn Temple and Natalie Schilling-Estes 2003. *African American English: Structure and Clinical Implications*. Rockville, MD: American Speech–Language–Hearing Association.

Allen, Harold B. (ed.) 1973. *The Linguistic Atlas of the Upper Midwest*. Minneapolis: University of Minnesota Press.

Ash, Sharon 2003. A National Survey of North American Dialects. *Publication of the American Dialect Society* 88(1): 57–73.

Auer, Peter (ed.) 2007. *Style and Social Identities: Alternative Approaches to Linguistic Heterogeneity*. Berlin: Walter de Gruyter.

Bailey, Guy and Cynthia Bernstein 1989. Methodology for a Phonological Survey of Texas. *Journal of English Linguistics* 22: 6–16.

Bailey, Guy and Jan Tillery 2004. Some Sources of Divergent Data in Sociolinguistics. In Carmen Fought (ed.), *Sociolinguistic Variation: Critical Reflections*. Oxford University Press, 11–30.

Bailey, Guy, Tom Wikle, Jan Tillery, and Lori Sand 1991. The Apparent Time Construct. *Language Variation and Change* 3: 241–264.

Bailey, Guy, Jan Tillery, and Tom Wikle 1997a. Methodology of a Survey of Oklahoma Dialects. *SECOL Review* 21: 1–30.

Bailey, Guy, Tom Wikle, and Jan Tillery 1997b. The Effects of Methods on Results in Dialectology. *English World-Wide* 18: 35–63.

Bamberger, Robert and Samuel Brylawski 2010. *The State of Recorded Sound Preservation in the United States: A National Legacy at Risk in the Digital Age*. Washington, DC: National Recording Preservation Board.

Barrett, Rusty 1995. "Supermodels of the World, Unite!": Political Economy and the Language of Performance among African American Drag Queens. In William Leap (ed.), *Beyond the Lavender Lexicon: Authenticity, Imagination, and Appropriation in Lesbian and Gay Languages*. Newark, NJ: Gordon and Breach, 203–223.

Bauer, Laurie 2002. Inferring Variation and Change from Public Corpora. In J.K. Chambers, Peter Trudgill, and Natalie Schilling-Estes (eds.), *The Handbook of Language Variation and Change*. Malden, MA: Blackwell, 97–114.

Baugh, John 2003. Linguistic Profiling. In Sinfree Makoni, Geneva Smitherman, and Arnetha F. Ball (eds.), *Black Linguistics: Language,*

Society and Politics in Africa and the Americas. London/New York: Routledge, 155–168.

Becker, A.L. 1995. *Beyond Translation: Toward Modern Philology*. Ann Arbor, MI: University of Michigan Press.

Bell, Allan 1984. Language Style as Audience Design. *Language in Society* 13: 145–204.

2001. Back in Style: Reworking Audience Design. In Penelope Eckert and John Rickford (eds.), *Style and Sociolinguistic Variation*. Cambridge University Press, 139–169.

Bell, Allan and Gary Johnson 1997. Towards a Sociolinguistics of Style. *University of Pennsylvania Working Papers in Linguistics* 4(1): 1–21.

Benor, Sarah 2001. The Learned /T/: Phonological Variation in Orthodox Jewish English. *Penn Working Papers in Linguistics (Selected Papers from New Ways of Analyzing Variation 29)* 7: 1–16.

2004. Talmid Chachams and Tsedeykeses: Language, Learnedness, and Masculinity among Orthodox Jews. *Jewish Social Studies* 11: 147–170.

Bernard, H. Russell 2006. *Research Methods in Anthropology: Qualitative and Quantitative Approaches*. 4th edn. Walnut Creek, CA: Altamira Press.

Bernstein, Basil 1961. Social Class and Linguistic Development: A Theory of Social Learning. In A.H. Halsey, J. Floud, and C.A. Anderson (eds.), *Education, Economy and Society*. New York: Free Press, 288–314.

1972. A Critique of the Concept of Compensatory Education. In C. Cazden, Vera John, and Dell Hymes (eds.), *Functions of Language in the Classroom*. New York: Teachers College Press.

Bickerton, Derek 1980. What Happens When We Switch? *York Papers in Linguistics* 9: 41–56.

Bird, Steven and Gary Simons 2003. Seven Dimensions of Portability for Language Documentation and Description. *Language* 79(3): 557–582.

Blake, Renee and Meredith Josey 2003. The /ay/ Diphthong in a Martha's Vineyard Community: What can we Say 40 Years after Labov? *Language in Society* 32(4): 451–485.

Blanton, Phyllis and Karen Waters 1996. *The Ocracoke Brogue*. Raleigh: North Carolina Language and Life Project.

Blom, Jan-Petter and John Gumperz 1972. Social Meaning in Linguistic Structures. In John Gumperz and Dell Hymes (eds.), *Directions in Sociolinguistics*. New York: Rinehart and Winston.

Boersma, Paul and David Weenink 2012. *Praat: Doing Phonetics by Computer*. www.praat.org/.

Bourhis, Richard and Howard Giles 1976. The Language of Co-Operation in Wales: A Field Study. *Language Sciences* 42: 13–16.

Bourhis, Richard, Howard Giles, and Wallace E. Lambert 1975. Social Consequences of Accommodating One's Style of Speech: A Cross-National Investigation. *International Journal of the Sociology of Language* 6: 11–32.

Briggs, Charles L. 1986. *Learning How to Ask: A Sociolinguistic Appraisal of the Role of the Interview in Social Science Research*. Cambridge University Press.

Bucholtz, Mary 1996. Geek the Girl: Language, Femininity, and Female Nerds. In Jocelyn Ahlers, Leela Bilmes, Melinda Chen, Monica Oliver, Natasha Warner, and Suzanne Wertheim (eds.), *Gender and Belief Systems*. Berkeley Women and Language Group, 119–132.

1999. Why Be Normal? Language and Identity Practices in a Community of Nerd Girls. *Language in Society* 28: 203–223.

2001. The Whiteness of Nerds: Superstandard English and Racial Markedness. *Journal of Linguistic Anthropology* 11: 84–100.

2003. Sociolinguistic Nostalgia and the Authentication of Identity. *Journal of Sociolinguistics* 7(3): 398–416.

2011. *White Kids: Language, Race, and Styles of Youth Identity*. Cambridge University Press.

Butters, Ronald R. 2000. "What is about to Take Place is a Murder": Construing the Racist Subtext in a Small-Town Virginia Courtroom. In Peg Griffin, Joy Peyton, Walt Wolfram, and Ralph Fasold (eds.), *Language in Action: New Studies of Language and Society*. New York: Hampton, 362–389.

Cameron, Deborah, Elizabeth Frazer, Penelope Harvey, Ben Rampton, and Kay Richardson (eds.) 1992. *Researching Language: Issues of Power and Method*. London: Routledge.

1993. Ethics, Advocacy and Empowerment: Issues of Method in Researching Language. *Language and Communication* 13(2): 81–94.

Campbell-Kibler, Kathryn 2010. Sociolinguistics and Perception. *Language and Linguistics Compass* 4(6): 377–389.

Cannadine, David 1988. *Class in Britain*. London: Penguin.

Cedergren, Henrietta 1973. The Interplay of Social and Linguistic Factors in Panama. PhD, Cornell University.

1984. *Panama Revisited: Sound Change in Real Time*. New Ways of Analyzing Variation (NWAV) 13. Philadelphia.

Chambers, J.K. and Peter Trudgill 1998. *Dialectology*. 2nd edn. Cambridge University Press.

Cheshire, Jenny 1982. *Variation in an English Dialect: A Sociolinguistic Study*. Cambridge University Press.

Coupland, Nikolas 1980. Style-Shifting in a Cardiff Work Setting. *Language in Society* 9(1): 1–12.

1984. Accommodation at Work: Some Phonological Data and Their Implications. *International Journal of the Sociology of Language* 46: 49–70.

2001a. Dialect Stylization in Radio Talk. *Language in Society* 30(3): 345–375.

2001b. Language, Situation and the Relational Self. In Penelope Eckert and John Rickford (eds.), *Style and Sociolinguistic Variation*. Cambridge University Press, 185–210.

2007. *Style: Language Variation and Identity*. New York: Cambridge University Press.

Cukor-Avila, Patricia and Guy Bailey 2013. Real and Apparent Time. In J.K. Chambers and Natalie Schilling (eds.), *The Handbook of Language Variation and Change*. 2nd edn. Malden/Oxford: Wiley-Blackwell.

Cutillas-Espinosa, Juan Antonio, Juan Manuel Hernández-Campoy, and Natalie Schilling-Estes 2010. Hyper-Vernacularisation and Speaker Design: A Case Study. *Folia Linguistica* 44(1): 31–52.

Cutler, Cecilia A. 1999. Yorkville Crossing: White Teens, Hip Hop, and African American English. *Journal of Sociolinguistics* 3(4): 428–442.

Davies, Bronwyn and Rom Harré 1990. Positioning: The Social Construction of Selves. *Journal for the Theory of Social Behavior* 20: 43–63.

Douglas-Cowie, Ellen 1978. Linguistic Code-Switching in a Northern Irish Village: Social Interaction and Social Ambition. In Peter Trudgill (ed.), *Sociolinguistic Patterns in British English*. London: Edward Arnold, 37–51.

Drager, Katie 2010. Sociophonetic Variation in Speaker Perception. *Language and Linguistics Compass* 4: 473–480.

Du Bois, John W. 2007. The Stance Triangle. In Robert Englebretson (ed.), *Stancetaking in Discourse: Subjectivity, Evaluation, Interaction*. Amsterdam: John Benjamins, 139–182.

Duranti, Alessandro 1997. *Linguistic Anthropology*. Cambridge University Press.

Eckert, Penelope 1989. *Jocks and Burnouts: Social Identity in the High School*. New York: Teachers College Press.

1997. Age as a Sociolinguistic Variable. In Florian Coulmas (ed.), *The Handbook of Sociolinguistics*. Oxford/Malden: Wiley-Blackwell, 151–167.

1998. *Vowels and Nail Polish: The Emergence of Linguistic Style in the Preadolescent Heterosexual Marketplace. 1996*. Berkeley Women and Language Conference, Berkeley, CA, Berkeley Women and Language Group.

2000. *Linguistic Variation as Social Practice*. Malden, MA: Blackwell.

2001. Style and Social Meaning. In Penelope Eckert and John R. Rickford (eds.), *Style and Sociolinguistic Variation*. Cambridge University Press, 119–126.

2003. Elephants in the Room. *Journal of Sociolinguistics* 7(3): 392–397.

2005. Three Waves of Variation Study: The Emergence of Meaning in the Study of Variation, manuscript.

2008. Variation and the Indexical Field. *Journal of Sociolinguistics* 12(4): 453–476.

2012. Three Waves of Variation Study: The Emergence of Meaning in the Study of Variation. *Annual Review of Anthropology* 41: 87–100.

Eckert, Penelope and Sally McConnell-Ginet 1992. Think Practically and
    Look Locally: Language and Gender as Community-based Practice.
    Annual Review of Anthropology 21: 461–490.
Eckert, Penelope and John R. Rickford (eds.) 2001. *Style and Sociolinguistic
    Variation.* Cambridge University Press.
Erickson, Frederick 1986. Qualitative Methods in Research on Teaching. In
    Merlin C. Wittrock (ed.), *Handbook of Research on Teaching.* New York:
    Macmillan, 119–161.
Fasold, Ralph 1972. *Tense Marking in Black English: A Linguistic and Social
    Analysis.* Arlington, VA: Center for Applied Linguistics.
    1984. *The Sociolinguistics of Society.* Oxford: Basil Blackwell.
Feagin, Crawford 2013. Entering the Community: Fieldwork. In
    J.K. Chambers and Natalie Schilling (eds.), *The Handbook of Language
    Variation and Change.* 2nd edn. Malden/Oxford: Wiley-Blackwell.
Fuller, Janet M. 1997. Pennsylvania Dutch with a Southern Touch:
    A Theoretical Model of Language Contact and Change. PhD, University
    of South Carolina.
Gal, Susan 1979. *Language Shift: Social Determinants of Linguistic Change in
    Bilingual Austria.* New York: Academic Press.
Garrett, Peter 2010. *Attitudes to Language.* Cambridge University Press.
Giles, Howard, Nikolas Coupland, and Justine Coupland 1991.
    Accommodation Theory: Communication, Context, and Consequence.
    In Howard Giles, Nikolas Coupland, and Justine Coupland (eds.),
    Contexts of Accommodation: Developments in Applied Sociolinguistics.
    Cambridge University Press, 1–68.
Goffman, Erving 1963. *Behavior in Public Places: Notes on the Social Organization
    of Gatherings.* New York: The Free Press.
    1974. *Frame Analysis.* New York: Harper & Row.
    1981. Footing. *Forms of Talk.* Philadelphia: University of Pennsylvania
    Press, 124–159.
Graff, David, William Labov, and Wendell A. Harris 1986. Testing Listeners'
    Reactions to Phonological Markers of Ethnic Identity: A New Method
    for Sociolinguistic Research. In David Sankoff (ed.), *Diversity and
    Diachrony.* Amsterdam: John Benjamins, 45–58.
Grieser, Jessica 2012. *[T]inking About Takoma: Race, Style, and Identity at
    DC's Border.* Symposium About Language and Society – Austin (SALSA) 20.
    Austin, TX.
Grimes, Drew 2004. *Celebrating Muzel Bryant.* Raleigh: North Carolina
    Language and Life Project.
Gumperz, John J. 1982. Fact and Inference in Courtroom Testimony. In
    John J. Gumperz (ed.), *Language and Social Identity.* Cambridge
    University Press, 163–195.
Harré, Rom and Luk van Langenhove 1999. *Positioning Theory.* Malden, MA:
    Blackwell.

Hewitt, Roger 1982. White Adolescent Creole Users and the Politics of Friendship. *Journal of Multilingual and Multicultural Development* 3(3): 217–232.

Hindle, Donald M. 1979. The Social and Situational Conditioning of Phonetic Variation. PhD, University of Pennsylvania.

Hoffman, Michol F. and James A. Walker 2010. Ethnolects and the City: Ethnic Orientation and Linguistic Variation in Toronto English. *Language Variation and Change* 22: 37–67.

Hopper, Paul J. 1987. *Emergent Grammar*. 13th Annual Meeting, Berkeley Linguistic Society, Berkeley, CA.

Horvath, Barbara 1985. *Variation in Australian English*. Cambridge University Press.

Hutcheson, Neal 2001. *Indian by Birth: The Lumbee Dialect*. Raleigh: North Carolina Language and Life Project.

2003. *Celebrating Princeville*. Raleigh: North Carolina Language and Life Project.

2004. *Mountain Talk*. Raleigh: North Carolina Language and Life Project.

2005. *Voices of North Carolina*. Raleigh: North Carolina Language and Life Project.

Hymes, Dell 1974. *Foundations in Sociolinguistics: An Ethnographic Approach*. Philadelphia: University of Pennsylvania Press.

Irvine, Judith 2001. "Style" as Distinctiveness: The Culture and Ideology of Linguistic Differentiation. In Penelope Eckert and John Rickford (eds.), *Style and Sociolinguistic Variation*. Cambridge University Press, 21–43.

Jaffe, Alexandra M. (ed.) 2009. *Stance: Sociolinguistic Perspectives*. Oxford University Press.

Jamsu, Jermay, Patrick Callier, and Jinsok Lee 2010. *A Diachronic Study of Monophthongization in Washington, DC*. New Ways of Analyzing Variation (NWAV) 38. Ottawa, Canada.

Jamsu Reynolds, Jermay, 2012. Language Variation and Change in an Amdo Tibetan Village: Gender, Education and Resistance. PhD, Georgetown University.

Johnson, Keith 2012. *Acoustic and Auditory Phonetics*. 3rd edn. Malden, MA: Wiley-Blackwell.

Johnstone, Barbara 1996. *The Linguistic Individual: Self-Expression in Language and Linguistics*. Oxford University Press.

1999. Uses of Southern-Sounding Speech by Contemporary Texas Women. *Journal of Sociolinguistics* 3(4): 505–522.

2000a. *Qualitative Methods in Sociolinguistics*. New York: Oxford University Press.

2000b. The Individual Voice in Language. *Annual Review of Anthropology* 29: 405–424.

Johnstone, Barbara and Judith Mattson Bean 1997. Self-Expression and Linguistic Variation. *Language in Society* 26: 221–246.

Johnstone, Barbara and Scott Kiesling 2008. Indexicality and Experience: Exploring the Meanings of /aw/- Monophthongization in Pittsburgh. *Journal of Sociolinguistics* 12: 5–33.

Josey, Meredith 2004. A Sociolinguistic Study of Phonetic Variation and Change on the Island of Martha's Vineyard. PhD, New York University.

Kendall, Tyler 2007. Enhancing Sociolinguistic Data Collections: The North Carolina Sociolinguistic Archive and Analysis Project. *Penn Working Papers in Linguistics* 13(2): 15–26.

2008. On the History and Future of Sociolinguistic Data. *Language and Linguistics Compass* 2(2): 332–351.

2013. Data in the Study of Language Variation and Change. In J.K. Chambers and Natalie Schilling (eds.), *The Handbook of Language Variation and Change*. 2nd edn. Malden/Oxford: Wiley-Blackwell.

Kerswill, Paul 1996. Children, Adolescents, and Language Change. *Language Variation and Change* 8: 177–202.

2013. Koineization. In J.K. Chambers and Natalie Schilling (eds.), *The Handbook of Language Variation and Change*. 2nd edn. Malden/Oxford: Wiley-Blackwell.

Kerswill, Paul and Ann Williams 2000. Creating a New Town Koine: Children and Language Change in Milton Keynes. *Language in Society* 29: 65–115.

2002. "Salience" as an Explanatory Factor in Language Change: Evidence from Dialect Levelling in Urban England. In Mari C. Jones and Edith Esch (eds.), *Language Change: The Interplay of Internal, External, and Extralinguistic Factors*. New York: Mouton de Gruyter, 84–110.

Kiesling, Scott 1998. Men's Identities and Sociolinguistic Variation: The Case of Fraternity Men. *Journal of Sociolinguistics* 2(1): 69–99.

2009. Style as Stance: Stance as the Explanation for Patterns of Sociolinguistic Variation. In Alexandra Jaffe (ed.), *Stance: Sociolinguistic Perspectives*. Oxford University Press, 171–194.

Kretzschmar, William A. 1994. *Handbook of the Linguistic Atlas of the Middle and South Atlantic States*. University of Chicago Press.

Kurath, Hans. 1949. *Word Geography of the Eastern United States*. Ann Arbor: University of Michigan.

Labov, William 1963. The Social Motivation of a Sound Change. *Word* 19: 273–309.

1966. *The Social Stratification of English in New York City*. Washington, DC: Center for Applied Linguistics.

1969. The Logic of Non-standard English. In James E. Alatis (ed.), *Georgetown Monograph on Languages and Linguistics 22*. Washington, DC: Georgetown University Press, 1–44.

1972a. Some Principles of Linguistic Methodology. *Language in Society* 1: 97–120.

1972b. *Language in the Inner City: Studies in the Black English Vernacular.* Philadelphia: University of Pennsylvania Press.

1972c. *Sociolinguistic Patterns.* Philadelphia: University of Pennsylvania Press.

1982. Objectivity and Commitment in Linguistic Science: The Case of the Black English Trial in Ann Arbor. *Language in Society* 11: 165–202.

1984. Field Methods of the Project on Linguistic Change and Variation. In John Baugh and Joel Sherzer (eds.), *Language in Use.* Englewood Cliffs, NJ: Prentice-Hall, 28–53.

1994. *Principles of Linguistic Change Volume I: Internal Factors.* Malden/ Oxford: Wiley-Blackwell.

2001a. Applying Our Knowledge of African American English to the Problem of Raising Reading Levels in Inner-City Schools. In Sonja Lanehart (ed.), *African American English: State of the Art.* Philadelphia: John Benjamins, 299–318.

2001b. *The Anatomy of Style-Shifting.* In Penelope Eckert and John R. Rickford (eds.), *Style and Socioinguistic Variation.* Cambridge University Press, 85–108.

2006. *The Social Stratification of English in New York City.* 2nd edn. Cambridge University Press.

2008. Unendangered Dialect, Endangered People. In Kendall A. King, Natalie Schilling-Estes, Lyn Fogle, Jia Jackie Lou, and Barbara Soukup (eds.), *Sustaining Linguistic Diversity: Endangered and Minority Languages and Language Varieties.* Washington, DC: Georgetown University Press, 219–238.

Labov, William and Wendell A. Harris 1986. De Facto Segregation of Black and White Vernaculars. In David Sankoff (ed.), *Diversity and Diachrony.* Philadelphia: John Benjamins, 1–24.

Labov, William, Sharon Ash, Maciej Baranowski, Naomi Nagy, Maya Ravindranath, and Tracy Weldon 2006a. Listeners' Sensitivity to the Frequency of Sociolinguistic Variables. In Michael L. Friesner and Maya Ravindranath (eds.), *Penn Working Papers in Linguistics: Selected Papers from NWAV 34,* Volume 12.2. Philadelphia: Penn Linguistics Club, 105–129.

Labov, William, Sharon Ash, and Charles Boberg (eds.) 2006b. *The Atlas of North American English: Phonetics, Phonology and Sound Change.* Berlin: Mouton de Gruyter.

Ladefoged, Peter 1993. *A Course in Phonetics.* 3rd edn. Fort Worth: Harcourt, Brace, and Jovanovich.

Ladefoged, Peter and Keith Johnson 2010. *A Course in Phonetics (with CD-ROM).* 6th edn. London: Wadsworth.

Lambert, Wallace E., R.C. Hodgson, R.C. Gardner, and S. Fillenbaum 1960. Evaluational Reactions to Spoken Language. *Journal of Abnormal and Social Psychology* 60: 44–51.

Lave, Jean and Etienne Wenger 1991. *Situated Learning: Legitimate Peripheral Participation.* Cambridge University Press.

Le Page, Robert B. and Andrée Tabouret-Keller 1985. *Acts of Identity: Creole-Based Approaches to Language and Ethnicity.* Cambridge University Press.

Lee, Sinae 2011. *High and Mid-Back Vowel Fronting in Washington, DC, Metropolitan Area.* New Ways of Analyzing Variation (NWAV) 40. Washington, DC.

Lippi-Green, Rosina 1994. Accent, Standard Language Ideology, and Discriminatory Pretext in the Courts. *Language in Society* 23: 163–198.

Lippi-Green, Rosina L. 1989. Social Network Integration and Language Change in Progress in a Rural Alpine Village. *Language in Society* 18: 213–234.

Locklear, Hayes Alan, Walt Wolfram, Natalie Schilling-Estes, and Clare J. Dannenberg 1996. *A Dialect Dictionary of Lumbee English.* Raleigh, NC: North Carolina Language and Life Project.

Lou, Jia Jackie 2009. Situating Linguistic Landscape in Time and Space: A Multidimensional Study of the Linguistic Construction of Washington, DC, Chinatown. PhD, Georgetown University.

2010a. Chinese on the Side: The Marginalization of Chinese in the Linguistic and Social Landscapes of Washington, DC, Chinatown. In Elana Shohamy, Monica Barni, and Eli Ben-Rafael (eds.), *Linguistic Landscape in the City.* Bristol: Multilingual Matters, 96–114.

2010b. Chinatown Transformed: Ideology, Power, and Resources in Narrative Place-Making. *Discourse Studies* 12(5): 625–647.

Lucas, Ceil, Robert Bayley, and Clayton Valli 2001. *Sociolinguistic Variation in American Sign Language.* Washington, DC: Gallaudet University.

Macaulay, Ronald K.S. 1977. *Language, Social Class, and Education: A Glasgow Study.* Edinburgh University Press.

2002. Extremely Interesting, Very Interesting, or only Quite Interesting? Adverbs and Social Class. *Journal of Sociolinguistics* 6: 398–417.

2009. *Quantitative Methods in Sociolinguistics.* Palgrave Macmillan.

Mallinson, Christine and Becky Childs 2004. African American English in Appalachia: Dialect Accommodation and Substrate Influence. *English World-Wide* 25: 27–50.

2007. Communities of Practice in Sociolinguistic Description: Analyzing Language and Identity Practices among Black Women in Appalachia. *Gender and Language* 1(2): 173–206.

Matsuda, Mari J. 1991. Voices of America: Accent, Antidiscrimination Law, and a Jurisprudence for the Last Reconstruction. *The Yale Law Journal* 100(5): 1329–1407.

McDavid, Raven I., Jr. and Raymond K. O'Cain (eds.) 1980. *Linguistic Atlas of the Middle and South Atlantic States.* University of Chicago Press.

McFadden, Jennifer L. 2011. Indexicality and Sociolocation in a Bangladeshi Market: A Sociolinguistic Ethnography. PhD, Georgetown University.

Milroy, James 1981. *Regional Accents of English: Belfast. Dundonald,* Belfast: Blackstaff Press.

Milroy, James and Lesley Milroy 1985. Linguistic Change, Social Network and Speaker Innovation. *Journal of Linguistics* 21: 339–384.

Milroy, Lesley 1980. *Language and Social Networks.* Oxford: Blackwell.

1987. *Observing and Analysing Natural Language.* Malden/Oxford: Wiley-Blackwell.

Milroy, Lesley and Matthew Gordon 2003. *Sociolinguistics: Method and Interpretation.* Malden MA: Blackwell.

Modan, Gabriella Gahlia 2007. *Turf Wars: Discourse, Diversity, and the Politics of Place.* Malden, MA: Blackwell.

Montgomery, Michael 2000. Isolation as a Linguistic Construct. *Southern Journal of Linguistics* 24: 41–53.

Neuman, W. Lawrence 1997. *Social Research Methods: Qualitative and Quantitative Approaches.* 3rd edn. Boston: Allen & Bacon.

Nichols, Patricia C. 1983. Linguistic Options and Choices for Black Women in the Rural South. In Barrie Thorne, Cheris Kramarae, and Nancy Henley (eds.), *Language, Gender and Society.* Cambridge, MA: Newbury House, 54–68.

Niedzielski, Nancy 1999. The Effect of Social Information on the Perception of Sociolinguistic Variables. *Journal of Language and Social Psychology* 18: 62–85.

Nielsen, Rasmus 2010. "I Ain't Never Been Charged with Nothing!": The Use of Falsetto Speech as a Linguistic Strategy of Indignation. *University of Pennsylvania Working Papers in Linguistics* 15(2): 111–121.

Nylund, Anastasia 2010. *Styling "Factualness" in Interaction: The Intersection of Stop Release and Velar (-ing).* Sociolinguistics Symposium 18. Southampton, UK.

2011. Connecting Discourses of Language and Place in Washington, DC. *Texas Linguistics Forum* 54: 120–130.

2012. *L-Vocalization in Washington, DC: Understanding Regional and Ethnoracial Identities in a Contested City.* Annual meeting of the American Dialect Society. Portland, OR.

Ochs, Elinor 1992. Indexing Gender. In Alessandro Duranti and Charles Goodwin (eds.), *Rethinking Context.* Cambridge University Press, 335–358.

Parrott, Jeffrey K. 2002. Dialect Death and Morpho-Syntactic Change: Smith Island Weak Expletive "It." *University of Pennsylvania Working Papers in Linguistics: Selected Papers from NWAV 30* 8.

Patrick, Peter L. 2002. The Speech Community. In J.K. Chambers, Peter Trudgill, and Natalie Schilling-Estes (eds.), *The Handbook of Language Variation and Change.* Malden, MA: Blackwell, 573–597.

Pederson, Lee, Susan Leas McDaniel, Guy Bailey, and Marvin Bassett (eds.) 1986. *Linguistic Atlas of the Gulf States.* Athens: University of Georgia Press.

Plichta, Bartłomiej. "Akustyk." http://bartus.org/akustyk.

Plichta, Bartłomiej, Dennis R. Preston, and Brad Rakerd 2005. The /ay/s Have It. *Acta Linguistica Hafniensa* 37: 107–130.

Podesva, Robert J. 2004. *On Constructing Social Meaning with Stop Release Bursts.* Sociolinguistics Symposium 15. Newcastle upon Tyne.

2006. Phonetic Detail in Sociolinguistic Variation: Its Linguistic Significance and Role in the Construction of Social Meaning. PhD, Stanford University.

2007. Phonation Type as a Stylistic Variable: The Use of Falsetto in Constructing a Persona. *Journal of Sociolinguistics* 11(4): 478–504.

2008. *Linking Phonological Variation to Discourses of Race and Place in DC.* Annual meeting of the American Anthropological Association. San Francisco, CA.

Podesva, Robert J. and Sinae Lee 2010. *Voice Quality Variation and Gender in Washington, DC.* New Ways of Analyzing Variation (NWAV) 39. San Antonio, TX.

Podesva, Robert J., Sarah Roberts, and Kathryn Campbell-Kibler 2002. Sharing Resources and Indexing Meanings in the Production of Gay Styles. In Kathryn Campbell-Kibler, Robert J. Podesva, Sarah Roberts, and Andrew Wong (eds.), *Language and Sexuality: Contesting Meaning in Theory and Practice.* Stanford, CA: CSLI Publications, 175–189.

Podesva, Robert J., Jermay Jamsu, Patrick Callier, and Jessica Heitman forthcoming. Constraints on the Social Meaning of Released /t/: A Production and Perception Study of U.S. Politicians. *Language Variation and Change.*

Pope, Jennifer, Miriam Meyerhoff, and D. Robert Ladd 2007. Forty Years of Language Change on Martha's Vineyard. *Language* 83: 615–627.

Preston, Dennis R. 2013. Language with an Attitude. In J.K. Chambers and Natalie Schilling (eds.), *The Handbook of Language Variation and Change.* 2nd edn. Malden/Oxford: Wiley-Blackwell.

Purnell, Thomas, William Idsardi, and John Baugh 1999. Perceptual and Phonetic Experiments on American English Dialect Identification. *Journal of Language and Social Psychology* 18(1): 10–30.

Queen, Robin 2007. Sociolinguistic Horizons: Language and Sexuality. *Language and Linguistics Compass* 1(4): 314–330.

Rampton, Ben 1995. *Crossing: Language and Ethnicity among Adolescents.* London: Longman.

1999. Styling the Other: Introduction. *Journal of Sociolinguistics* 3(4): 421–427.

Reaser, Jeffrey 2006. The Effect of Dialect Awareness on Adolescent Knowledge and Attitudes. PhD, Duke University.

Renn, Jennifer and J. Michael Terry 2009. Operationalizing Style: Quantifying the Use of Style Shift in the Speech of African American Adolescents. *American Speech* 84(4): 367–390.

Rickford, John R. 1986. The Need for New Approaches to Social Class Analysis in Sociolinguistics. *Language and Communication* 6: 215–221.

1997a. *Suite for Ebony and Phonics*. Discover. New York: Kalmbach.

1997b. Unequal Partnership: Sociolinguistics and the African American Speech Community. *Language in Society* 26(2): 161–197.

Rickford, John R. and Faye McNair-Knox 1994. Addressee- and Topic-Influenced Style Shift: A Quantitative Sociolinguistic Study. In Douglas Biber and Edward Finegan (eds.), *Sociolinguistic Perspectives on Register*. New York: Oxford University Press, 235–276.

Rickford, John R. and Angela E. Rickford 1995. Dialect Readers Revisited. *Linguistics and Education* 7(2): 107–128.

Romaine, Suzanne 1978. Post-Vocalic /r/ in Scottish English: Sound Change in Progress. In Peter Trudgill (ed.), *Sociolinguistic Patterns in British English*. London: Edward Arnold, 144–157.

1980. A Critical Overview of the Methodology of Urban British Sociolinguistics. *English World-Wide* 1(163–198).

Sankoff, David and Suzanne Laberge 1978. The Linguistic Market and the Statistical Explanation of Variability. In David Sankoff (ed.), *Linguistic Variation: Models and Methods*. New York: Academic Press, 239–250.

Sankoff, David, Gillian Sankoff, Suzanne Laberge, and Marjorie Topham 1976. Méthodes D'échantillonnage Et Utilisation De L'ordinateur Dan L'étude De La Variation Grammaticale. *Cahiers de linguistique de l'Université du Québec* 6: 85–125.

Sankoff, Gillian 1980. *The Social Life of Language*. Philadelphia: University of Pennsylvania Press.

2006. *Apparent Time and Real Time*. Encyclopedia of Language and Linguistics. Keith Brown. Oxford: Elsevier. 1: 110–116.

Santa Ana, Otto 2002. *Brown Tide Rising*. Austin: University of Texas Press.

2009. "Did You Call in Mexican?" The Racial Politics of Jay Leno Immigrant Jokes. *Language in Society* 38(1): 23–45.

forthcoming, 2013. *Juan in a Hundred: The Representation of Latinos on Network News*. Austin: University of Texas Press.

Saville-Troike, Muriel 2003. *The Ethnography of Communication*. 3rd edn. Malden, MA: Blackwell.

Schegloff, Emanuel A. 1997. "Narrative Analysis" Thirty Years Later. *Journal of Narrative and Life History* 7(1–4): 97–106.

Schiffrin, Deborah 2006. *In Other Words: Variation in Reference and Narrative*. Cambridge University Press.

2009. Crossing Boundaries: The Nexus of Time, Space, Person, and Place in Narrative. *Language in Society* 38: 421.

Schilling, Natalie 2011. Language, Gender, and Sexuality. In Raj Mesthrie (ed.), *The Cambridge Handbook of Sociolinguistics*. Cambridge University Press, 218–237.

2013. Investigating Stylistic Variation. In J.K. Chambers and Natalie Schilling (eds.), *The Handbook of Language Variation and Change*. 2nd edn. Malden/Oxford: Wiley-Blackwell.

Schilling, Natalie and Jermay Jamsu 2010. *Real-Time Data and Communal Change in Washington, DC, African American Vernacular English*. New Ways of Analyzing Variation (NWAV) 39. San Antonio, TX.

Schilling-Estes, Natalie 1998. Investigating "Self-Conscious" Speech: The Performance Register in Ocracoke English. *Language in Society* 27: 53–83.

2004. Constructing Ethnicity in Interaction. *Journal of Sociolinguistics* 8: 163–195.

2007. Sociolinguistic Fieldwork. In Robert Bayley and Ceil Lucas (eds.), *Sociolinguistic Variation: Theory, Methods and Applications*. Cambridge University Press, 165–189.

2008. Stylistic Variation and the Sociolinguistic Interview: A Reconsideration. In Rafael Monroy and Aquilino Sánchez (eds.), *25 Años De Lingüística Aplicada En España: Hitos Y Retos (Proceedings of AESLA 25)*. Murcia, Spain: Servicio de Publicaciones de la Universidad de Murcia, 971–986.

Schilling-Estes, Natalie and Walt Wolfram 1994. Convergent Explanation and Alternative Regularization Patterns: *Were/Weren't* Leveling in a Vernacular English Variety. *Language Variation and Change* 6(3): 273–302.

Schneider, Edgar W. 2013. Investigating Variation and Change in Written Documents: New Perspectives. In J.K. Chambers and Natalie Schilling (eds.), *The Handbook of Language Variation and Change*. 2nd edn. Malden/Oxford: Wiley-Blackwell.

Sclafani, Jennifer 2009. Martha Stewart Behaving Badly: Parody and the Symbolic Meaning of Style. *Journal of Sociolinguistics* 13(5): 613–633.

Seals, Corinne under review. Phonological Cues for Identity Expression: Examining the Linguistic Meaning of Palatalization Amongst Multilingual Ukrainian Youth.

Shuy, Roger W. 1996. *Language Crimes: The Use and Abuse of Language Evidence in the Courtroom*. Malden/Oxford: Blackwell.

1998. *The Language of Confession, Interrogation and Deception*. London: Sage.

2005. *Creating Language Crimes: How Law Enforcement Uses (and Misuses) Language*. Oxford University Press.

Shuy, Roger W., Walt Wolfram, and William K. Riley 1968. *Field Techniques in an Urban Language Study*. Washington, DC: Center for Applied Linguistics.

Smitherman, Geneva 1981. "What Go Round Come Round": King in Perspective. *Harvard Educational Review* 51(1): 40–56.

Soukup, Barbara 2011. Austrian Listeners' Perceptions of Standard-Dialect Style-Shifting: An Empirical Approach. *Journal of Sociolinguistics* 15(3): 347–365.

2012. Current Issues in the Social Psychological Study of "Language Attitudes": Constructionism, Context, and the Attitude–Behavior Link. *Language and Linguistics Compass* 6(4): 212–224.

Stenström, Anna-Brita, Gisle Andersen, and Ingrid Kristine Hasund 2002. *Trends in Teenage Talk: Corpus Compilation, Analysis and Findings.* Amsterdam: John Benjamins.

Strand, Elizabeth 1999. Uncovering the Role of Gender Stereotypes in Speech Perception. *Journal of Language and Social Psychology* 18(1): 86–99.

Stuart-Smith, Jane 1999. Glasgow: Accent and Voice Quality. In P. Foulkes and G.J. Docherty (eds.), *Urban Voices: Accent Studies in the British Isles.* Leeds: Arnold, 203–222.

Tagliamonte, Sali A. 1998. *Was/Were* Variation across the Generations: View from the City of York. *Language Variation and Change* 10(2): 153–191.

2006a. *Analysing Sociolinguistic Variation.* Cambridge University Press.

2006b. "So Cool, Right?": Canadian English Entering the 21st Century. *Canadian Journal of Linguistics* 51(2/3): 309–331.

Tannen, Deborah 1989. Constructing Dialog in Conversation: Towards a Poetics of Talk. *Talking Voices: Repetition, Dialogue and Imagery in Conversational Discourse*, 98–133.

Thelander, Mats 1982. A Qualitative Approach to the Quantitative Data of Speech Variation. In Suzanne Romaine (ed.), *Sociolinguistic Variation in Speech Communities.* London: Edward Arnold, 65–83.

Thibault, Pierrette and Diane Vincent 1990. *Un Corpus De Français Parlé.* Montréal: Recherches Sociolinguistiques.

Thomas, Erik R. 2002. Sociophonetic Applications of Speech Perception Experiments. *American Speech* 77(2): 115–147.

2011. *Sociophonetics: An Introduction.* Basingstoke: Palgrave Macmillan.

2013. Sociophonetics. In J.K. Chambers and Natalie Schilling (eds.), *The Handbook of Language Variation and Change.* 2nd edn. Malden/Oxford: Wiley-Blackwell.

Thomas, Erik R. and Jeffrey Reaser 2004. Delimiting Perceptual Cues Used for the Ethnic Labeling of African American and European American Voices. *Journal of Sociolinguistics* 8(1): 54–87.

Trudgill, Peter 1972. Sex, Covert Prestige and Linguistic Change in the Urban British English of Norwich. *Language in Society* 1(2): 179–195.

1974. *The Social Differentiation of English in Norwich.* Cambridge University Press.

1981. Linguistic Accommodation: Sociolinguistic Observations on a Sociopsychological Theory. In Carrie S. Masek, Roberta A. Hendrick, and Mary Frances Miller (eds.), *Papers from the Parasession on Language and Behavior.* Chicago Linguistic Society, 218–237.

1983. Acts of Conflicting Identity: The Sociolinguistics of British Pop-Song Pronunciation. In Peter Trudgill, *On Dialect: Social and Geographical Perspectives.* Oxford: Blackwell, 141–160.

1988. Norwich Revisited: Recent Linguistic Changes in an English Urban Dialect. *English World-Wide* 9(3): 33–49.

1989. Contact and Isolation in Linguistic Change. In Leiv Egil Breivik and Ernst Håkon Jahr (eds.), *Language Change: Contributions to the Study of Its Causes.* Berlin/New York: Mouton de Gruyter, 227–237.

Tseng, Amelia 2011. *"I Can Tell She's Gonna Be Bilingual, and Pretty Good at It Too": /ae/ Realization, Situated Identity Construction, and Latino Immigration in Washington, DC.* New Ways of Analyzing Variation (NWAV) 40. Washington, DC.

Van Hofwegen, Janneke 2012. The Development of African American English through Childhood and Adolescence. In Sonja Lanehart, Lisa Green and Jennifer Bloomquist (eds.), *The Oxford Handbook on African American Language.* Oxford University Press.

Vincent, Diane, Marty Laforest, and Guylaine Martel 1995. Le Corpus De Montréal 1995: Adaptation De La Méthode D'enquête Sociolinguistique Pour L'analyse Conversationnelle. *Dialangue* 6: 29–46.

Watson, Mark 2006. Post-Revolutionary Cuban Spanish: Changes in the Lexicon and Language Attitudes Motivated by Socio-political Reforms. PhD, Georgetown University.

Weinreich, Uriel, William Labov, and Marvin I. Herzog 1968. Empirical Foundations for a Theory of Language and Change. In Winfred P. Lehmann and Yakov Malkiel (eds.), *Directions for Historical Linguistics: A Symposium.* Austin, TX: University of Texas Press, 95–188.

Wells, John Christopher 1982. *Accents of English.* Cambridge University Press.

Willemyns, Michael, Cynthia Gallois, Victor J. Callan, and Jeffrey Pittam 1997. Accent Accommodation in the Job Interview: Impact of Interviewer Accent and Gender. *Journal of Language and Social Psychology* 16(1): 3–22.

Williamson-Ige, Dorothy K. 1984. Approaches to Black Language Studies: A Cultural Critique. *Journal of Black Studies* 15(1): 17–29.

Wolfram, Walt 1969. *A Sociolinguistic Description of Detroit Negro Speech.* Washington, DC: Center for Applied Linguistics.

1971. *Sociolinguistic Aspects of Assimilation: Puerto Rican English in East Harlem.* Washington, DC: Center for Applied Linguistics.

1993. *Ethical Considerations in Language Awareness Programs.* American Association of Applied Linguistics Ethics Symposium. Atlanta, GA.

1995. Delineation and Description in Dialectology: The Case of Perfective *I'm* in Lumbee English. *American Speech* 71: 5–26.

2013. Community Commitment and Responsibility. *The Handbook of Language Variation and Change.* 2nd edn. Malden, MA: Wiley-Blackwell.

302 *References*

Wolfram, Walt and Ralph Fasold 1974. *The Study of Social Dialects in American English*. Englewood Cliffs, NJ: Prentice-Hall.
Wolfram, Walt and Clare J. Dannenberg 1999. Dialect Identity in a Tri-Ethnic Context: The Case of Lumbee American Indian English. *English World-Wide* 20: 179–216.
Wolfram, Walt and Jeffrey Reaser forthcoming. *Tar Heel Talk: Voices of North Carolina*. Chapel Hill, NC: University of North Carolina Press.
Wolfram, Walt, Carolyn Temple Adger, and Donna Christian 1999. *Dialects in Schools and Communities*. Mahwah, NJ: Lawrence Erlbaum Associates.
Wolfram, Walt, Kirk Hazen, and Natalie Schilling-Estes 1999. *Dialect Change and Maintenance in Outer Banks English*. Tuscaloosa: University of Alabama Press.
Wolfram, Walt, Jeffrey Reaser, and Charlotte Vaughn 2008. Operationalizing Linguistic Gratuity: From Principle to Practice. *Language and Linguistics Compass* 2(6): 1109–1134.
Wolfram, Walt, Janneke Van Hofwegen, Jennifer Renn, and Mary E. Kohn 2011. The Progression of African American English in Childhood and Adolescence : A Longitudinal Study, ms.
Wolfson, Nessa 1976. Speech Events and Natural Speech: Some Implications for Sociolinguistic Methodology. *Language in Society* 5: 189–209.
Zentella, Ana Celia 1997. *Growing up Bilingual: Puerto Rican Children in New York*. Malden, MA: Blackwell.
Zubair, Cala 2008. *Discourses of History in a Gentrifying Neighborhood of Washington, DC*. Annual meeting of the American Anthropological Association. San Francisco, CA.
  2012. Register Formation among Sri Lankan University Youth. PhD, Georgetown University.

Index

(**bold** entries point to boxed summaries)

audience design approach (cont.)
  interviewer and 109, 124, 127–128,
    173, 254
  real-world contexts 142, 150
  referees 143, 154
  researcher control 149–150
  responsive style shifting 135, 137,
    141–143, 145, 153, 155
  second wave studies and 156
  topic effects 142, 145, 147, 149–150
audio recorders 219–222
  advantages of digital 219
  bit-rate 220
  bits 220
  built-in storage capacity 233
  dynamic range 220
  file formats 221–222
  frequency response 219
  minimum specifications **218**, 221
  quantization rate 220
  removable storage 233
  resolution 220
  sampling 219
  sampling rate 219–220, 237
  settings 237
audiological status 201–202, 214–215
Auer, P. 92, 168
authenticity 21–22, 66, 164–165,
    186–187, 196

Bailey, G. 34–35, 43, 63–64
Bangladesh 196–197, 202
Barrett, R. 29–30, 50, 161
batteries 234, 243
Baugh, J. 90, 274
Bayley, R. 201
Belfast 9, 22–23, 109, 191, 196
Bell, A. 14, 109, 141–143, 147–150, 174
Bernard, H.R. 258
Bird, S. 267
Blom, J. 142–143
Bourhis, R. 88
Briggs, C. 107, 132
Brittany, France 68, 282
Bucholtz, M. 24–25, 50, 63, 154
Butters, R. 276

cables, *see* connectors
Cameron, D. 214
Campbell-Kibler, K. 87, 89, 132–133

Canadian English 28
Cane Walk, Guyana 21, 25
Cardiff 111, 150
Chambers, J.K. 16
Cheshire, J. 109
Childs, B. 25, 110
Cochrane, L. 202, 282
communities of practice 24–26, 191
  definition of 24
  gender and 24–26, 30
  metadata 255
  practices vs. memberships in 24–25,
    54
  stratification in 53–54
  vs. speech community 63
community involvement 15–16,
    268–284
  advocacy 194–196, 214, 268, 270–276,
    281–282
  complications 277–280, 283
  empowerment 194–196, 214, 268,
    277–280
  ethics in 203, 268–269
  expressing thanks 281
  fitting in 198–201
  forms of 120–125, 194
  "giving back" 194–195, 277, 280–286
  interaction and 282
  Labov's principles for 269–270, 273,
    277
  limitations of 122–123
  necessity of 126, 268
  reasons for 268–270, 277
  volunteer service 188, 192, 280–281
  Wolfram's principle for 277
  see also ethics; linguistic
    discrimination; outreach;
    relationships with participants;
    researcher role
communicative competence 120,
    202–203
  non-native 110, 201
communicative norms
  for questions 107, 132
  local 80
compressed audio files 221–222, 233, 235
confidentiality 131, 263–265
  access and 15, 243, 249, 257, 265
  of participant identities 253–254, 258
  video data 264

in sociolinguistic interviews 106–108,
148–149, 162
in speech communities 20
style and 2, 13, 134, 141, 143,
148–149, 158
third wave studies and 160–161
interactional sociolinguistics 4, 8, 108,
129–130, 173
interview errors and mishaps
abrupt topic shift 207–208
blind adherence to questionnaire
208–209
closed-ended questions 212
excessive length of interview 211
failure to follow up 204
in recording 238
success despite 207–210, 212
Interview Report Forms 248, 253, 260
interviewer strategies
backchanneling 210
demeanor and 209–210
flexibility 211–212
following up 204
participating in talk 210
interviewers
from within the community 124–125
metadata **254–255**, 254–255
as producers of data 148–149, 210, 225
see also researcher role
introductions to community 177–183,
197
brevity and honesty in 178–179
vs. institutional descriptions 179–181
samples of 181–182

Jamsu Reynolds, J. 125, 211, 282
Japanese 113
Johnson, G. 147–150
Johnson, K. 266
Johnstone, B. 10
Josey, M. 57–59

Kajino, S. 96, 113, 187, 211, 281
Kendall, T. 252, 266
Kiesling, S. 10, 26, 158
Korean 84

Labov, William 15, 66, 144, 172
African American Vernacular English
9, 109, 120, 271, 284–285

apparent time 55
attention to speech approach 13,
98–104, 135–136, 138, 174
educational advocacy 270–271
group interviews 109
Martha's Vineyard 4, 7–9, 22, 55, 57,
86, 114, 156
methodologies 16, 212–214
narrative 100–102
New York City 20–23, 50, 79–83,
86, 97–98, 105, 120, 136–137,
155, 174
observer's paradox 66, 99
Principle of Error Correction 214, 270,
278, 284–285
Principle of the Debt Incurred 214,
270, 280
rapid and anonymous survey 79–84,
127
sociolinguistic interviews 6–7, 94, 97,
131, 174
speech community, definition of 20
vernacular principle 6, 98, 159
Ladefoged, P. 266
language attitudes 69, 85–92
see also perception studies
data types 92
as main sociolinguistic concern 85
language change and 86
problems eliciting 88–89
regional differences in 88–89
social justice and 87
LCDC project 95, 128–130, 179–181,
254–255
language maintenance 23
language varieties 133
"authenticity" of 21–22
evaluations of 88–89
local vs. standard 142–143
reification of 27, 62–63
as resources 167
Lee, J. 84–85
Le Page, R. 27
linguistic anthropology 4, 8, 108, 113,
115, 133
Linguistic Atlas of the United States and
Canada 4, 36, 70
linguistic convergence 153–155
alignment and 166–167, 171
among girls vs. boys 170

linguistic convergence (cont.)
  vs. divergence 153–155, 171
  with audience expectations 153–154
linguistic discrimination 194–195,
    269–270
  in education 270–273, 275
  in housing 273–275
  in media 275
linguistic market 48
linguistic profiling 91, 274
local categories 9–10, 41–43, 52, 63, 156
Lou, J. 187–188, 199, 281
Lucas, C. 201

Macaulay, R.K. 111–112, 127
Mallinson, C. 25, 110
markers 155
Martha's Vineyard 4, 7–9, 22, 55, 86,
    114, 156, 161
  re-studies of 5, 57–60
McFadden, J. 196–197, 202, 211
    (Endnote 1), 238, 281, 284
McNair-Knox, F. 145–147
Mennonites 198
mergers 34, 38, 57, 69, 74–77, 127
  near-mergers 76–77, 86
  unmergers 76–77
metadata 216, 243–244, 248, 252–256
  adding later 263
  interviewee 255–256
  interviewer **254–255**, 254–255
  links to data files 262–263
  see also Interview Report Forms
methods, diversity of 1, 8–11, 62, 66,
    128–130, 167, 173–174
microphone placement
  experimenting with 237
  in laboratory 246
  mounts for 226–227, 242
  participants and 241–243
microphone specifications 218, 222–223
  dynamic range 222–223
  frequency response 222–223
  impedance 223, 233
  signal-to-noise ratio (SNR), 226, 242
microphone types 223–226
  boundary 227
  built-in 222, 225, 227
  cardioid, *see* unidirectional
  condenser 223–224

dynamic 223–224
electret 224
lavalier 224–226
omnidirectional 225, 242
unidirectional 224–225, 242
USB 246
wireless 227
Milroy, J. 9, 22–23, 53, 109, 191, 196
Milroy, L. 9, 16, 22–23, 53, 109, 186, 191,
    196, 213

narratives 94, 100–102, 106, 112, 132
  performed speech in 138–140, 159
  "natural" speech 111, 127, 139–141, 245
New York City 50, 174
  Harlem 9, 23, 94–97, 120
  Lower East Side 20–21, 79–83, 86,
    136–137, 155
  Puerto Rican community in 23
New Zealand 142–143, 147–150
Niedzielski, N. 91–92
Nielsen, R. 168
Northern Cities Vowel Shift 38, 52–53,
    67, 156
Norway 142
Norwich, England 56–58, 76
Nylund, A. 260

"objectivity" 114–117, 283
observer effects 126
observer's paradox 66, 79, 99, 114–115,
    128, 178, 202
Ocracoke Island, NC
  elicitations and interviews 71, 94–97,
    108, 206
  entering 184
  participation in 121–122, 197–198
  performed speech in 159
  sampling 40
  social class and 48
outreach 15, 183, 194–195, 285
  balanced viewpoints in 279–280
  dialect awareness 276–280, 284–285
  legal 275–276

panel studies 55, 57, 59, 61
  truncated 55–56
Parrot, J. 78–81
participant-observation
  advantages of 121–122